THE THEOLOGY
OF ST. PAUL

D. E. H. WHITELEY
Fellow of Jesus College, Oxford

THE THEOLOGY OF
ST. PAUL

D. E. H. WHITELEY

Fellow of Jesus College, Oxford

OXFORD
BASIL BLACKWELL
1974

© BASIL BLACKWELL 1964

FIRST EDITION 1964
REPRINTED 1966, 1971, 1972
SECOND EDITION 1974
ISBN 0 631 15710 7

PRINTED IN GREAT BRITAIN
BY A. T. BROOME AND SON, 18 ST. CLEMENT'S, OXFORD
AND BOUND BY THE KEMP HALL BINDERY, OXFORD

PREFACE TO FIRST EDITION

I must first acknowledge my debt to the Rev. L. B. Cross, my predecessor in office at Jesus College, Oxford, and my Tutor in Theology, as well as to my previous teachers in Classics, Philosophy, and Ancient History at Pembroke College, Oxford.

I should also like to record my gratitude to the staff of Messrs. Basil Blackwell and Mott, Ltd., especially Mr. H. L. Schollick, and to Mrs. A. Wawerka of The New Typing Office, who typed out my badly-written manuscript and assisted in the compilation of indexes.

I am indebted to the University Presses of Oxford and Cambridge for permission to make use of the translation prepared for the *New English Bible, New Testament*, Copyright 1961, Oxford and Cambridge University Presses; and to Thomas Nelson and Sons, Ltd., acting on behalf of the National Council of the Churches of Christ in America, the copyright owner, to quote from the *Revised Standard Version of the Old Testament*, copyrighted 1952 and the *Revised Standard Version of the Apocrypha* copyrighted 1957; and especially to the editors of the *Journal of Theological Studies* for permission to reproduce, substantially unchanged, 'St. Paul's Thought on the Atonement', published by them in October, 1957, which constitutes pages 130–148 of this present work.

D. E. H. WHITELEY.

Jesus College, Oxford.
September, 1963.

PREFACE TO SECOND EDITION

I am greatly indebted to numerous scholarly friends who pointed out and corrected errors in the first edition of 1964 in time for me to incorporate the corrections in the second impression of 1966. My first wife, Muriel, who died in 1967, and my present wife Joan, helped me with constructive criticism of the text and lay-out. I wish to thank Mrs. Cipolla for her patient work in checking references and helping to compile the indexes, and the Oxford Theology Faculty Secretaries who carried out the tedious work of typing.

I am also grateful to the Publishers and Printers for producing this edition in spite of many difficulties, not least the astronomical rise in the price of paper.

CONTENTS

LIST OF ABBREVIATIONS

B	Arndt and Gringrich, *A Greek-English Lexicon of the New Testament*
A.V.	*Authorized (King James) Version*
P *B.A.S.O.R.*	*Bulletin of the American Schools of Oriental Research*
P *B.J.R.L.*	*Bulletin of the John Rylands Library* (Manchester)
Black N.T.C.	Black New Testament Commentary (London)
B	Blass-Debrunner-Funk, *A Greek Grammar of the New Testament* (E.T., R. W. Funk, 1961)
B *The Body*	J. A. T. Robinson *The Body*, S.B.T., no. 5, (London, 1952)
Charles (ed.)	*The Apocrypha and Pseudepigrapha of the Old Testament*, 2 vols. (Oxford, 1963²)
Christ	L. Cerfaux, *Christ in the Theology of St. Paul* (E.T. New York and Edinburgh, 1959)
Church	L. Cerfaux, *The Church in the Theology of St. Paul* (E.T., New York and Edinburgh, 1959)
C.N.T.	*Commentaire de Nouveau Testament* (Neuchâtel)
Danby	*The Mishnah*, E.T., H. Danby (Oxford, 1933¹, often reprinted)
E.T.	English Translation
E.VV.	English Versions
P *Exp.T.*	*Expository Times* (Edinburgh)
I.B.	*The Interpreter's Bible* (Nashville, Tennessee)
I.C.C.	International Critical Commentary (Edinburgh)
Introduction	A. Richardson, *An Introduction to the Theology of the New Testament* (London, 1958)
P *J.B.L.*	*Journal of Biblical Literature* (Philadelphia)
P *J.T.S.*	*Journal of Theological Studies* (Oxford). The New Series (N.S.) began in 1950
B *Judaism*	G. F. Moore, *Judaism in the Early Centuries*, etc.
Judaisme	J. Bonsirven, *Le Judaisme Palestinien au temps de Jésus-Christ* (2 vols., Paris, 1935)
London N.T.C.	London New Testament Commentary
LXX	Septuagint
Moffatt N.T.C.	Moffatt New Testament Commentary
M.T.	Massoretic Text
N.E.B.	New English Bible
P *N.T.S.*	*New Testament Studies* (Cambridge, England)
P *R.B.*	*Revue biblique* (Jerusalem)
R.V.	*Revised Version*
R.S.V.	*Revised Standard Version*
S.B.T.	Studies in Biblical Theology (London)
Strack-Billerbeck	H. L. Strack and P. Billerbeck, **Kommentar zum Neuen** Testament aus Talmud und Midrasch (Munich, 1922 f.)
Theology	R. Bultmann, *Theology of the New Testament* (E.T. London, vol. 1, 1952, vol. 2, 1955)
T.W.N.T.	*Theologisches Wörterbuch zum Neuen Testament*, ed. Kittel and Friedrich (Stuttgart, 1933 f.)

P = Periodical
B = see also *Bibliography*, pp. 315–22

INTRODUCTION TO SECOND EDITION

This second, enlarged, edition is not the book I should have liked to write, which would have been far longer: it is a book students can afford to buy as a paper-back and libraries in the cased form. In the interests of students I have referred mainly to books available in English.

Though students have been my main concern, this new edition may also be useful to those teaching in various forms of education, to clergy, and to instructed members of the laity, including professional theologians whose speciality is not the N.T. Even Pauline experts may find something of interest in this new Introduction and in the appended notes. I have retained the text of the first edition unchanged to avoid confusion. New material has been indicated by a dagger (†) and is to be found in the Additional Notes at the end of the book. As it is not easy to turn to a new discussion and remember the argument, I have, I hope, inserted adequate connecting links for clarity.

The new material, which is to be found in this second Introduction and in the appended notes, has been arranged so that it can be seen how Pauline research and my own studies have developed in the last ten years. For reasons of space I have stressed the topics on which I have most to say.

I am glad that it is now possible to help the student by indicating my own position in N.T. criticism and in the systematic theology of the 1970's. In criticism I am broadly in accord with W. Marxsen[1] though I normally find my conclusions more 'conservative' than his. In systematics I have much sympathy with W. Pannenberg's recent summary of his thought *The Apostles' Creed*.[2] I often feel that there is special pleading on some points and that I should have welcomed further qualification; but I am deeply impressed by this combination of charity and truth when writing about the Jews and Martin Luther, as well as by his frank admission of the faults of his own and all other branches of the Church. I could have wished for consideration of Pentecostalism

---

[1] *Einleitung in das Neue Testament* (Gütersloh, 1964³), E.T. *Introduction to the New Testament* (Oxford, 1968; second unchanged impression 1970).

[2] E.T. (London, 1972) of *Das Glaubensgekenntnis ausgelegt und veranwortet vor den Fragen der Gegenwart* (Hamburg, 1972).

and other searches after God and about the many attempts by those rightly dissatisfied with contemporary materialism who find the answer in the wrong place. Serious students of N.T. criticism should use the latest edition of W. G. Kümmel's *Introduction to the New Testament*,[3] which is frequently being revised; and the most convenient exponent of the 'conservative' view is D. Guthrie.[4] I am glad to note that in Paul's theology I find myself much closer to the 'conservative' exposition of L. Morris as expressed in the third edition of *The Apostolic Preaching of the Cross*[5] than I did in the case of the first.[6] I feel that scholars have failed to realize that Morris's third edition is very different from his first. As I have argued later, Morris and I have certainly modified our language, and probably also our views, and in so doing have drawn closer together.

E. Best[7] says that Bultmann's exposition of Paul is 'alive' but 'wrong', mine 'right' but 'dead'. Best is not hostile to Bultmann or myself: he uses us as examples to illustrate the inherent difficulty of writing about Paul. He suggests that each 'side' should try to modify its approach to meet the demands of the other. Naturally, I have consulted many University teachers in Theology about what they and their students would like to see in a new edition of this book. All would like to see more emphasis laid upon practical moral problems. I have tried to show that answers to problems of our own day cannot be read off from the Bible as if from a slide-rule: we must become in our own day the kind of man Paul was in his to give in this century moral decisions as truly Christian as the Apostle gave in his time.

For practical reasons of book-production it is possible in an Introduction to consider books and comments which appeared after the additional material had been irretrievably committed to the printers. C. P. M. Jones in his Bampton Lectures of 1970, which he has not yet had published, said that I was wrong in maintaining that Paul was not a 'systematic theologian'. Therefore I consulted him, and found we were in complete agreement: Paul produced what was in substance 'systematic theology', but, even in *Romans*, he did not do so according to a Scholastic or

---

[3] London, S.C.M. Press.
[4] *Introduction* to various parts and later to the whole of the N.T. (London, various dates; future revisions can reasonably be expected).
[5] (London, 1965). [6] (London, 1955).
[7] *Expt. T.*, vol. lxxx, 1968–69, no. 6, March, pp. 165–6.

Reformation framework, and we must always consider what problem Paul himself was facing, and not force him into the mould of our own later thought.

Another friend, A. E. Harvey, has given me permission to expound briefly a thesis he has not yet had time to develop in full. (It is confidently expected that it will appear in the *J.T.S.*) He adduces evidence that 'elders' (*zᵉquenim* in Hebrew) were not an official order; Josephus[8] does indeed mention them as a constituent of the Sanhedrin, but Harvey suggests that they were merely lay members of wealthy or noble families, whose sympathies were with the Sadducees. This makes good sense of Acts xxiii where Paul plays off the Pharisees, who support him, against the Sadducees. The party of fanatics who volunteered next morning to murder Paul approach 'the high priests and elders', who presumably were Sadducees.

Having produced sound evidence (still to be published) that elders were not an established order in Judaism, Harvey goes on to make his main contribution, which I have gathered chiefly from a paper he has kindly lent me. In the ancient world the stability of society was maintained largely by the wisdom and experience of those who had lived a long time. I may add on my own account, without committing Harvey, that when technological change was less rapid, and when, owing to lack of adequate public hygiene and medical skill, fewer men survived even to middle age, sheer length of life and experience was a great asset. Nowadays, on the contrary, when new techniques make skill and knowledge obsolete in a few years, when more men survive to middle and old age, and when younger men, with their more flexible minds, can more easily adapt themselves to new conditions, the advantage of seniority has suffered a significant decline.

In Paul's day, however, age and experience were of the greatest value. Harvey suggests that Paul appointed some of his first converts to be elders to carry out the function of maintaining stability. Cf. Acts xiv. 23, 'They also appointed elders for them in each congregation.' Normally, of course, they would be men who were old chronologically, but occasionally a young man might be appointed to a position of authority because of his personal suitability. This sort of situation seems to lie behind 1 Tim. iv. 12,

---

[8] *Wars of the Jews*, Bk. 2, ch. xvii, sect. 3 (Whiston's E.T.), 411 in Niese (Loeb Edition, *Josephus*, ed. H. St. J. Thackeray, vol. 1, Bk. 2, p. 484, facing p. 485).

'Let no one despise you because you are young'. Harvey suggests that, at least in the N.T., elders usually deserved their title both because they were so appointed and because of their age. They are closely connected with and contrasted with younger men in 1 Tim. v. 1, 'Never be harsh with an elder; appeal to him as if he were your father. Treat the younger men as brothers'; and 1 Pet. v. 1–4 exhorts the elders how they ought to tend the flock of God whose shepherds they are, which makes clear that they hold an office, while the next verse reads, 'In the same way you younger men must be subordinate to your elders'.

The cornerstone of Harvey's case is 1 Clement, 42,§4b ... 'They appointed their first converts, testing them by the Spirit, to be bishops and deacons of the future believers' (. . . *Kathistanon tas aparchas autōn, dokimasantes tō pneumati, eis episkopous kai diakonous tōn mellontōn pisteuein*).[9] Such is Harvey's case, and I find it both plausible and original, especially because the leading men (*hoi dunatoi*) are not expressly called elders, though it is not clear that the gathering was a formal meeting of the Sanhedrin: it was rather a special meeting; but it is natural to suppose that it consisted mainly of Sanhedrin members.[10]

There are a number of books which I have been unable to discuss: some because students should read them for themselves; and others, to my great regret, because they were not translated into English, and therefore not available to many students, until after I had written the main body of the new material. They will be found in the additional bibliography, p. 321.

My interest in Pauline studies began almost forty years ago as a reaction against the view held at that time and propounded by a famous evangelist, but explicitly, though not consistently, disavowed by L. Morris. My present position on the important question of the work of God in Christ is found in the additional notes. I have paid great attention to those who have written on this subject, especially if their views are not in accordance with my own.

[9] *The Apostolic Fathers*, ed. Kirsopp Lake, Loeb Edition, vol. 1 (London and Cambridge, Mass., 1912, often reprinted), pp. 80f. The best collection of material is still that of J. B. Lightfoot, two volumes (London, 1890). The edition by W. K. Lowther Clarke (London, 1937) is useful. No serious student of the early history of the ministry can afford to neglect *The Didache, Études Bibliques*, (Paris, 1958), by A. Audet. See also note on p. xvii.
[10] Whiston, *Wars of the Jews*, Bk. 2, ch. xvii, sect. 3, Loeb Edition, ed. H. St. J. Thackeray, p. 484, facing p. 485, 411 in Niese's numbering.

There are, of course, other writers with whom I cannot be in agreement. I feel that the difference is this. I lay more stress than they do upon the fact that all statements about God and His work are of necessity analogical. I agree that the actual language of Scripture has its roots, in some cases, in practices which we should now regard as sacrificial in a crude sense, and which we often interpret within the framework of Medieval or Reformation theology. But St. Paul, although he had his own framework of reference, had not the same framework of reference which we have inherited. For this reason he employs a wealth of metaphors, all of which point at the mystery of God's work in Christ. I doubt if he was conscious of the fact that he was speaking metaphorically, but the mere fact is that he used many metaphors which are in a sense incompatible with each other at their own level (the linguistic analyst would say that they: 'cannot be placed on the same map'). The Apostle himself reminds us at the end of 1 Cor. xiii that we now see only 'puzzling reflections in a mirror'.

Note. *Pisteuein* (see p. xvi) is a present infinitive. I suggest that its aspect is linear, not punctilinear, and should render: 'Continue in loyalty'.

Erratum
Professor John C. Hurd Jr. has noted that, on p. 244, 1 Cor. v. 19 (at the end of line 21) should read 1 Cor. v. 9.

INTRODUCTION TO FIRST EDITION

The aim of this book is to expound the Theology of St. Paul. No attempt has been made to consider the 'realities behind' his thought or to apply Pauline teaching to the needs of our own day. These objectives are, of course, legitimate and indeed essential; but there is a grave risk of reading our own concerns into the thought of the Apostle and so of distorting his message. I have therefore confined myself to the limited task of trying to discover what he actually intended to convey to his fellow-Christians when he composed his epistles.

It is not, however, possible to discuss the Apostle at all without employing the technical language of Theology, and this language has acquired overtones and associations because of the use made of it in later centuries. The very word 'creation', for example, suggests to us theories about the origin of the universe which lay beyond the horizon of first century thought. For this reason later theories have been noted where necessary in order to prevent them from misleading us by reason of associations derived from subsequent ecclesiastical controversies.

It is impossible to avoid the problem of which epistles among those traditionally ascribed to him are really the work of St. Paul. To discuss this important question with the thoroughness it deserves would require a separate book. I must therefore say what I have taken for granted so far as the present book is concerned, without stating my reasons for doing so. I have not used the Pastoral epistles, although I believe that they embody Pauline material. I have been unable to convince myself that St. Paul himself wrote or dictated *Ephesians*, though it is in an important sense a 'Pauline' writing. My task would have been much easier if I could have passed over this difficulty and treated *Ephesians* as if it were actually the work of the Apostle. But it seemed that I should then have been creating a theological synthesis of my own based mainly on St. Paul and partly on the Epistle to the Ephesians. This epistle has not been used without support from the others to 'prove a point', but whenever an 'Ephesian' passage has seemed to run counter to my arguments, I have tried to discuss it with due consideration.

The Rev. A. Q. Morton has investigated the authorship of the 'Pauline' epistles with the aid of a computer. His conclusions are the same as those reached on independent grounds by F. C. Baur, namely that the Apostle wrote only *Rom.*, *1* and *2 Cor.*, *Gal.* and *Philem.* If Mr. Morton is correct, the consequences for the structure of St. Paul's theology are less serious than some might suppose, since so much of the teaching found in the 'rejected' epistles is also substantiated in those that are genuine. So far as this book is concerned only those doctrines would have to be abandoned as non-Pauline which are found in *1* and *2 Thess.*, *Phil.* and *Col.* alone, without support from *Rom.*, *1* and *2 Cor.*, *Gal.* and *Philem.*

St. Paul's theology is very closely integrated. It seems to 'coinhere' in such a way that it can be made to centre equally well upon the doctrines of, e.g., Christ, the Cross, the Church, and the Last Things. For this reason the traditional 'chronological' order of presentation has been adopted. First we have described St. Paul's treatment of the created universe, which includes human nature, angels and evil powers. Then follows the Fall and its results, such as 'Natural Theology' and the Wrath of God. We next turn to God's plan of salvation, and it is at this point that Predestination is considered. The Person of Christ and the Work of Christ follow naturally, and after this we examine the means of appropriating the benefits of Christ's work, that is to say, Faith and the Sacraments. This brings us to our present condition as members of the Church with its ministry and to St. Paul's teaching on morality, which receives fuller treatment than has been customary in recent years. The last chapter is devoted to God's future fulfilment of His purpose, and includes such subjects as the resurrection body, the 'sleep of the soul', the 'Man of Sin', Christ's Second Coming and the ultimate fate of non–Christians.

The most obvious omission, of course, is that of the Holy Spirit. This vital subject is so all-pervasive that instead of treating it separately I have tried to deal with it as it occurs in such sections as those devoted to Christology, Baptism, Morality, etc. Again, I have passed lightly over certain aspects of the doctrine of the Church because they have already been expounded by Paul S. Minear in *Images of the Church in the New Testament* (London, 1960) and for the important subject of *Agape* I have made reference to existing standard works (p. 232, n. 64).

Chapter One falls outside this scheme; in it is considered the background to St. Paul's thought, Jewish, Greek and Christian. This again, like the problem of authorship, really requires a separate book. It seemed impossible to omit it completely, since the background of St. Paul's thought is so closely integrated with the very structure of his theology; however, this subject is treated more briefly than the others.

New Testament quotations are taken from the *New English Bible* unless otherwise indicated. Since this rendering is idiomatic and represents the thought of the original instead of presenting a word for word translation, the Greek word *corresponding* to the original has been quoted where necessary. For example, at Rom. ix. 22 *orgē*, literally *corresponds* to "his retribution at work" in the *N.E.B.* Quotations from the Old Testament and Apocrypha are given in the words of the Revised Standard Version. However, in the index of names and subjects such phrases derived from the older versions as 'Man of Sin' have been used to make reference easier. In most cases the index of Biblical references will be the most effective guide. All Hebrew and Greek words have been transliterated.

The interests of students as well as of scholars have been considered in the references. For example, in the case of passages taken from the intertestamental writings, reference has been made to the volume and page of R. H. Charles's *Apocrypha and Pseudepigrapha of the Old Testament*. Again, references to the *Manual of Discipline* are not given only by column and line, which would be sufficient for scholars; reference is also made to the page in T. H. Gaster's translation, *The Scriptures of the Dead Sea Sect*, for the benefit of students and members of the general public.

This book is devoted to an examination of St. Paul's own thought, and not to an appraisal of recent literature on the subject, though such books have their due place. The references to current literature have therefore been cut to the minimum. This has been possible because of the recent development of bibliographical aids. We may note especially Bruce M. Metzger, *Index to Periodical Literature on the Apostle Paul* (Leiden, 1960); *Bibliographie biblique* (Montreal, 1958) which lists some 9,000 books and articles covering the whole bible written by Roman Catholics in Latin, French and English; and a valuable periodical, *New Testament Abstracts* (Weston, Mass., U.S.A., 1956–). Also worthy of mention are the bibliographical notes in Bultmann, *Theology of the New Testament* (E.T., London, 1, 1952; 2, 1955) and in Stauffer, *New Testament Theology* (E.T., London, 1955).

CHAPTER ONE

THE BACKGROUND
OF ST. PAUL'S THEOLOGY

i. The Problem and its Overtones

Although this book is devoted to an exposition of St. Paul's theology, it is essential to begin by examining very briefly the background to his thought. If we are to understand what he means, it is first necessary to realize what questions he was trying to answer. Again, false views about the background to St. Paul's thought go hand in hand with misleading theories concerning the substance of his theology.

In this initial chapter we shall treat the background of his beliefs in a summary fashion, before going on to a closer examination of the Apostle's convictions in the remaining nine chapters.

When the 'man in the street' hears the Apostle's name mentioned, it oftens conjures up in his mind certain half-formulated ideas which are very closely related to the problem of background. For example, it is commonly thought that St. Paul was the man who ruined Christianity: Christ, it is said, preached the true Gospel, and the church perverted it, St. Paul being the chief offender. It is thought, for instance, that St. Paul introduced false ideas derived from 'Greek thought' or from the Mystery Religions, or, on the other hand, that he dragged back the infant church into the morass of Judaism from which Our Lord had freed it.

We shall see that St. Paul did not borrow wholesale from the Mystery Religions, though it is true that St. Paul and the devotees of the Mystery cults held in common certain presuppositions which the majority of twentieth-century men do not share; this makes them appear to have been more alike than they really were. Again, we shall see that there is almost nothing in St. Paul's writings which could not have been derived from Judaism or from the apostolic church. On the other hand, we must not imagine that Jews and Gentiles were living wholly apart. On the contrary, they borrowed much from each other. Above all, we must maintain that the authority of St. Paul's writings does not depend upon their background. As James Barr[1] has pointed out, ' "Semitic" language and thought is not as such necessarily superior to that of other language-groups. Throughout most of their history the people of God had to strive not against Hellenism at all, but against the Baalim and other gods worshipped by those who were just as "semitic" as themselves'. St. Paul's thought is *in fact* mainly Jewish in origin, but that is not the reason why we accept its authority.

ii. ST. PAUL'S GENTILE BACKGROUND

(a) *St. Paul not indebted to the Mystery Cults*

This subject need be considered only at the level of popular misconceptions. Most of our extant evidence for the mystery cults comes from after the time of St. Paul. For example, Apuleius, whose *Golden Ass* is one of our sources for these cults, wrote in the third quarter of the second century A.D. The magical papyri and the hermetic writings, at least in their present form, are also too late to have influenced St. Paul. It is of course true, that so far as chronology is concerned, St. Paul might have borrowed from an earlier form of mystery-religion, but the evidence for this hypothetical earlier form no longer exists, if indeed it ever did.

Further, St. Paul does not seem to have been the sort of man that we should expect to borrow from pagan sources. He was brought up as a strict Jew (Phil. iii. 5). Col. ii. 8, 'Do not let your minds be captured by hollow and delusive speculations (*dia tēs philosophias kai kenēs apatēs*),' is a warning against the kind of thought which we find in the Mystery Religions: it is not directed against philosophy in any modern sense of the word, as some have imagined being misled by the rendering of the *A.V.*, 'Philosophy and vain deceit'. In 1 Cor. x. 21f. St. Paul condemns those who become partners with demons; and this does not suggest that he would have borrowed consciously from the Mysteries. If he had in fact done so, we should have expected that his 'Judaizing' opponents would have attacked him for it, and that he would have been compelled to defend himself. But no defence on this score is to be found in the Pauline Epistles.

It is noteworthy on the negative side that St. Paul never speaks of Christians being 'born again' in Baptism; the Pauline equivalent

[1] *The Semantics of Biblical Language* (Oxford, 1961), p. 19.

is perhaps 'being risen with Christ' (Col. iii. 1): if the Apostle was aware of a Mystery Cult which spoke about 'being born again' he may have avoided the phrase of set purpose in order to obviate the danger that Christianity might be confused with cults of that nature. Again, we do not find in his writings such catch-words of the mysteries as *mustēs*, initiated, or *telestheis*, made perfect.

Since, however, this subject is peripheral and preliminary to our main concern, we must be content to refer to *The Origin of Paul's Religion*, by J. Gresham Machen,[2] and to F. Prat's *Theology of St. Paul*.[3] †

(b) *St. Paul's Hellenistic Background*

Among the most scholarly protagonists of the Hellenistic background in recent years has been W. L. Knox. He presented his case in *St. Paul and the Church of Jerusalem*, esp. pp. 136-49; this case, at present out of fashion, is put forward with moderation and discrimination. He develops the subject more fully in *St. Paul and the Church of the Gentiles*.[4] He concentrates more explicitly on this particular theme in *Some Hellenistic Elements in Primitive Christianity*.[5]

His treatment is often most illuminating; we shall see this, for example, when we come to deal with astrology.[6] It is clear that the thought-world of St. Paul and that of contemporary Hellenistic culture had much in common. But when all is said and done, though there is much that *could* have been derived from Hellenistic sources, there is hardly anything which could have come *only* from Hellenistic sources: what the Apostle shares with the Gentile world is for the most part not *peculiar* to the Gentiles; it is found in that large area of belief and language which was shared by Jew and Gentile alike. On the other hand, there is hardly anything in St. Paul which it would not have been possible for him to derive from Jewish sources, and a great deal which could have been taken from Jewish sources and from nowhere else.

The word *suneidēsis*, remorse, though not specifically Stoic,[7] as some have supposed, belongs to the language of Greek popular

---

[2] Grand Rapids, Michigan, 1947².
[3] E.T., 2 vols. in 1, London, 1959, vol. 2, pp. 37–41.
[4] First published, Cambridge, 1939.
[5] London, 1944, being the Schweich Lectures of the British Acadamy for 1942.
[6] cf. p. 23 f.
[7] *Conscience in the New Testament*, S.B.T. 15, (London 1955), pp. 13–15.

proverbial philosophy,[8] as C. A. Pierce has shown. It hardly belongs to the LXX, being found at Eccles. x. 20; Wisd. of Sol. xvii. 11; and, as a variant, at Ecclus. xlii. 18. It is found fourteen times in the Paulines, being confined to *Romans* and 1 and 2 *Corinthians*, and six times in the Pastorals.

Dupont[9] has made good his case that the word *Parousia*, 'coming', is Greek in origin, although adapted to express a Jewish idea; it was in fact passed to and fro among Greeks and Jews. It is found in St. Paul bearing a technical eschatological sense eight times. It is significant that we are reduced to considering such shreds of evidence as this when we attempt to find material in St. Paul which could be drawn only from Hellenistic sources.

iii. St. Paul's Jewish Background

(a) *Bibliography*

When, on the other hand, we turn to the problem of St. Paul's Jewish background, we are faced with the opposite difficulty: it is impossible to estimate the extent of the Apostle's debt to Jewish and Christian sources without undertaking a detailed examination of his entire theology. Indeed, we shall inevitably be making constant reference to his Judaeo-Christian background throughout this book. Otherwise, it would not be possible to understand his thought at all. At this point we must be content to refer to some of the literature. *St. Paul and Contemporary Jewish Theology*,[10] though very old, is still of value for its lively and thorough presentation of St. Paul's affinities with apocalyptic Judaism. It must not, of course, be supposed that different types of Judaism, Pharisaic, apocalyptic or Essene existed in water-tight compartments; there were many strands of thought, and they are all related to each other. *Paul and Rabbinic Judaism*[11] is well described by its title, and is one of the best books ever written on St. Paul. It includes a valuable bibliography (pp. 342-51). The additional notes to the second edition[12] (pp. 352-67) bring the subject down

---

[8] ibid., pp. 15–17.
[9] *L'Union avec le Christ suivant Saint Paul* (Louvain and Paris, 1952), pp. 49–64.
[10] H. St. John Thackeray (London, 1900).
[11] W. D. Davies, (London, 1948[1]).
[12] The second edition, London, 1955, is an exact reproduction of the first, including the pagination, except for the additional notes, which are not covered in the indexes.

to the beginning of 1955, and after this time the ground is covered by *New Testament Abstracts*. Among more recent writers, F. C. Grant (1962)[13] shows that St. Paul's background was basically Jewish; he believes that St. Paul's Judaism was that of the Western Diaspora.[14] It is maintained by van Unnik that St. Paul's background was not that of Tarsus at all, but of Jerusalem.[15] Finally, H. J. Schoeps in *Paul, the Theology of the Apostle in the light of Jewish Religious History*,[16] shows how the matter stands in the eyes of a distinguished Jewish scholar.

(b) *Jewish and Gentile Cross-fertilization*

That the background to St. Paul's thought was mainly Judaeo-Christian has long been accepted in academic and popular circles alike. But popular circles have hardly yet assimilated the further point that Jewish and Gentile thought were not wholly separate, but were subject to cross-fertilization. Again, 'Jewish' and 'Greek' are sometimes opposed in an emotive way as if the Jewish were good *because* it is Jewish and the Greek bad *because* it is Greek. We must add that the 'bad word' 'Greek' is normally applied in such circles to one of the aspects of Greek thought which differs from the Jewish. Elements of Greek thought which agree with the Jewish are simply disregarded.

The contemporary tendency to abandon the old dichotomy between Jewish and Hellenistic thought must be illustrated and defended in greater detail, since it has not yet become part of popular theology, unlike the previous insistence upon an almost exclusively Jewish background to St. Paul's thought.

It must be remembered that Jewish and Hellenic thought both grew up together in the Eastern end of the Mediterranean. Both owed a little to Egypt and a great deal to the civilization of the Tigris-Euphrates valley. Both alike derived something from Aegean culture. A vivid picture of what Greek and Jew share in common as part of their ancient heritage is presented by Cyrus H. Gordon in *Before the Bible*.[17] After the fall of the monarchy the Diaspora was a link between Jewry and other civilizations;

[13] Frederick C. Grant, *Roman Hellenism and the New Testament* (Edinburgh and London, 1962).
[14] op. cit. p. 146.
[15] W. C. van Unnik, *Tarsus or Jerusalem?* (E.T. London, 1962).
[16] H. J. Schoeps, (E. T. London, 1961), being a revision of the German original, (Tübingen, 1959).
[17] London, 1962.

some Jews became assimilated, while others reacted violently against the Gentiles. The Maccabean war did involve fighting against the Syrians, but it was also a war between Jews, between those who were prepared to adopt foreign ways of life and those who were not. Herod the Great was both a Jewish king and a Hellenistic prince.

The Sanhedrin itself, the supreme religious authority, was known by a Greek name. The Greek *sunedrion*, council, was transliterated into an Hebraic form in the Mishnah, and is only one of a number of such loan-words which have been recorded by S. Krauss.[18] In the time of Bar Kochba, the Jewish patriots exchanged letters in Greek, the language of the Eastern half of the Empire they were opposing.[19] The Jews infiltrated the whole of the Eastern half of the Empire and also Rome itself and the Western Mediterranean seaboard. Nevertheless, they retained their identity and seem to have persuaded many Gentiles to adopt the Jewish way of life.[20]

The influence of Jewish and Gentile culture upon each other has long been recognized. W. L. Knox, for example, laid stress upon it in 1925.[21] Since that time discoveries at Nag Hammadi and Qumran have strengthened this impression by providing examples of 'missing links'.

The thirteen coptic papyri found at Nag Hammadi in Egypt in 1945 include what is probably a translation of the Greek *Gospel of Truth* attributed to the heresiarch Valentinus by Irenaeus.[22] It must be emphasized that the interpretation of these documents has not yet been completed, and that any conclusions which we may draw from them are still to some extent provisional. For a general survey, including bibliographies, we may cite *The Jung Codex*,[23] *The Gnostic Problem*,[24] *Gnosticism and Early Christianity*,[25] and *Newly Discovered Gnostic Writings*.[26]

[18] *Griechische und lateinische Lehnwörter im Talmud, Midrasch und Targum* (Berlin, 1898).
[19] ch. Yadin, Y., *Biblical Archaeologist*, XXIV, (1961), pp. 34–50 and 86–95.
[20] For a concise account of the Jewish Diaspora in the Roman Empire and of Syncretism see C. Guignebert, *The Jewish World in the Time of Jesus* (E. T. London, 1939), pp. 211–52.
[21] *St. Paul and the Church of Jerusalem* (Cambridge, 1925), 126.
[22] *Adversus Haereses*, iii. 11, 12.
[23] H. C. Puech, G. Quispel and W. C. van Unnik, tr. and ed. F. L. Cross (London, 1955).
[24] R. McL. Wilson, London, 1958.
[25] R. M. Grant, Oxford, 1959.
[26] W. C. van Unnik, E.T., S.B.T. no. 30, (London, 1960).

From our angle two points are important. First, whether we can date it precisely or no, the *Gospel of Truth* presents a form of proto-Gnosticism which is nearer to the New Testament than is fully developed Gnosticism which we find in the *Pistis Sophia,* written in the third century A.D. For example, the *Gospel of Truth* contains no reference to such foundation stones of later Gnosticism as the enumeration of aeons and a distinction between the Unknown God, and a lower 'demiurge' who made the world. This suggests that later Gnosticism grew from Christianity and from non-Christian mythologies, as opposed to the view that St. Paul 'copied from Gnosticism'. But, granted that St. Paul did not borrow from Gnosticism in its later form, it is possible that in *Colossians* he presented the Gospel to men whose mental background was the seed-bed from which Gnosticism developed. This does not mean that St. Paul was a Gnostic, but it does mean that he had to some extent to use their intellectual framework in order to counter their teaching: otherwise he would have been like an elephant fighting a whale, unable to make effective contact with his adversary. The language of *Colossians* may owe something to Gnosticism, but the thought is Christian. That such typical 'Gnostic' (in a wide sense) writings as *Poimandres* and *The Sacred Discourse of Hermes Trismegistus* borrowed independently of each other from the Book of Genesis has already been shown by Dodd.[27] We may therefore suppose that Gnosticism borrowed from Christianity. But it is only fair to say that the Gnostics did raise important questions, and in order to answer them the church was compelled to some extent to recast Christianity in a Gnostic mould.

The Qumran discoveries lay renewed emphasis upon the fact that Judaism was far from being homogeneous. It included some who shared the dualism which we normally associate with Greece and Persia; it may indeed have been from these sources that the Qumran sectaries derived their dualistic tendencies. On this point I have nothing to add beyond what W. D. Davies has said in *Christian Origins and Judaism.*[28] In spite of the great importance of the Qumran documents for this subject, the upshot can be stated very briefly. In the Judaism of the first century A.D. there were men whose cast of thought included some 'typically Greek'

---

[27] *The Bible and the Greeks* (London, 1954²), pp. 170–234.
[28] London, 1962, Chs. v. and vii.

C

elements.[29] St. Paul probably derived his 'Hellenistic' elements *directly* from his fellow-Jews; it is, of course, possible that their ultimate source may have been Gentile.

It is, perhaps, a natural professional temptation for theologians to concentrate too much upon the specifically religious side of Jewish culture, and to cut religion off from life. This, above all in the case of Judaism, is to misunderstand both. It is well to bear in mind the possibility that Judaism in the first century A.D., the century of Philo and Josephus, was less inward looking, less 'ghetto-minded' than it was in the days when Rabbi Judah compiled the Mishnah: in between there fell the two destructions of Jerusalem in the days of Titus and of Hadrian. This appears reasonable from *Sotah* ix. 14, 'During the war of Titus they forbade . . . that a man should teach his son Greek'.[30] This point should not be pressed too far; Rabbi Judah himself is said to have spoken Greek. But it is natural that the traumatic experience of two terrible wars should weaken the links between Jew and Gentile. If we may not neglect general history, we must also remember the common life, as it can be reconstructed from surviving artifacts. On this basis E. R. Goodenough[31] has provided evidence that the Jews did not live in a state of cultural isolation, but that their art had much in common with that of their Gentile neighbours.

iv. St. Paul and Apostolic Christianity

The closeness of the connexion between St. Paul and his Christian predecessors and contemporaries has been emphasized by Hunter.[32] He defends the Apostle against the charge of being the great innovator or the great corrupter.[33] Two difficulties of method confront us when we ask ourselves whether St. Paul was an innovator. First, we do not know precisely what the 'original' pre-Pauline Christianity was, so that we have no sure basis for comparison; this makes it hard to answer Hunter's question one

---

[29] cf. T. Francis Glasson, *Greek Influence in Jewish Eschatology* (London, 1961).

[30] *Sotah* (The suspected adulteress), ix. 14, *Danby*, p. 305.

[31] *Jewish Symbolism in the Greco-Roman Period* (New York, 1953).

[32] *St. Paul and his Predecessors* (London, 1940¹). The 2nd. ed., 1961, includes an Appendix, pp. 116–150, noting further evidence in support of Hunter's case which has come to light after twenty years.

[33] op. cit., p. 150.

way or the other. Secondly, an estimate of the amount of innovation is inevitably somewhat subjective, since we have no agreed method of measuring it. Two scholars might agree exactly on what St. Paul had added or changed, and yet one might call him a traditionalist and the other a great innovator. Some believe that all change is bad simply because it is change. Others contend that a movement must change under new conditions to avoid fossilization. Quite apart from these emotive preferences, the nature and degree of change is a matter on which agreement is not easy.

One of the chief arguments used by Hunter is that St. Paul and the other first century Christians took over the content of 'the kerygma'. This argument is fundamentally sound, although certain qualifications are desirable.

The basic work on this subject was published as long ago as 1903 by Alfred Seeberg.[34] Since then it has been developed and refined by Dibelius,[35] Dodd,[36] and Hunter himself,[37] to mention only a few. Since this theory is so generally accepted we need not do more than refer to some of the literature. We can not maintain that there was a set, official form of preaching. We can say only that in Christian preaching and worship certain themes were dominant, and that they are reflected in the speeches of *Acts*,[38] in various passages in the Pauline Epistles,[39] and elsewhere in the New Testament.[40] The content of the kerygma varies according to the opinion of different scholars. We might summarize it as follows: (1) The Prophecies have been fulfilled. (2) The Messiah has been born. (3) And crucified. (4) And buried. (5) God has raised Him from the dead. (6) And exalted Him to His right hand. (7) The Spirit has been sent. (8) The Messiah will return in Judgement. (9) Therefore repent and accept Baptism. But this list is only a hypothetical reconstruction. Seeberg, for example, argues that the original kerygma included the Subjection of Angels, on the basis of Eph. i. 20; Phil. ii. 11; Col. ii. 20,[41] and the acknowledgement of Jesus as Lord, because of Rom. x. 9; 2 Cor. iv. 5,[42] though

[34] *Der Katechismus der Urchristenheit* (Leipzig, 1903).
[35] *From Tradition to Gospel*, E. T. 1933², (London, 1934).
[36] *The Apostlic Preaching and its Developments* (London, 1936), *Gospel and Law* (Cambridge, 1951).
[37] op. cit. esp. the Appendix to 1961².
[38] Acts ii. 14–40, iii. 13–24, iv. 9–12, v. 30–31, x. 37–43, xiii. 17–39.
[39] e.g., Rom. i. 1–5; 1 Cor. xv. 3–5; Phil. ii. 5–11.
[40] e.g., Eph. i. 20–2; 1 Pet. i. 20–2, iii. 18–iv. 6; Rev. i. 4–7.
[41] *Der Katechismus der Urchristenheit* (Leipzig, 1903), p. 78.
[42] op. cit., pp. 179f.

he agrees that the Resurrection of the Faithful, as opposed to that of Christ, was not part of the kerygma in the time of St. Paul.[43] On the other hand, there are those like Glasson[44] who do not believe that the Second Coming figured in the kerygma; this is not unreasonable, in view of the weak attestation of this 'article of the kerygma' in Acts. But it would be very difficult to argue against the 'hard core' of the kerygma, the Fulfilment of Prophecy, the Messiah, the Crucifixion and the Resurrection. Since more and more was added to this basic group, it is somewhat arbitrary to draw a line and to say 'this belongs to the kerygma but that does not'. We can be sure that kerygma regarded as an *activity* of proclamation gradually included within itself an ever-increasing content. We are concerned to maintain only this: that St. Paul took over from his predecessors in Christ the activity of kerygma or 'Proclamation' and some of its content, at least that recorded in 1 Cor. xv. 3-5.

The dominant position of the kerygma has been challenged by C. F. Evans.[45] He points out, fairly enough, that this theory has been accepted too readily, and that the kerygma regarded from the point of view of content, that is, as a hypothetical reconstruction of the main recurring themes of the preaching of the Apostles, has been accorded too much authority as the unchallengeable dogmatic core of the Biblical Revelation. It is most important to be clear what the upshot of Evans' article really is. It is not that there was no such thing as a kerygma, a basic core of early preaching: it is that we ought not to accept at their face value the presentations of the hypothetical kerygma which we find in the speeches in *Acts*. Evans' view of *Acts* is comparable to that of Dibelius.[46] Evans is on the whole more guarded in his judgement. His general line is that the author of *Acts* was writing for his own day, and not always recording just what actually took place.

It is not, however, necessary for us to enter into the contemporary discussions on *Acts*.[47] All we are concerned to argue is

---

[43] op. cit., p. 263.

[44] T. F. Glasson, *The Second Advent. The Origin of the New Testament Doctrine*, (London, 1963³).

[45] 'The Kerygma', *J.T.S.*, N.S., 7, Pt. II, (1956), pp.24–41.

[46] *Studies in the Acts of the Apostles*, (E. T. London, 1956). The original articles were published between 1923 and 1947.

[47] cf. H. Conzelmann, *The Theology of St. Luke* (E. T. London, 1960); J. C. O'Neill, *The Theology of Acts in its Historical Setting* (London, 1961); and C. K. Barrett, *Luke the Historian in Recent Study* (London, 1961).

that some at least of the basic kerygmatic convictions were derived
by St. Paul from earlier tradition: it does not matter, for our purpose, how that material was employed, if at all, in *Acts*. Seeberg
and Hunter have given us good reason to believe that some of the
Pauline phrases in kerygmatic passages are *pre*-Pauline. This contention Evans does not challenge or even discuss. He says that
the attempt to reconstruct the kerygma includes an examination of
passages in the Pauline Epistles which appear to be pre-Pauline.
He says that they may provide the more definite evidence, but that
he is concerned with the passages in *Acts*.

That St. Paul's teaching was basically the same as that of the
other Apostles is, after all, only what he himself would seem to
claim in 1 Cor. xv. 3, 'I handed on (*paredōka*, virtually a technical
term) to you the facts which had been imparted (*parelabon*, also
virtually technical) to me', and 1 Cor. xv. 11, 'This is what we all
proclaim'. But this would appear to be countered by Gal. i. 11-12,
'The gospel you heard me preach is no human invention. I did
not take it over (*parelabon*, the same virtually technical term) from
any man; no man taught it me; I received it through a revelation
of Jesus Christ'.

If we suppose that the same body of facts is comprised both
by 'the gospel you heard me preach' in Gal. i. 12, and by 'the facts
imparted to me' of 1 Cor. xv. 3, then we are driven to conclude
that what differed was St. Paul's attitude to this body of facts.
Lagrange, for example, suggests that St. Paul had become familiar
with the facts from the preaching of the Christians he had persecuted. What he received from Christ was a spiritual understanding (*intelligence spirituelle*) of the significance of those same
events.[50] But against all such views we must maintain that 'gospel'
can hardly mean anything but content.

Fridrichsen[51] has put forward a most attractive proposal.
There was, he believes, a 'Petrine Gospel' and a 'Pauline Gospel'.
The hard core of the kerygma, as we have it, for example, in 1
Cor. xv. 3f., was common to both. Typical of the Petrine Gospel
was the belief that Christ was the Jewish Messiah; we find this
emphasis in the Petrine speeches of *Acts*, for example, in Acts
iii. 12-26. The Pauline Gospel was characterized by the belief
that Christ had been exalted to be Lord of *all* peoples, not of the

[50] *Epître aux Galates* (Paris, 1925²), pp. 10–11 on i. 12.
[51] Anton Fridrichsen, *The Apostle and his Message* (Uppsala, 1947).

Jews alone. St. Paul received this 'Gospel', according to Frid-richsen, in the course of a vision. This was not his vision on the road to Damascus, but some other; a vision is mentioned at Acts xxii, 17. and no doubt there were others, as we can infer from 2 Cor. xii. 1f. Fridrichsen finds support for his theory in Eph. iii. 1-12, which is probably due to a follower of the Apostle, and in Rom. xvi. 25-7. It is unfortunate that some manuscripts place these verses at the end of Ch. xiv. and Papyrus 46 at the end of Ch. xv. This *may* mean that the verses are not by St. Paul, though it is more probable that the conflict of evidence is due to the fact that there was more than one recension of *Romans*. Fridrichsen can claim support from Col. i 25-7. 'The task assigned to me by God for your benefit: to deliver his message in full . . . to make known how rich and glorious it is among all nations', from Gal. i. 16, 'In order that I might proclaim him among the Gentiles', and from Gal. ii. 8, 'For God whose action made Peter an apostle to the Jews, also made me an apostle to the Gentiles'.

Any suggestion that there was tension between St. Peter and St. Paul causes some to raise the alarm-cry 'Tübingen'. It is true, of course, that the Tübingen-theory with its artificial schematiza-tion does not fit the facts. In particular, St. Peter was not a Judaizer, but in all probability, as Cullmann[52] has suggested, a man of insight and sensitivity, more articulate than his fellow-apostles, and accordingly their spokesman, who changed both his attitude and his sphere of activity in response to changing circum-stances. But this does not mean that apostolic Christianity was completely homogeneous. Judaism at this time embraced a rich variety of thought and practice. Christianity was a new move-ment, and wide divergencies had not yet taken place, but the New Testament itself bears witness to the variety of thought and prac-tice among those who acknowledged Jesus as Lord. St. Paul and the other apostles were united, we may conclude, upon most points; nevertheless, there were serious clashes. This is simply what the Apostle himself tells us in Gal. ii. 9. 'James, Cephas, and John, accepted Barnabas and myself as partners', and in Gal. ii. 11, 'But when Cephas came to Antioch, I opposed him to his face.' When Hunter claims that St. Paul was not a great innovator or corrupter[53] he means that the Apostle was not an innovator in

---

[52] *Peter, Disciple, Apostle and Martyr*, E.T. (revised), London, 1962[2], pp. 41 ff.   [53] *St. Paul and his Predecessors* (London, 1961[2]), p. 150.

the bad sense. We can agree that he was not a corrupter, and Hunter himself would surely agree that in the good sense St. Paul was the greatest innovator that the Christian church has known.

v. THE OLD TESTAMENT

The importance of the Old Testament for the background of St. Paul's thought cannot, of course, be exaggerated. It is, however, a major study in itself, and we can here accord it only the most cursory treatment; Amsler[54] has dealt with the matter clearly and concisely. Ellis[55] has discussed it lucidly and well, and his appendices are a most convenient source for statistical information. He recognizes about ninety quotations[56] from the Old Testament in the Paulines, apart from Ephesians and the Pastorals, which he himself includes with the rest, and nearly as many allusions.[57] It is not necessary to be too precise about actual figures: the tables produced by Ellis illustrate very adequately the well-known fact that St. Paul's writings are steeped in the O.T., especially in certain sections of his epistles. Ellis notes thirteen[58] cases where St. Paul would seem to agree with the LXX against the Hebrew. It is not possible, however, to attach too much weight to this last point, since there was no fixed text of the LXX universally accepted in St. Paul's day, so we cannot employ his use of the LXX as evidence for a Hellenistic element in his background. J. Bonsirven has shown clearly that St. Paul's technique of O.T. exegesis finds close parallels in Rabbinic sources.[59]

St. Paul's use of the O.T. provides clear evidence for the Jewish nature of his background. Can we maintain that it also sheds light upon his relation with the rest of the apostolic church? Perhaps a sixth of St. Paul's O.T. quotations are paralleled in the remainder of the N.T. It is not easy to assess the significance of

[54] S. Amsler, *L'ancien Testament dans l'Eglise* (Neuchâtel, 1960), pp. 44–62. There is a brief but excellent bibliographical footnote on p. 44, and an extended bibliography, pp. 231–8.
[55] E. Earle Ellis, *Paul's Use of the Old Testament* (Edinburgh, 1957).
[56] op. cit., Appendix I (A), pp. 150–2.
[57] op. cit., Appendix I (B), pp. 153–4.
[58] e.g., Rom. iv. 3, x. 16; 1 Cor. vi. 16; Gal. iii. 6, op. cit., Appendix I (A) pp. 150–2.
[59] *Exégèse rabbinique et exégèse paulinienne* (Paris, 1939). The tables, pp. 277–90. are useful. Especially valuable is Table II, pp. 284–90, which lists the quotations and allusions under the O.T. books. This shows in a vivid manner that St. Paul, like most Christian writers, had a preference for *Psalms, Isaiah.* and the Pentateuch.

this evidence. We can hardly attach weight to the fact that the Ten Commandments are quoted both at Matt. xix. 18, and at Rom. xiii. 9. But the remaining quotations suffice to show that in his use of the O.T. St. Paul had something in common with his fellow-Christians, in fact that there was a common Christian tradition of O.T. quotation and exegesis which St. Paul shared with the other N.T. writers and with the Church Fathers.[60] These facts have been explained in different ways by Rendell Harris[61] and B. P. W. Stather Hunt,[62] who support the Testimony Book hypothesis; by C. H. Dodd,[63] who has argued that the early church had a special predilection for certain parts of the O.T.; by K. Stendahl,[64] who thinks of a 'school' of writers; and by B. Lindars[65], who agrees both[66] with Dodd and with Stendhal. For our present purpose, however, it does not matter how much each of these factors may have influenced the growth of the Christian tradition of O.T. quotation and exegesis. We are concerned only with a section of the data which each of these theories seeks to explain, namely the overlap between St. Paul and the other N.T. writers in their use of the O.T., and this overlap is great enough to justify us in concluding that St. Paul is rightly to be placed in the Judaeo-Christian tradition. †

When we consider the substance of St. Paul's exegesis of the O.T. we pass from the background of his thought, the concern of the present chapter, to the body of his theology; and to this the remainder of the book will be devoted. Yet it is essential at this stage to say something about typology.

This word is employed in more than one sense, and to some readers its emotive overtones are good, to others bad. In the Bampton Lectures for 1814 van Mildert declares: 'It is essential to a type in the scriptural acceptation of the term that there should be competent evidence of the divine intention in the correspondence between it and the Antitype'.[67] Now that so much of what still seemed in 1814 to be history in the most objective sense is

---

[60] Ellis, op. cit., Appendix II, pp. 156–85, and Appendix iv, p. 187.
[61] *Testimonies*, (Cambridge), vol. i. (1916), vol. ii, (1920).
[62] *Primitive Gospel Sources* (London, 1951).
[63] *According to the Scriptures* (London 1952).
[64] *The School of St. Matthew* (Uppsala, 1954).
[65] *New Testament Apologetic* (London, 1961).
[66] These explanations are not mutually exclusive. Stendahl, for example (op. cit., p. 217), agrees that there may have been oral or even written testimonia but maintains that they cannot have come first in the development of quotations.
[67] Oxford, 1815 (no title except 'van Mildert's Bampton Lectures'), p. 239.

regarded as sacred legend, or as history transmuted by cultic use, it is difficult to be dogmatic. It requires some considerable degree of intellectual hardihood to maintain that God created one man Adam, or that He made the waters of the Red Sea a wall to the Israelites on the right hand and on the left (Exod. xiv. 29) with the purpose, at least in part, of foreshadowing Christ or Baptism. It is not surprising that typology fell into disrepute in the course of the last century when we remember that it was conceived in such a manner, and that the 'correspondences' were often trivial and artificial.

There is, however, a sense in which St. Paul's thought can fairly be called 'typological', though some of the associations of the word 'typology' are to be regretted.

In O.T. times the Jews believed in One God whose will was sovereign in all the world. He knew the end from the beginning. When he gave commandments to Moses or to David, He was well aware whether they would be obeyed or no. Although He allowed Himself, within limits, to be defied, yet His purposes were sure. His covenant-loyalty towards Israel, which had led to the Exodus, would lead, and did lead, to the return from the Babylonian Exile. It was therefore natural to refer to the Return by means of Exodus-language, and to speak of the achievement of His purpose for the end of history by means of language applied to the creation.

Such an attitude to the O.T. and to history was inherited from Judaism by the early Christians, St. Paul among them. As Christians they also believed that God's purposes all converged upon Jesus Christ and would reach in Him their fulfilment. It was only natural that they should apply to Christ, both during His incarnate life and at the return in glory, language derived from the O.T. accounts of God's great acts of salvation performed in the distant past; there is reason to suppose that Christ Himself did the same. For us this raises questions of fundamental importance, including the nature of the inspiration of Scripture and the authority of Christ. For St. Paul and the early Christians these questions did not exist. It could never have occured to St. Paul to doubt that the first man Adam and the last Adam were alike historical figures. He had not asked himself whether God *caused* the 23,000 to sin and perish as a warning to the Christians. He believed on the basis of the O.T. that they had in fact sinned and perished, and that nothing could take place without the will of God. He therefore concluded in 1 Cor. x. 11, 'All these things that happened to them were symbolic, and were recorded for our benefit as a warning.' St. Paul did not accept either predestination or typology as those doctrines were later developed, but there is a legitimate sense in which the words 'typological' and 'predestinarian' can be applied to the Apostle's theology, and it was in part his writings which gave rise to the later doctrines.

CHAPTER TWO

THE CREATED ORDER

i. CREATION

We shall misunderstand St. Paul if we imagine that he specu-
lated, as we are bound to do, about the origin of the physical
universe. Such cosmogonic enquiries fall within the legitimate
sphere of the scientist, who may fairly ask whether the universe
had a beginning in time, or whether we are to accept a 'steady-
state' theory, according to which the expanding universe has
always existed, and atoms of hydrogen always have been and
always will be spontaneously created. The systematic theologian,
indeed, must not neglect such matters and Mascall[1] has done well
to maintain that the Christian doctrine of creation, which is concerned with the sovereignty of God, is not bound to either a
'steady state' explanation of the universe or to what is popularly
known as the 'big bang' theory: both are consistent with the sovereignty of God, so that the systematic theologian should not attempt to choose between them, but should leave the decision to
the scientist. This question has been raised solely in order to show
by contrast what St. Paul was not concerned with.

Bultmann,[2] on the other hand, is probably going too far when
he says that God's creatorship is for St. Paul a proposition that
explains man's existence. It is true that St. Paul is interested in
the doctrine of creation mainly because of its practical and religious consequences for mankind: since the earth is the Lord's
and everything in it, therefore the Corinthians may eat anything
sold in the meat market without raising questions of conscience
(1 Cor. x. 26, referring back to Ps. xxiv. 1). But it is a mistake
to confuse what follows from a belief with the belief itself. It is
most improbable that St. Paul had ever doubted or even questioned the biblical account of the creation of the world as recorded
in *Genesis*.We may, as twentieth-century systematic theologians,
hold different views ourselves, but we must beware of the temp-

---

[1] E. L. Mascall, *Christian Theology and Natural Science* (London, 1956),
pp. 132–6, esp. 161–2.
[2] *Theology*, vol. i, p. 228.

tation to read back our own conclusions into the Epistles of St. Paul.

When the Apostle says, 'In Him (i.e. Christ) everything in heaven and on earth was created' (Col. i. 15) he presumably wishes to assert that there was no pre-existent matter which was organised and arranged to form the world, but that all things were created by God in Christ out of nothing (*ex nihilo*) to use the language of later traditional theology. Since matter has been created by God, who 'saw that it was good', St. Paul is able to say, Rom. xiv. 14, 'Nothing is impure in itself'. This was a matter of some importance in a world where it was widely taken for granted that matter in itself, if not actually evil, was at least tainted.

St. Paul's insistence that everything was created by God through or in Christ also countered any belief that the world was made by some such intermediary as the 'demiurge'. We are not justified in supposing that St. Paul actually developed his theory of the creation of all things in Christ because of the need to combat a belief in intermediaries of this nature held at Colossae. This theory is already found in a germinal form in 1 Cor. viii. 6, 'There is one Lord, Jesus Christ, through whom all things came to be'. It is always important to distinguish between the situation which merely evoked a particular expression or development of some belief and a situation which actually gave rise to the belief itself. Conditions at Colossae may well have evoked the expression of St. Paul's belief which is attested in Col. i. 15f., but the previous existence of the belief itself is made clear by 1 Cor. viii. 6.

ii. The 'Supernatural' Creation

(a) *Introductory*

Col. i. 16, 'In him everything in heaven and on earth was created, not only things visible but also the invisible orders of thrones, sovereignties, authorities and powers', makes it clear that not only what we should call the physical, material universe was made by God in Christ but also the 'spiritual' world of devils, angels etc. That all these beings were made by God is suggested in Rom. viii. 38-9, where 'the realm of spirits or superhuman powers' etc. is taken up in the words, 'Nothing in all creation that can separate us from the love of God in Christ Jesus our Lord'.

The question of 'evil spirits' is always liable to fan latent pre-
judices into flame. There are some who are misled by the false
glamour of 'science' and 'enlightenment' and laugh all such questions out of court without waiting to hear the evidence. Others
are led astray by the equally false glamour of a belief that to
'believe in devils' is a sign of being up with the latest theological
developments. Whatever the contemporary theological fashion
may be, it is our task to ask only what St. Paul believed. In recent
times attempts have been made by systematic theologians to apply
the term 'demonic' to such forces as nationalism, the cult of
wealth, friction between successive generations and clashes and
adjustments between the 'overprivileged' and the 'underprivileged': wherever human beings are the victims of powerful evil
forces which are not due to the conscious sin of persons now alive,
it is suggested, the situation may fairly be described as 'demonic'.[3]
Such suggestions may be a legitimate reapplication of Pauline
terminology, and it may even be the case that if St. Paul had been
alive today he would himself have applied these terms to the problems which now confront us, but such speculations are not
exegesis. We are concerned only with what St. Paul meant in the
epistles he wrote nearly two thousand years ago.

It is first necessary to draw a distinction. As MacGregor[4] has
pointed out, the 'devils' which Jesus cast out in the familiar nar-
ratives preserved in the Synoptic Gospels are not to be identified
with the principalities and powers etc. of *Colossians* and *Ephesians*,
though Schlier[5] would appear to deny this. The demons of the
Synoptic Gospels are the putative cause of afflictions which come
upon individuals and are now treated, with varying success, by
physicians and psychiatrists. The 'principalities and powers' are
the concern of politicians, sociologists, and others. The only passage in which it can possibly be argued that St. Paul speaks of
evil spirits as we know them from the Synoptic Gospels is 1 Cor.
x. 20f. The Greek word *daimonion*, which is so common in the
Gospels, does not occur in the Paulines or in *Ephesians* apart from
this passage.[6] Ling[7] reminds us that St. Paul is here referring

[3] cf. P. Tillich, *The Interpretation of History* (E.T. New York, 1936), pp.
77f.

[4] G. H. C. MacGregor, *N.T.S.*, i (1954), ' Principalities and Powers', pp.
17–28.

[5] H. Schlier, *Principalities and Powers in the New Testament* (Freiburg,
1961), p. 15.

[6] It is found in the Pastorals only at 1 Tim. iv. 1.

[7] Trevor Ling, *The Significance of Satan* (London, 1961), pp. 36–7.

back to the LXX of Deut. xxxii. 17, which teaches that worship of an idol is no better than worship of an evil spirit. Ling further remarks[8] that St. Paul thinks of the demons not as separate beings, but as a society. We may add that St. Paul employs the term only in order to express his detestation of idols, so that 'individual demons', which play a central role in the synoptics, occur only marginally in a single passage in the Pauline Epistles.

We may now pass on to consider 'principalities and powers'. The question naturally arises, Do such powers really exist, or are they examples of the use of mythological language to describe something which it is difficult to express precisely in literal terms? This question belongs to the sphere of systematic theology, as does the question, How are the realities referred to in the Bible by means of such conceptions as principalities and powers to be presented in twentieth century thought forms? I personally believe that, whatever may be said about the demons of the Synoptics, St. Paul, consciously or otherwise, was using mythological language. In other words, there *are* no principalities or powers, but St. Paul employs this language to express something which is both true and important. It is necessary for an author to be explicit on this point, so that the reader may be able to allow for his prejudice, but our present task is the descriptive, historical task of seeking to unravel the thought of St. Paul.[9]

(b) *The Old Testament background*

For this end it is essential to consider the evidence of the Old Testament, which at first sight appears to contain very little teaching on demons or on principalities and powers, especially when we view it against the background provided by the demon-ridden world of Mesopotamia. Closer investigation, it is true, shows that there are more references to non-human forces of evil than might at first appear. But when all allowances have been made, the fact remains that demons do not loom large in the Old Testament. Yet we do find various figures subordinate to Yahweh, who correspond to the gods of the heathen.[10] 'Sons of God' are beings partaking of the nature of divinity; this is an example of the very familiar Hebrew idiom which employs the phrase 'son of . . .' to

---

[8] ibid., p. 37.
[9] On this point I am, I believe, fundamentally in agreement with G. B. Caird, *Principalities and Powers* (Oxford, 1956), pp. x–xi.
[10] cf. G. B. Caird, *Principalities and Powers* (Oxford, 1956), pp. 1–11.

do the work of an adjective. 'Sons of God' are mentioned at Gen.
vi. 3, Deut. xxxii. 8, (LXX)[11] and Job i., where the satan[12] is num-
bered among them. We also read of beings whom Yahweh has appointed as his agents in the world. Deut. iv. 19 speaks of the heavenly
bodies which the Lord 'has allotted to all the peoples under
heaven', and we find quite explicitly in Ecclus. xvii. 17, 'He
appointed a ruler for every nation, but Israel is the Lord's own
portion.' In Dan. x. it is taught that the prince (*sar:* clearly a
supernatural being) of Persia and the prince of Greece, though
presumably appointed in the beginning by God, were actually
resisting His purposes; but we are left in no doubt of the fact that
these rebellious figures, who remind us of disloyal satraps in the
Persian Empire, will at last be brought to heel. The importance of
this teaching for our purpose is that St. Paul had before him in the
Old Testament spiritual beings who owed their existence and their
power to God, and nevertheless rebelled against Him, but would
at last be compelled to submit themselves to His will.

In the inter-testamental period such beliefs flourished exceed-
ingly.[13] Even more significant is the fact that according to the
Synoptic Gospels Christ Himself took for granted the belief in
demons which was widespread in contemporary Palestine, and that
His beliefs were shared by the early Church.

(c) *Evil Powers: their sphere of action*

In the thought of St. Paul the evil powers, like everything else,
owed their creation to God. (Col. i. 16, Rom. viii. 38). It is therefore natural that they have power in the physical world, including
power over the human body. A key passage for this problem is 2
Cor. xii. 7, 'And so to keep me from being unduly elated by the
magnificence of such revelations, I was given a sharp pain in my
body (*skolops tē sarki*) which came as Satan's messenger to bruise
me; This was to save me from being unduly elated'.

Ever since the time of Tertullian[14] it has been generally

---

[11] The M.T. reads 'sons of Israel'. The rendering of the LXX has now
received support from a Hebrew MS. found at Qumran. cf. Skehan, *B.A.S.O.R.*
no. 136 (Dec. 1954), 'A Fragment from the "Song of Moses".' I owe this
information to G. B. Caird, op. cit., p. 5, n. 1.

[12] In Job i. and Zech. iii. the word *sātān* is used with the article and refers to
an office. In 1 Chron. xxi. 1. '*Sātān*' is found for the first time without the
article, and may therefore be regarded as a proper name. '*Sātān*' occurs in the
O.T. in these three passages only.

[13] J. Bonsirven, *Judaïsme*, vol. i, pp. 239–46.

[14] *De Pudicitia*, xiii. 17.

supposed that St. Paul referred in this passage to some physical malady. Menoud[15] has suggested that the *skolops tē sarki* (lit., splinter for the flesh) was not a physical affliction at all, but a deep personal grief, due to the failure of Israel to respond to the Gospel. That this failure on the part of his own people was a deep sorrow for the Apostle is clear from Rom. ix. 3, 'For I could even pray to be outcast from Christ myself for the sake of my brothers, my natural kinsfolk (*tōn sungenōn mou kata sarka*, lit. 'my kinsmen according to flesh")'. But does St. Paul refer to this sorrow in the verse under consideration? Such a theory involves understanding flesh (*sarx*) to mean 'fellow-countrymen', i.e. the Jews. This supposition seems to gain support from Rom. ix. 14, 'I try to stir emulation in the men of my own race, lit. "in my own flesh" (*sarx*).' But in these two passages the word *sarx* is seen to be applied to the Jewish race only because of the context. We are not justified in giving the same interpretation to *sarx* in another passage where the context gives no such guidance. This 'theological' interpretation of 2 Cor. xii. 7 really relies upon supplying a context from another Epistle, namely Romans, which was not written until after 2 *Cor.* We may therefore accept the general view that St. Paul was here referring to some physical malady; the evidence of the New Testament and the speculations of scholars have been carefully reviewed by Allo,[16] who points out that all the data are consistent with malaria.

If Satan and his hosts are responsible for disease, it is only natural that he should be connected with death, since disease may be regarded as a 'mild attack' of death. Accordingly we find in 1 Cor. v. 5, 'This man is to be consigned to Satan for the destruction of the body (*sarx*)'. We must resist the temptation to see Satan wherever the Apostle speaks of disease or vice versa. In Gal. iv. 12–16 we hear about illness, but there is no mention of Satan. Equally, when St. Paul tells us in 1 Thess. ii. 18 that Satan thwarted his intention of going to Thessalonica, we cannot be sure that an attack of illness prevented him, though this is perfectly possible; it may have been the travelling arrangements which broke down.

This latter suggestion, which is of course mere guesswork, is consistent with the fact that for St. Paul all human life is under a

---

[15] Ph. H. Menoud, 'L'Echarde et l'Ange satanique', in *Studia Paulina*, Essays in honour of J. de Zwaan (Haarlem, 1953), pp. 163–71.

[16] Le Père E.-B. Allo, *Seconde Epître aux Corinthiens* (Paris, 1956²), Excursus xvi., pp. 313–23.

curse, though he does not always specify the cause of this evil; when, for example, he speaks of 'this present age of wickedness' (Gal i. 4) he does not make it clear whether we are to blame the fall of Adam or the activities of the powers of evil, and the same must be said about Col. i. 13, 'He rescued us from the domain of darkness.' Indeed, St. Paul is among the earliest writers to connect Satan, i.e. the Devil, with the Serpent who tempted Adam and Eve. These two figures were at first completely separate. The 'disloyal civil servant' Satan (in Greek *diabolos*, devil) was first indentified with the Serpent in Wisd. of Sol. ii. 24, 'But through the devil's (*diabolos*) envy death entered the world.' We find this same identification in Rom. xvi. 20, 'The God of peace will soon crush Satan beneath your feet', which refers back to Gen. iii. 15, where the Lord God promises that the seed of Eve shall bruise (crush) the serpent's head.

(d) *Did St. Paul use astrological language?*

This would suggest that St. Paul was more concerned with the fact of evil than with analysing its causes, so we need not be surprised that he employs the language of Astrology. Indeed, for St. Paul astrological forces are so closely merged with principalities and powers that it is not possible for us to disentangle them. This of course was not St. Paul's intention: he was eager to maintain that all things evil were to be overcome by Christ, no matter what their cause might be and no matter what terminology men might use to describe them.

For his readers, on the other hand, it was a matter of no small importance that Christ should be victorious over astrological forces. It would be superfluous to illustrate the widespread influence of astrological teaching, at all intellectual levels, in the world of St. Paul; for this we need only refer to the writings of Cumont. For St. Paul it was perhaps no more and no less 'superstitious' to believe in astrological forces than it was to believe in principalities and powers. It must again be stressed that astrological influences and 'spiritual forces' were alike originally good in the eyes of St. Paul, since God had created them, though they had gone astray, and men had wrongly submitted to their power.

The *magoi* who came to worship Christ according to Matt. ii. were of course, astrologers, as the New English Bible makes clear; earlier translations, not to mention Christmas carols, have obscured

D

this fact by speaking of 'Wise men' or 'kings'. St. Ignatius,[17] it is true, while recognizing the astrological background to the story of the Magi, regards it as an event which destroys sorcery and spells. Stendahl,[18] however, is correct when he points out that *Matthew* does not regard the Magi as evil. We may think of *Matthew* as saying, 'Scripture, the greatest of all authorities, bears witness to Christ. So, for that matter, does astrology, but Scripture is my concern'.

That St. Paul did include astrological influences among the spiritual forces which were to be made subject to Christ is a hotly disputed point. There are several relevant passages, of which one stands alone, namely Rom. viii. 38–9, 'For I am convinced that there is nothing in death or life, in the realm of spirits or superhuman powers (*archai*), in the world as it is (*enestōta*) or the world as it shall be (*mellonta*), in the forces of the universe, in heights (*hupsōma*) or depths (*bathos*)—nothing in all creation that can separate us from the love of God in Christ Jesus our Lord.' Now *hupsōma* and *bathos* were technical terms in astrology, denoting the highest and lowest point reached by a heavenly body. Lietzmann,[19] who defended this interpretation, himself doubted whether the Apostle would have known the meaning of these technical terms. Very probably he did not. In this case the sense of the passage would be, 'I do not know what these things are, but one thing I do know: whatever they may be, they cannot separate us from the love of God'. W. L. Knox[20] remarks that *enestōta* and *mellonta* also refer to the present and future position of heavenly bodies, and finds it difficult to suppose that so many technical terms borrowed from astrology could have come together in so short a space by accident.

The other 'astrological' passages are:

(1) Gal. iv. 3, 'We were slaves to the elemental spirits of the universe (*ta stoicheia tou kosmou*)'.

(2) Gal. iv. 9–10, 'How can you turn back to the mean and beggarly

[17] *Ephesians*, xix. 3, Lightfoot and Harmer (London, 1898), pp. 110–11 E. T. ib., p. 142.

[18] *Peake's Commentary on the Bible* (London, 1962), pp. 771–2 on Matt. ii. 1–12.

[19] Handbuch zum N.T., *An die Römer* (Tübingen, 1938³), p. 88. *hupsōmata kai tapeinōmata*, highest and lowest points, are employed astrologically in Plutarch, *Septem Sapientium Convivium*, 3, p. 149a, Teubner, *Plutarchi Moralia*, vol. i (Leipzig, 1925), p. 305.

See Arndt and Gringrich, *s.v. hupsos* and *bathos*.

[20] *St. Paul and the Church of the Gentiles* (1939),[1] reprinted without change 1961, pp. 106–7 and notes.

spirits of the elements? ... You keep special months and seasons and years.'

(3) Col. ii. 8, 'The elemental spirits of the world (*ta stoicheia tou kosmou*)'.

(4) Col. ii. 20–1, 'Did you not die with Christ and pass beyond reach of the elemental spirits of the world? (Greek as in (3)).[21]

The alternative explanation is that *stoicheia*, literally 'letters' and so 'elements', refers to 'elementary instructions concerning material objects', such as Jewish food laws. Lightfoot[22] rejects the 'astrological' interpretation on the ground that 'we' must include Jews. But astrology and magic, though officially forbidden among the Jews, were actually practised.[23] Certainly both astrology and obedience to the Torah could be regarded by St. Paul as things which the Christians ought to have 'grown out of', and that both would lead to a meticulous regard for times and seasons (Gal. iv. 10). But it is difficult to see how 'elements of the world' (*stoicheia tou kosmou*) can refer to the Torah or to teaching *about* the material world. It is true that in Heb. v. 12 *stoicheia* certainly means elementary teaching, and that it is followed by a genitive of the subject taught; but in that passage God's oracles are more clearly a subject for instruction.

It may well be that too much space has been devoted to a matter of minor importance. But, as Bruce[24] remarks, the vital fact is that Christ offers freedom from the 'elements' and from all half-realized forces, whether known or unknown: whatever influences or powers may come upon us, St. Paul maintains, Christ is their master.

The sphere of the activity of evil spirits extends over the whole universe, including 'the heavenlies', (*ta epourania*); this is made quite explicit in Eph. vi. 12, which speaks about 'superhuman forces of evil in the heavens' (*epourania*). In this century we tend to associate 'the heavenlies' or 'the spiritual' exclusively with the good. For St. Paul the 'spiritual' like the earthly, and like Man himself, was part of the created order and was capable of acting against God's will.

[21] Some spirits say to Solomon, 'We are the thirty-six *stoicheia*, the world rulers (*kosmocratores*) of this darkness', and their leader goes on, 'I am the first decan (*dekanos*, an astrological technical term) of the Zodiacal circle', in the *Testament of Solomon*, ed. C. C. McCown (Leipzig 1922), pp. 51–2. This composite work probably dates from early in the 3rd century A.D.).

[22] J. B. Lightfoot, *St. Paul's Epistle to the Galatians* (London, 1881⁷), on iv. 3.

[23] For evidence, see J. Bonsirven, *Judaisme* vol. ii, pp. 187–90.

[24] F. F. Bruce, London N.T.C., *Commentary on the Epistles to the Ephesians and the Colossians* (London, 1957), pp. 240–1.

(e) *The Activities of Evil Powers*

Accordingly, even 'religion' is not exempt from the activities of the spiritual forces of evil. This applies even to the Christian Church, as we find quite clearly in 2 Cor. xi. 14–5, 'Satan himself masquerades as an angel of light. It is therefore a simple thing for his agents to masquerade as agents of good'. In Gal. i. 8 the Apostle condemns any 'gospel' at variance with his own, even if proclaimed by 'an angel from heaven'; this may, however, be merely a forceful way of saying 'anyone at all, even if it were (which of course is impossible) an angel from heaven'. Much the same applies to 1 Cor. xii. 3, 'No one who says "A curse on Jesus!" can be speaking under the influence of the Spirit of God'; the meaning may be that such a person is speaking under the influence of an evil spirit, the situation presupposed by 1 John iv. 1–3, 'Test the spirits to see whether they are from God', etc. On the other hand, St. Paul may have thought that such a man was speaking merely from the evil of his own heart.

The influence of such evil forces is naturally apparent in pagan religion and culture, as we can see from 2 Cor. iv. 4, 'Their unbelieving minds are so blinded by the god (*theos*) of this passing age'[25] . . . A similar view of the state of the world is attested in Gal. i. 4, 'This present age of wickedness', Phil. ii. 15, 'A warped and crooked generation,' and Col. i. 13, 'The domain of darkness'.[26] It is not clear whether this state of affairs is due to the sin of Adam or to the activities of evil spirits; St. Paul is here concerned with the actual condition of human beings not with the causes which have led to it. The theory that evil spirits are behind the world and worldly culture receives a classic expression in 1 Cor. ii. 6–8, 'This passing age, nor to any of its governing powers (*archontes*) which are declining to their end.' Caird[27] makes the interesting suggestion that 1 Cor. xi. 10, 'Therefore it is woman's duty to have a sign of authority (*exousia*) on her head, out of regard for the angels,' means that Christian women must conform to the normal conventions of society, which are regarded as being under the control of 'angels' for the time being.

From spiritual beings thought of as 'spirits' of the age it is a very

---

[25] cf. the 'Prince (*Archōn*) of this world', John xii. 31, xiv. 30, xvi. 11.
[26] This view is found again in Eph. ii. 2, v. 16, and perhaps in Col. ii. 18, which may, however, attest only false beliefs among men.
[27] G. B. Caird, *Principalities and Powers* (Oxford, 1956), pp. 17–18.

short step to the theory that such forces are active in the political sphere and lie behind the power of the state; such theories will be examined in Ch. ix.[28]

St. Paul is more concerned with the all-pervasive large-scale effects of the demonic-complex as a whole than he is with the activities of 'individual' evil spirits. It was the serpent that seduced Eve (2 Cor. ix. 5), and the serpent is to be identified with Satan, as we gather from a comparison with Rom. xvi. 20.[29] The Crucifixion was due to the powers (*archontes*) that rule the world, and they are almost certainly evil spirits. Illness and death can also be connected with such influences, as we have already seen.[30] Satan tempts us in the moral sphere, exploiting our natural weakness (1 Cor. vii. 5), and also resorts to trickery (2 Cor. ii. 11, xi. 4), especially in the intellectual sphere (2 Cor. x. 4, 5).

(f) *Good Angels*

Richardson[31] roundly maintains that there are no good angels in St. Paul. This is almost accurate, and perhaps it may need to be said as a corrective to that over-sentimental regard for Angels which was one of the many strands of Victorian religion. But as a description of St. Paul's theology it is somewhat too sweeping. The archangel (*archangelos*) of 1 Thess. iv. 16 must surely be 'good'. It is also probably good angels who are referred to in 2 Thess i. 7, 'When our Lord Jesus Christ is revealed from heaven with his mighty angels (*met' angelōn dunameōs*) in blazing fire'. The phrase 'angel of light' tells in the same direction (2 Cor. xi. 14).[32] The angels of 1 Cor. xiii. 1 are neutral. Gal. iv. 14, 'You welcomed me as if I were an angel (*angelos*) of God', is probably irrelevant, since *angelos* could well mean merely 'messenger', and have no reference to superhuman beings. When St. Paul tells us in Gal. iii. 19 that the Law was given through angels he is really concerned to stress the superiority of Christ over the Law: he is not concerned at all with angels as such.[33]

[28] cf. pp. 229–31.
[29] cf. supra, p. 23.
[30] cf. supra, p. 22.
[31] *Introduction*, p. 209.
[32] 'The angels who are his chosen' (1 Tim. v. 21), are clearly good. 'His own' (tois hagiois) at 2 Thess. i.10 may well be good angels.
[33] M. Dibelius, *Die Geisterwelt im Glauben des Paulus* (Göttingen, 1909), p. 31, concludes that all the above passages refer to 'good' angels, and says the same about 'those that are his own' (*hagiōn*) in 1 Thess. iii. 13).

(g) *The 'reality' of Spiritual Powers*

We must face the question whether St. Paul believed in the real existence of 'spiritual beings' or whether for him they were merely a convenient way of speaking about God and human beings. In theological language we may ask whether they were hypostatized or whether they were mere personifications. We may phrase the question in the language of the market place by asking whether they were 'real' only in the sense that the British Lion or the Russian Bear are 'real', or whether St. Paul thought that they were real, though not physical, in the sense that a bear or a lion at the zoo is real. There is a natural temptation to 'save the credit' of St. Paul, and incidentally, to escape from the problem of de- or re-mytholog-ization, by supposing that for St. Paul they were only figurative, like the British Lion. It is most improbable that St. Paul had ever posed the question to himself consciously in explicit terms. We must keep quite separate the problem of what we ourselves believe, which is a matter of systematic theology, and the problem of what St. Paul believed. If we are to disagree with the Apostle, we should do so with our eyes open.

We can be sure that the resurrection body of Christ, though transmuted into spiritual substance, was in St. Paul's eyes completely real. It is therefore difficult, though perhaps not wholly impossible, not to suppose that when St. Paul paints a picture of our Lord's return in glory to judge the world, he believes that the glorified body of Christ and all the 'bodies' of those who play a part in the scene are 'real', that is to say hypostatized. 1 Thess. iv. 16 joins together the Lord Himself and the 'archangel's voice'; it seems probable that 'archangel' and 'voice' could be seen and heard like Christ Himself; the same may be said of the 'mighty angels' mentioned in 2 Thess. i. 7. 1 Cor. iv. 3, 'We are to judge angels,' points in the same direction. I would put no weight on the remaining ten[34] passages in the Paulines where *angelos* is found and *archangelos* occurs in the New Testament only at 1 Thess. iv. 16 and at Jude 9.

1 Cor. x. 21, 'You cannot drink the cup of the Lord and the cup of demons', would suggest that the 'Lord' and demons are alike real. It is less easy to be confident about 1 Cor. viii. 4–5, 'Of course, as you say, "a false god has no existence in the real world. There is

[34] Rom. viii. 10; 1 Cor. iv. 9, xi. 10, xiii. 1; 2 Cor. xi. 14, xii. 7; Gal. i. 8. iii. 19, iv. 14; Col. ii. 18.

no god but one" (almost certainly a quotation from the Corinthians' letter to Paul). For indeed if there be so-called gods—as indeed there are many "gods" and many "lords"....' St. John Thackeray[35] is probably correct when he says, 'The divinity of these powers is denied, not their existence'. It is likely that St. Paul does assert the objective, though not physical, existence of evil spirits, falsely believed to be 'gods' by those who worship them. On the other hand, it is possible that he believes in the real existence not of evil spirits, but of idols, that is to say physical objects, and that when he says that there are gods, he means only that there are many cults of such beings as Zeus, Aphrodite etc., in which case he is asserting the existence not of gods, but of names of gods. The classic exposition of this 'unreal' interpretation is by J. B. Lightfoot.[36] Satan is mentioned by St. Paul on eight[37] occasions, and the parallel figure of the Serpent (*ophis*) once[38]; it is hard to imagine that he is speaking figuratively.

It would seem that St. Paul did believe in the 'real' existence of a 'personal' Satan and probably of other personal demons. 'Satan' and 'Belial' (2 Cor. vi. 15) are the only 'personal' names accorded to 'devils' in the New Testament. The devil (*diabolos*) does not occur in the acknowledged Paulines, but is found in Ephesians at iv. 27 and vi. 11. All these figures are 'real' and personal. It is less easy to reach a conclusion about the possibly astrological 'elements' of Gal. iv. 3[f], and Col. ii. 2, 20 and the 'height' and 'depth' of Rom. viii. 38 or the 'cosmic powers and authorities', again in all probability astrological, of Col. ii. 15. Are they 'real' like Satan, though not personal, or are they 'figurative' like sin in Rom. v. 13, 'Sin was already in the world before there was law,' which we take to mean that men sinned before God gave the Law on Sinai, not that an external force called 'Sin' compelled them to do so? †

(h) *The fate of the Evil Powers*

I have failed to find a single passage in St. Paul's writings where 'demonic forces' as opposed to 'personal' demons are referred to which does not say either (1) that these forces have been overcome or (2) that they will be overcome or (3) that they are something which

---

[35] H. St. John Thackeray, *The Relation of St. Paul to Contemporary Jewish Thought* (London, 1900), p. 145.

[36] *Saint Paul's Epistle to the Galatians* (London, 1881[7]), p. 167, on iv. 3.

[37] Rom. xvi. 20; 1 Cor. v. 5, vii. 5; 2 Cor. ii. 11, xi. 14, xii. 7; 1 Thess. ii. 18; 2 Thess. ii. 9. [38] 2 Cor. xi. 3.

the Christian ought to have 'grown out of', apart from Col. i. 16, which makes it clear that all these powers were created through Christ and for Him.

That a victory has already been achieved is made clear in Gal. i. 3–4. 'Our Lord Jesus Christ, who sacrificed himself for our sins, to rescue us out of this present age of wickedness,' if we are correct in seeing here a reference to demonic forces at all. No such doubt arises with Gal. iv. 3^f, 'During our minority we were slaves to the elemental spirits of the universe but . . . God sent his own son . . . to purchase freedom for the subjects of the law'. The thought is continued in Gal. iv. 8. We read in Col. i. 13, 'He rescued us from the domain of darkness and brought us away into the kingdom of his dear Son, in whom our release (*apolutrōsis*, sometimes rendered "redemption") is secured,' in Col. ii. 15, 'On that cross he discarded the cosmic powers and authorities like a garment,' and in Col. ii. 20, 'Did you not die with Christ and pass beyond reach of the elemental spirits of the world?' These passages have been quoted in full to underline the obvious, but supremely important fact that the victory already achieved over the forces of evil is closely bound up with the cross of Christ.

This past victory on the part of Christ has moral and spiritual repercussions for those who are Christians; in view of Christ's victory, asks St. Paul in Gal. iv. 9, 'How can you turn back to the mean and beggarly spirits of the elements?' The same sentiment is repeated in Col. ii. 8, 18.

Christ has already won a victory over evil spirits at the cross, and He is destined to win another at the Second Coming. This is clear from Rom. xvi. 20, 'The God of peace will soon crush Satan beneath your feet,' 1 Cor. vi. 3, 'We are to judge angels,' 1 Cor. xv. 24, 'Then comes the end, when he delivers up the kingdom of God the Father, after abolishing every kind of domination, authority, and power,' and Phil. ii. 10, 'At the name of Jesus every knee should bow—in heaven, on earth, and in the depths.'

The 'past' victory is stressed, without reference to the cross, at Eph. i. 20–23 (where the resurrection is mentioned), ii. 1–2. and iii. 10–12. A further victory by Christians through Christ's power, over evil spirits is the theme of Eph. vi. 10–19.

On the subject of principalities and powers one final question remains: are they merely defeated, or are they in some sense saved? At this point we, as twentieth century Christians are bound to declare an interest. It would be a great practical convenience for us if we could say that these powers were to be saved, since that would give us a biblical ground for maintaining that such modern 'principalities and powers' as nationalism, loyalty to a social class, whether high or low, and the techniques of mass communication and consumer-persuasion, though sometimes demonic in their effects, are nevertheless capable of redemption. Such a belief may well be true, but it is a grave mistake to suppose that *all* truth is to be found in the Bible, since it tempts us to read into the Bible teaching which simply is not there.

There is nothing surprising in the belief that these powers should be saved. After all, it was when we were sinners in a state of enmity with God that Christ died to save us. Richardson[39] maintains that the cosmic forces were to be saved. He says that in 2 Cor. v. 19, 'God was in Christ reconciling (*katallassōn*) the world (*kosmos*) to Himself,' *kosmos* (world) includes all creation, not excepting the elements (*stoicheia*) etc. This is true, but we may fairly doubt whether St. Paul was aware of this, since he continues, 'No longer holding men's misdeeds against them, and that he has entrusted us with the message of reconciliation.' Cerfaux[40] argues that the powers are defeated, while mankind is saved, not overcome, and that the Church cannot be stretched to include the powers. The key verse is Col. i. 20, 'Through him God chose to reconcile the whole universe (*ta panta*) to himself . . . whether on earth or in heaven'. Moule[41] compares Romans viii. with its apparent promise of redemption for Nature as well as Man. It may be that St. Paul is more concerned with the completeness of Christ's victory than with the fate of the powers. If he envisaged the redemption of demonic forces, he did so only out of the corner of his eye: the redemption of mankind held the centre of his field of vision.

iii. The Human Creation

(a) *Introductory*

Theological students frequently gain the impression that the biblical view of man is 'unitary', and to be accepted; while the Greek theory, which is to be rejected, can be summed up in the phrase

[39] A. Richardson, *Introduction*, p. 213.
[40] L. Cerfaux, *Church*, p. 339.
[41] C. F. D. Moule, *The Epistles of Paul the Apostle to the Colossians and to Philemon* (Cambridge, 1957), ad loc.

'*sōma sēma*', which means that the body (*sōma*) is a tomb (*sēma*).
This is a gross oversimplification and it presupposes a false manner
of asking the question, but it does do justice to this vital fact that
for St. Paul sin is not a taint due to 'flesh' (*sarx*) or body (*sōma*)
which is inherently evil, but is due to wrong willing by the whole
personality, though this wrong willing often takes place in the
sphere of flesh. This is made abundantly plain in Gal. v. 19–21,
'Anyone can see the kind of behaviour that belongs to the lower
nature (*sarx*, flesh): fornication, impurity, and indecency; *idolatry*
and *sorcery*; *quarrels*, a *contentious temper*, *envy*, *fits of rage*, *selfish
ambitions*, *dissensions*, *party intrigues*, and *jealousies*; drinking bouts,
orgies, and the like.' The sins represented by the words which
have been italicized above might well be committed by disembodied
spirits, though the remainder are sins committed in the sphere of
the body. Thus the 'deeds of the flesh' are not necessarily physical,
so that the 'body' is not the cause of all sin, even though it is the
sphere of many sins.

(b) *Dualism*

It will help to avoid confusion if we first examine the word
'dualism', which is susceptible of several different applications:

(1) *Anthropological dualism*, that is the view that in human beings
there are two elements which can be separated. These are distinguished as (a) body or flesh and (b) soul or spirit; as (a) extended
substance, *res extensa* and (b) thinking substance, *res cogitans*; or
in our own day this division has been expressed by one of its leading
opponents, Gilbert Ryle,[42] in the phrase 'the ghost in the machine'.

(2) *Metaphysical dualism*. We shall reserve this term for the
belief that 'flesh 'or 'body' is by its very nature evil and the cause
of evil. From this it might follow that an incarnate being was
bound to sin simply because he was incarnate. Such views no doubt
lay behind the docetist theory that Christ had only an apparent,
'seeming' body, since if His body had been 'real' He would inevitably have sinned.

(3) *Cosmogonic dualism* is the belief that two different 'forces',
generally opposed as 'good' and 'evil' created the universe.

(4) *Moral dualism* is the belief that sin matters, and that conduct
is not unimportant.

It is clear that the Manichaeans were strongly dualistic in each

[42] *The Concept of Mind* (London, 1949), p. 15, and *passim*.

of the four senses distinguished above. All Jews, Christians, and Moslems are moral dualists, but this has not been true of some idealists. It is possible to be a dualist in the anthropological but not in the metaphysical sense, that is to say, it is perfectly possible to believe that the soul or spirit is separable from the body, and alone survives death, which is a form of anthropological dualism, and yet to reject the belief that matter or the body are evil as such: this is probably the position of many Christians.

In recent years theologians have become increasingly opposed to both metaphysical and anthropological dualism as defined above, largely through a realization of the Hebrew background of the New Testament. This tendency has been reinforced by certain other factors. First, some have reacted against 'nineteenth-century idealism' or 'Greek thought' merely because it is 'Greek' or 'nineteenth century': criteria of this nature should not be allowed to weigh in the balance on one side or the other.

Secondly, the monistic view, the theory that man is an 'ensouled body', not a 'ghost in a machine', has gained support from the need for Christians to cope with the opportunities and dangers which arise from technological advances and our growing control over our natural environment. When human beings were at the mercy of disease and famine it was hardly surprising that Christianity, like the other world religions, should accept the view that the only real life is the life of the spirit and that the material world is something evil from which we should be glad to escape. Now that antibiotics and tractors make it feasible to overcome famine and disease, we have become more aware of our duties towards our neighbour in material matters, simply because it is now easier to perform them. Since we are more aware of these duties we listen to William Temple's aphorism 'Christianity is the most materialistic of all religions' and lay stress upon the unity of our human nature.

A third factor is the rapid advance in the biological sciences. Diseases formerly regarded as 'mental' are now being treated, not without success, by brain surgery and drugs. Some forms of idiocy can be cured by supplementing the defective secretions of endocrine glands. Others are due to diseases in pregnancy or to the unforeseen side-effects of drugs administered to the mother during that period. Further, the science of genetics has made such strides that it has become easy for the man in the street to suppose that we are 'determined by our parents' genes'.

All these newly discovered facts have influenced popular opinion in the direction of 'Materialism'. The facts must, of course, be accepted: they must not be 'explained away' or glossed over. They raise formidable problems concerning the freedom of the will and life after death. These questions must be referred to the systematic theologian, who has to consider in addition the contributions made by philosophers, psychologists and students of parapsychology. For our immediate purpose it is only necessary to register the fact that advances in technology and in theoretical biology have predisposed us to accept a monistic view of man, and to reject both metaphysical and anthropological dualism.

It is these factors, in addition to a praiseworthy awareness of Hebrew background which have caused so many students to form the oversimplified opinion that Greek thought is 'dualistic' and 'bad', while Hebrew thought is 'unitary' and 'good'.

(c) The Greek doctrine of man

When we say that Greek thought is 'dualistic', we are applying the word both in the anthropological and in the 'metaphysical' sense. That is to say, according to the 'Greek' view, the 'soul' or 'spirit' is good and is the essential part of man, while the 'flesh' or 'body' is inherently sinful. This is a fair description of one strand only in Greek thought. The Homeric view of life after death, as we find it in Odyssey xi. is not unlike the Sheol-theory of the Old Testament. Even Plato does not maintain that soul (*psychē*) is good without qualification. The 'desiring' (*epithumētikon*) part of the soul is the source of sexual feeling, hunger and thirst, while the 'passionate' part (*thumoeides*) is responsible for anger and courage; both are separate from and inferior to the rational part.[43]

(d) The Hebrew doctrine of man

The teaching of the Old Testament on the nature of man is well known, but is too important to be taken for granted. First, there is little or none of the anthropological dualism which is a marked feature of some Greek thought. The word *nephesh* (Greek *psychē*), 'soul' is actually applied to dead bodies in such passages as Num. v. 2.[44] Again, physical organs, such as 'heart', 'liver' and

---

[43] *Republic*, iv. 439e–441b.
[44] W. David Stacey, *The Pauline View of Man* (London, 1956), p. 87.

'kidneys' are thought to be the seat of feeling and will, while the soul can be the seat of physical sensation. Exod. xiv. 4, 'I will harden Pharaoh's heart', impresses us less than it ought to, because here, as so frequently happens, the English language has been moulded by the Bible, so that 'heart' is commonly used among us in a figurative sense; but in Exod. xiv. 4 and many similar passages such words as 'heart' (Heb. *lēb*, Greek *kardia*) are employed in a sense which is quite literal, even though 'non-physical' functions are ascribed to a physical organ.[45] 1 Kings xvii. 22, 'And the soul of a child came into him again and he revived', may be a case of the 'return' of a 'separable' soul, or it may be that 'his soul returned' means simply 'he revived'. Eccles. iii. 21, 'Who knows whether the spirit (*ruaḥ*) of man goes upward, and the spirit of the beast goes down to the earth', shows that the writer was familiar with anthropological dualism; but that he probably rejected it. If dualism of this kind is to be found in the Old Testament at all, it is merely peripheral: the basic teaching of the Old Testament is anthropological monism.

The Old Testament never teaches metaphysical dualism, the belief that 'flesh' and matter are evil, although in a very few non-typical passages 'flesh' (*bāsār*, *sarx*) is associated with weakness. Isa. xxxi. 3, 'The Egyptians are men, and not God; and their horses are flesh, and not spirit,' is the *locus classicus*, and the same thought occurs in Gen. vi. 3, and in 2 Chron. xxxii. 8.

It is only too easy when studying the Old Testament to be led astray by the availability of certain kinds of evidence and by our own interests. F. H. Bradley suggested that for a dog 'What smells is real' because of the acuteness of the dog's sense of smell. We are naturally tempted to lean too hard upon the valuable assistance which we can obtain from the Concordance. It is true that we learn much about Old Testament anthropology by examining the use made of such words as *bāsār*, flesh, *nephesh*, neck and so breath, 'soul' and 'person', but we must not overlook the even more vital fact that God made men and requires them to obey[46] Him.

There are certain commonplaces of Old Testament Theology which it would be wasteful to substantiate here, but they are so

[45] cf. H. Wheeler Robinson, *The Christian Doctrine of Man* (London, 1926³), p. 22f.
[46] It is in the light of this basic insight that W. Eichrodt views man in *Man in the Old Testament* E.T., S.B.T., no. 4, (London, 1951).

important that it is essential to recall them in outline. First, the
Old Testament speaks of Man aspectivally, not partitively. We
speak of a man partitively when we split him up into head, trunk
and legs, or into body, soul and spirit: we speak of him aspectivally
when we call him an Englishman, not a German, or a Methodist,
not a Congregationalist; the whole man is Methodist, so that
Methodism is not part of the man, but an aspect of the whole
man. It is fair to say that the anthropological language of the
Biblical writings is aspectival, not partitive. Thus ' heart', 'soul'
and 'flesh' are not typically three constituents which can be
combined with others and tied together to make up a complete
man. They can each of them be applied alone to the complete
man, but they are typically employed under different circumstances: 'heart' is used to refer to the whole man when willingness
or obedience is thought of; 'soul' is used when the life of the person
is in question. Ezek. xviii. 20, 'The soul (*nephesh*) that sins shall
die', makes it clear that these terms are not used exclusively.
'Soul' is employed when both obedience, which is 'typical' of the
heart and life are in question. Man then is a whole, whose different
activities are spoken of by means of different terms, and it is God
who made him and requires his obedience. Also, as will appear
later, man is not an isolated individual, but exists in solidarity
with his fellowmen and with his physical environment.

In the intertestamental writings we encounter anthropological
and metaphysical dualism, which it is hardly possible to detect in
the Old Testament. 2 Esdras vii. 78, 'When the decisive decree
has gone forth from the Most High that a man shall die, as the
spirit leaves the body to return again to him who gave it . . .'
presupposes a degree of separation between body and spirit which
makes it impossible to withhold the description of anthropological
dualism, and the same must be said about the Apocalypse of
Moses, xxxii. 4, 'Rise up Eve, for behold, Adam thy husband hath
gone out of his body. Rise up and behold his spirit borne aloft to
his Maker'.[47] Wisd. of Sol. ix. 15, 'For a perishable body (*phthar-
ton sōma*) weighs down the soul', does at least lay stress upon the
limitations imposed by the body, though it would be going too far,
as Goodrick[48] points out, to see evidence in this verse for the view
that the body is inherently evil. The thought of Qumran associates

[47] Charles, vol. ii. p. 149.
[48] A. T. S. Goodrick, *The Book of Wisdom* (London, 1913), ad loc.

flesh not only with weakness but with sin. In the Psalm with which the Manual of Discipline concludes we read:

'But I belong to wicked mankind
To the company of erring flesh . . .
And if I stumble in the iniquity of flesh. . .[49]

Here again, we cannot say that flesh is regarded as inherently evil, but we cannot blink the fact that evil and the flesh are very closely associated.

(e) St. Paul's unitary view of man

St. Paul himself differs very little from the Old Testament in respect of anthropological and metaphysical dualism. A man who believed as St. Paul did in the creation of all things by God could not in any case hold either anthropological or metaphysical dualism in an extreme form. Since God created body and 'soul', neither of the two could be of themselves wholly evil or wholly independent of each other. Equally, no one who believed in God as creator could accept anthropological monism in its extreme physical form, which we should describe as biological mechanism.

The fundamental conclusion, although some qualification will be necessary, is that St. Paul did not accept either anthropological or metaphysical dualism. Rom. xii. 1, 'Offer your very selves (*sōmata*, lit. "bodies") to him', and Rom. xiii. 1, 'Every person (*psychē*, lit. "soul") must submit to the supreme authorities', illustrate the fact that for St. Paul, as for Old Testament writers, 'soul' and 'body' so far from being discrete, mutually exclusive parts of the human being, could each by itself be applied to the entire personality.

A most illuminating passage is 1 Thess. v. 23, 'May God himself, the God of peace, make you holy in every part, and keep you sound in spirit, soul and body, without fault when our Lord Jesus Christ comes'. The language is trichotomistic, it is true: the thought is monistic, both in the anthropological and in the metaphysical sense. The threefold formula may be due to some liturgical tradition, but St. Paul employs it to express the prayer that the whole man will be preserved and kept holy. If he had

[49] *Manual of Discipline*, col. xi. lines 9 and 12, in Millar Burrows, *The Dead Sea Scrolls* (New York, 1956), p. 388 and Theodore Gaster, *The Scriptures of the Dead Sea Sect* (London, 1957), pp. 128–9. For discussion and reference to literature, see W. D. Davies, *Christian Origins and Judaism* (London, 1962), pp. 149–52.

been a metaphysical or anthropological dualist, he would have prayed that when the sinful body perished the spirit, and perhaps also the soul, would soar aloft to its natural abode, being liberated from the defiling influence of the body. Again, 2 Cor. v. 4, 'We do not want the old body stripped off (as a dualist would have done). Rather our desire is to have the new body put on over it', and Phil. iii. 21, 'He will transfigure (*metaschēmatisei*. Not cast off and replace, which would be dualistic) the body belonging to our humble estate', make it clear that the Apostle's thought is basically monistic.

(f) *St. Paul's modifications of the unitary view*

There are, however, other passages which show that his teaching is not unqualified anthropological monism. Phil. i. 23-4, 'What I should like is to depart and be with Christ; that is better by far; but for your sake there is greater need for me to stay on in the body (*sarx*, lit. "flesh")', demonstrates his conviction that he is not so completely dependent upon his own physical body that he cannot survive apart from it. Even if, as some suppose, he would be 'asleep', i.e. not conscious, with Christ, at least he would *exist* with Christ and without his earthly body. The same conclusions arise from 2 Cor. v. 1-10.[50] 1 Cor. v. 3, 'Though I am absent in body (*sōma*), I am present in spirit (*pneuma*)', and Col. ii. 5, 'For though absent in body (*sarx*), I am with you in spirit (*pneuma*)', prove nothing, since *pneuma* may mean merely ' in thought or intention',[51] though it is not easy to parallel this meaning.

Far more important is 2 Cor. xii. 3, 'This same man (whether in the body [*en sōmati*] or out of it [*chōris tou sōmatos*] I do not know—God knows) was caught up into Paradise'. The fact that he does not know makes it clear that this experience was an experience of the real person not a mere 'invented' illustration, and that for St. Paul it was not impossible that a human being should undergo an 'out of the body' experience and return to the body again. This, we must surely admit, is a case of anthropological dualism. It is peripheral, not central or normative in the Apostle's thought, but it is there, and we ought not to ignore it.

2 Cor. xii. 3 shows that his anthropology was not completely homogeneous. It is also shown how easy it is for us to be misled by

---

[50] Cullmann and Ellis believe in the ' sleep of the soul '. Their theories are discussed in Chapter x., pp. 262-70.

[51] So Allo, *Première Épître aux Corinthiens* (Paris, 1956), ad loc.

our own terminology. It is beyond question that for St. Paul the human being is more than his physical body. When we say that St. Paul was an anthropological monist, we do not mean that, in his opinion, man consists of only a single factor, for example the physical body, which is what the word 'monist' would naturally suggest. We mean that, in his view, the constituent parts of man are closely linked together; the more loosely the parts are linked, the more suitable the term 'dualistic' becomes. When, as in the case of a compound like water, the constituent elements are so closely bonded that the eye cannot distinguish them, the word 'monistic' is suitable. A 'man-on-a-horse' would naturally be described in dualistic language. Yet it is possible for the oxygen and hydrogen which make up the compound water to be split up, so that what is usually 'monistic' must now be described in dualistic terms. St. Paul's anthropology is 'close-knit' and may reasonably be called 'monistic'. But on rare occasions, when dealing with non-normal situations, such as death and a possible out-of-the-body experience, he employs dualistic language.

(g) 'Flesh' and sin

It cannot be said that St. Paul is a metaphysical dualist; that is, he does not believe that flesh is inherently evil. The word *sarx* (flesh) is found eighty-one times in the Paulines, and nine times in *Ephesians*. Often *sarx* is used in a purely physical sense, as in 1 Cor. xv. 39, 'All flesh is not the same flesh; there is flesh of men, flesh of beasts etc.' Clearly in this application the word is devoid of ethical overtones. On other occasions, as in Rom. i. 3, 'On the human level (*kata sarka*, lit. 'according to the flesh') he was born of David's stock,' the word refers only to racial or social matters and has nothing 'metaphysical' about it. Sometimes also the word is used to mean 'the lower ethical level', as in Gal. v. 24, 'Those who belong to Christ Jesus have crucified the lower nature (*sarka*, lit. "flesh") with its passions and desires.' Gal. v. 19f[52] makes it clear that when 'flesh' is used in a moral sense it does not necessarily have any physical meaning, since most of the sins ascribed to the lower nature (*sarx*) could well be practised by a disembodied spirit. The main argument for the view that St. Paul did not regard the flesh as inherently evil is this: *sarx* sometimes means 'flesh' and sometimes lower nature or sin; the mere fact that the same word

[52] *supra*, p. 32.

E

can mean both 'sin' and 'flesh' does not justify us in concluding that
flesh is inherently sinful. W. D. Davies has listed the occurrences of
sarx in the physical and in the ethical senses of the word.[53] Fundamentally, this is a sound conclusion, but just as 'flesh' (*bāsār*) in the
Old Testament is associated with weakness, so 'flesh' (*sarx*) in the
New Testament is associated with sin.

This association of sin with the physical body is clear from Rom.
viii. 12–13, 'It follows, my friends, that our lower nature (*sarx*,
flesh) has no claim upon us; we are not obliged to live upon that
level (*kata sarka*)'. So far we could maintain the *sarx* in this
passage merely refers to the lower nature, and does not associate
this lower nature with the 'flesh' which is its primary meaning.
But St. Paul continues immediately, in Rom. viii. 13, 'If you do so
you must die. But if you by the spirit put to death all the base
pursuits of the body (*sōma*), then you will live'. As a contrast to
spirit (*pneuma*) we should have expected *sarx*, which might have
had only an ethical sense, without any physical reference: we find
instead *sōma* which must have a physical meaning, and this shows
that for St. Paul the physical and the ethical connotations of *sarx*
were to some extent associated. This association of flesh with sin
and evil was probably connected with the fact that, for St. Paul, as
will appear from the next chapter, the created universe was
associated with the sin of Adam (Rom. viii. 19–23). We are justified
in seeing an association of sin with flesh in Gal. v. 19 and 24, and
in Rom. vii. 14, 'I am unspiritual (*sarkinos*).' The word *sarkinos*,
to judge from its formation ought to mean 'made of flesh' with a
primarily physical connotation, while '*sarkikos*' ought to mean
'flesh-directed' and to have an ethical application. Here *sarkinos*,
literally 'made of flesh', clearly bears an 'ethical' meaning. It
would be unwise to lay too much emphasis on this point, since
the connotations of the two words overlap, and they are confused in
manuscripts.[54] But the mere fact that such overlapping and confusion do occur justifies us in supposing that the two applications of
the word *sarx* were linked in the thought of St. Paul. It is fatally
easy for non-typical passages, which have to be discussed precisely
because they are non-typical, to create a misleading impression. St.
Paul did *not* believe that flesh is inherently evil: he was not a

[53] *Christian Origins and Judaism* (London, 1962), p. 153.
[54] See Arndt and Gringrich on both words, and also Blass-Debrunner-Funk,
section 113 (2), p. 62.

metaphysical dualist any more than he was an anthropological dualist. But just as, in unusual circumstances, he employs, though only rarely, the language of a loose-knit as opposed to a close-knit anthropology, so, though rather infrequently, he tends to associate flesh with evil.

(h) *St. Paul's anthropological terminology*

We must now briefly review the words which St. Paul employs to express his thought on the nature of man. These are flesh (*sarx*), body (*sōma*), spirit (*pneuma*), heart (*kardia*), mind (*nous*), remorse or conscience (*syneidēsis*), soul (*psychē*), and inner man (*esō anthrōpos*). These terms have been subjected to a valuable analysis by Wheeler Robinson,[55] Bultmann,[56] Ryder Smith,[57] and Stacey.[58]

The connotations of these words are not naturally exclusive, but overlap to a considerable extent. 'Flesh' can possibly be used, like 'body' and 'soul', to refer to the whole person. Stacey[59] compares 2 Cor. vii. 5, 'Even when we reached Macedonia there was still no relief for this poor body (*sarx*) of ours' with 2 Cor. ii. 12, 'When, I came to Troas . . . I still found no relief of mind (*pneuma*)'; it may be, however, that the passages are not exactly parallel, and that complementary aspects of the Apostle are being stressed in each case.

'Flesh' can mean 'on the human level,' as in Philem. 16, 'As a dear brother, very dear indeed to me, and how much dearer to you, both as a man (*en sarki*, lit. "in the flesh") and as a Christian'. Flesh also suggests dullness of apprehension, as in Rom. vi. 19, 'To use words that suit your human weakness (*sarx*)'. It would be superfluous to repeat or expand what has already been said on the subject of 'flesh'.

The word 'body', *sōma* must be discussed further when we come to consider eschatology.[60] In the Greek of the New Testament it normally refers to the human body, alive or dead. St. Paul applies it to the human body in Gal. vi. 17, 'I bear the marks of Jesus branded on my body'. This 'purely physical' use is found in Rom. i. 24, iv. 19, vi. 12; 1 Cor. vi. 13; 2 Cor. x. 10. The word

[55] H. Wheeler Robinson, *The Christian Doctrine of Man* (Edinburgh, 1926³), esp., pp. 104–15.
[56] R. Bultmann, *Theology*, vol. i, esp., pp. 190–246.
[57] C. Ryder Smith, *The Bible Doctrine of Man* (London, 1951).
[58] W. David Stacey, *The Pauline View of Man* (London, 1956). An illuminating chapter is devoted to each of the main anthropological terms used by St. Paul.
[59] op. cit., p. 157.   [60] cf. *infra*, p. 248–60.

is applied to the human being as a whole in 1 Cor. vi. 15, 'Do you
not know that your bodies (*sōma*) are limbs and organs of Christ?'
which Stacey[61] compares with 1 Cor. xii. 27, 'Now you (*humeis*)
are Christ's body, and each of you a limb or organ of it'.

We must mention at this point some Pauline uses of the word
'body' which are not really anthropological. Since 'body' comes
to mean 'an organized whole' the Apostle can speak of the body or
sōma of sin (Rom. vi. 6) . The specifically Pauline application of
the word ' body ' to the Church will be examined in Ch. viii.[62]

The most important uses of the word 'spirit', *pneuma*, do not
fall within the sphere of anthropology at all, but are found in
passages concerned with the Third Person of the Trinity or with
the doctrine of salvation. 'Spirit' is a common word in the LXX
and in secular Greek. In the New Testament it is applied to new
situations and gradually acquires new shades of meaning. Most
often it refers to the Third Person of the Trinity, as in Rom. v. 5,
'Through the Holy Spirit he has given us', Rom. viii. 4, etc.[63]
Sometimes St. Paul employs 'spirit' in situations where systematic
theologians of a later age might use such language as 'in a state of
grace' or even 'the grace of humility', etc.[64]

It has been maintained that the spirit is something which only
Christians 'possess'. Since all the Pauline Epistles are addressed
to Christians, it is never easy to be certain whether by their spirit,
as opposed to the Holy Spirit, St. Paul means something which
they possess simply because they are human beings, and which
they share with Jews and even with pagans, or something which
only Christians possess. Philem. 25, 'The grace of the Lord Jesus
Christ be with your spirit', is indecisive, and so are passages like
1 Thess. v. 23, Gal. vi. 18, and Phil. iv. 23. It would be easy to fall
into the trap of reifying 'spirit' and to think of spirit as a 'thing' or
element which Christians 'possess'. In St. Paul's view for a man
to 'have' a spirit meant that the word 'spirit' could be applied to
either the whole man or an aspect of his life; it was not a 'part' of
him. 1 Cor. ii. 11, 'Among men, who knows what a man is, but
the man's own spirit (*to pneuma tou anthrōpou*) within him?'
strongly suggests that ' spirit ' can be applied to a human being
as such, and not to Christians only. It is possible, but only just

---

[61] *The Pauline View of Man*, London, 1956, p. 183.
[62] cf. p. 190 f.
[63] cf. Chapter v. pp. 124–9.
[64] cf. Chapter ix. p. 213

possible, that St. Paul was thinking solely of Christians. 2 Cor. vii. 1, 'Let us therefore cleanse ourselves from all that can defile flesh or spirit', points in the same direction, as do 1 Cor. xvi. 18; 2 Cor. ii. 13, vii. 13, where St. Paul speaks of relief of 'spirit' (*pneuma*; rendered 'mind' in the N.E.B. in each of these three passages). 1 Cor. v. 5, 'This man is to be consigned to Satan . . . so that his spirit may be saved', is indecisive. Since the sinful Corinthian in question was a member of the Church, it could be argued that his 'transformed' nature was in question. 1 Cor. vi. 17, 'He who links himself with Christ is one with him spiritually', does seem to refer to the 'renewed' or transformed spirit. In most cases it is not possible to be certain whether the Apostle refers to the Holy Spirit, the 'natural' spirit of a man or the 'renewed' spirit of a man who has become a Christian. The problem has been well studied by Allo[65] and Stacey,[66] both of whom seem to me more definite than the evidence permits.

Stacey[67] deals concisely and well with the Pauline use of the word *psychē*, soul. He quotes Rom. ii. 9, 'There will be grinding misery for every human being (*psychē*) who is an evildoer'. The word can refer, like 'body' to the whole person, and can be employed when sin is in question. No more need be said about the anthropological sense of this word.

Mind (*nous*) is also used with reference to all men, not to Christians alone. This is clear from Rom. xii. 2, 'Let your minds (*nous*) be remade'. Phil. iv. 7 and 1 Cor. xiv. 14 probably use the word in the same sense. Robinson[68] points out that in Col. ii. 18, which speaks of 'worldly minds' (lit. 'mind of the flesh') St. Paul uses 'mind' to refer to the whole human being, when engaged in thought, in this case in wrong thought; Rom. i. 28, 'He (God) has given them up to their own depraved reason', (*nous*) shows that 'mind' is not as such a privileged part or rather aspect of man. 1 Cor. xiv. 14, 'The spirit in me prays but my intellect lies fallow', makes it clear that 'mind' or 'intellect' is not the same as 'spirit'; I cannot agree with the N.E.B. which here seems to refer *pneuma* to the Holy Spirit, since it spells 'Spirit' with a capital letter.[69]

[65] *Première Epître aux Corinthiens* (Paris, 1956²), Excursus v., pp. 87–115, esp. pp. 92–3.

[66] *The Pauline View of Man* (London, 1956), pp. 133–5.

[67] op. cit., p. 123f.

[68] J. A. T. Robinson, *The Body* S.B.T., no. 5, (London, 1952), p. 25, n. 2.

[69] These last two points I owe to Stacey, op. cit., pp. 200 and 203.

'Heart' (*kardia*) refers to the personality in general in 2 Thess. ii. 16–7, 'And may our Lord Jesus Christ . . . still encourage and fortify you (lit. "your hearts") in every good deed and word'. 'Heart' is applied to men as thinking, knowing beings in Rom. ii. 15, 'They display the effect of the law inscribed on their hearts'. Rom. ii. 5, 'In the rigid obstinacy of your heart', and 2 Cor. ix. 7, 'Each person should give as he has decided for himself (lit. 'in his heart'),' show that the word is also used of human beings when willing or deciding. The N.E.B., by omitting the word 'heart' makes it clear that *kardia* is not a 'part' of man which 'excludes' other parts, but a way of speaking about the whole personality under certain circumstances. The same applies to *suneidēsis*, 'conscience'. It is not a part of man, and does not really belong to the sphere of anthropology at all. It means 'remorse' and tells us how man reacts to his own sin, not how man is constituted.[70]

The examination of individual words used by St. Paul to describe human nature is necessary and valuable, but we shall fail to see the wood for the trees unless we emphasize in conclusion three vital points which arise from the fact that his theology of creation is based upon Genesis.

First, behind all St. Paul's thought lies the fundamental conviction that man was created by God to obey Him, and that man is wholly subject to God, so that even when he sins he cannot evade God's purpose; man shares the fact of being God's creature with the physical, natural world and with the 'supernatural' world of good and evil spirits.

Secondly, each individual man is a unity. He is not, of course, a 'simple substance' and in rare cases the Apostle's anthropology tends to be 'loose-knit' but in most cases it is close-knit, and therefore typically biblical. Most emphatically, his thought is not dualistic but unitary.

Lastly, we must add that mankind as a whole, like each individual man, is a unity. This is a fact of cardinal importance, since it is the foundation stone for St. Paul's theology of the Fall and restoration of the human race: as in Adam all men die, so in Christ all will be brought to life. This unity of the human race is especially significant for the doctrine of the Fall of Man, which is the subject of the next chapter.

[70] cf. *infra*, p. 210 f.

CHAPTER THREE

THE FALL AND ITS RESULTS

i. THE FALL

(a) *Solidarity in Adam*

It is one of the main contentions of this book that many of St. Paul's fundamental doctrines can be properly understood only if we realize that he took for granted the presupposition of human solidarity. 1 Cor. xv. 21, 'As in Adam all men die, so in Christ all will be brought to life', makes the matter clear enough: our involvement in sin and death and our salvation through Christ depend upon our being in some sense 'one with' both the first man, Adam, and the last Adam. This subject cannot be expounded adequately by means of preliminary discussion alone. It will be necessary to see how the concept of solidarity sheds light upon St. Paul's teaching about topics like the Atonement, Baptism and the Church, which will be considered in subsequent chapters.

'Corporate personality', 'extended personality' and 'solidarity' are concepts widely accepted among contemporary theologians. In Great Britain the pioneer work was done by Wheeler Robinson[1] and A. R. Johnson[2]. J. A. T. Robinson[3] has made a further valuable contribution, although some of his conclusions are controversial. R. P. Shedd has carried out a clear and illuminating examination of the subject in *Man in Community*[4], a study of St. Paul's application of Old Testament and Early Jewish conceptions of human solidarity. The fact that such theories are now fashionable should put us on our guard against adopting them too readily. It is fatally easy, when a theory is in vogue, to read it into the Bible, in a manner which would have astonished the sacred writers, and to find evidence for our belief in a mere turn of phraseology[6]. It is easy to

---

[1] *The Christian Doctrine of Man* (Edinburgh, 1934³).
[2] esp. *The Vitality of the Individual in the Thought of Ancient Israel* (Cardiff, 1949).
[3] *The Body* S.B.T. no. 5, (London, 1952).   [4] London, 1958.
[6] For example, Shedd draws our attention to 2 Kings v. 27, where Elisha says that Naaman's leprosy will cleave to Gehazi and his descendants for ever. Shedd asks whether this is a genuine instance of the corporate extension of punishment to future generations or merely a case of Hebrew hyperbole. op. cit., p. 16.

see these faults in scholars of an earlier generation, and it is wise to heed the words 'I am no better than my fathers'. We need not, however, reject a view just because it is popular. We are now beginning to realise that even the nineteenth-century scholars on whom it has been fashionable to pour scorn made a solid and lasting contribution to theological learning, and this is not invalidated by a certain number of exaggerations and false guesses. In the same way it is reasonable to hope that the emphasis which we now lay upon solidarity, although it also may be exaggerated, will be accepted as a permanent enrichment of theological learning.

It would be tedious to develop the topic of solidarity at length. It is very familiar and it has been adequately expounded by Shedd and the other writers mentioned above. It will be sufficient, by way of illustration, to recall the account of Achan recorded in Joshua vii. Achan alone was guilty of taking some of the devoted things (v.1) but the Lord said to Joshua, 'Israel has sinned; *they* have transgressed my covenant.' And Israel punished Achan and his family. In 1 Sam. xiv. we find that Jonathan, who alone ate honey, was thought to have brought disaster upon all Israel. In this chapter both Jonathan and the people took a rationalistic, 'commonsense' view, and opposed the 'old-fashioned taboos' which Saul and the priest tried to impose. This should warn us against supposing that Israelite thought on this matter was uniform. †

(b) '*Sin*' *and* '*guilt*' *distinguished*

Before examining St. Paul's thought about the Fall and Original Sin it is essential to clarify some of the terms employed and to sketch in the Old Testament background. The expressions 'sin', 'guilt', and 'sense of guilt' demand careful consideration. Neither in the Bible nor in subsequent theology is there a standard definition universally accepted. If we do adopt a definition of 'sin' or 'guilt', we adopt it mainly as a yardstick for our own use: the Bible has no such standardized terminology. As a first approach it will be wise not to attempt definitions, but to consider the situations in which these words are used. We shall use 'Sin' with a capital letter when we talk about a man who is in a wrong relationship with God and his fellow men and 'scarce safe grounded in himself'. We shall speak of 'sins' with a small 's' when we wish to refer to individual acts of rebellion against God or injury to human being. The word 'sin' is normally reserved for conscious, purposeful violation of a known law. It is possible to do 'wrong' acts, that is, for a Christian, acts contrary to God's will, without knowing that they are wrong or without intending to do them. In such cases, although the acts are 'wrong' we should not describe them as 'sinful'.

Let us suppose, for the sake of illustration, that a man has been made sinless and is in a right relationship with God and man, and that he sins no more. Let us suppose further that reparation has been made. Can we say that even when sin has been done away there is a sense in which 'guilt' (Latin *reatus*) still remains? Within the Christian tradition it will generally be agreed that there is a sense in which guilt does still remain.

What then is this guilt? It must be distinguished from consciousness of guilt or sin. A man who has lost his memory has no more consciousness of sin or guilt, but there is a sense in which it can be claimed that his guilt remains[7].

We may suggest that guilt, as opposed to sin, and distinguished from conciousness of sin or guilt, refers to the fact of having sinned or to the status which results from having sinned or to liability for punishment.

It is thus clear that 'guilt' is a concept derived from law, and that it expresses a man's relationship to his fellow citizens or to the state. It is of limited use in describing our relationship to a personal God. 'Merit' is on the positive side what 'guilt' is on the negative, and it will be agreed by all that merit has no place in St. Paul's thought. Inevitably, this matter will be discussed further in Ch. vi, which is concerned with the work of Christ: the Fall and Sin are related to the work of Christ as disease to cure.

It would be too simple to say that guilt, like merit, has no place at all in St. Paul's theology: St. Paul does deal with a guilt situation: he deals with the fact that we are all sinful and in a state of rebellion against God. This is the kind of situation which later western thought would deal with by means of such depersonalized abstractions as 'guilt'. That is what is meant by calling it a 'guilt' situation. But in St. Paul's thought it is God Who deals with this 'guilt situation', and His manner of doing so is described by means of more personal, less abstract language, derived not from Roman Law, but from the Old Testament. His manner of dealing with it is explained by such words as reconciliation, forgiveness, 'freely' (*chariti*, by grace), setting in a right relation-

[7] cf. St. Augustine, *Contra Jul. Pel.*, Book VI., Ch. 19.

ship (*dikaiosunē*, justification), etc. St. Paul's thinking appears paradoxical to us because he faces a situation which we should view against a background of guilt, merit, etc., and presents an explanation in terms of the free, unmerited action of a personal God.

(c) *The Old Testament teaching*

In the Old Testament such distinctions were not made. Genesis iii. offers an explanation for death and drudgery. It can hardly be said that it offers a theory of the origin of sin. Even universal sinfulness is not stated in theoretical terms in the Old Testament: concrete acts of sin are denounced, however, in vigorous words. We are now familiar with the fact that rapid changes in technology and culture are connected with a rise in the crime rate. We are therefore tempted to see in the accounts of Cain and Abel and of Tubal-Cain, who made instruments of bronze and iron, figures like Prometheus; we are tempted to suppose that the Bible itself teaches us that changes in culture are connected with sin. But the Old Testament writers themselves were probably concerned only to explain the rise of food-producing and metallurgical techniques, and, above all, to connect them with their national history and with the God of Israel.

(d) *The Fall in the intertestamental writings*

The Old Testament provides merely the background for St. Paul's thought. It is in the intertestamental writings that we first find specific teaching about the Fall and Original Sin. Ecclus. xxv. 24, 'From a woman sin had its beginning and because of her we all die', attributes death, and probably also sinfulness, which is the cause of death, to Eve. 2 Cor. xi. 3, 'As the serpent in his cunning seduced Eve, I am afraid your thoughts may be corrupted', is not really parallel. St. Paul compares possible sin at Corinth with the Fall of Eve: he does not say that Eve's Fall caused her descendants to sin and to die, although he may have held this belief. 1 Tim. ii. 14, 'It was not Adam who was deceived; it was the woman who, yielding to deception, fell into sin', does follow the line of thought found in Ecclus. xxv. 24. But the writer of this letter, even if he was St. Paul, which is on balance unlikely, is not here concerned to present theories about the origin of sin or death: he is concerned mainly with the practical task of inducing women to live modestly, and quietly.

According to 1 Enoch lxix. 4f.[8] it was fallen angels who deceived Eve and led human beings astray by teaching them the art of writing. A similar theory is found in the *Manual of Discipline*[9] where we read 'All who practise perversity are under the domination of the Angel of Darkness'.

The chief share of the blame is laid not upon Eve or upon the Fallen Angels, but upon Adam in 2 Esdras vii. 118–9, 'O Adam, what have you done? For though it was you who sinned, the fall was not yours alone, but ours also who are your descendants. For what good is it to us, if an eternal age has been promised to us, but we have done deeds that bring death?' Here, as in 2 Esdras iii. 4f. it is not stated in so many words that Adam's fall made sin and death inevitable for all, but it is clearly suggested that, as a result, the vast majority do in fact sin and therefore die. This comes very close to the Pauline view that because of Adam's sin all human beings are delivered over to sin and death. This theory was not universal in Judaism, as we can tell from Ecclus. xv. 15, 'If you will you can keep the commandments, and to act faithfully is a matter of your own choice'. The Syriac Apocalypse of Baruch liv. 19,[10] 'Adam is therefore not the cause, save only of his own soul. But each of us has been the Adam of his own soul', can easily be misunderstood to mean that Adam's fall had no effect on his descendants. That this is not so is clear from liv. 15,[11] 'For though Adam first sinned and brought untimely death upon all . . .' The fall of Adam did have results; but they were purely physical, being limited to death. Sin was the result of each man's own abuse of freedom. There would appear no reason in principle why a man should not avoid sin altogether. Indeed, in ix. 1[12] we are told that Jeremiah was free from sin.

The rabbinical writings do not differ significantly. Billerbeck distinguishes two emphases: death is a fate which came upon men because of the sin of Adam; and death is the punishment for the sins of each individual man. These two emphases which are not sharply opposed, are sufficiently substantiated in Billerbeck's treatment of Rom. v. 15.[13] We may illustrate the latter from the story of Chanina ben Dosa, the wonder-working holy man who is

---

[8] Charles, vol. ii. p. 233.
   [9] *The Scriptures of the Dead Sea Sect*, ed. and tr. T. H. Gaster (London, 1957), p. 53.
   [10] Charles, op. cit., p. 512.   [11] ibid., p. 511.   [12] ibid., p. 484.
   [13] Strack-Billerbeck, vol. iii. pp. 227–9.

said to have flourished about 70 A.D. He was bitten by a water-serpent, but it was the serpent that died. Said ben Dosa: 'It is not the serpent that brings death, but sin.'[14]

(e) *Original Sin*

St. Paul's fundamental teaching is expressed in Rom. v. 12, 'It was through one man that sin entered the world, and through sin death, and thus death pervaded the whole human race, inasmuch as all men have sinned (*eph hō pantes hēmarton*)'. It is now generally agreed that *eph hō* means ' because '. St. Augustine, indeed, understood St. Paul to mean that all sinned in Adam, ' because they were all in him when he sinned' (*quia in illo fuerunt omnes quando ille peccavit*).[15] St. Augustine takes *eph* to mean 'in' and supposes that *hō* refers back to Adam, i.e. the 'one man'. The Pelagian view was that death, not sin, pervaded the whole race.

In favour of an Augustinian view it could be argued that after the time of Adam men did not sin culpably until the Law was introduced through Moses. St. Paul says in Rom. v. 13–14, 'For sin was already in the world before there was law, though in the absence of law no reckoning is kept of sin. But death held sway from Adam to Moses even over those who had not sinned as Adam did by disobeying a direct command'. Between Adam and Moses men did wrong acts, that is they were materially sinful, but they were not formally sinful, because they were not aware of the commandments. St. Paul knew that all men die, and that all are sinful, and he connected the two facts.

The sin of Adam had the following results. Death entered the world, but could not have struck down a sinless man. But man was also involved in sin, as was the material universe, so that all men were liable to die because they were sinful. This is clear from Rom. vi. 23, ' For sin pays a wage, and the wage is death', and from Rom. v. 19, 'For as through the disobedience of one man the many were made sinners (*hamartōloi katestathēsan*)'.

It is important to stress the fact that, in the eyes of St. Paul, the reason why all men die is that, since the Law was given, all men are sinners, and even before that, all were wrong-doers. There is no question of innocent children being punished: there are no

---

[14] ibid., vol. ii. p. 169 on Luke x. 19.

[15] *Contra duas Epistolas Pelagianorum*, Bk. IV, Ch. iv, sect. 7. cf. Bright, *Anti-Pelagian Treatises of St. Augustine* (Oxford, 1880), p. 354.

'innocent' children. All, thanks to Adam, are in a state of potential rebellion against God, even though this potential rebellion has not, in the case of small children, crystallized out into conscious actual sin.

St. Paul does believe in Original Sin, but not in Original Guilt. He does not say that the guilt of Adam's sin was imputed to his innocent descendants, but that through Adam's sin all men were made sinful, even though before Moses this sin was not conscious. He does not mention the case of children who die too young to be aware of the law, but clearly they would be in the same position as the generations of men who lived between Adam and Moses.

St. Paul is probably describing the condition of those who lived between Adam and Moses when he says in Rom. vii. 9, 'There was a time when, in the absence of law, I was fully alive; but when the commandment came, sin sprang to life and I died'. It has often been supposed that in this passage St. Paul was speaking of himself, either when he was still a Jew, or after he had become a Christian. But such a negative view of the Law was hardly common among Jews; the typical attitude is found in Ps. cxix., and St. Paul himself claims that he had been, according to Phil. iii. 6, 'In legal rectitude faultless'. Rom. vii. 9, therefore can hardly refer to his pre-conversion period; it is difficult to believe that the Apostle was speaking of a time after his conversion, because of such passages as Gal. ii. 20, 'The life I now live is not my life, but the life which Christ lives in me'. It is of course true that, if St. Paul is describing not his own life, but the history of the human race, then he is painting an unduly favourable picture of the time of man's 'innocent wrong-doing', but this is consistent with what he says about the Law. He is, in any case, concerned to describe in telling phrases the condition of men in his own day, not to trace with historical accuracy the stages by which this condition had been reached.

We find in Rom. i. 18–32 what is almost a parallel version of the fall, a presentation of the same realities by means of different symbols. In Gen. iii. we are told that mankind failed to obey God, and was therefore turned out of the Garden, and that God further punished man by cursing the ground because of him. In Gen. iii. the results of the Fall are purely material and do not include moral deterioration, although this is added in the intertestamental writings. In Rom. i. God does not punish men for refusing to honour him as God, by turning them out of the Garden, and giving them over to death and drudgery. Instead, according to Rom. i. 28, 'Because they have not seen fit to acknowledge God, he has given them up to their own depraved reason'. This passage will be considered again when we come to deal with the Wrath of God. St. Paul was not a social scientist, and the connexion which he sees between idolatry and sin is not based upon statistics showing a higher incidence of crime among polytheists. The Apostle sees and detests both sin and idolatry. When he says that God 'gives men up' to sin, he is concerned to preserve the sovereignty of God, not to say that God causes sin, though he comes very near to doing so. This matter will be examined further in Ch. iv. when we treat of Predestination.

It will be convenient at this point to recapitulate St. Paul's teaching:

(1) Adam's sin introduced into the world death, which we may think of as a deadly virus, killing those who are susceptible to it, namely those who are 'in sin'.

(2) By his sin Adam made all who are in Adam, that is to say all human beings, to be 'in sin' and therefore victims of death.

(3) The phrase 'in sin' includes the following classes:

(a) Those who are guilty of 'actual' sin in the traditional sense of the term, that is to say, those who came after Moses and whose sin was formal as well as material since they were aware of the Law which they were breaking.

(b) Those who lived between Adam and Moses. They were not guilty of actual sin in the ordinary sense of the word, though they were guilty of actual wrong-doing. Their sin was solely 'original' not actual, though their wrong-doing was actual.

(c) We may presume that for St. Paul, who never considers this question in his extant writings, those who died, before or after Moses, too young to have committed a wrong act for which they could be held responsible, would be classed along with those who lived between Adam and Moses.

(4) In Rom. i. 18–32, St. Paul gives us what is almost a parallel account of the origin of sin. Just as the 'primal' sin of rebellion by Adam led to his expulsion from the Garden, so the 'primal' sin of idolatry lead to sin of every kind.

(5) In Rom. vii. we find reference to the various stages of man's

religious history, the age of 'original' sin and actual wrong-doing before Moses, and the period after Moses when wrong-doing was conscious and therefore sinful.

(f) *Actual sin*

For St. Paul sins, that is actual sin, count less than Sin, that is original sin. Because of 'original sin', a phrase which St. Paul does not use, we became God's 'enemies', and St. Paul's main contention is that we were reconciled to him through the death of his son, and that we shall be saved through his life (Rom. v. 10). 'Actual' sin, however, must be considered briefly. Just as original sin brings death (Rom. v. 12, etc.) so the actual sin of failing to discern the body is the reason why so many at Corinth are feeble and sick, and a number have died (1 Cor. xi. 29–30). Although the physical flesh is not evil as such, yet the physical body is a natural sphere for the working of sin, as we can tell from Rom. vi. 12, 'Sin must no longer reign in your mortal body (*sōma*), exacting obedience to the body's (*autou*) desires', and from Rom. vii. 5, viii. 13. But there is no part of our being which has escaped the taint of sin: we are totally depraved in the sense that all of our nature is affected, though St. Paul does not deny the actual virtues of the pagans (Rom. ii. 14). The power of the intellect is distorted according to Rom. i. 21, 'All their thinking has ended in futility, and their misguided minds are plunged in darkness'. Mind (*kardia*, lit. heart) is here very much the 'practical' reason, and this passage is linked with Rom. vii. 21, 'when I want to do the right, only the wrong is within my reach'.

ii. GENERAL REVELATION

(a) *Introductory*

Since the whole world and every part of each individual human has been affected by the Fall of Adam, it follows that, apart from what God has done in Israel under the old dispensation, and later in Christ, all human life and every human activity has to be regarded as 'fallen'. The state can be regarded as an organization whose purpose is to enable fallen men to make the best of a fallen world. It is worth noting that Thomas Hobbes held a not dissimilar view of the state. The state, however, must be examined in Ch. ix. In Ch. iv. under the general title of Preparation for the

Gospel, we shall consider how God dealt with the problem created by Adam's fall; this will involve an examination of Israel and the Gentiles, the Law, and Predestination. The remainder of this chapter will be devoted to a consideration of the results of the Fall, which include General Revelation, commonly called natural religion, morality outside the Judaeo-Christian tradition, generally known as natural morality and the Wrath of God.

'Natural religion' is a difficult subject because different denominations are to some extent committed, both by loyalty and by inherited tradition, to hold opposing views. Further, 'natural religion' normally comprises two separate propositions, either or both of which can be accepted in conjunction with different beliefs on other questions, and they are placed in a very different light by the context.

First, 'natural religion' always includes the belief that some awareness of God is available to all mankind, and is not witheld from them on the ground that they are outside, for example, the Mosaic Covenant, or the New Covenant in Christ. Secondly, 'natural religion' also normally holds that this 'awareness of God' is due to a 'finding' by man of a God Who passively waits to be found. He may indeed have left 'clues' to guide man to Him, but His action in the present is passive, though He was active in the past when He 'actively created', e.g. the physical universe. The belief that God is passively discovered by man apart from revelation, as the result, perhaps, of contemplating the heavens or arguing back to a 'First Cause' could be held by a man who denied any revelation whatsoever. It was held on the other hand by men like Thomas Aquinas and Bishop Butler who believed that God both allowed Himself to be passively discovered by pagans, and also actively revealed Himself through such men as Moses, and, supremely, in Jesus Christ.

The problem is further bedevilled in our own day by what used to be called the missionary situation, that is by the relation of Christians to non-Christians both in Western countries like Great Britain and in the developing countries. If we are trying to find some common ground, so that conversation becomes possible with a non-Christian, whether he lives in an English housing estate or as a member of some African tribe, we readily think in terms of 'natural religion' that is, of some realization of the super-natural shared in common by the non-Christian in question and ourselves.

St. Paul looked at matters from an entirely different angle. In Rom. i. 18f., the only passage in his epistles where 'natural religion' can be sought, he is not concerned to find common positive ground with the pagans to serve as a basis for agreement. He was concerned only to show that the Gentiles, like the Jews, had sufficient knowledge of God to be blameworthy. Further, though St. Paul does hold the first article of the natural religion creed, namely that awareness of God is available to all men, he does not hold the second, that God passively waits to be found; Rom. i. 19, 'God himself has disclosed (*ephanerōsen*) it to them', makes this clear enough, and, in any case, St. Paul's God was 'active', not passive. It is therefore easier to restate the question by dropping the misleading expression 'natural religion' and speaking instead, with Richardson[16] and Nygren,[17] about 'general revelation'. Many supporters of 'natural religion' would be perfectly happy to accept this less ambiguous phrase. On the other hand, the general revelation does appear to differ from the special revelation in character and content, quite apart from the fact that it is directed towards the 'Gentiles', whereas the 'special revelation' is confined to the 'Old Israel' and to the Church. The general revelation is implicit, while the special revelation is couched in explicit terms.

(b) *Why the Gentiles were blameworthy*

After this preliminary clarification of our own terminology we turn to St. Paul. He was not concerned in the least with the theoretical problems which we have just posed. His intention was solely to make it clear that the Gentiles, like the Jews, deserved God's condemnation. When we ask what St. Paul thought about the reality or otherwise of general revelation we are really asking what we can infer from his manner of speaking about the matter which really concerned him. The important verse is Rom. i. 19, 'For all that may be known (*to gnōston*) of God by men lies plain before their eyes; indeed, God Himself has disclosed it to them'. Two questions arise: (1) What was disclosed to men? Was it the existence of God for example or the fact that He created the world out of nothing or the fact of man's creaturely status and sinfulness? (2) Does St. Paul refer to a real knowledge which mankind actually

---

[16] *Introduction*, pp. 50–53.
[17] A. Nygren, *Commentary on Romans* (E.T., London, 1952), pp. 105–8 on Rom. i. 18f.

F

attained, or to a possible knowledge which men failed or refused to attain?

The answer to the second question must surely be that a real knowledge of God was actually achieved by men apart from the biblical revelation, though that knowledge was disregarded and rejected. First, this passage is an integral part of the argument of the Epistle: otherwise, the bulk of the human race would not stand under the judgement of God. Again St. Paul says that *to gnōston* is 'plain before their eyes' because God himself has disclosed (*ephanerōsen*) it to them. We must take account of the fact that the 'possibility' theory is supported by some very sober critics such as Barrett[18] and Michel.[19] If a baby is born alive but strangled at birth, we may say that its life was actual, that its survival was an unrealized possibility, and that the person who strangled it was guilty of murder. In the same way the revelation was actually made and 'instantly' rejected; this 'crime' laid guilt upon all who perpetrated it. We might argue that mankind 'had all the evidence available' but 'refused to draw the conclusion'. When we say that a man 'refuses' to draw a conclusion, we normally mean that he *has* drawn it, dislikes it, and smothers it at once.

It is probably unwise to base anything upon the precise meaning of *gnōston*, which is found here only in the Pauline writings. An adjective of this type, formed from a verb and ending in -*tos*, would naturally mean 'known' or 'capable of being known'. But it is very doubtful whether *gnōstos* does mean 'knowable' as opposed to 'known'. In many passages 'knowable' is impossible, and in none in the Greek Bible is it certain. If we could stress the aspect of 'possibility' the meaning might be inclusive, i.e. 'all that can be known'. It might on the other hand mean that what could be known was placed before them but disregarded, with the result that in fact they did not know God. Such minutiae must be examined, but it is unwise to build anything upon them: the plain meaning of the passage is that the Gentiles knew enough to be culpable, and beyond that it is dangerous to speculate.

Owen[20] maintains that according to St. Paul, the Gentiles knew that God existed, but did not know that He was the creator.

---

[18] *The Epistle to the Romans* Black N.T.C., (London, 1957) pp. 35–36.
[19] *Der Brief an die Römer* Meyer-Kommentar, (Göttingen, 1955[10]), pp. 54 and 56.
[20] H. P. Owen, 'The Scope of Natural Revelation in Rom. i. and Acts xvii.', *N.T.S.*, v. (1959), pp. 133–43.

From *Romans* alone it is hardly possible to be certain that the Pagans knew God to be Creator or that they did not. On general grounds, however, it is possible that the pagans whom St. Paul had in mind, not a specific group but 'gentiles' as a type, would be held to have possessed or suppressed a knowledge of God, but not to have regarded Him as creator. The word 'God' is a single word, but to it there are attached a number of beliefs, overtones, etc., and for different men different beliefs are attached to this single word. To the Jew, who knew his Bible, God was a 'living' God and the creator of the world. For St. Thomas the creation of the world was part of 'natural' not of 'revealed' theology. Owen[21] is probably correct when he suggests that in New Testament times the *existence* of God might well be part of the 'general revelation', but God's *creatorship* was part of revealed theology, being known through the Bible, and by faith (Heb. xi. 3).

Miss Hooker[22] goes further in stressing what is essentially the same point, namely that St. Paul's mental framework was not that of contemporary pagans or of eighteenth-century philosophical theologians. A philosopher of that century would find it easy to speak in terms of abstractions such as natural religion, revealed religion and natural morality. If we had to translate eighteenth-century ideas into biblical thoughtforms, we should replace abstractions by persons and events. Natural morality would be represented by the covenant with Noah, revealed religion by the giving of the covenant on Mount Sinai, and natural theology perhaps by use of the figure of Adam.

Miss Hooker starts from the view, fairly widely held, that Rom. i. 23, '*Exchanging the splendour* of immortal God *for an image* shaped like mortal man, even for images like birds, beasts and creeping things', is based upon Ps. cvi. (LXX., cv.) 20, the words italicized being the same in the LXX and in *Romans*. But some of the words which are *not* taken from Ps. cvi. are to be found in *Genesis*, namely birds (*peteina*) and creeping things (*herpeta*) in Gen. i. 20; beasts (*tetrapoda*) corresponds to cattle (*ktēnē*) in Gen. i. 24. St. Paul was well aware, so Miss Hooker's argument continues, that moral evil was rife in the world, especially idolatry and sexual vice. She suggests that in Rom. i. 18–23 he was describing these facts with Gen. i.–iii. in mind. According to Gen. i. 26, God made

[21] ibid.
[22] Miss M. D. Hooker, 'Adam in Romans I.', *N.T.S.*, vi. (1960), pp. 297–306.

Man in his own image and gave him domination over fish, birds, beasts and reptiles. St. Paul saw that all these, apart from fish, were commonly worshipped; he therefore argued that, by worshipping the image of a creature, man lost the privilege of being made in the image of God, so that rebellion against God, worshipping images of created beings, and the general loss of a proper place in the world were closely linked together.

Miss Hooker mentions other connexions between Rom. i. and Genesis which are sufficient to make her general case extremely probable. She links the sexual faults with the rabbinic tradition which associated the Fall with sexual desire. But St. Paul speaks in Rom. i. 26–7 only of homosexual vice. Gen. i. 27, 'God created man in his own image, male (*arsen*) and female (*thēlu*) he created them', may provide the clue. It could be urged that when God created human beings male and female he meant them to behave accordingly, so that males had natural intercourse with females. St. Paul says that human beings gave up the natural intercourse. In other words, they moved away from the natural functions which God gave them at the creation as 'male and female'.

Be that as it may, the important point about Rom. i. 18–32 is that all those who are 'in Adam' are sinful. Directly St. Paul wishes to show that all men are fallen and stand under the wrath of God: indirectly, in order to preserve human responsibility, he has shown his belief that all men have had some knowledge of God revealed to them.

iii. NATURAL MORALITY

Just as Rom. i. 19 is the *locus classicus* in St. Paul's epistles for 'natural religion', so the *locus classicus* for natural morality is Rom. ii. 14, 'When Gentiles who do not possess the law carry out its precepts by the light of nature, then, although they have no law, they are their own law, for they display the effect of the law inscribed on their hearts'. Just as the Pauline foundation stone for natural religion was not part of the Apostle's direct intention, but came in indirectly to guarantee universal human blameworthiness, so we must note that 'natural morality' also is not part of what he positively wishes to say: it comes in indirectly to emphasize the blameworthiness of the Jews. This would suggest that the Epistle to the Romans is gloomy beyond description. But in fact the centre of the epistle is a great blaze of light. In Rom. iii. 21–viii. 39 he describes what God has done and will do in Christ for men. For this blaze of light a lamp-black background is provided by the description of human sin which we find in Rom. i. 18–iii. 20. This dark background includes the two dim glimmers of 'natural religion' and 'natural morality' in Rom. i. 19 and ii. 14.

A verse which has received less attention than it deserves is Rom. i. 32. 'They know well enough the just decree of God, that those who behave like this deserve to die, and yet they do it; not only so, they actually applaud such practices'. This makes it quite clear[23] that the Gentiles had conscious knowledge of what God had laid down. When in Rom. ii. 14 we are told that they 'carry out its precepts' we can be sure, in the light of Rom. i. 32, that the Gentiles are not just obeying the law by mistake: their occasional obedience (*hotan*, 'when', in Rom. ii. 14 suggests that obedience is the exception) like their general disobedience is a conscious reaction to a known divine command. The Apostle, then, gives recognition to the fact that pagan morality, both in theory and in practice, partly overlapped with the moral requirements of the Jewish law.

Rom. xiv. 23, 'What is not of faith is sin' (*A.V.*) must be considered because it has led to serious misunderstanding, although it is really quite irrelevant, as we can see from the rendering of the N.E.B., 'Anything which does not arise from conviction is sin'. The meaning is clear. If a man eats certain foods because of his conviction that Jewish food laws are not binding upon a Christian, then he is free from blame. If, however, he believes that to eat such food is contrary to God's will, so that his eating is due to greed and not to conviction, then he is to be blamed; this is the point of the passage added to Luke vi. 3 by the Codex Bezae, 'On the same day (Jesus) saw a man working on the Sabbath, and said to him "How blest are you if you know what you are doing; but if you do not know, you are accursed and a transgressor of the Law".' Unfortunately, on the basis of Article xiii. it has been supposed that the good works of those who have not faith in Christ are not pleasing to God, but have the nature of sin

[23] A comparison of Rom. i. 32, which says in general terms that the Gentiles disobey the Law, with Rom. ii. 14f. which says that some of them, occasionally at least, obey part of it, should warn us that when the Apostle uses general, sweeping language he does not invariably wish to be understood in an all-inclusive sense.

on the ground that, according to Rom. xiv. 23, *A.V.*, 'What is not of faith is sin'. This false interpretation of the verse would run counter to any theory of natural morality. Properly understood, Rom. xiv. 23 is not relevant.

The exegesis of Rom. ii. 14–16 has been made more difficult because it is germane to two great questions, the problem of universalism, and the problem of ethical relativism. Rom. ii. 15, 'Their own thoughts argue the case on either side, against them or even for them (lit. "or even defending (*apologoumenōn*) them")' does not *necessarily* mean that pagans are acquitted at the judgement; to 'defend' is not the same as to 'acquit' and it *may* be that the defence will never be successful and that all pagans will be condemned. But at least we cannot say that pagans are to be condemned unheard just because they are pagans. It is hardly possible that St. Paul is here speaking of former pagans who have become Christians: Christians have more to guide them than the 'light of nature'. When we consider that the majority of human beings since the world began have died before becoming adults, and that for most human beings Christianity has never been a 'live option' because of social conditioning, it is clear that the judgement of non-Christians raises a problem of the greatest weight. We shall consider it in the next chapter under 'Predestination'. Here we need say only that Rom. ii. 15 does not foreclose the matter.

In our own day great problems are raised by ethical relativism. Among Christians, Catholics and Protestants differ to some extent in the moral rules which they acknowledge. Communists differ from non-Communists. In a society where rapid technological progress produces rapid social change, there are differences in emphasis between the moral code of one generation and the next. It would be a great convenience if there were some standard acknowledged to be binding upon all mankind. For example, is monogamy something specifically 'Christian' and 'western' which is binding only upon Christians, or is it part of the 'natural law', and ought Christians to enforce it upon a non-Christian minority? Questions of this nature are very far from being trivial. No solution can be based upon Rom. ii. 14f. alone; this verse by itself does not tell us the content of the law inscribed on the hearts of the gentiles; it does not deal with the fact that various communities at different times had different 'codes of law' inscribed on their hearts. For this problem we must call in also the aid of sociologists, economists and many others. All St. Paul does is to tell us that in his day the provisions of the Jewish law overlapped in part with the moral codes acknowledged by the Gentiles, who sometimes obeyed them and thus put to shame those Jews who failed to observe the Law.

iv. THE WRATH OF GOD

(a) *The points in question*

For subsequent theology 'natural religion' and 'natural morality' have been important issues. In St. Paul's writings the verses which have been held relevant to these doctrines are merely incidental to the main theme of this part of the Epistle to the Romans, which is the wrath of God. This portion of the Epistle may be regarded as a diagnosis of the disease, while the remainder is devoted to an exposition of the cure.

The wrath of God is a matter about which theologians feel deeply, but little precision of thought and language has been attained. It is clear that divergences of opinion exist and that they are important, but their nature and extent stand in need of clarification. Dodd says that St. Paul 'retains the concept of "the Wrath of God" . . . to describe an inevitable process of cause and effect in a moral universe'.[24] Tasker,[25] on the other hand, reproduces this passage from Dodd and regards his view as inadequate. He quotes with approval the saying that 'The Wrath of God is an *affectus* as well as an *effectus*, a quality of the nature of God, an attitude of the mind of God towards evil'.[26] John Knox[27] maintains that the wrath of God is not 'merely an automatic effect of sin' but 'also an imposed penalty for sin'. I find it difficult to understand how Knox can apply this to Rom. i. 18–32. We can accept that when men reject God and worship idols, they do in fact fall into further sin. But sin is contrary to God's will. It is hard to see why God, who hates sin, should impose upon those who have sinned the penalty of committing further sin.

There are, of course, some points on which all would agree,

[24] C. H. Dodd, *The Epistle to the Romans* Moffatt N.T.C., (London, 1932), p. 23 on Rom. i. 18.
[25] R. V. G. Tasker, *The Biblical Doctrine of the Wrath of God*, Tyndale Lecture for 1951 (London, 1957[2]), p. 16.
[26] ibid.   [27] *I.B.*, vol. ix. p. 397 on Rom. i. 18.

and it is important that they should not be overlooked merely because they are non-controversial. All agree that God is personal, and that if the wrath of God is impersonal, it is the impersonal effect upon sinners, who are themselves personal, of disobeying a personal God. None would doubt that God hates sin, or the gravity of continuing in sin. Tasker is clear that the Wrath of God is not fickle or wayward,[28] and Morris, who follows the same general line on this matter, makes it clear that 'wrath', like 'love', when applied to God, is free from human imperfections, and that the Wrath of God is no vindictive passion.[29]

After noting these areas of agreement, and before examining the Pauline texts it will be convenient to consider some typical points of a general nature which have been raised by twentieth century writers on the subject.

First, Morris[30] remarks that, 'The idea of God's wrath is unwelcome to many moderns'. It is true that the idea is unwelcome to many moderns and that it is welcome to many others. The fact that it is welcome or unwelcome is quite irrelevant to whether it is true or false; on this point Morris would no doubt agree.

Secondly, Tasker[31] would seem to suggest that in recent years the severity of biblical Christianity has largely been lost sight of with disastrous results. It is most difficult to generalize on such matters. Any statements of this nature should be accompanied by full statistical information. This ought to be based on facts which can be objectively measured, and care should be taken to see that misleading correlations are not made: social science is no affair for amateurs. In default of a properly conducted enquiry, which is much to be desired, we should be well advised to leave this matter alone.

Thirdly, A. G. Hebert maintains that, 'On the level of divine love, the Love of God demands as its correlative the Wrath of God'.[32] Hebert makes it clear that God is personal, and that He does care; he reminds us that the Psalms confront us with our duty to Him, as creatures owing adoration and love to their

[28] op. cit., Preface, p. vii.
[29] *The First and Second Epistle to the Thessalonians* London N.T.C., (London, 1959), p. 65.
[30] ibid., p. 64.
[31] op. cit., Preface. p. vii.
[32] *The Authority of the Old Testament* (London, 1947), p. 252. This passage is quoted with approval by Tasker, op. cit., p. 28.

Creator. All this is well said. But what are we to make of the statement that 'the Love of God demands as its correlative the Wrath of God'? He has already insisted on the previous page, that 'The opposite of love is not wrath but indifference'. What does he mean by 'correlative'? If a man is loving it does not necessarily follow that he is wrathful, though human beings who are by nature intense are often capable of extremes of both love and hatred. This is a matter of psychological fact in some human beings: it does not follow logically. Again, it might be urged that human beings are not aware of love unless they can contrast it with wrath or indifference. Even if this is so in all cases, and even if it applies in the case of God's qualities, it does not follow that love and its opposite or its correlative must be qualities of the same being: men could well learn from *human* wrath or indifference to appreciate the love of God. Probably Hebert did not intend what would appear to be a piece of false logic. In all likelihood he was merely trying to express in crisp language his conviction that God is personal and loving, and that His Wrath is the result of His Love. But if this is so the word 'wrath' will require careful definition, and Hebert never says what he means by the Wrath of God.

Fourthly, and this may shed light upon the issue raised by Hebert, Morris[33] points out that, 'There is an implacable divine hostility to everything that is evil.' This hostility he would appear to identify with God's Wrath, and he adds that God did not destine His own to experience His wrath. What is meant by 'everything that is evil'? If it includes sinful persons, that would include God's own. For we are all alike sinful and therefore evil. If, on the other hand, 'everything evil' means sin rather than the sinner, we come to the doctrine that God loves all *men*, not because of our merits—we have none!—but because of His own nature. Just as His love is infinite, so is His hatred of the sin and evil that is in us. His hatred of sin does not lead Him to destroy sinners. A doctor who hates disease does not 'destroy' the patient, even though he has brought the disease upon himself: he seeks to 'destroy' the disease. God's hatred of sin did not lead Him to send armies of angels to slay the sinners: it led Him to send His Son to die for us.

[33] *The First and Second Epistles to the Thessalonians*, London N.T.C., (London, 1959), p. 160.

(b) *The word orgē (wrath) in the LXX*

In the LXX the wrath (*orgē*) of God is frequently mentioned and there can be no doubt that a 'feeling' (*affectus*) on the part of God is intended. Exod. iv. 14, 'The anger of the Lord was kindled against Moses' (lit. the Lord, being enraged, *thumōtheis*, with anger, *orgē*) is typical. No other verse of this nature will be quoted here. The reason for this is that all scholars are in agreement about this matter. But, though only one quotation has been made, it must be remembered that there are many others.

The LXX also speaks of *orgē* not as a feeling (*affectus*) of God, but as an activity (*effectus*). This use is found already in Exod. xv. 7, 'Thou didst send forth (*apesteilas*) thy fury (*tēn orgēn sou*), it consumed them like stubble'. It tends to be more frequent in the later parts of the Bible. 2 Chron. xxx. 2, 'Because of this, wrath has gone out (*orgē egeneto*) against you from the Lord', and Judith ix. 9, 'Behold their pride, and send thy wrath (*aposteilon tēn orgēn sou*) upon their heads', are typical instances of the *effectus* use of the word *orgē*: they describe, not what God feels, but how He acts. Indeed, the 'wrath' of God has very nearly become hypostatized. These two passages have been quoted for illustration only; the evidence will be found in *The Wrath of the Lamb*,[34] which is certainly the best book to date on the Wrath of God in the Bible. But it must be emphasized that although the 'impersonal' use of wrath is more frequent in the later books, it never in the LXX supplants the use of 'wrath' to describe how God feels. Hanson[35] refers us to a passage in Josephus[36] where it is said that disasters may have occurred 'because God was angry (*dia tou Theou mēnisantos*)', and in the Apocalyptic writings *orgē* is frequently referred to the coming woes, as in Isa. xxvi. 20, 'Hide yourselves for a little while until the wrath is past'. Yet the 'apocalyptic' wrath is in some ways nearer to the impersonal *effectus* type than to the vivid *affectus* wrath which is characteristic of the earlier strata.

(c) *Orgē in St. Paul*

When we turn to the writings of St. Paul we notice a complete change. In every case in his Epistles where we find the word wrath

[34] A. T. Hanson, (London, 1957), esp. pp. 21–26 and 41f. Cf. for a similar treatment G. H. C. MacGregor, 'The Concept of the Wrath of God in the New Testament', *N.T.S.*, vii. (1961), pp. 101–9.   [35] op. cit., p. 64.
[36] *Antiquities of the Jews*, Book XV. Ch ix. sect. I (299 in Niese).

(*orgē*) applied to God, the sense is such that if it had occurred in the LXX, it would have been classified without hesitation as an *effectus* use, describing how God acts. One reason why this important fact has received comparatively little attention is that in the LXX the *effectus* nature of wrath is made clear by contrast with such *affectus* passages as Joshua vii. 1, 'The anger of the Lord burned against Israel (lit. 'the Lord was enraged, *ethumōthē* with anger, *orgē*'): in St. Paul these *affectus* passages are nowhere to be found. Such verbs as 'be enraged' are not found with God as the subject. *Thumoomai*, used of God in Joshua vii. 1, is applied in the N.T. only to King Herod when he slew the Holy Innocents (Matt. ii. 16). It is suggestive that although *orgē* is found seventeen times in the Paulines (apart from three occurrences in *Ephesians* and one in the Pastorals) St. Paul speaks of the wrath *of God* twice only, at Rom. i. 18 and Col. iii. 6; the phrase recurs at Eph. v. 6. In most of these seventeen cases St. Paul certainly meant the wrath 'of God', but his infrequent use of the phrase may be due to an unconscious awareness of the fact that he was employing the word in an impersonal sense. In some passages the wrath of God is applied to the future and clearly refers to the judgment. It does not make sense to say that God *does not yet* feel anger for our sin, but will *begin* to feel anger in the future. On the other hand, it makes excellent sense to say that certain *results* (i.e. wrath, *orgē*) will begin to take place only at the end of the world. Where the wrath of God has *a content*, as it appears to do in Rom. i. 18–32, it must be an *effectus*, not an *affectus*.

All the passages in the Paulines and in *Ephesians* where the word *orgē* occurs must now be examined. Col. iii. 8 and Eph. iv. 31 may be eliminated at once, since they refer to human wrath, which is to be put away.

1 Thess. i. 10, 'Wait expectantly for the appearance from heaven of his Son Jesus, whom he raised from the dead, Jesus our deliverer, from the 'terrors of judgement' (*orgē*, lit. 'wrath') to come', is clearly a case of 'eschatological' wrath. Neil[37] well remarks that 'it is not the present retribution for sin as elsewhere in Paul . . . but is its complement, and equally impersonal'. To what has been said above it is necessary to add only this: it would be inept to say that Christ delivers us from the 'future feeling ' of an

---

[37] W. Neil, *Thessalonians* Moffatt N.T.C., (London, 1950), ad loc., p. 32. His treatment of this whole passage, pp. 29–32, is most valuable.

omniscient God; but it makes excellent sense to say that Christ rescues us from the future results of God's hatred of sin. 1 Thess. ii. 16, 'All this time they have been making up the full measure of their guilt (*hamartias*, lit. "sins") and now retribution (*orgē*, lit. "wrath") has overtaken (*ephthasen*) them for good and all', raises many problems. The sixth century Codex Claromontanus, followed by G, and strongly supported by Old Latin MSS. reads 'wrath *of God*', which is certainly the correct interpretation, though it is not probable that this is textually original. Whether we are to understand that the *orgē has*[38] come upon them, as Milligan[39] and Bicknell[40] suggest, or that it *will* come upon them, as Frame[41] seems to hold, it is hardly possible to understand wrath as a feeling of God. 1 Thess. v. 9 also seems to refer to the final fate of the wicked when it speaks of *orgē*.

Rom. i. 18, 'For we see divine retribution revealed from heaven (lit. the "wrath", *orgē*, of God is being revealed, *apokalup-tetai*)' is both difficult and important. It is vital to note that the wrath has a 'content', that is, the disasters which are described in Rom. i. 18–32; these disasters take the form of sinning. The fact that the 'content' of God's wrath is the continual sinning which is going on all around us seems to tell against both the theory that *orgē* is future and the view that it is an *affectus* of God. The language is assuredly eschatological, as Michel[42] points out. But we have here a case of realized eschatology. The 'wrath' is normally thought of as future. The fact that it is happening before our eyes shows that God is already active. Lagrange[43] makes the valuable point that 'revealed from heaven' leads us to suppose that the wrath is 'like something separate sent from God (*la colère est comme un object distinct envoyé par Dieu*). He quotes as parallels Exod. xv. 7[44] and Num. M.T. xvi. 46 (LXX. xvii. 11), 'For wrath has gone forth from before the face of the Lord.' This to some extent

[38] This interpretation gains in probability if we can accept the perfect *epthaken*, which is read by *Codex Vaticanus*.

[39] G. Milligan, *St. Paul's Epistles to the Thessalonians* (London, 1908), p. 32, ad loc.

[40] E. J. Bicknell, *The First and Second Epistles to the Thessalonians* (London, 1932), pp. 27–8, ad loc.

[41] J. E. Frame, *The Epistles of St. Paul to the Thessalonians* (Edinburgh, 1912), pp. 113–4 ad loc. Frame believes that the aorist *epthasen* is proleptic.

[42] O. Michel, *Der Brief an die Römer* Meyer-Kommentar, (Göttingen, 1955¹⁰), p. 52.

[43] *Epître aux Romains* (Paris, 1915), ad loc., pp. 21–22.

[44] *v. supra.* p. 64.

anticipates the position of which Dodd and now Hanson are protagonists. Barrett[45] is doubtful whether we can accept the view that 'Paul thought of the divine wrath in impersonal terms, as an almost automatic force which resists evil'. He adds that 'Wrath is God's personal (though never malicious or, in a bad sense, emotional) reaction against sin'. St. Paul did not, of course, consciously ask himself whether he was using personal or impersonal language. When he says 'wrath' he means 'wrath of God', though he seldom includes the words 'of God'. In referring to what *we* should call 'impersonal, automatic' processes, he employs 'personal' language.

The word *orgē*, literally 'wrath', is represented in the N.E.B. by means of the word 'retribution' at Rom. ii. 5, 8; v. 9. This is clear from the use of the future tense in all three cases, as in Rom. v. 9, 'We shall all the more certainly be saved, *sōthēsometha*, through him from final retribution (*Tēs orgēs*; 'final' is a justifiable explanation, especially since the article is present, but it does not answer directly to any word in the Greek). In the same way Rom. iii. 5, 'Is it unjust of God . . . to bring retribution (*ho epipherōn tēn orgēn*), upon us?' is probably a reference to future judgement. Rom. iv. 15, 'Law can only bring retribution', may well be a reference to the future; however, it does not really enlighten us about wrath but about law, which is what the Apostle intended. He means 'Law brings wrath'. He is not concerned with the nature of wrath, but solely with the fact that it is an inevitable result of law. In all the five cases mentioned in this paragraph *orgē* refers to future judgement wherever its meaning can be defined at all: in no instance is there any reason to suppose that St. Paul had in view an *affectus* on the part of God.

Rom. ix. 22, 'But what if God, desiring to exhibit, *endeixasthai*, "his retribution at work" (simply *tēn orgēn*; "at work" corresponds to no actual word in the Greek. It is a gloss, and in my view a correct gloss) tolerated very patiently those vessels which were objects of retribution, *skeuē orgēs*, due for destruction', raises many problems, not all of them being relevant at this point. Two facts must be stressed. First, God has already exhibited his *orgē*. Secondly, He has effected this exhibition of His *orgē* by doing something, namely tolerating the *skeuē orgēs*. It could be the case

[45] C. K. Barrett, *The Epistle to the Romans* Black N.T.C., (London, 1957), ad loc., p. 33.

that his *orgē* is a feeling and that God wishing (a) to show how He feels and (b) to show His power has acted in a certain way. But since *orgē* normally refers to judgement in the future, we are surely justified in supposing that already in the past God has made a partial display of the judgement which will be consummated in the future; in other words, this is an instance of 'realized eschatology'; God has now begun to do what Israel for generations past has longed for Him to do. In this case His *orgē* is not the cause of His display of power, but identical with it: both His wrath and His power consist in His direction of the course of history.

Hanson[46] makes the interesting suggestion that *skeuē orgēs* etc. means not '*recipients* of wrath prepared for destruction' but '*instruments* of wrath forged for destruction'. If Hanson's suggestion is correct, then Rom. ix. 22 is parallel to Jer. l., (LXX xxvii.) 25, 'The Lord has opened his armory and brought out the weapons of his wrath (*skeuē orgēs*)' or to Ps. vii. 13, (LXX vii. 13), 'He (God) has prepared his deadly weapons (*skeuē thanatou*)'. Against Hanson's interpretation must be set *skeuē eleous* in Rom. ix. 23, which the N.E.B. renders, 'Vessels which were objects of mercy'. This seems more probable than 'instruments for making known his mercy', though this would apply to St. Paul himself, and it cannot be ruled out as impossible. Again, the *skeuē* are fitted *eis apōleian*, that is as objects, or according to Hanson, as instruments of destruction. Now we read in Rom. ix. 21, 'Is he not free to make out of the same lump two vessels (*skeuē*) one to be treasured (*eis timēn*) the other for common use (*eis atimian*)?' *Eis* in v. 21 seems to mean 'destined to receive', not 'destined to confer'. Both these facts militate against Hanson, though not decisively, since a phrase used in one sense might suggest to St. Paul a similar phrase used in another sense.

In either case, *orgē* is more likely to refer to God's providential ordering of history than to His feelings.

Rom. xii. 19, 'Do not seek revenge, but leave a place for "divine retribution" (*orgē*)' may refer to the final judgement or to God's purpose working out in history. Whichever it may be, it can hardly refer to feelings. The Romans are forbidden to seek active revenge: they are not bidden to avoid resentment; and the *orgē* for which they are to stand aside would therefore naturally consist in action, not in feeling.

[46] *The Wrath of the Lamb* (London, 1957), p. 90.

Rom. xiii. 4, 'They are God's agents of punishment, for retribution (*eis orgēn*) on the offender', gives *orgē* a content. God's wrath here takes the form not of sinning, as in Rom. i. 18-32, but of suffering punishment at the hands of the Roman authorities, and the same applies to *orgē* in Rom. xiii. 5.

Col. iii. 6, 'Because of these (the sins mentioned above) God's dreadful judgement (*orgē tou Theou*) is impending', probably refers to the future, and the same applies to Eph. v. 6. Whether *erchetai* means 'Will come' or 'comes' it suggests something sent from or by God rather than His feeling. Col. iii. 8 and Eph. iv. 31 are concerned with the putting away of human wrath, and are not relevant to our present enquiry. Eph. ii. 3, 'In our natural condition, we, like the rest, lay under the dreadful judgement of God (lit., We were by nature children of wrath, *ēmetha tekna phusei orgēs*),' is no doubt correctly interpreted by the N.E.B., 'We were the kind of people on whom God's judgement rests'.

We have now reviewed all the passages where St. Paul employs the word *orgē*, 'wrath'. In none of them is it necessary to suppose that *orgē* refers to a 'feeling' or '*affectus*' on the part of God, directed against sinners; indeed, there is no case where this explanation is even very plausible. In all cases *orgē* refers to what He will do or is already doing. It must be emphasized, however, that 'wrath' is the action of a personal God Who hates sin. He is far from being 'emotionally' neutral, but loves sinners.

Some other passages must now be considered. *Thumos*, anger, is mentioned in Col. iii. 8, Eph. iv. 31, where it is a human failing and is to be overcome. In Rom. ii. 8 St. Paul speaks of the *thumos*, anger, of God. In the Bible, as Hanson[47] has shown, *thumos* and *orgē* do not differ in meaning. *Thumos* in Rom. ii. 8 adds nothing to *orgē* except emphasis, and its presence is probably due to a memory, perhaps unconscious, of Ps. lxxviii (LXX lxxvii), 49.[48]

†, †

(d) '*Enemies*' of God

Far more important are the passages where St. Paul speaks about human beings as 'enemies of God', for example, Rom. v. 10, 'For if, when we were God's enemies (*echthroi*) we were reconciled to him. . . .' The question arises, does *echthroi* mean *hated* by God or *hating* God? The passive sense, 'hated by God'

[47] *The Wrath of the Lamb*, (London, 1957), Appendix 3, pp. 206-9.
[48] Hanson, op. cit., p. 87.

has been defended on the basis of Rom. xi. 28, 'In the spreading of the Gospel they are "treated as God's enemies" (simply *echthroi*, lit. "enemies"; "treated as" is a "gloss", which I personally accept) for your sake, but God's choice stands, and they are his friends (*agapētoi*) for the sake of the patriarchs'. It is argued that because '*agapētoi*' means 'loved by', therefore *echthroi* must mean 'hated by'. But this is quite unsound, because the two statements are on different levels. In any case, purpose, rather than feeling is in question. God's ultimate purpose, his 'strategic aim' is to save Israel, hence they are called *agapētoi*. His immediate aim, His tactical method, includes dealing with them as an opposed group, keeping them 'out' to bring the Gentiles 'in'. On the ultimate level, Israel is beloved. On the level of the immediate situation, Israel was in opposition to God. It was the immediate situation in 'ecclesiastical politics', not any feeling of animosity on God's part, that St. Paul had in mind in Rom. xi. 28.[49]

Commenting on Rom. v. 10, 'When we were God's enemies we were reconciled to him', Murray says, 'If we dissociate from the word "enmity" in this case all that is malignant and malicious, it means the removal of God's holy enmity against us'.[50] But verse 10 must be read in the light of verse eight, 'But Christ died for us while we were yet sinners, and that is God's own proof of his love towards us'. God had no enmity towards us, not even 'holy enmity'; sending His own Son in a form like that of our own sinful nature was no act of enmity: it was the supreme act of love. In this act of love Father and Son were not divided, as St. Paul himself tells us in 2 Cor. v. 19, 'God was in Christ reconciling the world to himself'. On the other hand, *echthroi* in Rom. v. 10 cannot mean 'hating' God, since the attitude of men was not at once changed by the death of Christ. *Echthros*, I suggest, does not refer to the 'feelings' either of God or of man, but to the relation[51] between God and Man. The third passage which must be considered together with Rom. xi. 28 and v. 10 is Col. i. 21, 'Formerly you were yourselves estranged from God; you were his enemies in heart and mind'. Lightfoot is probably correct when he

[49] So Leenhardt, *C.N.T.*, *Romans*, xi. 28.

[50] John Murray, *The Epistle to the Romans*, vol. i. Chapters 1–8, London N.T.C., (London, 1960), p. 172.

[51] I am here, of course, applying to 'enemy' an interpretation analogous to that accorded to 'reconcile' by Dom Jacques Dupont in 'La réconciliation dans la théologie de Saint Paul', *Analecta Lovaniensia Biblica et Orientalia*, ser. ii fasc. 32; Bruges-Paris, 1953.

maintains that *echthroi* is here active. But need it mean 'consciously hating'? Lightfoot's word 'hostile' should be understood to mean 'opposed to'. The Gentiles were not *motivated* by hatred of God; but their lives were a defiance of His will.

Certainly the most illuminating illustration of the meaning of *echthros* is Matt. v. 43–45, 'You have heard that they were told "Love your neighbour, hate your enemy". But what I tell you is this: Love your enemies and pray for your persecutors; only so can you be children of your heavenly Father'. *Echthroi* means here 'those who are opposed to you'. It is possible to hate such. We often do. But Christ tells us to love those who are opposed to us. To say that a man is an 'enemy', an *echthros*, does not tell us anything by itself about our feelings towards him. They may be feelings of anger, but they will be feelings of love if we are really children of our heavenly Father. We then were ' enemies ' of God, estranged from Him. Nevertheless, He loved us, and showed His love by sending His Son to effect reconciliation, making known to us the love which He already bore us.

(e) *Conclusion*

This discussion of God's wrath has been made to hinge on the question of whether it is solely an *effectus*, or whether it is both an *effectus* and an *affectus*. The proponents of both views feel themselves under an obligation to maintain certain vital convictions. But on many of these points they are really in agreement. Those who uphold the *affectus* theory are scrupulously careful to make it clear that there is nothing 'malicious' about the wrath of God. They also insist, quite rightly, that God is personal, and that He does not condone sin, but will bring judgement. With all this the upholders of the *effectus*-theory agree from the heart; they might perhaps envisage judgement differently, but they would not deny its extreme gravity. They would also agree with Tasker's contention that all language can be applied to God only in the analogical sense.[52]

We must distinguish between the referend, that is, the reality referred to, and the language which is used to refer to it. It is our conclusion that the reality referred to, the wrath of God, is an impersonal *effectus* due to a personal God, but that St. Paul when

[52] *The Biblical Doctrine of the Wrath of God* (London, 1951), preface, p. vii.

G

he referred to this reality, used the word *orgē* which sometimes in the LXX is used for an impersonal *effectus*, but more frequently for a personal *affectus* of God.

Richardson rejects the impersonal theory with the words: 'We can rationalize the idea in that way, if we like, but it would be a mistake to suppose that the N.T. writers did so'.[53] This opinion must be read in the light of what Morris[54] says about the thought of the Bible. He maintains that the 'Prophets and the psalmists know nothing of an impersonal process of retribution', and that 'In the thought of the New Testament writers there is no place for an impersonal agency which can act in independence of God, for "all things are of God" '. We hasten to agree that nothing can act, or, we may add, exist in absolute independence of God; but many beings do act in a relative independence of God, though ultimately they will be made subject to Him (1 Cor. xv. 28). This 'relative independence' is most obvious when God is not obeyed. But we must maintain, first, that the Bible tends to use personal language where we should employ impersonal language. It is not that the New Testament writers had no place for an impersonal agency: rather, they described 'impersonal agency' by means of personal language. Secondly, it is clear that even in the LXX *orgē* is sometimes used impersonally as in Judith ix. 9, 'Send down thy wrath'. But we can agree that the impersonal wrath is ultimately under the control of a personal God, and that, as Morris points out, 'God is responsible when these consequences do follow'.[55]

The wrath of God, then, His *orgē*, is an *effectus* which is ultimately under the control of an *affectus*; and this *affectus* is His love.

[53] *Introduction*, p. 76.
[54] *The First and Second Epistles to the Thessalonians*, London N.T.C. (London, 1959), p.64.
[55] op. cit., p. 65.

CHAPTER FOUR

PREPARATION FOR THE GOSPEL

i. Introductory

Under this traditional heading we shall examine St. Paul's teaching on the Jews and the Law, the Gentiles and the Promise, and Predestination. An alternative title for this chapter might have been 'God's Lordship over History', which has a contemporary ring. The word 'history', as used in present day theology, includes both fact and 'interpretation'. We may add 'sacred legend', as a third element. The distinction between objective fact, sacred legend, and 'inspired interpretation' is sometimes irrelevant, since, as most of us would agree, God has revealed Himself by means of each one of them. For example, it is probably a brute, objective fact of history that some at least of the ancestors of the Israelites escaped from Egypt in what we call the Exodus. That a rock followed them is sacred legend, and that the rock was Christ (1 Cor. x. 4) is interpretation. The value of St. Paul's teaching is not vitiated by the fact that he is here giving his own interpretation of a sacred legend. But it is a most serious error to suppose that, merely because history is held to include interpretation, objective fact does not matter: if St. Paul and the other apostles did not recognize Jesus Christ as an objective reality after He rose from the dead, then 'our gospel is null and void' (1 Cor. xv. 14).

When we say that God is 'Lord of history', we must not imagine that 'history' is an abstraction. We mean that God's will is effective in the lives of human beings. We shall consider in this chapter how God dealt with the Jews before the time of Christ, and what His purpose was for both Jew and Gentile after the Incarnation. It will be necessary to look forward to the very end of history, since it is only then that His purpose is to be fulfilled. In the next chapter and those which follow we must retrace our steps and see how the fulfilment of God's purpose took shape through the person and work of Christ, how that work became effective for us through faith and the sacraments, and how the Christian life is to be lived out in the fellowship of the Church.

ii. THE JEWS

It is only too easy to think of Judaism as a dark backcloth intended to show up by contrast the light of the Gospel. Apart from the ever-present danger of anti-Semitism, this prevents us from appreciating the response of faith. The Jews did not fail to see what was obvious: they failed to rise to a very great challenge, and this failure is quite easy to understand, as will appear when we come to examine St. Paul's teaching on the Law.

The Apostle himself was a Jew, and proud of it, as we tell from 2 Cor. xi. 21, 'But if there is bravado (and here I speak as a fool), I can indulge in it too. Are they Hebrew? So am I . . . . ,' and from Phil. iii. 5, 'Circumcised on my eighth day, Israelite by race, of the tribe of Benjamin, a Hebrew born and bred; in my attitude to the law, a Pharisee; in pious zeal, a persecutor of the church; in legal rectitude, fautless.' His extremism is emphasized by Gal. i. 13–14, 'You have heard what my manner of life was when I was still a practising Jew: how savagely I persecuted the church of God, and tried to destroy it; and how in the practice of our national religion I was outstripping many of my Jewish contemporaries'. There may be further evidence for this pre-conversion Jewish extremism in Gal. v. 11, 'If I am still advocating circumcision. . . '. It is possible that when still a Jew he had been a powerful advocate of conversion to Judaism, and therefore of circumcision. The word 'still' (*eti*) is absent in a wide range of manuscripts, but probably ought to be retained, since the passage would be easier to understand without it; it is obvious why it should be left out if original, but there is no good reason why it should be included if it was not.

But be that as it may, St. Paul had unquestionably been a devout Jew, and very conscious of it, before his vision on the road to Damascus. Even after his conversion, being himself an Israelite, of the stock of Abraham, he was unable to believe that God had rejected his people (Rom. xi. 1.) His deepest desire and prayer to God was for their salvation (Rom. x. 1). Indeed, he could even pray to be outcast from Christ himself for the sake of his brothers, his natural kinsfolk (Rom. ix. 3). He fully realized that Jews were sinful (Rom. ii.), and that they had been 'rejected' by God, like branches lopped out of a tree (Rom. xi. 15, 17). He could use the strongest language against those who tried to force circumcision upon his Gentile converts (Gal. v. 12), and yet I have failed to find a passage where he expresses hatred of Judaism as such. St. Paul was deeply conscious of the historical privileges of Israel, as we can see from Rom. iii. 1, 'Then what advantage has the Jew? What is the value of circumcision? Great, in every way. In the first place, the Jews were entrusted with the oracles of God,' and from Rom. ix. 4, 5, 'They are Israelites: they were made God's sons; theirs is the splendour of the divine presence, theirs the covenants, the law, the temple worship and the promises.'

All this teaching is firmly rooted in such Old Testament passages as Deut. xiv. 1, 'You are the sons of the Lord your God', 1 Kings viii. 11, 'For the glory (Hebrew *kābōd*, Aramaic *shekināh*, Greek *doxa*, presence) of the Lord filled the House of the Lord,' etc. We naturally ask how it is possible to reconcile the emphasis which St. Paul places upon the ordinances given by God to Israel with his insistence upon the actual, historical disobedience and rejection of Israel. It is true that the Apostle speaks from the heart, and makes no attempt to integrate his thought into a neat, consistent system. But there is no need to suppose that there was a flagrant contradiction in his theology.

St. Paul believed that two things were necessary for salvation: neither was effective alone, but both were essential. In the technical language of logic each was a necessary but not sufficient condition. If a woman wishes to light a gas-jet she must both turn on the gas and also strike a match. The match and the turning on of the gas are each necessary but not sufficient conditions. For salvation it was necessary in St. Paul's thought both to have a covenant with God and to observe its terms. The covenant was a necessary condition, but not sufficient without obedience. The privileges of the Jews were all of the 'covenant' type: they constituted a link with God, but did not make obedience possible. Rom. ii. 25, 'Circumcision (the seal of the covenant) has value, provided you keep the law; but if you break the law, then your circumcision is as if it had never been,' is a key verse. The Jews had been given a covenant, but not the power to observe its terms, although such a power is promised in Ezek. xxxvi. 27, 'I will put my spirit within you, and cause you to walk in my statutes'.

It might be objected that God had given the Jews 'enough rope to hang themselves with'. St. Paul recognized the plain fact that Jews, like all other human beings, were sinful. He believed that God was all-powerful and that the religious heritage of Israel was

His gift. He believed that God was a God not of the Jews alone, but of Gentiles also (Rom. iii. 29). Why then had God given to the Jews the covenant only, and not the power to fulfil it? He had witheld the power to fulfil the covenant in order that the Gentiles also might be brought in. This is a natural understanding of Gal. iii. 22, 'But Scripture has declared the whole world to be prisoners in subjection to sin, so that faith in Jesus Christ may be the ground on which the promised blessing is given'. The Gentiles could not be saved, because they were outside the covenant. In Christ God gave the Gentiles a new covenant, so that they now possessed the first condition for salvation, which they had never done before. In Christ also God offered both Jew and Gentile for the first time the power to fulfil the covenant. St. Paul might have argued thus: if God had given Israel the power to keep the law, then the Kingdom of God would have come, and the Gentiles would have been left out. If he had been asked why God had not given to all men, Jews and Gentiles alike, both the covenant and the power to obey it, he might have replied that this was a pointless question, since, as everyone knew, the Gentiles were in fact outside the covenant, and it would be presumptuous to ask how matters might have developed if God's plan had been different.

iii. THE LAW

(a) *The Torah in Judaism*

St. Paul's statements about the Law would appear to be in flat contradiction with each other. In its favour he says that it is one of the privileges of Israel (Rom. ix. 4), and that it has been a kind of tutor (*paidagōgos*) in charge of us till Christ should come (Gal. iii. 24). Against it he urges that it intruded to multiply law-breaking (Rom. v. 20), and that those who rely on obedience to it are under a curse (Gal. iii. 10).

In subsequent Christian theology the word 'law' has been associated almost exclusively with moralism. This one-sided emphasis makes it difficult to understand the ambivalent, 'love-hatred' attitude of St. Paul to the law. We must not regard the law as an independent entity, but consider its place in the total life-pattern of those who used, or sometimes abused, the law as a lamp to their feet and a light to their path (Ps. cxix. 105).

In pre-exilic Israel the law, the Torah, included the national history, myths and legends.[1] It included in its scope not only legal and religious matters as we should now define them, but also what we might describe as the 'Israelite way of life'. Their customs, feasts and sacred places were often those of their neighbours and of their predecessors. But there was a vital difference. The Israelite came to regard a place as holy because Yahweh had recorded his name there by appearing to one of the patriarchs. The fact that the place had been sacred to the pre-Israelite inhabitants became something to cover up, and was finally irrelevant. Feasts which had originally been observed as part of the agricultural year were associated with some historic act of salvation wrought by Yahweh on behalf of Israel, just as in Europe certain midwinter observances have been associated with the Incarnation and have therefore been given a new meaning.

In respect of content the Torah included stirring accounts of what God had done for Israel. The fact that the legal ordinances were set in the framework of the Exodus makes it fair to say that the law was not mere 'moralism' but included the moral requirements of God, placed in a framework of salvation-history, and in particular of God's covenants[2] with His people. Before the Exile the Law was probably not regarded as an external burden. It would be associated with the scenery, since it told how God had given the people the hills and valleys which they saw around them. It was the expression, whether oral or written, of their daily way of life, and was the means of keeping alive their sense of God, together with the cultic persons and places, especially the Temple at Jerusalem and the sacrifices which were offered there by or on behalf of the king.

For those who went into exile in Babylon all was changed. The king was no more and the Temple was burned with fire. They could offer no sacrifice in a strange land. The scenery and the on-going life of the people around them were no longer closely bound up with Yahwism. Their environment was no longer Israelite, but pagan. One thing remained: the Law and its regulations which were binding upon the individual Jew, and upon his family. Indeed, the Jewish family became a 'micro-environment' in which the fear of the Lord could be practised. Is it surprising that the

[1] H. J. Schoeps, *Paul* (E.T. London, 1961), pp. 213–15.
[2] cf. G. F. Moore, *Judaism*, vol. 1, pp. 226–34, and Schoeps, *Paul* (E.T. London, 1961), pp.220–9.

Law seemed to swallow up within itself all the ordinances of religion and to become *the* link with God? The sabbath, being distinctive, became even more important as a means of keeping Israel 'holy' and distinct from the people around. Circumcision, we may suppose, received greater emphasis precisely because it was not practised by the people of Babylon.

The re-establishment of Jewry which we associate with the name of Ezra naturally laid stress upon the Law. Ezra has often been criticized for 'narrowness', but if his narrowness was wrong, we must admit that this particularistic zeal was a means of keeping Judaism alive, and that, under God, Judaism and Christianity would not be potent forces in the world today if it had not been for 'narrow zealots' like Ezra and those who followed in his path at the time of the Maccabees and later, not excluding Saul of Tarsus. When Saul became Paul, it must have seemed to some of his former associates that he was wantonly throwing away the religious and national heritage which his ancestors in the time of Antiochus Epiphanes had defended with their life's blood. These well-known facts must be kept in mind if we are to appreciate the Apostle's zeal for the Law before his conversion.

We must also resist the temptation to force Judaism into a narrow mould and forget its rich variations. Side by side with particularism there was a strand of universalism[3]. To some, the *Torah* was a joy and a delight, as we can tell from Ps. cxix, which must always be taken into account by all, especially by us Christians, when we try to understand the Jewish attitude to the Law. Another reaction is seen in Mal. i. 13, 'What a weariness this is, you say, and sniff at me, says the Lord of Hosts.' Clearly, the attitude expressed in Ps. cxix is somewhat idealized. It would be useless to speculate about what proportion of the Jews at any one time adopted either of these two attitudes towards the Law. It is sufficient to remember that in this, as in other respects, the Jewish nation was not homogeneous.

Again, a doctrine of salvation by works was held in Judaism, as we may gather from the reward promised in the Syriac Apocalypse of Baruch, li. 7 to 'Those who have been saved by their works, and to whom the law has been now a hope.'[4] Sometimes, no doubt,

---

[3] c.f. G. F. Moore, *Judaism*, vol. I, pp. 226–34, and Schoeps, *Paul* (E. T. London, 1961), pp. 220–9.

[4] Charles, vol. ii. p. 509.

this led to the kind of smugness which is attacked in our Lord's parable of the Pharisee and the Publican (Luke xviii. 9–14). But although there was no doubt smugness among the Jews, many of them were quite well aware of their sin, as we find in 2 Esdras iv. 38, 'But all of us also are full of ungodliness.' Schoeps[5] quotes several cases of rabbis who thought that it was not even possible to fulfil the Law.

(b) St. Paul's teaching on the Law

The Greek word *nomos*, law, is sometimes employed by St. Paul to mean simply 'Holy Scripture', without any emphasis upon God's requirements. This use is found in 1 Cor. xiv. 21, 'We read in the Law: . . .' and then follows a quotation from Isa. xxviii. 11. This sense is also found at 1 Cor. xiv. 9, 34; Gal. iv. 21. Sometimes also *nomos* means principle or norm,[6] as in Rom. vii. 21, 'I discover this principle, *nomos*, then, that . . . .' This meaning also occurs in Rom. vii. 23, viii. 2.

But by far the most important use of the word *nomos* is that by which it is applied to the Torah as God's supreme self-revelation. This is very nearly hypostatized. The substructure of the Apostle's thought about the Torah included four basic convictions. The first, shared with all Jews, was that the Law was God's gift and therefore good. The second, shared with many Jews, was that no one in fact obeyed the Law. The third, which a significant minority of the Jews also accepted, was that God's plan included the good of the Gentiles as well as that of Israel. The fourth, which cut him off from Judaism and made him a Christian, was that God had raised from the dead the Messiah of Israel, whom the rulers of the nation had given over to be crucified.

The excellence of the Law is fundamental to St. Paul's thought. Gal. iii. 19–20, 'It was promulgated through angels, and there was an intermediary', is intended, we must agree with Klausner[7] and Ridderbos,[8] to reduce the prestige of the Law. But this is balanced by Rom. vii. 12f., 'Therefore the law is in itself holy, and the commandment is holy and just and good. Are we to say then that this good thing was the death of me? By no means. It was sin that

[5] *Paul* (E.T. London, 1961), pp. 176–8, and 185–7.
[6] Arndt and Gringrich, *s.v.*, 2a.
[7] *From Jesus to Paul* (E.T. London, 1942), p. 501.
[8] Herman N. Ridderbos, *Epistle to the Galatians*, London N.T.C., (London, 1961³), p. 138 on iii. 19.

killed me, and thereby sin exposed its true character. . . . We know
that the law is spiritual; but I am not: I am unspiritual, the
purchased slave of sin. . . '. This passage makes it perfectly clear
that the law in itself was good, and that it was sin, not the law, that
was evil.

The passages in which St. Paul might seem to argue that the
law is evil fall broadly into two classes. The first class, which must
be discussed later, comprises the verses in which it is taught that
God purposely allowed the Jews to go on sinning, since He 'with-
held' the power to obey the law which He had given them by
covenant, in order to bring the Gentiles in. The Jews were forced
to hold back, as it were, to give the nations time. It was made
impossible to achieve salvation by obeying the Law, which was
peculiar to the Jews, in order that all alike, both Jew and Gentile,
might enter in together as members of Christ Jesus, in whom is
neither Jew nor Gentile.

The second class consists of those passages which speak of the
Law as a moral indicator, making it possible to realize the gravity
of sin. We may cite Rom. iii. 20, 'No human being can be justified
in the sight of God for having kept the law: law brings only the
consciousness of sin,' vii. 7, 'But except through the law I should
never have become acquainted with sin' (cp. also Rom. v. 13).

Rom. v. 20, 'Law intruded into this process to (Gk. *hina*, which
normally expresses purpose) multiply law-breaking', presents us
with a problem, but this problem is largely solved if we continue to
read what immediately follows, 'But where sin was thus multiplied,
grace immediately exceeded it, in order that, as sin established its
reign by way of death, so God's grace might establish its reign in
righteousness, and issue in eternal life through Jesus Christ our
Lord'. The intention of God in giving the Law by Moses was to
turn mere unconscious wrong-doing into conscious sin, by making
clear His will: sin is the conscious defiance of the known will of
God. Nathan did much the same to David when he said in 2 Sam.
xii. 7, 'You are the man'. If God is to deal with wrong-doing (so
St. Paul seems to believe) it must be crystallized into conscious sin,
like a boil that is brought to a head by hot fomentations in order to
be pricked. St. Paul probably means that God gave the law with
the immediate intention of transforming unconscious wrong-doing
into conscious sin, and with the ultimate intention of overcoming
that sin altogether.

Unconscious wrong-doing can be dealt with effectually only by being transformed into sin, that is, conscious defiance of God's will, made known to us by the Law. But conscious sin which has not yet been dealt with is even more serious. The giving of the Law is part of the ultimate purpose of God, which is to conquer sin altogether, but during the intervening period wrong-doing is all the more serious because it has now become conscious sin. This accounts for 1 Cor. xv. 56, 'The sting of death is sin, and sin gains its power from the law:' the law for the time being makes ignorant transgression into conscious sin, and therefore far more heinous. This, if we accept the rendering of the N.E.B., is the force of Gal. iii. 19, 'Then what of the Law? It was added to make wrong-doing a legal offence (lit. "because of transgressions" *tōn parabaseōn charin*).' Rom. vii. 8, 'In the absence of law sin is a dead thing,' belongs to the same line of thought. If it were not for the law, sin would not be sin at all since it would not be contrary to the known will of God; it would be mere ignorant transgression: but it must become conscious sin before it can be conquered.

We have seen, then, that for St. Paul, as for all Jews, the Law was very good because God had given it. In those places where he seems to be speaking against the Law, always excluding a class of passages which is reserved for later treatment, he means that the Law makes us aware of sin; that it is, because Law makes known to us the will of God, it transforms 'innocent' wrong-doing into conscious sin, and God has brought this about in order to overcome sin.

He also believed, like many other Jews, that it is not possible to keep the Law. From this he draws the un-Jewish conclusion that it is not possible to be saved by doing the works of the Law. Gal. iii. 21, 'If a law had been given which had power to bestow life then indeed righteousness would have come from keeping the law,' makes it clear that there is nothing wrong with the Law as such. If we may think of the Law as an aeroplane, obedience to it as the fuel, and the moon as righteousness, then we must say that the aeroplane has nothing wrong with it. The fuel is bad enough by itself to wreck the entire enterprise, since we render the Law ineffective by our failure to obey it: 'What the Law could never do, because our lower nature robbed it of all potency, God has done' (Rom. viii. 3.). But supposing that the impossible had taken place, and a human being (apart from Christ) had kept the Law, would he have obtained righteousness? In fact such things do not happen, as we know from Gal. ii. 16, 'But we know that no man is ever justified by doing what the law demands' (so Rom. iii. 21, ix. 31; Gal. iii. 11). But is it theoretically possible? The question does not arise: it is not God's purpose that any individual should attain righteousness for himself by keeping the Law; God's purpose is to offer righteousness to all through faith in Jesus Christ.

The third fundamental conviction which underlies St. Paul's teaching about the Law is that God is not a God of the Jews only, but of the Gentiles also. He does not mean merely that the Gentiles can enter the covenant by becoming Jews: they can share in all the present and future privileges of Israel while remaining un-circumcised. In this he went beyond Philo, and indeed beyond normative Judaism altogether.

St. Paul's conviction on this matter was in direct conflict with Jewish practice. We are so much accustomed to reading *Genesis* in the light of *Galatians* that we tend to forget how completely his conviction denied the plain teaching of Scripture as recorded in Gen. xvii. 14, 'Any uncircumcised male who is not circumcised in the flesh of his foreskin shall be cut off from his people; he has broken my covenant'. For St. Paul to say or even to imagine that Scripture could be 'wrong' was quite impossible. If he felt that the 'apparent' meaning of certain passages was wrong, all he could do was to extract the 'true' meaning by normal exegetical methods from the same or other texts.[9]

Before we examine St. Paul's treatment of the texts, we must face some fundamental problems. Bonsirven says roundly that exegesis of this kind does not come from the text: (*Evidemment de pareilles exégèses ne découlent pas du texte*). It could be put forward only by a believer inspired from above (*Ne peut les proposer qu'un croyant célestement inspiré...*).[10] Schoeps objects that the hypothesis of inspiration cannot be proved, and suggests that St. Paul was undertaking a firm polemic against Jewish exegesis.[11] We must distinguish two questions, those of origin and validity.

It is clear that St. Paul sometimes reads a meaning into the Old Testament (Eisegesis). We Christians accept such teaching because we believe that the New Testament, as well as the Old, is

---

[9] So Schoeps, *Paul* (E.T. London, 1961), p. 170.
[10] J. Bonsirven, *Exégèse rabbinique et exégèse paulinienne* (Paris, 1939), p. 307.
[11] *Paul* (E.T. London, 1961), p. 250. n.1.

a medium of God's self-revelation. Exod. iii. 6, 'I am the God of your father, the God of Abraham, the God of Isaac and the God of Jacob,' clearly means 'I am the God worshipped by your father Amram and by your ancestors Abraham, Isaac and Jacob'. When our Lord quoted part of this verse, adding 'God is not God of the dead but of the living' (Mark xii. 26–7), He was putting forward the doctrine of resurrection on his own authority. He was not proving it by Scriptural exegesis, any more than He 'proved' doctrine by means of parables. The parables put men into a situation in which, if they have ears to hear, they apprehend new truth. St. Paul's exegesis of some passages will not be regarded as valid by a Jew or by anyone who is not a Christian. One who is a Christian already will see his convictions given form in St. Paul's exegesis.

We can be sure that St. Paul was not driven to regard circumcision as non-essential for salvation by his exegesis of the Old Testament: it was his rejection of the necessity for circumcision that led him to interpret the Old Testament as he did. The validity of St. Paul's teaching is a question which lies within the sphere of the doctrines of inspiration and faith; it lies outside the scope of biblical scholarship as such, though few would in fact devote their time to biblical scholarship if they did not, as persons, hold positive views about faith and about the Old and the New Testaments as a means of revelation. With regard to the origin of St. Paul's exegesis we cannot be certain whether it was a reply to Jewish exegesis or no.

The lines of exegesis which St. Paul employs in order to integrate his new conviction with Scripture may be divided for purposes of convenience into those connected with death and those connected with history.

(c) *Abrogation of the Law: arguments connected with death*

Foremost among the passages connected with death stands Gal. iii. 13–14, 'Christ bought us freedom from the curse of the law by becoming for us an accursed thing (*genomenos huper hēmōn katara*)'; for Scripture (i.e. Deut. xxi. 23) says 'For a hanged man is accursed by God'. This passage has often been regarded as a foundation stone of the substitutionary theory of the Atonement. It has been supposed that the task He undertook was to free mankind from sin and guilt and therefore from death. But this problem was not in St. Paul's mind, for he continues in the next verse, Gal. iii. 14,

'And the purpose of it all was that the blessing of Abraham should in Jesus Christ be extended to the Gentiles, so that we might receive the promised Spirit through faith'. St. Paul is here describing not how Christ saved mankind from sin, but how he saved the Gentiles from the Law, and not the Gentiles only, but the Jews also. The Gentiles stood condemned by the Law because they were strangers to the covenants, including the 'covenant sign' of circumcision; the Jews stood condemned because, although they were within the covenant, they failed to obey its terms. The Law was a pistol pointed at the heart of Jew and Gentile alike. Christ caused the curse of the Law to be 'fulfilled' and therefore 'exhausted'.

Schoeps, following Klein,[12] understands the passage in the following way. Deut xxi. 23 gives a ruling on what is to be done when a man who has been executed for some crime is, after death, hanged on a tree, just as the bodies of criminals in England were formerly submitted to public exhibition as a warning to others. Deut xxi. 23 says that such a corpse must not be left on the tree all night lest it defile the land, since 'a hanged man is accursed by God'. It was the Law which pronounced a curse upon a man who was hung up after death. Christ's death, not quite parallel, was due to the fact that He hung on the cross. Since Christ has done that which the Law says brings a curse, Christ has incurred the curse of the Law and exhausted its power, like one who explodes a mine and destroys its power at the cost of physical annihilation.

To some this may seem trivial argumentation. To Jews who did not share St. Paul's belief about the Gentiles, it must have appeared wholly unconvincing. To St. Paul himself, and to others who shared his conviction that Gentiles could enter into the heritage of Israel without submitting to the yoke of the Torah, such an exposition of Deut. xxi. 22–3 must have brought a great feeling of relief, since it enabled them to reconcile their belief about the Gentiles with their belief in the authority of the Torah, and to do so by methods which were in accordance with the current techniques for introducing new truth by reading it into the Old Testament.

Such expositions of the Bible, in spite of the present revival of interest in typology, are a hindrance today, just as they were a

---

[12] *Studien über Paulus* (Stockholm, 1918), pp. 62–7. I owe this reference to Schoeps, op. cit., p. 179.

help in the first century A.D. What is of permanent value, independently of all changes of fashion in the use of Scripture, is St. Paul's conviction about the Gentiles. Since Christians have for many centuries taken St Paul's conviction on this point for granted they have applied Gal. iii. 13 not to freedom from the curse of the Law but to liberation from sin, which, unlike the Law, is a permanent problem, common to all centuries. It is possible that St. Paul may in his own thinking have used the explanation of Deut. xxi. 23 which we find at Gal. iii. 13 in connection with liberation from sin. In this case the thought would be parallel to that found in 2 Cor. v. 21, and the Church in general has understood Gal. iii. 13 in this way. But actually in Gal. iii. 13–14 St. Paul is concerned primarily with victory over the Law, not victory over sin.

Another line of argument, still connected with death, is used by St. Paul to put forward his conviction that the Law no longer had power to exclude those who did not accept it. He argues in Rom. vii. that liability to the claims of law ceases with death. This generalisation is illustrated by the fact that a wife's obligation to her husband ceases when he dies, at least to the extent that she is now free to marry another man. He argues that Christ's death makes Him free from the Law, 'So you, my friends, have died to the law by becoming identified with the body of Christ (lit. 'through the body of Christ', *dia tou sōmatos tou Christou*)'. The 'identification' of the Christian with Christ in His death and freedom from the Law is more concisely expressed in Gal. ii. 20, 'I have been crucified with Christ: the life I now live is not my life, but the life which Christ lives in me'. This argument, again, would not convince anyone not ready to accept it, but it might reconcile the traditional teaching of the Torah with the conviction of a man who already believed, consciously or unconsciously, that Christ ends the law and brings righteousness for everyone who has faith.

(d) *Abrogation of the Law: arguments connected with history*

Other arguments are based upon historical or chronological factors. Abraham's faith was counted as righteousness (Rom. iv. 9). This refers back to Gen. xv. 6, when the patriarch was still uncircumcised, since it was not until Gen. xvii that his circumcision was recorded.

Again, once a will has been executed, no one else can set it aside or add a codicil. It makes no difference to St. Paul's argument whether *diathēkē* means 'will', or 'covenant', as J. B. Light-foot[13] maintained. *Diathēkē* is in any case the normal LXX rendering of the Hebrew *berîth*, covenant. St. Paul states that a covenant or a will cannot be overridden by a Law introduced 430 years later (Gal. iii. 15–18.).

Further, an heir, when still legally a minor, may be subject to guardians and trustees. Judaism was subject to the elemental spirits of the universe (Gal. iv. 3), which are closely associated with the *Torah*.[14] But when the time fixed by God in His providence had elapsed God sent His own Son to purchase freedom for the subjects of the law, in order that we might attain the status of sons. Here again, the argument is basically chronological.

(e) *The Torah in the Church*

Some further points must be considered briefly. St. Paul never makes any explicit distinction between the moral and the ritual law.[15] On the other hand, some at least of the content of the 'moral' law is insisted upon in certain passages. In Rom. xiii. 8 St. Paul tells us that he who loves his neighbour has satisfied every claim of the law; he then refers briefly to the prohibition in the decalogue of adultery, murder, theft, and covetousness. Essentially the same point is made in Gal. v. 14.

Gal. vi. 2, 'Help one another to carry these heavy loads, and in this way you will fulfil the law of Christ', on the other hand, probably refers to something else. It may point not to a survival of part of the content of the Old Law, but to a new law of a different order altogether. The phrase occurs here alone in the New Testament. The only parallel so far noticed in the Rabbinic writings is 'The Torah which a man learns in this world is vanity compared with the Torah of the Messiah'.[16] It may be that some belief of this kind lay behind St. Paul's language.†

iv. THE GENTILES

St. Paul's teaching on Jews and Gentiles has been illuminated by Munck[17] in an article entitled 'Israel and the Gentiles in the New Testament'. He starts from the apparently anti-Gentile

---

[13] *St. Paul's Epistle to the Galatians* (London, 1881⁷) on Gal. iii. 15.

[14] So B. Reicke, *J.B.L.*, lxx. (1951), pp. 259–76. This most important article is a translation from the Swedish original in *Svensk Exegetisk Arsbok* (1942). The English title is 'The Law and this World according to Paul'.

[15] So W. Gutbrod, *T.W.N.T.*, iv. p. 1063, E.T., *Law*; (London, 1962), p. 106.   [16] See Strack-Billerbeck, iii. p. 577 on Gal. vi. 2.

[17] *J.T.S.*, N.S., ii. Pt. i. (1951), pp. 3–16.

sentiments attributed to Christ in such passages as Matt. x. 5, 'Do not take the road to gentile lands, and do not enter any Samaritan town; but go rather to the lost sheep of the house of Israel'. This is contrasted with the 'liberal' attitude of St. Paul.

In order to put the problem into sharp focus two 'classical' solutions are propounded. The first is that of F. C. Baur. He maintained that the original 'universalism' of Jesus Christ was completely obscured by the Early Church, which took the Jewish line, represented by Matt. x. 5 until the original teaching of Christ was rediscovered by St. Paul. But if all the twelve apostles and other early Christians had been so firmly Jewish in their views, it is hard to imagine how St. Paul could ever have succeeded.

The second 'classical' theory is that of Adolf Harnack.[18] He maintained that the teaching of Christ was almost exclusively 'Jewish',[19] the only exception being the pericope of the Syro-Phoenician Woman; and it is made abundantly clear that this event was exceptional.[20] The mission to the Gentiles was originated by St. Stephen and others,[21] but it was St. Paul[22] who made it really effective. In that case it would have been even more difficult for St. Paul and his predecessors to succeed.

Munck himself holds that Christ and St. Paul both accepted as their final purpose the 'universalistic' aim of preaching the Gospel to all mankind, and that they both took for granted a presupposition which we can best express in the words of Rom. xi. 16, 'If the first portion of dough is consecrated, so is the whole lump'. Christ, then, concentrated exclusively upon Israel, because this, in His view, was the only way to save the world in time. If the pilot of a ship has fainted, someone must grasp the rudder; to pay attention to any other part of the ship is a waste of time. To save the rest of the ship it is essential to gain control of the rudder. Christ, according to Munck, regarded Israel as the rudder of the world. St. Paul accepted the same presupposition with a vital difference: to him the rudder of the world was not Israel but the Gentiles. He therefore preached to the Gentiles to convert the Jews as well, just as Christ had preached to the Jews alone with the hope of winning the Gentiles also. St. Paul believed that the Jews had in fact rejected the Gospel, so that the function of being the rudder of the

---

[18] *The Expansion of Christianity in the First Three Centuries*, (E.T. London and New York, i. 1904, and ii. 1905).
[19] Op. cit., i. pp. 40–45.   [20] ibid., p. 41.
[21] ibid., pp. 54–55.   [22] ibid., p. 63

H

world was given to the Gentiles. A key passage for Munck is Rom. x. 18, 'But, I ask, can it be that they (Israel) never heard it (the good news)? Of course they did: "Their voice has sounded all over the earth, and their words to the bounds of the inhabited world" ' (from Ps. xix. 4). It is true, of course, that the Gospel had not been preached in every single locality inhabited by Jews, but, as Munck remarks, 'The parts to which they have preached stand for the whole, the Jewish people'.[23]

This principle of 'representative universalism' is also applied to the Gentile mission, as we can see in Rom. xv. 19, 'I have completed the preaching (*peplērōkenai*) of the Gospel of Christ from Jerusalem as far round as Illyricum'. Now in point of fact he had done nothing of the kind, if 'preaching the gospel fully' means preaching it in every village. But St. Paul's claim is correct if we understand it as Munck suggests. St. Paul had indeed presented Christianity to a representative sample of the Gentiles who lived in the north-east segment of the Roman Empire from Jerusalem to the Balkans. It was his aim to go on to the west, to Rome and to Spain. This also makes good sense if we suppose that by doing so he expected to fulfil God's purpose by preaching 'representatively' to all the Gentiles, so that the whole world could be turned towards God including His ancient people, the Jews.

Munck's important thesis covers many points which lie outside the scope of this book, but at least it gives a convincing explanation for St. Paul's attitude to Jews and Gentiles as expounded in the Epistle to the Romans. It naturally leads on to the subject of Predestination, but before we embark upon this it remains to complete St. Paul's thought concerning the Gentiles.

About these it must be said that although they were destined to play an important role in the future, thanks to Grace, as the rudder of the world, and although through the Gentile mission they had already begun to do so, yet those Gentiles who had not yet responded to the Gospel, and were therefore still 'in the state of nature', were lying under the 'Wrath of God'. This appears from Col. i. 21, 'Formerly you were yourselves estranged from God; you were his enemies in heart and mind and your deeds were evil,' and also from 2 Cor. iv. 4. Yet in the case of Jew and Gentile alike God 'in his forbearance has overlooked the sins of the past' (Rom. iii. 25; cp. Acts xiv. 16, xvii. 30).

[23] *J.T.S.*, N.S., ii. Pt. i. (1951), p. 8.

v. PREDESTINATION

(a) *Clarification of problems*

St. Paul's thought concerning Predestination cannot be usefully considered without a preliminary examination of more recent theories. The meaning of the words that have to be used, and, far more important, their emotional associations, have been decisively affected by the thought of St. Augustine and his successors.

When the 'man in the street' thinks of Predestination, what he has in mind is a kind of popularized Augustinianism which he often associates exclusively with Protestantism, and especially with the name of John Calvin. What he has in mind is that the belief that God, without any reference to merits, predestined some human beings, most would say a small minority, to salvation. The remainder were left to perish in the 'mass of perdition' or actually predestined to perish eternally, even though God could have saved them all. It is as if God had allowed a man (Adam) to get on to a ship which both knew was doomed to sink. Adam did not know, though God did, that his conscious disobedience would involve countless others in disaster. God then rescued some men from the sinking ship but left the rest to perish, although it was in His power to save them all.

To any practising and believing Christian this must seem a blasphemous parody of the doctrine of Predestination. Few contemporary Christians hold the doctrine in its most extreme Augustinian form; but the 'parody' sketched in above is an understandable caricature of the teaching of Western Christendom, both Protestant and Roman Catholic, since early in the fifth century. The 'man in the street' robs the doctrine of a dimension by taking it out of its setting as the work of God in Christ. But we cannot accuse him of ignorance in this respect. His caricature is excusable.

Before we turn to the Pauline texts, some further points must be clarified. It is now generally recognized that when a man makes a confession of his religious belief, he is not *only* saying something which he believes to be factual. He is not merely speaking about God, for example, but also expressing his attitude towards God. St. Augustine and Calvin, when they wrote about Predestination, were not only stating their belief about God's plan for the future of human beings: they were expressing their awe of God, and pledging themselves to obey a Master; strange as it might seem to the ' man in the street', for them the doctrine of Predestination was a vehicle of worship. St. Paul's thought on this same subject is also in part an expression of attitude, but it is more than that. St. Paul is to some extent concerned in his teaching on Predestination with attitude-towards-God, but he is also concerned with belief-about-God.

If a man has a pain in some part of his body, the real cause of the trouble may lie somewhere else. In a similar manner, when theologians speak about, for example, the future fate of the wicked, they may well be primarily concerned, not so much with the fate of any human beings as with God and His sovereignty. St. Paul was certainly concerned with the sovereignty of God, but this does not exclude a concern for the future of human beings also. Again, it is possible to have an unqualified belief in the power of God without claiming to know in detail how that power is to be employed. St. Paul certainly held such a belief about God's power, but he does not say anywhere what future God has in store for all individuals.

Modern theologians are in general familiar with theories of Predestination, viewed as complete systems. They realize that if they hold one belief it 'entails' or perhaps merely suggests another. If they hold one theory, they are aware of the difficulties which it raises, and for these they are ready to offer at least a provisional solution. But St. Paul, though he unquestionably believed in some sense in Predestination, had no clear answer to all the problems which this doctrine naturally raises.

When the 'man in the street' hears that a theologian is a strong believer in Predestination, he is apt to conclude that he also believes in Eternal Punishment, and that 'Predestination' means predestination to salvation; eternal punishment seems to many to be the 'natural completion' of predestination. But in fact a believer in predestination may also believe either in eternal punishment or in the ultimate salvation of all men, or that the wicked are reserved not for eternal punishment but for annihilation. St. Paul, as we have said, certainly believed in Predestination. How did he 'complete' this teaching? 2 Thess. i. 9, 'They will suffer the punishment of eternal ruin,' suggests everlasting punishment. Rom. vi. 23, 'For sin pays a wage, and the wage is death,' in itself, apart from other passages, would lead to a belief in annihilation, while Rom.

ix–xi would naturally lead us to suppose that St. Paul believed in the ultimate salvation of all men. We cannot say that the Apostle was firmly committed to any one of these three possiblities. He used at different times language which suggested each of these three incompatible theories, but he did not decisively adopt any one of them. Again, for St. Paul Predestination was normally predestination for service, not predestination to salvation.

(b) *Predestination to service*

The issue is made unnecessarily difficult if we concentrate our attention exclusively upon dubious matters which have proved hot-beds of contention. 'Predestination' and 'calling' should be viewed first of all in the context of matters which are not seriously in dispute.

Gal. i. 15, 'But then in his good pleasure God, who had set me apart from birth and called me through his grace, chose to reveal his Son to me and through me in order that I might proclaim him among the Gentiles,' shows us Predestination as God's calling of St. Paul to his special mission; we find a similar thought in Rom. i. 1; Gal. i. 1 etc., Col. iii. 12, God's chosen people (*eklektoi*) applies 'predestinarian' language to the Church, the Israel of God; and 1 Cor. vii. 21, 'Were you a slave when you were called?,' means, were you a slave when you became a Christian? This use recurs in Rom. i. 7; 1 Cor. i. 2. A doctrine of providence can be found in 1 Cor. x. 13, 'God . . . when the test comes he will at the same time provide a way out, by enabling you to sustain it,' and 2 Cor. i. 9, 'Indeed we felt in our hearts that we had received a death-sentence. This was meant to teach us not to place reliance on ourselves, but on God who raises the dead,' is a Pauline form of the belief that God 'brings good out of evil', and the same may be said about Rom. viii. 28.

(c) *Human 'cooperation'*

There are some passages which suggest that if God has called us, that is enough: others would leave us to suppose that human co-operation is also necessary.

In both cases, we have to deal not with categorical statements designed to answer a carefully formulated question, but with the implication of statements concerned with some other matter. Among the first class we may notice Rom. xiv. 4, 'And stand he will, because his Master has power to enable him to stand,' and Rom. xvi. 25, 'To him who has power to make your standing sure (*humas stērixai*) . . . .' These both *suggest* a belief that God's power alone is sufficient but they cannot be held to prove it.

1 Cor. i. 9, 'It is God himself who called you, . . . and God keeps faith,' naturally suggests that, as Calvin argues, 'calling' is calling to salvation, that the spirit is the sure witness of election, on which perseverance depends. About this verse Calvin adds that it was important for St. Paul to write this to prevent the Corinthians from being dejected when they came face to face with all the faults that he was to reveal to them later on. Much the same must be said about 1 Cor. x. 13, 'God keeps faith', and about 1 Thess. v. 24, 'He who calls (*kalōn*, present tense) you is to be trusted; he will do it'.

About such verses there is an element of attitude-towards-God; we are to rely upon Him. But there is also an element of belief-about-God; we are to rely upon Him (attitude) just because He is reliable (belief). It is clear that St. Paul's thought on this point is parallel to Theism, not to Deism. He does not believe that God called us in the past and that the past calling is enough, but he lays stress upon the continuing activity of God. The God who has called us, 'sustains' us, just as he 'sustains' the world, which He has created. In the words of Phil. i. 6, 'The One who started the good work in you will bring it to completion by the Day of Christ Jesus'.

On the other hand, 1 Thess. ii. 12, 'To live lives worthy of the God who calls you into his kingdom and glory,' suggests that God's call ought to be matched by our response, and this verse is supported by Eph. iv. 1, 'I entreat you . . . live up to your calling,' though this is probably not by St. Paul. Phil. ii. 12–13, 'You must work out your own salvation in fear and trembling; for it is God who works in you, inspiring both the will and the deed,' lays emphasis upon the same point. Just because God loves and calls men made in His own image, persons created to obey Him, His rule over us differs from His rule over the sub-personal creation.

This last passage, Phil. ii. 12–13, highlights the falsity of the belief that each human being is an encapsulated unit, hermetically sealed against outside influence: 'For all of us are the parts of one body' (Eph. iv. 25). In an ordinary human body the same few pints of blood, laden with fuel, oxygen, hormones, etc., circulate through all the different organs. Each individual organ is 'open' to the influence of what other parts of the body supply. When a muscle contracts, it is the action of that particular muscle, even though it could not act without sugar and oxygen, which come to it through the digestive and respiratory systems. In the same way, our actions are in an important sense our own, in spite of the fact that we could not have done those actions if God had not been working in us.

The error of Pelagius lay partly in this, that he seems to have taken it for granted that each human being is more independent and less 'open' than is actually the case. If we speak about 'synergism' or 'cooperation' we must not think of God and man as co-equal partners: God is different in kind from ourselves, and belongs to a higher order. In such matters language must of necessity be analogical. We are probably as near as possible to the thought of St. Paul if we say that our good actions are 'ours' in the same way that the contraction of a muscle is the action of that muscle when it obeys the command of the will. It is the muscle that acts, but its action is dependent upon the 'impulses' which come from the brain, and upon what other parts of the body supply. Our actions are our own, but we are dependent upon the life of the Body to which we belong, and 'It is God who works in you, inspiring both the will and the deed'.

(d) Romans viii. 29—30

We must now at last examine the three great passages upon which the Christian doctrine of Predestination has been founded, Rom. viii. 29–30, Rom. ix.-xi. 36, and Eph. 1. We moderns look upon each of them as a *locus classicus* for the doctrine of Predestination. We therefore tend to approach them asking ourselves, What answer does St. Paul give to the problem why some men are predestinated to salvation and others are not? But St. Paul did not intend these three passages to be answers to any such question. In Rom. viii. 29-30 he is concerned rather with the doctrine of Assurance: since our salvation is due to God, none can challenge it. Rom. ix–xi is concerned with the difficulty caused by Israel's rejection of the Gospel. Eph. i. is devoted to God's purpose. None of these three passages is directly focussed upon the problem of who is predestinated to salvation and who is not. It is clear that the three passages inevitably give rise to this question, but they do not inevitably lead us to any one answer. The doctrine of Predestination, in the broad sense in which it was held in common, despite their differences, by St. Augustine, St. Thomas and John Calvin, is not an exposition of St. Paul's thought. It is rather one attempt to solve a problem which is inevitably raised by the Pauline writings.

Rom. viii. 29, 'For those whom he foreknew (*proegnō*) he also predestinated (*proōrise*) to be conformed to the image of his Son' (R.S.V.), makes it clear that the 'security' of the Christian is based upon the eternal purpose of God. It is wholly gratuitous to read into this passage the doctrine that Christians are predestinated by God because He foresees their merit.[24] St. Paul certainly says that certain people, before they were created, had been foreknown, predestinated, called, justified and glorified. He does not say whether those glorified might later lapse by apostasy. He presumably supposed that some of those predestined had not yet heard or responded to the Gospel; otherwise he would not have continued his missionary preaching. He does not say whether those foreknown were a large or small portion of the human race. In Rom. ix. 25–32 he seems to believe that all men would be saved, which would suggest that all men had been foreknown, but that not all had yet heard the Gospel or accepted it. But in Rom. viii. 29f. this question is not raised. St. Paul is content to argue that the Christians have nothing at all to fear, since their hope is founded upon divine Predestination. Indeed, to use later traditional language, Rom. viii. 29f. is concerned not with the doctrine of predestination, but with the doctrine of assurance.

(e) Ephesians i

If Rom. viii. 29f. may be regarded as a basis for the doctrine of assurance applied to the individual, then Eph. i. is a warrant for the application of this doctrine to the church. 'In Christ he chose us (*exelexato*) before the world was founded . . . ; and he destined us (*proorisas*) such was his good will and pleasure . . .' (Eph. i. 4–5). 'Before the world was founded' does exclude predestination according to foreseen works, though it is unlikely that it was intended to do so. Its purpose probably was to associate the church with what had

---

[24] We may accept this without further discussion. The Roman Catholic Lagrange (*Epître aux Romains* (Paris, 1915), ad loc.) and the Conservative Evangelical Murray (*The Epistle to the Romans*, London N.T.C., (London, i. 1960), ad loc.), both agree.

been 'created before creation' a 'mark of honour' which in Judaism
showed the sovereignty of God. In 1 Pet. i. 20 this is ascribed to
Christ, in Rev. xiii. 8 and in the similar verse Rev. xvii. 8 to the
predestination of those whose names were written in the Lamb's
Book of Life. In Eph. i. the main thought is that the church is
securely based upon the power of God. The question is never
raised who is at last to be a member of the church and who is
not. God's hidden purpose was that the universe (*ta panta*) . . . .
should be brought into unity with Christ (Eph. i. 10). This could
be understood as an indication of eventual universal salvation, but
that would be to take the words as an answer to a question which
has not been asked. We are justified in seeing below the surface the
thought that 'Israel', for which we must here read 'the church' is
predestined to be saved. But this does not raise the question of who
is and who is not to be an Israelite. Born Israelites could be guilty
of apostasy, and Gentiles could be converted. It is true that if we
take the principle which *Ephesians* applies to the church, and
ourselves apply it to individuals, which is what later theologians
have done, we arrive at a very 'high' doctrine of predestination
indeed; but this *Ephesians* fails to do. All we find is the conviction
that the hope of the church is firmly based on the will of God.

(f) Romans ix—xi

Rom. ix–xi is mainly concerned with Israel's rejection of the
Gospel. This historical fact presented two problems for the
apostolic church. First, if Israel, God's own people, did not accept
Jesus, how could He be the Messiah? Secondly, assuming that
Jesus was the Christ, the Messiah whom Israel expected, why had
God allowed His own people to miss the promised salvation? It
was this second problem which exercised the mind of St. Paul, and
to him it was no merely theoretical problem, but a difficulty which
rent his heart in twain.

Here above all, we can hardly overestimate the importance of
viewing St. Paul's teaching against the background of his own
thought, not that of St. Augustine and his successors. In Great
Britain in the middle-ages it frequently happened that an ancient
church, perhaps Saxon in origin, was incorporated into a new
building. The old church became the chancel of a new, cruciform
structure. Since it now forms part of an intelligible architectural
pattern, the architectural ignoramus can easily fail to see that it

once had an independent existence. In the same way, we are so familiar with the present map of the U.S.A. that it is hard to remember that it was once limited to the Eastern sea-board and that Texas was part of Mexico. It is just as hard to realize that Rom. ix–xi once had an independent existence as a section of *Romans* apart from the Predestinarian systems in which it has been included, and which are possible completions of it in the sense that they provide answers to questions which St. Paul had left unanswered. For example, Rom. ix. 13, 'Jacob I loved and Esau I hated' (quoted by St. Paul from Mal. i. 2–3) does not refer to the damned who are lost eternally: it refers to the ancient people of God, to Israel after the flesh; they have not yet become true sons of Isaac, but it is God's purpose that they shall be.

We must now turn to the text of Rom. ix–xi. St. Paul is most deeply concerned for his non-Christian natural kinsfolk the Jews; he could even pray to be outcast from Christ himself for their sake (ix. 3). Their failure to respond to the Gospel does not mean that the word of God has proved false. Rom. ix. 7, 'Through the line of Isaac your posterity shall be traced' (Gen. xxi. 12) shows that God knew, and had foretold in Scripture, the fact that some of His people would prove false.

God, according to Rom. ix., knew that Pharaoh would be stubborn. God himself had predestined Pharaoh to afflict Israel (Rom. ix. 18) in order to make His power known in dealing with this tyrant. It should be noted that Pharaoh is predestined to afflict Israel: nothing is said about damnation. We naturally ask, Did God really cause the King of Egypt to sin? The answer would appear to be that He did, because of Rom. ix. 19. 'Why does God blame a man. . . . Surely the potter can do what he likes with the clay.' The objection, 'Then why does God blame a man?' hardly makes sense unless St. Paul supposed that God had predestined Pharaoh to commit sin. But St. Paul is well aware that this line of thought has dangerous consequences. Rom. ix. 20, 'Who are you, sir, to answer God back?,' is less an assertion of predestination than a warning against pushing thoughts too far. St. Paul did venture along the path of asserting that God predestines some to sin in order to show His mercy on others. He does not in this section consider the ultimate fate of those who are predestined to sin: he is concerned with the past sin of Pharaoh and the present sin of Israel, not with the future fate of either. This problem is reserved for a later chapter (x). Predestination to damnation, as opposed to predestination to sin, can be read into the present passage, but not out of it.

As we proceed to Ch. xi, we remember St. Paul's problem, which is that the majority of Israel, we might fairly say 'Israel as a whole' had failed to respond to the Gospel. This is clear from Rom. xi. 7, 'What Israel sought, Israel had not achieved, but the selected few have achieved it'. This verse describes the present situation. The future is disclosed in Rom. xi. 15f., 'For if their rejection has meant the reconciliation of the world, what will their acceptance mean? Nothing else than life from the dead! If the first portion of dough is consecrated, so is the whole lump.' The 'first portion' would seem to be the church, the 'whole lump' the human race, Jew and Gentile alike.

(g) Will all be saved?

Are we to conclude then that all will be saved? This is a natural sequel to the Apostle's present line of thought, just as predestination to damnation is a natural sequel to Rom. ix. 22f. But in both cases St. Paul sees where his line of thought is leading and draws back, as we can tell from Rom. ix. 22–23, 'Observe the kindness and the severity of God—severity to those who fell away, divine kindness to you, if only you remain within its scope; otherwise you too will be cut off, whereas they, if they do not continue faithless, will be grafted in.' This is a doctrine of 'conditional damnation.' Some human beings, Jew and Gentile alike, will be lost if they refuse God's offer. It is not said that they will in fact refuse it. St. Paul does not here *foretell* apostasy by the Romans; he firmly warns them against it. Universal salvation, according to this verse, is not ruled out, but it is certainly not inevitable. Yet damnation is assuredly not due to predestination but to human defiance of God's will.

The theme is repeated in Rom. xi. 25–6, 'This partial blindness has come upon Israel (that is according to natural descent) only until the Gentiles have been admitted in full strength: when that has happened the whole of Israel will be saved.' The 'whole of Israel' clearly refers to the Christian church in its final state. Will it include every Jew and every Gentile, or merely some Jews and some Gentiles? Barrett[25] inclines to the view that only some are to

[25] *Romans*, Black N.T.C., (London, 1957) ad loc., p. 223.

be saved. He refers us to the Mishna[26], *Sanhedrin* x. 1, 'All Israelites have a share in the world to come,' which is followed by a list
of exceptions. It should be noted that the various exceptions are
ascribed to two other authorities, Rabbi Akiba and Rabbi Judah.
In *Romans* we have a continuous passage due to a single author, not
an amalgam consisting of quotations from three different sources.
Further, there is this great difference between the Mishna and
St. Paul, that the Mishna carefully specifies exceptions, but St.
Paul mentions no exceptions whatsoever. Barrett does not claim
that St. Paul *does* refer only to a few; he rightly points out that he
does not *necessarily* refer to all. But if this is so, then we are left
with a sense of anticlimax. The church *already* consisted of some
Jews and some Gentiles. It seems strange that this great passage
should mean merely that the proportion is to be increased.

If we are taken back to Rom. ix. 18, 'Thus he not only shows
mercy as he chooses, but also makes men stubborn as he chooses,'
an 'open' statement which reserves all power to God, but does not
say what use He will finally make of it, we may conclude with St.
Paul's final words in this section, before he passes over into adoration, Rom. ix. 32, 'God's purpose was to show mercy to all mankind'.
As will appear later, St. Paul does not teach universal salvation,
although he sets out along paths which lead in that direction.
Neither does he teach that any are predestined to damnation: when
he finds that the natural logic of his thought would compel him to
adopt that conclusion, he ceases to follow it. In St. Paul's thought
predestination is connected with the tendency towards universal
salvation. Damnation, whatever form it may take, is due not to
predestination by God, but to wilful sin on the part of man himself.

We have followed St. Paul's exposition of God's purpose to
the very end, to the consummation which even in our own day
has not yet been achieved. God's purpose was to be accomplished
in Jesus Christ, and it is to St. Paul's teaching on the Person of
Christ that we must now proceed.

[26] Danby, p. 397.

CHAPTER FIVE

'THE LORD AND THE SPIRIT'

i. JESUS IS LORD

The full humanity of Christ is an essential element in the thought of St. Paul, although he does not assert it in a self-conscious manner, since it can never have occurred to him to question it. That Christ was human is inevitably presupposed in the Pauline teaching on salvation; it is impossible to deny the centrality of Christ's death to Paul's soteriology, and Christ could not have died if He had not been human. 'On the human level (lit. according to the flesh, *sarka*) he was born of David's stock' (Rom. i. 3) and 'flesh' in this passage, as in Rom. ix. 5, must refer not merely to His physical body, but to His complete human nature. A human body in the straightforward physical sense is ascribed to Christ in Col. ii. 9, 'For it is in Christ that the complete being of the Godhead dwells embodied', and in Rom. vii. 4.[1] The manhood of Christ is asserted in 2 Cor. viii. 9, 'He was rich, yet for your sake he became poor', in Gal. iv. 4, 'Born of a woman, born under the law', and in Phil. ii. 7–8, where we are told that he 'Made himself nothing, assuming the nature of a slave. Bearing the human likeness . . .'[2] while the cardinal importance of His humanity for our salvation is made abundantly clear in 1 Cor. xv. 21, 'For since it was a man who brought death into the world, a man also brought resurrection of the dead'.

A special interest attaches to Rom. viii. 3, 'In a form like that of our own sinful nature, and as a sacrifice for sin', to 2 Cor. v. 21, 'Christ was innocent of sin, and yet for our sake God made him one with the sinfulness of men', and to Gal. iii. 13, 'By becoming for our sake an accursed thing' all of which Stauffer[3] classifies as

---

[1] The term 'body' of Christ is employed eucharistically in 1 Cor. x. 16, xi. 24, 27 and in the ecclesiological sense in 1 Cor. xii. 27 and Eph. iv. 12, while in Col. ii. 17 it means 'reality', and in Col. i. 22 it bears a soteriological sense, and provides only indirect evidence for St. Paul's belief that Christ had a physical body.

[2] Neither 'form' nor 'likeness' gives the slightest warrant for a docetist interpretation. Cp. the commentaries of Bonnard, *C.N.T.*, (Neuchâtel, 1950), and Beare, Black N.T.C., (London, 1959), ad loc.

[3] *New Testament Theology*, E.T. (London, 1955), p. 343.

'paradoxical incarnation formulae'. These passages have frequently been interpreted as evidence for a substitutionary theory of the Atonement, and this problem must receive the careful consideration which it deserves in a subsequent chapter.[4] To anticipate the results of a later enquiry, we may say at this stage that, whereas 2 Cor. v. 21 probably does employ sacrificial language in order to illuminate the apostle's thought on redemption, yet Rom. viii. 3 and Gal. iii. 13 are primarily incarnational. 2 Cor. v. 21 states that Our Lord 'knew', that is to say, 'practised',[5] no sin, and may be regarded as the Pauline counterpart of Heb. iv. 15, 'One who because of his likeness to us, has been tested every way, only without sin'. In Rom. viii. 3 St. Paul wished to say that Christ was wholly identified with us, that He took upon Himself our nature, or, to use the language of the Bible, that He was sent in our flesh. Yet since the Fall of Adam our flesh had been sinful, and Christ was not sinful; so the Apostle shrinks from saying that God sent His son in our [sinful] flesh, and has to say that He sent Christ in flesh like our sinful flesh [yet without sin], in order to deal with sin.[6] Schneider makes it abundantly plain that no ghost of docetic thought lurks behind the Word 'likeness'.[7]

St. Paul displays no interest of a 'biographical' nature in the earthly life of Jesus considered as past history; he is concerned with the acts and teaching of Our Lord only so far as they are relevant to the present and the future. There is no evidence at all for the view that he had known Jesus during His earthly ministry. 2 Cor. v. 16, 'Even though we have known Christ after the flesh (R.V.), yet now we know *him* so no more,' does not mean 'Even though I once knew Him during His life in Palestine': it means 'Even if my knowledge of Christ was formerly a merely fleshly, sinful knowledge, it is now no longer such'; this passage has been accorded what we may venture to regard as a definitive treatment by Allo.[8] St. Paul does indeed claim to know 'Words of the Lord', and we have every reason to believe that his claim was justified: 1 Cor. vii. 10, 'A wife must not separate herself from her husband', and 1 Cor. ix. 14 reproduce the substance of Mk. x. 1–12 and

[4] Cp. *infra*, p. 134 ff.
[5] So Bultmann, *Theology*, vol. i, p. 264 and Héring, *C.N.T.* (London, 1962), ad loc.
[6] So Lagrange, *Epître aux Romains*, (Paris, 1950), ad loc. Vincent Taylor, *The Person of Christ*, (London, 1958), pp. 39–40.
[7] *T.W.N.T.*, v., p. 196.
[8] *Seconde Epître aux Corinthiens*, (Paris, 1956), Excursus XI, pp. 179–82.

Mt. x. 10 respectively. But St. Paul is concerned with such teaching only because of its authority for the Church, and would appear to have been wholly indifferent to any 'human interest' in the earthly life of his Master.

We must now investigate those elements in his Christology which writers of a later period subsumed under the heading of the divine nature of Christ. Contemporary scholars very properly approach this subject by examining the titles and other terms which St. Paul applies to Him, words, that is to say, such as 'Lord', 'Christ', 'Son of God', 'Image of God', 'Glory' and many others. It has not always been sufficiently realized that these terms, for the most part, have one thing in common: in the Old Testament and in subsequent Jewish writings they connote a person or a 'theologumenon' through or in whom pre-eminently God is viewed as acting upon earth. For example, 'Son of God' refers to Israel, to the king of Israel and to the righteous Israelite, in all of whom God was revealing Himself to the world, by acting in and through them in so far as they proved worthy of their calling and were obedient to Him. Again, 'glory' is shown by a study of its septuagintal background to evoke ideas of the brightness of God's presence and of His saving activity as displayed in His 'wonderful acts' performed on behalf of His people.[9] In the Old Testament God Himself is called Lord, and the application of this word to Christ by St. Paul carries with it the conviction that 'God was in Christ' (2 Cor. v. 19). 'Christ' in the sense of 'Messiah' is not to be found in the Old Testament; but in later literature it represents a man through whom God will cause His will to be done on earth. Although these terms are never employed as mere synonyms, their connotations overlap, and they are linked together in a web of associations. 'Glory', for instance, in the LXX of Num. xii. 8 represents *temunah*, which properly means 'shape' (Deut. iv. 12) but is here employed in the secondary sense of 'appearance'.[10] It is thus very closely linked with image; we must not, of course, fall into the error of supposing that Greek words can be regarded as interchangeable merely because the writers of the LXX used them to translate the same or similar words in the M.T. Such words as 'glory' and 'image' are not identical in meaning; but still less are

---

[9] So Brockington in *Studies in the Gospels*, ed. Nineham, Oxford, 1955, pp. 4–5.

[10] cp. Brockington, ib., pp. 7–8.

they mutually exclusive: their semantic fields overlap, so that they reinforce and enrich each other.

But although any serious study of St. Paul's Christology must be firmly based upon an accurate examination of the language which he employs, nothing must be allowed to obscure the fact that it was his Christology which called the language into use, rather than the words which gave rise to his Christology. We must never give the impression that the Apostle's linguistic habits somehow generated his thought about Jesus Christ, rather as fragments of coloured paper are formed into a coherent pattern by means of a kaleidoscope. The contemporary reaction against any tendency to explain his theology in psychological terms, as a result, it may be, of his experience on the road to Damacus, should on no account cause us to forget that his words were a means for the expression of his beliefs, although we must agree that the formulation of his beliefs was due in part to the words and thought forms which were available to him as a Jew who knew his Old Testament and as a member of the Christian Church.

Further, it must be remembered that the meaning of a word is not fixed and unalterable, but changes and develops when the word receives a novel application; this happens above all when something radically new comes into being and has to be described. To take a trivial case, the English word 'car' acquired a significant extension of meaning through the introduction of the internal combustion engine. Infinitely more radical in its effect upon the relevant language was the Incarnation of Jesus Christ: the meaning of the words which the Christians applied to Him was not merely extended, but basically transformed. Outstanding cases of such a transformation are provided by 'Christ' (=Messiah) and by 'Son of God'. In pre-Christian days the Messiah was a human figure; he had, indeed, a special part to play in God's purpose, but he himself was purely human, and he was expected to die like other men.[11] In later Christian thought the word carries suggestions of divinity in its own right, precisely because it was applied to Jesus Christ. Much the same must be said about 'Son of God'. It did indeed apply to supernatural figures, that is to say to angels, in Gen. vi. 2 and other passages; if it ever possessed any polytheistic associations, they had long passed into oblivion among the Jews of

[11] cp. Mowinckel, *He That Cometh*, E. T. Anderson, (Oxford, 1956,) pp. 325–32.

the first Christian century, for whom its natural meaning when used of contemporaries was 'righteous Israelite', (Ecclus iv. 10; Wisd. of Sol. ii. 18; Lk. xxiii. 46, 'This man was innocent' is probably a correct interpretation of Mk. xv. 39, 'A son of God'). Yet for the patristic writers 'Son of God' referred to Christ's divine nature and 'Son of Man' to His human nature, whereas in first century Judaism the phrase 'Son of Man' probably suggested a supernatural figure, and 'Son of God' certainly referred only to a natural, purely human figure. In Christ St. Paul was a new creation, and his vocabulary also was created anew as familiar words were enhanced by novel applications.

Of all the Pauline designations of Jesus Christ, Lord, *kurios* is most frequently employed. The word is in form an adjective, and makes its earliest appearance with Pindar and the Attic tragedians in the fifth century B.C. It is not possible to distinguish rigidly between *kurios* (lord) and *despotēs* (master); but in general it may be said that 'master' suggests arbitrary power while 'lord' is employed when legitimate authority is in question. It is tempting to suppose that this may have been one reason for the use of the word by the writers of the LXX to translate JHVH and *Adonai*, since Judaism regarded God as a lawful ruler whose rights were based upon a series of covenants, above all the covenant made on Sinai, a ruler who did not issue His fiat in accordance with some arbitrary whim, but with the revelation of His nature and His will which He had made through Moses in the Torah.[12] In classical Greek *kurios* is normally a 'related word', whether used as an adjective or as a noun; for example, it is frequently followed by a genitival phrase indicating the sphere of mastery. Dodd points out that 'It seems to be most frequent and characteristic in relation to Isis *kuria* and Serapis, i.e. to deities who were not merely the official deities of this or that city, but gathered in various places throughout the world groups of worshippers who felt themselves to be in a peculiar personal relationship with the deity. It may be that Jews in the Hellenistic world felt themselves to be in an analogous relation to their own God, bound to Him by 'covenant', and therefore adopted the current term *kurios* to translate Adonai'.[13] In matters of this kind it is hard to avoid falling into the snare of

[12] cp. *T.W.N.T.*, iii. p. 1081, E. T. Kingdon, *Lord.*, Bible Key Words, viii. (London, 1958), p. 83.
[13] *The Bible and the Greeks*, 2nd impression, virtually unchanged, 1954, p. 10.

I

subjectivity, but it would certainly appear that *kurios* normally refers not to the status of an individual in isolation from all other beings, but to his relationship of mastery either over a group of men or over a sphere of life. But in Graeco-Roman, as opposed to Semitic usage, the sense of relatedness fades away precisely when the title is applied not to a human being, but to a god. Foerster remarks that 'This situation is connected with the fundamental structure of Greek theology, namely that for the Greeks the gods are in principle only the 'basic forms of reality'. . . . Since gods and men 'breathe from one mother' their mutual relationship cannot be described by *kurios-doulos* (lord-slave) terminology'.[14]

The word lord was especially applied both in Greek and in Latin to the Roman Emperors and to other sovereigns. Cerfaux has established the fact that in Aramaic a clear distinction was drawn between *maran* or *marana* (lord) and *elaha* (god): the former was applied to a living ruler, the latter to one who had already received apotheosis.[15] Among Greeks in the East the same distinction was observed between *kurios* and *theos*.[16] In the Roman imperial epoch, Foerster reminds us, the noun *kurios* has nothing in common with emperor-worship, yet though the emperor is not *kurios* as god, he can, as *kurios*, be god.[17] Cullmann accepts this conclusion, but qualifies it by saying that the word when employed to designate an emperor must have carried with it religious overtones.[18]

Two septuagintal uses are relevant to our purpose. It occasionally refers to a human master (Heb. '*ādhon*), and in this sense it is applied to Esau (Gen. xxxii–xxxiii *passim*) and to Joseph (Gen. xliv–xlvii *passim*). Above all, it is applied with the greatest frequency to God Himself, being the regular equivalent of the divine tetragrammaton.

Sufficient has now been said on the background of this word to justify us in turning to St. Paul's own writings. Three questions must be asked. First, how did *kurios* enter the vocabulary of the Early Church and of the Apostle? Secondly, what meaning or meanings does it bear in the Pauline Epistles? Thirdly, at what 'point in time', if any, did St. Paul believe that Christ achieved lordship?

---

[14] *T.W.N.T.*, iii. p. 1046, E.T., *Lord* (London), 1958, p. 15.
[15] *Receuil Lucien Cerfaux* (Gembloux, 1954), vol. i. p. 19. [16] ibid., p. 35.
[17] *T.W.N.T.*, iii. pp. 1054–5, E.T., *Lord* (London, 1958), pp. 30–31.
[18] *The Christology of the New Testament*, E. T. Guthrie and Hall (London, 1959), p. 198.

To the first question a clear answer is provided by Bultmann:
'It is highly improbable that the title *Kyrios* as applied to Jesus is
derived from the LXX . . . Rather, the term *Kyrios* used of Christ
is derived from the religious terminology of Hellenism, more
specifically from that of oriental Hellenism. . . This origin of the
Kyrios-title comes clearly into view in the antithesis of 'one Lord
Jesus Christ' to the 'many "lords" ' in 1 Cor. 8: 5f. . . . *Kurios*
indicates the respective deity not primarily in his divine majesty
and power, but in his 'master' relation to the speaker (the corresponding term for the worshipper is 'slave', *doulos*).'[19] The generally
accepted counter to this thesis is to say that 1 Cor. xvi. 22, Maranatha (=Aramaic *Maran-atha*, 'Our Lord comes' or *Marana-tha*,
Our Lord, come) can have arisen only in a Palestinian background,
as Kuhn maintains.[20] This is hardly conclusive: the Aramaic
language was not confined to Palestine, and it is possible that the
Eucharistic prayer *maranatha*, for it occurs in Didache x. 6[21] in a
Eucharistic context, first arose in Syria: this, however, is not very
probable, since an Aramaic formula which first arose in a bilingual
area would be unlikely to attain such fixity that it remained un-
translated,[22] although it must be remembered that Palestine also
was a bilingual area and that a liturgical formula had a greater
chance of becoming fixed in the original language. Further, the
Aramaic word *mar* (lord) would not necessarily refer to a divine
being. Bultmann faces this objection:[23] 'The eschatological prayer
'Maranatha' . . . certainly comes out of the earliest Church, but it
is likewise no proof that the earliest Church invoked Jesus as
Lord; for it can originally have meant God, even though it was
later taken to refer to Jesus (cf. Rev. 22: 20).[24] Bultmann's view
can not be formally refuted, but it fails to carry conviction,
especially since *kurios* is applied to Christ with such frequency in
the two Thessalonian epistles, which were written barely twenty
years after the Resurrection.[25] †

It is important to note that the early Christians were most
reluctant to call Jesus God, whereas Lord is applied to Him in

---

[19] *Theology*, vol. i, pp. 124–5.
[20] *T.W.N.T.*, iv., pp. 473–4.
[21] In *The Apostolic Fathers*, ed. Lightfoot and Harmer, (London, 1898),
p. 222, E.T., ib., p. 233.
[22] So Cullmann, *The Christology of the New Testament*, E. T. Guthrie and
Hall, (London, 1959), p. 214.
[23] *Theology*, vol. i, pp. 51–2.   [24] *Come, Lord Jesus.*
[25] cp. Vincent Taylor, *The Names of Jesus* (London, 1953), p. 47.

many passages which in their present literary form date from the very middle of the first century. He is called God only in the Johannine writings and in the Pastorals, with the possible exception of Rom. ix. 5. The reason presumably is that for a Jew the word God could mean One Person only, while *kurios* might be used of human beings; in using it they confessed their personal relation to Christ.[26] The use of the word God would have seemed to be an infringement of monotheism, whereas by calling Jesus Lord they confessed that He was associated with His Father in the exercise of authority. Cerfaux remarks that: 'Christ is Lord because he is God's vice-gerent, exercising a power that belongs to God'.[27]

The quotation from Cerfaux which concludes the preceding paragraph provides in summary form the answer to our second question, that of the meaning which *kurios* bears in the Pauline Epistles when applied to Jesus Christ. This problem is illuminated by Cerfaux's own examination of the Old Testament texts and phrases containing the word *kurios* which St. Paul applies to Jesus Christ.[28] We shall now consider afresh some of the same passages. The most enlightening is Rom. x. 13. 'Everyone who invokes the name of the Lord will be saved.' That 'Lord' here refers to Jesus Christ is made abundantly plain by what precedes: Rom. x. 9, 'If on your lips is the confession "Jesus is Lord", and in your heart the faith that God raised him from the dead, then you will find salvation.' The words cited from Rom. x. 13 correspond exactly to the LXX of Joel iii. 5 (M.T., Joel. ii. 32) with the addition of the connective 'for'; it has never been doubted that the words refer in *Joel* to Yahweh, and we may add that neither in *Romans* nor in the LXX is there any significant textual variant. It is perfectly clear what has happened: St. Paul has transferred to Jesus as Lord words which in the LXX are applied to God as Lord. In both cases the subject-matter is eschatological. The Apostle has not identified Christ with His Father: he has ascribed to Him one of the functions of God.

This is no isolated phenomenon, as we can see from 2 Thess. i. 8-10, 'Then he will do justice upon those who refuse to acknow-

---

[26] ibid., p. 45.

[27] *Christ in the Theology of St. Paul*, E. T. Webb and Walker (New York, 1959), p. 466.

[28] *Recueil Lucien Cerfaux*, (Gembloux, 1953), '*Kyrios dans les citations pauliniennes de l'Ancien Testament*', vol. i, pp. 173–181, originally published in *Ephemerides Theologicae Lovanienses*, 20 (1943), pp. 5-17.

ledge God and upon those who will not obey the Gospel of our
Lord Jesus. They will suffer the punishment of eternal ruin, cut
off from the presence of the Lord and the splendour of his might,
when on that great Day he comes to be glorified among his own
and adored among all believers.' Here we find reproduced with
omissions the formula which occurs three times in the LXX of Is.
ii. in verses 10, 19 and 21: 'From the face of (the fear of) the Lord,
and from the glory of his might when he shall arise (to shatter the
earth).' The remainder of the passage reflects the language of Ps.
lxxxviii. 7 in the LXX (M.T., lxxxix. 7) and of other Old Testament passages, though it would be hazardous to suppose that there
is conscious quotation. But in the case of Is. ii. 10, etc. no such
doubt arises, and we can safely claim that here again St. Paul applies
to Jesus words which the Old Testament uses of God, and that he
associates Jesus with God in the exercise of His function of judgement. The evidence is not so clear in the case of 2 Thess. i. 12,
'That the name of our Lord Jesus may be glorified in you.' It is a
loose quotation, at best, of Is. lxvi. 5, reflecting also Is. xxiv. 15
and Mal. i. 11, and we can not be certain that St. Paul intends
to quote. But the substance of the verse is very striking: any Old
Testament writer who said 'that the name of the Lord may be
glorified' would inevitably be speaking of Yahweh. Moreover, the
association of Jesus with God is not so strictly limited to function.
It is not indeed possible to make an absolute separation between
function and nature; but whereas in the passages considered above
the main emphasis was laid upon function, in 2 Thess. i. 12 there is
a shift in the direction of nature, for 'name' is universally agreed to
have been closely connected in Hebrew thought with what we
should call nature.

Cerfaux also draws our attention to the fact that St. Paul applies
to Christ phrases which in the Old Testament were habitually
applied to God. 1 Thess. ii. 19, 'Before our Lord Jesus at his
coming,' may be regarded as significant, and so may 1 Cor. i. 2,
'Who invoked the name of our Lord Jesus Christ,' as also may the
phrase 'do honour to the Lord' (2 Cor. viii. 19, etc.). We may note
at this point, although the word 'Lord' is not mentioned, 2 Cor.
v. 10, 'We must all have our lives laid open before the tribunal of
Christ'; the significance of this verse is underlined by a comparison
with Rom. xiv. 10, 'We shall all stand before God's tribunal', which
makes it clear that an important function of God Himself has been

ascribed to Christ; and 2 Cor. v. 10 finds a parallel in 2 Thess. i.
7-8, 'When our Lord Jesus Christ is revealed from heaven with
his mighty angels in blazing fire. Then will he do justice upon those
who refuse to acknowledge God'.

Since *kurios* speaks of Christ as sharing in the exercise of God's
authority it is not surprising that it should be closely connected
with the resurrection, the exaltation and the parousia.[29] In answer
to our third question it would not be very wide of the mark to say
that for St. Paul Christ attained to the exercise of Lordship at His
resurrection, although the term Lord is applied to Him during His
life on earth.[30] To say this is not to accuse St. Paul of displaying
an Adoptianistic emphasis, since *kurios* chiefly connotes sharing in
God's power, and it is a plain fact that Christ did not exercise such
a power to the full during the period of His humiliation.

In the Old Testament the term son of God is applied to
angelic beings (Gen. vi. 2, Job. i. 6, xxxviii. 7), but this usage is
barely relevant to our purpose and need not detain us. Its earliest
application was probably to the king. Ps. ii. 7, 'You are my son,
today I have begotten you'. and 2 Sam. vii. 14, 'I will be his father,
and he shall be my son', probably reflects the language of Canaanite
enthronement or 'accession-day' formulae, for the Israelites
'conquered' and used for their own purposes not only the territory
of Canaan, but also its sacred sites and its liturgical practices. The
application of the phrase to Israel in Exod. iv. 22, 'Israel is my
firstborn son', and in Hos. xi. 1, 'When Isreal was a child I loved
him,' would be a natural extension for Israelites, to whom the king
was so closely identified with his people that God could punish
Israel because of the sin of David (2 Sam. xxiv). It is most
important to note that in the thought of the Bible neither the king
nor the people of Israel is regarded as divine; their relation to God
was not essential, but was the obligation of obedience imposed upon
both people and king by covenant. Richardson is justified when
he lays stress upon the connection between sonship and obedience,
especially as the term is applied to righteous Israelites in Ecclus.
iv. 10 and Wisd. of Sol. ii. 18.[31] We may accept without qualification Vincent Taylor's summary: 'The significance of the phrase in

[29] cp. Cerfaux, *Christ*, p. 20.

[30] ibid., 469. Cerfaux draws our attention to the teaching of the Lord
given during his earthly life (I Cor. vii. 10, 15; ix. 1; xi. 23) and to the expression
'brother(s) of the Lord' (1 Cor. ix. 9, Gal. i. 19).

[31] *Introduction*, pp. 148–9.

Jewish thought is reasonably clear; it does not describe a divine
being, but characterises groups or individuals who stand in a
peculiarly close relationship with God'.[32]

It is worthy of note that in the Old Testament both the king
and Israel are called 'son of God', though not frequently, and that
the phrase is applied to both alike without qualification. St. Paul,
on the other hand, though he calls Christ 'Son of God' absolutely,
never uses the phrase of Christians without qualification. In Rom.
viii. 14–17 he limits the application of the phrase 'sons of God' to
those who are led by the spirit of God, who have received the
spirit of adoption which makes them heirs of God and joint-heirs
with Christ; the background of thought is baptismal, and the
meaning is that as we are associated with Christ by faith—baptism,
we are associated with His suffering, glorification and Sonship. In
view of the ethical stress which is apparent in vv. 12 and 13 we are
probably justified in seeing here also a connection between sonship
and obedience. 2 Cor. vi. 18, 'You shall be my sons and daughters,
saith the Lord Almighty,' is hardly relevant, since it occurs in a
strophic hymn compacted of Old Testament phrases; it may have
been taken over from some pre-Pauline source, and we can not be
sure that the Apostle would have accepted the implications of all
its phrases. Gal. iii. 26–27, 'For through faith you are all sons of
God in union with Christ Jesus. Baptized into union with him,
you have all put on Christ as a garment,' is analogous to Rom. vii.
14–17: we are sons of God not in our own right, but *qua* members
of Christ. The fact that St. Paul observes this distinction which
is not found in the Old Testament lends weight to the judgement
which Anderson Scott made upon the basis of a number of
passages: 'The language postulates a relationship which is independent of any historical experience, one which is pre-eminently
ethical in character, and seems to involve "a community of nature
between the Father and the Son" '.[33] It is clear that for St. Paul
Jesus fulfilled perfectly the vocation to obey God which had been
fulfilled imperfectly by Israel and its kings. Or rather, since Jesus
is regarded as Son of God in a pre-eminent sense, we may say that
St. Paul employed the calling to obedience of Israel and the kings
of Israel, a calling given by God, as a model for, or a pointer to,

[32] *The Names of Jesus*, London, 1953, p. 54.
[33] *Christianity according to St. Paul* (Cambridge, 1961[2]), p. 256. The passages
in question are Rom. viii. 3; viii. 31 and Col. i. 13.

the unique and inexpressible relation which subsists between God and Jesus Christ.

Col. i. 15, 'The first-born of all creation' (*R.S.V.*), *Prōtotokos pāsēs ktiseōs* is of special importance. The Arians and Theodore of Mopsuestia alike took *Prōtotokos pāsēs ktiseōs* to be a partitive genitive. The Arians said that of all created beings Christ was the first to be created. Theodore understood *Prōtotokos pāsēs ktiseōs* to refer to the new creation, with the result that for him the phrase meant the same as 'first-born from the dead' (*R.S.V.*) in *v.* 18. Neither of these interpretations will stand unless we deny the authenticity of *v.* 16, 'For in him all things were created' (*R.S.V.*) and for such a rejection there is no manuscript authority. The thought, moreover, is anticipated in 1 Cor. viii. 6, 'Yet for us there is one God, the Father, from whom all being comes, towards whom we move; and there is one Lord, Jesus Christ, through whom all things came to be, and we through him'. C. F. D. Moule[34] suggests that we should either understand *prōto-* in a temporal sense, quoting *prōtos mou ēn*, 'He was before me' (John i. 30) or take first-born to mean 'supreme over'. It is not impossible, as Moule agrees, that these two meanings were blended in the mind of St. Paul, since in contemporary Judaism 'pre-existence' was virtually a symbol for pre-eminence, and was ascribed in this sense to, e.g., the Law.[35]

Col. i. 15 leads naturally to a consideration of Wisdom. The familiar expression 'Wisdom Christology', although its use is wholly justified, can be misleading if it causes us to suppose that 'Wisdom Christology', 'Last Adam Christology', etc. were competing christologies in the same sense as Arian and Athanasian christologies. It would be nearer to the truth to say that they represented different verbal methods, partly alternative, partly complementary, of expressing the one christology which can be summed up in the phrase 'God was in Christ'. The word 'wisdom' is explicitly applied to Christ in 1 Cor. i. 24, 'He is the power of God, and the wisdom of God,' and in 1 Cor. i. 30, 'For God has made him our wisdom'. It is possible, but not probable that the concept of Wisdom also lies behind 1 Cor. x. 4, 'They all drank from the supernatural rock that accompanied their travels—and

[34] Cambridge Greek Testament Commentary, *Colossians and Philemon* (Cambridge, 1957), ad loc.
[35] Bonsirven, *Judaïsme*, vol. i., p. 250.

that rock was Christ,' since Philo, speaking of Deut. viii. 15, 'Who brought you water out of the flinty rock,' writes: 'The rock of flint is the Wisdom of God from which he feeds the souls that love him.'[36] Even more precarious is the theory that in Rom. x. 6–8, 'Who can go up to heaven?' (that is, to bring Christ down:) etc. St. Paul is employing language which, it is suggested, was commonly applied to Wisdom, on the ground that in Baruch iii. 29 we read:

'Who has gone up into heaven, and taken her [i.e. Wisdom] And brought her down from the clouds?'

In the opinion of Davies this interpretation fails to carry conviction.[37] But it is in Col. i. 15–18 that we find the most striking example of the use of Wisdom language to describe the work of Jesus Christ. It was Burney who first suggested that these verses are a Rabbinic exposition of the first word of the Book of Genesis, *berēshīth*, in—the beginning. *Be* can mean 'in', 'by' and 'unto', and in these verses we are told that all things were created 'in' Christ, 'by' Christ, and 'unto' Christ. *Rēshīth* can mean 'beginning', 'sum-total', 'head', and 'firstfruits', and in *Colossians* we are told that Christ is 'before' all things (beginning), that in him all things consist (sum-total), that he is the head of the body, and that he is the beginning, the first-born (firstfruits) from the dead; thus Christ fulfils every meaning which can be extracted from *rēshīth*. But, on the basis of Prov. viii. 22 and 30, 'beginning' was equated with 'Wisdom'; so Christ, according to Burney, is said in Col. i. 15–18 to have fulfilled all the functions of Wisdom.[38]

It is possible that scholars are too ready to speak of 'identifying' Christ with an 'hypostatized' wisdom through familiarity with later thought, especially that of the Cappadocian Fathers, losing sight of the commonplace but nevertheless vitally important fact that while Greeks of the 4th century A.D. tended to think in terms of ideas, Jews of the Biblical and inter-testamentary periods were inclined rather to think in terms of acts. For example, it is tempting to quote Ps. xxxiii. 6, 'By the word of the Lord the heavens were made,' and to say that the 'word of the Lord' has been hypostatized. But if we complete the verse,' And all their host by the breath of his mouth',

---

[36] *Leg. Alleg.* ii. 21, quoted by Davies, *Paul and Rabbinic Judaism* (London, 1955[2]), p. 153.

[37] ibid., p. 154.

[38] Burney, *J.T.S.*, xxxvii. (1926), p. 160f. His thesis is made clear in a table which is reproduced in Davies, *Paul and Rabbinic Judaism*, (London, 1955[2]), p. 152.

we are led to suspect that the Psalmist is merely reproducing or anticipating in a more vivid poetical form, the thought of Gen. i. 14–15, 'And God said, Let there be lights . . . and it was so'. Yet, although it is necessary to be cautious, we are justified in concluding that the figure of Wisdom was not merely personified but virtually, if not explicitly, hypostatized.[39] What is important for our purpose is that the figure of Wisdom had achieved a sufficient degree of independence for its attributes and functions to be transferred to someone other than God; and these functions were creation, revelation and redemption, which were credited to Wisdom as the agent of God. Creation is attributed to Wisdom in, for example, Prov. viii. 30, 'Then I was beside him like a master workman'; revelation supremely by her identification with the Torah in Ecclus. xxiv. 23, 'All this is the book of the covenant of the Most High God'; and redemption in Prov. viii. 35, 'For he who finds me finds life, and obtains favor from the Lord,' and in Wisd. of Sol. vii. 27, 'She makes them friends of God and prophets'. When St. Paul speaks of Christ in terms of Wisdom his intention is not to identify Him with an hypostatization of Wisdom, but to ascribe to Him the function of being God's agent in creation, revelation and redemption. In fact, the 'Wisdom Christology' of St. Paul may be summed up in these words: What Wisdom meant to the Jews was part of what Jesus Christ meant for St. Paul.

If we merely look up the word 'Adam' in a concordance we shall obtain a wholly inadequate notion of the vital importance of Adam in Pauline thought. The name occurs at three points only in St. Paul's epistles: it is found in Rom. v. 14, 'But death held sway from Adam to Moses, even over those who had not sinned as Adam did, by disobeying a direct command—and Adam foreshadows the Man who was to come' and the thought of the Adam —Christ antithesis dominates the entire section Rom. v. 10–21; in 1 Cor. xv. 22, 'As in Adam all men die, so in Christ all will be brought to life', and in 1 Cor. xv. 45, 'It is in this sense that scripture says "The first man, Adam, became an animate being", whereas the last Adam has become a life-giving spirit'. Some scholars have seen traces of the First-Last Adam scheme in other places. According to Richardson[40] it lies closely below the surface in Gal. iii. 28, 'There is no such thing as Jew and Greek (even the first

[39] cf. Job xxviii., Prov. viii., Ecclus. xxiv., Wisd. ix., Baruch iii, 9–iv. 4.
[40] *Introduction*, p. 246.

Adam was ancestor of both), slave and free man, male and female;
for you are all one person in Christ Jesus,' and Cullmann[41] finds it
in Col. iii. 9–10, 'Stop lying one to another, now that you have
discarded the old nature (gk *anthrōpon*, lit 'man') with its deeds
and have put on the new nature which is being constantly renewed in the image of its Creator (cf. Gen. i. 27) and brought to
know God'. To refuse to follow Richardson and Cullmann in this
judgement would be little short of perverse: in *Colossians* the
words 'image' and 'renewed' (lit 're-created') point strongly in
that direction; and the similarity of subject-matter strengthens
the case for Gal. iii. 28. There is, however, a difference of emphasis.
In *Galatians* the main stress is laid upon solidarity, while in
Colossians this is secondary, and the chief emphasis falls upon the
contrast between the old and the new. It is impossible to dispute
the 'Adamic' background to Phil. ii. 5–11, where the thought of
solidarity is completely absent. If we may take the Epistle to the
Ephesians into account it is legitimate to note also ii. 14f. and iv.
22f.

Far more important than the references, whether explicit or
subconscious, to Adam is that theme of the solidarity of the entire
human race which constitutes an essential presupposition for St.
Paul's thought of sin and salvation,[42] and for the Jew this solidarity
could be expressed by means of the word 'Adam'. It is a commonplace of Old Testament Theology that the same word can represent
both a group and an individual,[43] that 'Jacob' can be both a man
and an amphictyony of tribes. This applies above all in the case
of Adam, for while 'Jacob' etc. are proper names which can be
applied, in a collective sense, 'Adam' frequently means 'mankind'
in its own right. From the many cases which can be found in the
Old Testament we may quote Gen. vi. 1, 'When men (*hā'ādhām*)
began to multiply on the face of the ground, and daughters were
born to them, . . .' and Judges xvi. 17, where Samson says to
Delilah: 'If I be shaved, then strength will leave me, and I shall
become weak and be like any other man (*kekol-ha'ādhām*).'
Evidence has already been cited to show that the Jews conceived
the entire human race to be one in Adam.

---

[41] *The Christology of the New Testament*, (E.T. London, 1959), p. 174.
[42] cp. *supra*, p. 45 f. and *infra*, Ch. vi.
[43] cp. A. R. Johnson, *The One and the Many in the Israelite Conception of God*, (Cardiff, 1961²).

St. Paul's 'Last Adam' language can hardly be claimed to provide evidence for either the Humanity or the Divinity of Christ in the popular sense. It does show clearly that for St. Paul His humanity, though not quite impersonal in the later anhypostatic sense, is not individual but inclusive; indeed for St. Paul the humanity of every man is not individual but 'included': all men are included in Adam, and Christians are included in Christ. On the other hand, the soteriological, eschatological function of Christ is shown by the adjectives 'last' and 'new'. Last (*eschatos*) has this application only in 1 Cor. xv. 45. It does not in itself contain an eschatological meaning, since in its remaining Pauline occurrences its meaning is strictly temporal, if not pejorative, but in 1 Cor. xv. 45 its context gives it a soteriological flavour; it speaks of what God is to do in the 'last days', when He puts forth His power to judge and to save. The same may be said of 'new'; although its primary meaning is that of temporal posteriority, which is never completely lost, it acquired in the Old Testament religious overtones, suggesting the quality of God's acts, so that its meaning becomes qualitative as well as temporal. In the New Testament its meaning is even more closely defined. It has almost become a Christian technical term, referring to what God has done and will do in Jesus Christ and in the members of His body, the Church. 'Last Adam' and related language, then, show both that Christ is one with all Christians and that God is working in Him.

In two passages only does St. Paul speak of Christ as the image of God, and in each of them the word refers not to any divine status, but to his function of revealing God to men. 2 Cor. iv. 4, ' Their unbelieving minds are so blinded by the god of this passing age, that the gospel of the glory of Christ, who is the very image (gk. *Eikōn*) of God, cannot dawn upon them and bring them light,' speaks of the frustration of this God-revealing function of Christ in the case of unbelievers. Col. i. 15, 'He is the (visible) image of the invisible God', has the same force. But although St. Paul explicitly speaks only of the revelatory function of Christ, it may fairly be argued that this function could not have been performed if He had not possessed that metaphysical relation to God which is expounded in the Patristic writings.

Many scholars have found a connection between St. Paul's thought on the Last Adam and the oriental and Hellenistic myths of the Heavenly Man. This thesis has been rejected by a majority

of writers ever since it was first propounded by Bousset.[44] Among
English theologians Rawlinson attacked it, and is generally held
to have provided a successful refutation.[45] This, however, is a
reason for giving the theory a fair hearing, and we must note that
it is favoured by Bultmann[46] and Mowinckel,[47] and that it is taken
seriously by Cullmann[48] and by Riesenfeld.[49] The myth does not
exist in a standard form: it is known to us only in variant versions
which occur in relatively late documents, and if we attempt to
'reconstruct' a 'standard' form we may in fact have constructed
it for the first time in the twentieth century. Mowinckel has listed
fourteen features which recur with varying frequency in the
different forms of the myth.[50] His method is somewhat question-
begging, since he assumes the existence of ' the ' myth which he
finds in various forms: it may be that he has catalogued various
features derived from a number of closely related myths. Neither
the unity nor the multiplicity of the myth should be taken for
granted. In general the Heavenly Man is portrayed as a supernatural being who existed before and is closely connected with the
foundation of the world. He is the 'perfect' man, and his destiny
is a type of the destiny of mankind. He is a saviour who is incarn-
ated as a man, and in some Persian circles this is represented as
happening more than once. Bultmann points out that these speculations exhibit similarities to and contrasts with the teaching of the
New Testament; for example, Gnosticism cannot acknowledge
the real humanity of Christ.[51] Bultmann suggests that Christians
had to combat Gnosticism not as a foreign religion, but as a
phenomenon within Christianity,[52] and that it had infiltrated into
Christianity by way of a Hellenistic Judaism that was itself in the
grip of syncretism.[53] Of all the concepts which, in Bultmann's
opinion, were borrowed from Gnostic sources the one most
directly relevant to our present purpose is that of the Redeemer as
a cosmic figure.[54]

[44] *Kyrios Christos*, Göttingen, 1921².
[45] *The New Testament Doctrine of the Christ* (London, 1929²), pp. 125f.
[46] *Theology*, vol. i., pp. 164–83.
[47] *He that Cometh*, E. T. Anderson (Oxford, 1956), pp. 420–37.
[48] *The Christology of the New Testament*, E.T., (London, 1959), p. 176f.
[49] 'The Mythological Background of New Testament Christology,' in *The Background of the New Testament and its Eschatology*, (Cambridge, 1956), esp. p. 84.
[50] op. cit., pp. 427–9.   [51] *Theology*, vol. i, p. 168.
[52] ibid., p. 170.   [53] ibid., p. 171.
[54] ibid., p. 175.

It is essential to be perfectly clear about the nature of the question or questions which are at issue. The evidence compels us to agree that in the early Christian centuries, if not earlier, there existed a complex web of mythological speculations in which Adam, Christ, the Heavenly Man, and others were connected together in the minds of some men. It is quite another matter to suggest that St. Paul derived his thought about the Last Adam, or indeed about any of the concepts which he employs in order to portray Jesus Christ, from sources such as these; powerful arguments may be advanced to the contrary.

First, there is no evidence for the existence of a Heavenly Man myth as early as the First Century A.D., although the Bible itself contains elements which recur in the Heavenly Man speculations attested in later documents. This is an argument from silence and is therefore not conclusive: the Qumran discoveries have given us a healthy reminder of the fact that our evidence is not exhaustive. But although the existence of a pre-Christian 'Gnosticism' would appear to be confirmed by the *Manual of Discipline* with its incipient Gnostic tendencies, the general tone of the Scrolls would seem to militate against the existence at that early date of the full-blown Gnosticism described by Irenaeus and his successors.[55] The *Gospel of Truth* preserved in a fourth century Coptic version in the Jung Codex was probably written in Greek by Valentinus about the middle of the second century A.D. Its thought is nearer to that of the New Testament than to the mature Gnosticism of e.g. the *Epistle of Ptolemaeus to Flora*.[56] These discoveries at Nag Hammadi (1945) and at Qumran (1947 onwards) broaden the basis for an assertion that Gnosticism in its developed form is post-Pauline, and weaken the force of argument from silence insofar as new sources which might have provided evidence for the early occurrence of elaborate Gnostic thought have in fact failed to do so, although the *Manual of Discipline* confirms our belief that the hot-bed in which Gnosticism grew had already been prepared in the time of St. Paul.

Secondly, the speculations of the later cabbalistic literature concerning the First and Last Man and similar figures have no parallel in the older rabbinic literature.[57] Thirdly, St. Paul

---

[55] cp. B. Reicke, *N.T.S.* i. (1954), pp. 137–41.
[56] cp. *The Jung Codex*, Puech, Quispel and van Unnik, E.T. F. L. Cross, (London, 1955).
[57] Strack-Billerbeck, iii., p. 477.

would appear to be contrasting two men, the earthy and the Lord from Heaven, whereas Heavenly Man speculations tended to think rather of two phases of activity of the one Primal Man. Lastly, in order to give this verse an intelligible meaning which accords well with what the Apostle says elsewhere, it is not necessary to posit any source apart from the Old Testament and Christian teaching: Adam, the 'head' of the entire human race, is contrasted with Christ, the 'head' of those who are a new creation in Him. It is true that Adam is bound up with the Heavenly Man and linked with Him by intermediate figures, just as France is linked with Poland in the continent of Europe. But it would be fallacious to argue that wine imported from France had been imported from Poland on the ground that France and Poland are part of a continuous land-mass.

Equally precarious is the suggestion that St. Paul made use of a Son of Man Christology. This phrase is common in all the Gospels including the Fourth, but in the New Testament apart from the Gospels it occurs as a Christological title only at Acts vii. 56 and Rev. i. 13; xiv. 14. Cullmann[58] argues that although St. Paul does not use the phrase 'Son of Man', yet the simple word 'man' (*anthrōpos*) has the value of 'Son of Man'. He cites Rom. v. 15, 'The one man, Jesus Christ', and 1 Cor. xv. 45, where 'man' and 'Adam' are closely linked to Christ, as well as 1 Cor. xv. 21, 'A man also brought the resurrection of the dead'. It is true that *anthrōpos* can represent the Hebrew or Aramaic 'Son of Man' as in Is. lvi. 2. It would indeed be more revealing to say that 'Son of Man' in Hebrew and Aramaic can represent either an ordinary man or a 'messianic' figure. Cullmann urges that St. Paul may not have intended to exclude the technical christological sense when he used the word 'Man'. But it is wholly unnecessary to suppose that he meant anything more than 'man'.

It is likewise unnecessary to attach any great importance to the Servant of the Lord concept in St. Paul's thought. Jeremias[59] and Cullmann[60] have argued in the contrary sense. They agree that little weight can be attached to direct quotations, which are few indeed, but rest their case upon phraseological echoes and

[58] *The Christology of the New Testament*, E.T. (London, 1959), pp. 171–2.
[59] *T.W.N.T.* v., pp. 703 and 706, E. T. Knight, S.B.T. no. 20, (London, 1957), pp. 88 and 93. Jeremias agrees that there are but slight traces in the Pauline Epistles of the influence of the Servant-of-the-Lord concept.
[60] ibid., pp. 76–8.

upon the 'idea of vicarious suffering'. But it is dangerous to lean heavily upon small groups of common words, and vicarious suffering in the days of St. Paul was not associated exclusively with the Servant of the Lord. Stauffer[61] has drawn our attention to the importance of martyrdom in Jewish thought, and Barrett[62] has argued plausibly that it was martyrdom rather than Is. liii. which formed the background to Mk. x. 45, 'Surrender his life as a ransom for many'. Above all, Miss Hooker[63] has shown clearly that the identification of the Servant with Jesus Christ did not play any great part in the thought of St. Paul.

The Greek verbal adjective *Christos* means 'anointed', and it is the septuagintal equivalent to the Hebrew participle *mashiah*, which has the same meaning. The basic application of the word is to the anointing of a person to be king, as in Judges ix. 8, 'The trees once went forth to anoint a king over them'; but *christos* is employed to describe the High Priest in Lev. iv. 5, as well as the king in 1 Sam. xxiv. 7, where David speaks of Saul as *christos*. In *Isaiah*, *christos* is found only at xlv. 1, 'Thus says the Lord to his anointed, to Cyrus, whose right hand I have grasped'. It is illuminating to find the word applied to a Gentile ruler; it is indeed a 'functional' word, like 'Son of God' and may be used of anyone who is appointed to be the Lord's vicegerent. In the Old Testament there is no messiah or christ, and in our Lord's time no one doctrine of the Messiah or of the Last Things could claim to be standard. Indeed there was on these matters a diversity of opinions even within single groups.[64] The word 'Christ' was applied to Jesus by others, rather than by Himself. It is not easy to assess its significance in the writings of St. Paul, where it has virtually become a proper name, although the sense 'Messiah' is retained at least in Rom. ix. 5, 'From them in natural descent sprang the Messiah (*christos*)'.

Whether St. Paul called Jesus 'God' depends upon the punctuation of Rom. ix. 5. Deity is ascribed to Christ if we punctuate and render: 'Sprang the Messiah, supreme over all, God blessed for ever'. Some authorities, including the fifth century uncials A and

---

[61] *New Testament Theology*, E.T. (London, 1955), especially the evidence tabulated in Appendix i., pp. 331–4.
[62] *New Testament Essays, Studies in Memory of T. W. Manson* (Manchester, 1959), pp. 1–18.
[63] *Jesus and the Servant* (London, 1959), pp. 116–123.
[64] cp. Morton Smith, *J.B.L.*, lxxviii. (1959), p. 71.

C, place a stop after 'flesh' which yields: 'In natural descent sprang the Messiah. May God supreme above all be blessed for ever'. This is notoriously one of the most hotly debated passages in the New Testament. Too much weight should not be attached to the presence or absence of punctuation in the codices, since this is evidence for the interpretation given to the passage by the scribe and not for the intention of St. Paul. On stylistic grounds the preferable interpretation is that which ascribes deity to Christ, as Michel[65] maintains; he is careful to point out that the word *theos* does not involve any identification with God, but is to be understood in the light of 2 Cor. v. 19, 'God was in Christ . . . ', and similar passages.

The main stylistic argument in favour of referring the words 'Who is over all God blessed for ever' to Christ is as follows: if the words refer to God the Father, they constitute a doxology, and in the doxologies of the Bible and other semitic documents the word 'blessed' normally comes first, so that we should expect 'Blessed (*eulogētos*) be God', instead of finding that the word 'blessed' follows. The arguments against ascribing the words to the Father are fairly presented by Sanday and Headlam[66] and by Lagrange.[67] Sanday and Headlam, although they ascribe the disputed words to Christ with only slight hesitation, point out that the position of 'blessed' does not exclude the opposite interpretation. Both these commentaries contend that to address a doxology to God would be unsuitable at this point, on the ground that it would be out of keeping with the generally sad tone of the passage. This point fails to carry conviction. St. Paul can leap quickly from one point to another, and could easily give thanks to God for the privileges accorded to Israel, just as Job was able to say: 'The Lord gave, and the Lord has taken away; blessed be the name of the Lord (i. 21)'.

Vincent Taylor[68] ascribes the doxology to the Father on the ground that 'nowhere else does St. Paul call Christ God'; he adds that we must remember the subordinationist tone of 1 Cor. xv. 28 and other passages. But St. Paul had no closely integrated system, and it is not impossible that he should use subordinationist language in one place and call Christ 'God' in another.

[65] *Der Brief an die Römer*, Meyer-Kommentar, (Göttingen, 1955[10]), ad loc.
[66] *The Epistle to the Romans*, I.C.C. (Edinburgh, 1895), ad loc.
[67] *Epître aux Romains* (Paris, 1950), ad loc.
[68] *The Person of Christ* (London, 1958), p. 56.

K

Further, we must consider Rom. ix. 5 in close conjunction with 2 Thess. i. 12, 'According to the grace of our God and (the) Lord Jesus Christ'. It would not be methodologically sound to 'divide and conquer' denying the ascription of deity to Christ in each case on the ground that St. Paul nowhere calls Christ 'God'. On the other hand, as Rigaux[69] remarks, 'Lord Jesus Christ' without the article is an established phrase, so that it is on balance preferable to separate the two; the *Bible de Jérusalem* renders 2 Thess. i. 12, 'Of our God and of the Lord Jesus Christ'. This is probably correct. Rigaux[70] points out that St. Paul is not using careful language, since he prays in effect: 'that the name of our Lord Jesus may be glorified . . . according to the grace of . . . the Lord Jesus Christ'. This fact lends weight to Masson's[71] suggestion that St. Paul began by dictating 'the grace of our God . . .' and added 'and Lord Jesus Christ,' which is a set phrase, without realizing that strictly the article should have been inserted. We may conclude with some confidence that deity is not ascribed to Christ in 2 Thess. i. 12; the same is probably true of Rom. ix. 5, but no great confidence is possible, because of the unquestionable strength of the stylistic argument.

There are undoubtedly traces of subordinationist language in St. Paul's Epistles. This language does not, of course, carry anything even remotely approaching the force that it would have done in the fourth century. St. Paul is not giving a considered answer in a subordinationist sense to questions which had been explicitly raised: rather, what he says about the problems of his own day suggests subordinationist answers to problems of whose very existence the Apostle was completely unaware. On the other hand, it would be disingenuous to forget that language is often the unconscious revealer of thought. Without unduly anticipating a discussion of the view propounded by Cullmann, who maintains that the Christology of all the New Testament writers is exclusively functional and in no sense ontological, we may fairly say that St. Paul's main interest is concentrated not upon Christ's status but upon His work. From the point of view of 'traditionalism', the 'functional' Christology is two-edged: it forbids us to find a Chalcedonian doctrine ready made in the New Testament,

---

[69] *Les Epîtres aux Thessaloniciens* (Paris, 1956), ad loc.
[70] ibid.
[71] *Les deux Epîtres de Saint Paul aux Thessaloniciens*, C.N.T., (Neuchâtel, 1957), ad loc.

but it saves us from asserting that the 'nature' of Christ is inferior
to that of the Father. It is not unfair to say that the Pauline
epistles are concerned not with the subordination of Christ, but
with His obedience to the Father's will.

The first phrase which falls to be considered is Rom. xv. 6,
'The God and Father of our Lord Jesus', a liturgical formula
which recurs at 2 Cor. i. 3; xi. 31; Eph. i. 3, 1 Pet. i. 3. Attempts
to avoid the natural meaning of the phrase, and to understand
'He who is both God and the Father of our Lord' fail to convince.
Lagrange[72] interprets: 'God of Christ as having created his
humanity; Father, because the Father begat the Son'. But such
distinctions are frankly anachronistic when applied to St. Paul.
It is most unlikely that the Christians who used this phrase in
their worship during the middle of the first century A.D. had any
thoughts in their minds concerning the status of the Son relative
to the Father. If it is legitimate to guess what it meant to them
and to St. Paul we may suggest: 'Blessed be the God of Israel,
who is our God and our Father through adoption, because we
are one with Jesus Christ since we confessed Him as Lord in
baptism'.

1 Cor. iii. 23, 'You belong to Christ and Christ to God', calls
forth from Héring[73] the comment 'subordinationism, notwith-
standing the uncreated and eternal nature of the Son of God'.

1 Cor. xi. 3, 'While every man has Christ for his head, woman's
head is man, as Christ's Head is God', suggests a descending
hierarchical order: God, Christ, man, woman. The force of this
argument is weakened, though not destroyed, if we accept a
plausible interpretation which has been propounded by Bedale.[74]
He points out that *kephalē* (head) is not used to represent superior
rank in pre-Biblical Greek, and suggests that it must have
acquired this meaning by being employed in the LXX as an
equivalent for the Hebrew *rōsh*. But *rōsh* also means 'source' or
'beginning' as in Ezek xxi. 21, where the LXX renders it 'beginning' (*archē*). Bedale therefore suggests that *kephalē* in St. Paul's
Epistles may mean 'source of' rather than 'superior to'. In the
passage under consideration, we may say that the man is the
source of the woman in that Eve was taken from Adam, and that

---

[72] *Epître aux Romains* (Paris, 1950), on xv. 6.
[73] *The first Epistle of St. Paul to the Corinthians.* (London, 1962), ad loc.
[74] 'The Meaning of *kephalē* in the Pauline Epistles,' *J.T.S.*, N.S. v (1954),
pp. 211–5.

God is the 'source' of Christ, the 'fount of deity' as the Cappadocians said. Bedale's argument, though plausible, is not conclusive, since St. Paul does not elsewhere call God the source of Christ, whereas he does in other passages make use of subordinationist language.

The last passage of this type is 1 Cor. xv. 28, 'And when all things are thus subject to him, then the Son himself will also be made subordinate to God, who made all things subject to him, and thus God will be all in all'. To us these words inevitably suggest subordination, but Héring[75] may well be correct in supposing that St. Paul's intention was to counter any suspicion that Christ might be a 'revolutionary god' like Saturn, who dethroned Uranus only to be overthrown in his turn by Jupiter.

Yet even so the subordinationist language remains. Bonsirven[76] claims that any subordinationist Christology will always be shattered by 1 Cor. viii. 6, 'One Lord, Jesus Christ, through whom all things came to be, and we through him'. It is indeed impossible to confine St. Paul's thought in a single phrase or to extract from his writings the answers to questions which he had not raised; and the question whether Christ was equal or subordinate in status to the Father was foreign to the mind of the Apostle. The question which was alive for St. Paul was this: was there any other mediator between God and Man? To this question the answer was an uncomprising 'no': 'For it is in Christ that the complete being of the Godhead dwells embodied', (Col. ii. 9). There is no sphere of existence where Christ does not hold sway as God's vicegerent. This theme of the 'cosmological' extent of Christ's authority will be considered later when we come to examine the doctrine of the salvation of all mankind.[77] Phil. ii. 5–11 has been much discussed for the light which it may shed upon 'kenoticism', a doctrine which has been restated by Vincent Taylor[78] and attacked by Beare and Fairweather.[79] To enter into such a controversy would carry us too far afield, but the passage shows that Christ, unlike Adam, was completely obedient to God, with the result that God 'raised him to the heights' (Phil. ii. 9).

[75] *The First Epistle of St. Paul to the Corinthians.* (London, 1962), ad loc.
[76] *L'Evangile de Paul* (Paris, 1948), p. 73.
[77] cp. *infra*, p. 273, cp. also p. 29.
[78] *The Person of Christ* (London, 1958), Part ii.
[79] *The Epistle to the Philippians*, Black N.T.C., (London, 1959), ad loc., with appended note on 'The "kenotic" Christology' by Fairweather, pp. 159–74.

Again and again we have had occasion to remark that St. Paul
is concerned, not to say that Christ is the equal of the Father in
nature, but to assert that the Son is associated with the Father in
his functions of creation, revelation and redemption. He says not
that Christ is another Lord alongside God, but that He shares
fully in God's Lordship. Cullman brings this line of thought to
its logical conclusion, and maintains that the Christology of all
the New Testament writers, including St. Paul, is conceived wholly
in functional terms, 'Whereas the question of the two natures is a
Greek rather than a biblical one'.[80] 'Here lies the key to all New
Testament Christology. *It is only meaningful to speak of the Son
in view of God's revelatory action, not in view of his being*'. (Cullmann's italics).[81] 'Functional Christology is the only kind which
exists'.[82] This view is not a mere excrescence on Cullmann's
thought, but constitutes the very structure of his Christology, and
is integrated with his theology of salvation-history (*Heilsgeschichte*),
as expounded in 'Christ and Time'.[83] His thesis has lead to
understandable misgivings, but Benoit[84] points out that dogmatic
theology and biblical theology are not asking the same questions.

But further qualifications are essential. In our day we distinguish explicitly between a Christology of natures and a functional Christology, and we may consciously reject one in favour
of the other. St. Paul did not consciously reject a 'nature' Christology in favour of a purely functional Christology; and it is
improbable that he would have comprehended the distinction.
His framework of thought was not functional *as opposed* to metaphysical; it was rather an undifferentiated framework of thought,
almost entirely functional, which had to do duty for the concep-
tual, metaphysical framework which was foreign to biblical thought.
It might be said that he came as near to asserting a metaphysical
equality of community of natures as his non-metaphysical framework of thought permitted him to do. As Barrett[85] has pointed
out, the first exponents of Christology had to make some attempt
at expressing the inexpressible, and therefore drew on a wide
range of thought and vocabulary. This, he adds, was the reason
why the Church was in the end obliged to move on from a purely
functional to an essential Christology.

[80] *The Christology of the New Testament*, E.T. (London, 1959), p. 235.
[81] ibid., p. 293.   [82] ibid., p. 326; cp. pp. 181, 306.
[83] E.T. Marsh.   [84] *Revue biblique*, (1958), p. 274.
[85] *J.T.S.*, N.S. x. (1959), p. 379.

ii. THE HOLY SPIRIT

(a) *The Spirit the Hallmark of the Christian*

Although St. Paul cannot be said to have worked out a *doctrine* of the Spirit, yet the Spirit plays a dominant part in his teaching. In the Old Testament the spirit (a capital letter is hardly appropriate) is the spirit of God. The word 'spirit' is used on some of the occasions when the sacred writers wish to speak of the activity of God. In the Old Testament this 'activity word' is employed on special occasions, such as the Creation (Gen. i. 2), the stirring up of Gideon to sound the trumpet (Judges vi. 34) and above all when prophecy is in question. The spirit is never a permanent endowment of man, but always an 'occasional' activity of God. Joel ii. 28, 'And it will come to pass afterward that I will pour out my spirit upon all flesh', might suggest that in the Messianic Age the activity of God would be no longer 'fitful' but enduring. Psalms of Solomon xvii. 42 (37),[86] 'For God will make him mighty by means of his holy spirit', speaks of a permanent characteristic of the Messiah due to God's spirit.

Now for St. Paul the Christian was 'in Christ'. We must recall that although he employs a 'spatial metaphor' he does so in order to express a literal though not primarily physical truth which is basic to all his thought. But 'God was in Christ reconciling the world to himself' (2 Cor. v. 19). If God and the Christian were both in some sense (though not the same sense) 'in Christ', and if the language of 'corporate personality' and 'extended personality' does refer to something real in St. Paul's thinking, then there is a new relation between God and the Christian. To say that they are 'linked together in Christ' would obscure the fact that God and Man are not on the same level and the fact that the initiative is on the side of God. It would be possible to say that we 'come to share in the very being (*phusis*) of God' (2 Pet. i. 4), but St. Paul does not do this.

The Apostle is not conscious of the being of God so much as of His activity, which the Old Testament can express by means of the word 'spirit'. Moreover, the centre of all of St. Paul's theology is Jesus the Messiah. Since it was believed among contemporary Jews that in the Messianic Age God would pour

[86] Charles vol. ii, p. 650.

out His spirit on the Messiah and on His people, it was natural for St. Paul to express the relation of the Christian in Christ to God by means of the word 'spirit', which was no longer a temporary endowment of some of God's people, but a gift which God gave continuously to all His people, that is, to all who were in Christ.

It is therefore impossible to over-estimate the importance for St. Paul's thought of such passages as Rom. viii. 9–10, 'If a man does not possess the Spirit of Christ, he is no Christian', Rom. viii. 14–15, 'For all who are moved by the Spirit of God are sons of God', and others which will be quoted later because they illustrate other points as well. We are so much accustomed to think, at the popular level, of the Spirit as a special gift of particularly good or favoured Christians that it comes as something of a shock to read 1 Cor. xii. 13, 'For indeed we were all brought into one body by baptism, in the one Spirit . . . and that one Holy Spirit was poured out for all of us to drink'. This does not mean that the Corinthians were 'better' or 'more enthusiastic' Christians than we are, with the result that they 'had the Spirit' while we have not. It means that all of us, simply because we are Christians, have been given the Spirit, and St. Paul rates this gift higher than all the 'special' spiritual gifts of which the Corinthians were so proud. The teaching that the Spirit has been given to all Christians as such can be regarded as the fundamental teaching upon which all St. Paul's other utterances concerning the Spirit are based.

This is especially clear in cases where St Paul has Baptism in mind. Gal. iv. 6, 'To prove that you are sons, God has sent into our hearts the Spirit of his Son, crying "Abba! Father" ' (cf. Rom. viii. 15–16), suggests that we could not utter the baptismal response or indeed say the Lord's Prayer, if God had not sent His Spirit into our hearts. 1 Cor. xii. 3, 'And no one can say "Jesus is Lord!" except under the influence of the Holy Spirit', is seen to point in the same direction when we remember that 'Jesus is Lord' is a confession of faith, almost certainly baptismal, in Rom. x. 9. This does not mean that St. Paul had carefully considered whether a man could possibly make an insincere profession of faith, uttering the syllables without the guidance of the Spirit. He took it for granted that in fact those who were baptized were led by the Holy Spirit. In Gal. iii. 2 receiving the Spirit is ascribed to believing the Gospel message (cp. Gal. iii. 14) which would in fact issue in Baptism. 2 Cor. i. 21–22, 'And if you and we belong to Christ, guaranteed as his and anointed (*eis Christon kai chrisas*; lit., "into the Anointed One, and anointed") it is all God's doing; it is God also who set his seal upon us, and as a pledge (*arrabōn*) of what is to come has given the Spirit to dwell in our hearts', makes it clear that all Christians have been given the Spirit, the gift of God.

(b) *The Spirit Messianic*

Since the Spirit is the mark of those who belong to Christ, the seal used by God to distinguish His own, the Spirit is God's agent of sanctification (2 Thess. ii. 13, Rom. xv. 16). 1 Cor. iii. 16, 'You are God's temple where the Spirit of God dwells', shows once more how 'belonging to God' is expressed by means of the word 'spirit'.

'Belonging to God in Christ' is the main concept which 'Spirit' is used by St. Paul to express, and it is simply the Old Testament idea of God's power, exercised on rare occasions, which has been adapted to convey the belief that God's power is now in permanent possession of those who are 'in Christ' the Messiah and are therefore living under 'Messianic' conditions with the result that Messianic prophecies, including Joel ii. 28f., are fulfilled in them. This is the central concept from which all the others radiate outwards. Among these concepts, naturally enough in view of Joel ii. 28f., is the gift of prophecy, as we learn from 1 Thess. v. 19, 'Do not stifle inspiration (lit., "the spirit", *to pneuma*) and do not despise prophetic utterances', and 1 Cor. xiv. 12. 1 Cor. ii. 4, 'Demonstration of the Spirit and in power' (So R.S.V. for Greek *apodeixei pneumatos kai dunameōs*) probably refers to the Spirit as the agent of the 'mighty acts' of the Messianic Age. 1 Thess. i. 16, 'The welcome you gave the message meant grave suffering for you, yet you rejoiced in the Holy Spirit', may reflect a connection in St. Paul's mind between the Messianic Age with its characteristic joy (*chara*) and the Holy Spirit. The Thessalonians experienced at the same time 'great suffering' (Is it too much to see in this a reference to the Messianic woes?) and great joy. It is usual to say that the Christians were 'living at the same time in each of two overlapping ages'. This simply means that the Christians were subject to two sets of 'forces', those of the old age of evil and those of the 'new age', just as a man who has come out of the cold into a warm room is subject both to the cold which has numbed his hands and to the heat which is thawing them out. The cold is associated with the past, the warmth with the 'new age' of the present and the future. This is inevitably speculative, but the Spirit is certainly connected with joy at 1 Thess. i. 6, and Rom. xiv. 17, and again, less closely, at Gal. v. 22. It may well be the case that Spirit-joy-Messianic Age are all connected together.

In 1 Cor. ii. 10, St. Paul speaks of what God has revealed through the Spirit. Here, again, we may suppose that deeper knowledge is now possible for those who now 'belong more closely' to God, who are 'in the Messiah' (*en Christō*) and therefore 'in the Messianic age, and indwelt by the Spirit'. For the Spirit as giver of moral enlightenment, see below, p. 213. Rom. viii. 26, 'The Spirit himself is pleading for us', is set in a context dominated by the belief that those who are in themselves weak need have no fear, because they belong to Christ's family. Here also it may be that the Messianic status of the Christian, attested by the Spirit who dwells in him, is the reason for his 'access' to God in prayer. We have suggested that the activities of the Spirit and the Christian are 'Messianic'. This cannot of course be proved one way or the other, but it follows naturally from the fact that the Spirit in St. Paul's thought is the hallmark of all Christians.

(c) Is the Spirit Divine and Personal?

St. Paul would probably have found it hard to understand the later problem of the 'deity' of the Holy Spirit. He would have replied that the Holy Spirit is the Spirit *of God*. He could not have imagined the problem of a 'second' or 'third' divine being apart from, or in addition to the Father. The popular tritheism which sometimes masquerades as Trinitarianism would have been completely foreign to his thought. He would have said that the Father acts *in* the Son and *as* the Spirit. The difference suggested by 'in' and 'as' corresponds to the fact that the Second Person was incarnate in a complete human being, while the Third Person was not. Before we consider whether the Holy Spirit for St. Paul was 'distinct' and 'personal' it is well to remember that for Trinitarian orthodoxy the three Persons are not three separate personalities. St. Paul did not believe that the Spirit is 'impersonal'. The wind is an impersonal force. To St. Paul the Spirit is at least the Spirit of a Personal God.

(d) *Is the Spirit distinct from the Father?*

But granted that the Spirit is the Spirit of a Personal God, was He for St. Paul distinct from the Father? Gal. iv. 6, 'God has sent into our hearts the Spirit of his Son', does at least distinguish the First and the Third Person, as does Rom. v. 5, 'God's love has flooded our inmost heart through the Holy Spirit he has given us'. When we hear that 'God's Spirit dwells in us' (Rom. viii. 9) and that, 'When the Spirit pleads for us, God knows what the Spirit means', Rom. viii. 27, we can again say that the Spirit is distinguished from God. 1 Cor. ii. 11–12, 'Only the Spirit of God knows what God is. This is the Spirit that we have received from God . . .', suggests that the Spirit is and remains the Spirit of God and that the *same* Spirit extends into us and remoulds us, just as an ever-burning flame may ignite and 'extend into' inflammable material. The extension of Divine Personality is certainly presupposed by St. Paul.

The Holy Spirit, then, is clearly the Spirit of God, and God is Personal. In some passages, though they are a minority, St. Paul employs language which serves to distinguish the Spirit from God.

(e) *Is the Spirit distinct from the Son?*

This question is inevitably raised for us by the parallel language St. Paul employs about the Second and Third Persons of the Trinity. E. Schweizer[95] refers to the fact that in Rom. viii. 1–11, 'The Spirit of God in you' (viii. 9) alternates with 'Christ in you' (viii. 10) and 'You . . . in spirit' (viii. 9) with 'Those who are in Christ' (viii. 1) without any apparent difference in meaning. There is no need to labour the point since it is generally agreed that St. Paul often applies the same language both to the Son and to the Spirit.

Between Father and Spirit there is clear interaction. It is hard to find clear evidence for interaction between Son and Spirit. Rom. viii. 11, 'The Spirit of him who raised Jesus from the dead . . . will also give new life to your mortal bodies', does suggest that God and His Spirit were active in the Resurrection and that Christ Himself was passive.

Again the names of Father, Son and Holy Spirit are distinguished, for example, at 1 Cor. xii. 4–6 and 2 Cor. xiii. 13. Such

---

[95] *T.W.N.T.*, vi., p. 431, E.T., *Spirit of God*, 1960, p. 81.

traces of a Trinitarian ground-plan[97] are common enough. The question is whether what is said about Son and Spirit is so closely bound up that it *unites*, or different enough to *distinguish*. Gal. iii. 13–14, 'Christ bought us freedom . . . so that we might receive the promised Spirit', shows that, although the actions of Son and Spirit are naturally not opposed, since they are working to the same end, yet they are distinct, if only because the death of the Son comes before the receiving of the Spirit. The Spirit is not credited with the acts of the Incarnate Lord: He does not die, nor is He raised from the dead. We must conclude that the functions overlap, but do not coincide. Wainwright is therefore justified in maintaining that, although God, Christ, and the Spirit were in the forefront of St. Paul's mind he was not aware, like St. John, of a *problem* of the Trinity.[98]

[97] J. N. D. Kelly, *Early Christian Creeds* (London, 1960²), pp. 21f.
[98] A. W. Wainwright, *The Trinity in the New Testament*, (London, 1962), p. 249.

CHAPTER SIX

THE WHOLE WORK OF CHRIST

The Death of Christ

The purpose of this chapter is to inquire what theory St. Paul held concerning the *modus operandi* of the atonement through the death of Christ. It will be maintained:

1. That, if St. Paul can be said to hold a theory of the *modus operandi*, it is best described as one of salvation through participation: Christ shared all our experience, sin alone excepted, including death, in order that we, by virtue of our solidarity with him, might share his life.

2. That St. Paul does not hold a theory of substitution in the sense in which that term will shortly be defined. He believes that Christ made salvation possible for us at the great cost of his own life, not that God accepted his death instead of ours.

The 'participation' theory will be expounded and illustrated from St. Paul's writings. We shall then examine briefly a representative selection of those Pauline texts which seem to demand a substitutionary explanation. It will become apparent that the support which they lend to this theory is much less solid than some scholars have supposed, and that in none of them is it stated unambiguously. There are, however, passages in which the possibility of substitutionary thought cannot be excluded. It will be suggested that these verses, if there be in fact ideas of substitution behind them, describe, in language derived from the Old Testament, what Christ did, and not the means by which He accomplished it.

We must now define the term 'substitutionary', and it may be said at once that the words 'vicarious' and 'substitutionary' are employed in a variety of senses against the background of many different sets of presuppositions. For St. Paul the death of Christ was certainly vicarious: if He had not died on the cross, we should have perished eternally. Our death would have been due to our own sin, and could therefore have been described as penal. But the death which Christ died to save us from a penal death was not itself penal. Analogies derived from the sphere of human relationships can never be wholly satisfactory, since Christ was not merely a human being; but it is legitimate to describe the death of Christ in terms of human analogies, provided that we are aware of their limitations. Let us suppose that some man has been convicted of a crime. A friend may volunteer to be punished in his place, so that the criminal goes scot-free. This would be a penal, substitutionary transaction, and it is in such a sense that I demur at the application of these terms of the death of Christ. On the other hand, an innocent person may take the criminal into his home, endure his evil temper and suffer from his dishonesty; he may endure also the strain and the temptations due to the sinful nature of the man who is sharing his house: it is possible that the criminal will be reformed, and that the suffering of the innocent may prove to be redemptive. However, it would not be penal, and it should be described not as substitutionary, but as vicarious suffering endured to save another from the penal consequences of his own sin. This illustration is misleading in two respects, quite apart from the fact that Christ is divine, and that no human analogy can do justice to his work. Firstly, no human being is wholly innocent, and, secondly, Christ did not take us to share his life, but came down and took upon himself not only our life, but our nature. We might have suffered death as the result of our sin. But God is Love and Righteousness; this does not, of course, mean that the Father is righteous and the Son loving: since they are of one substance, both alike, together with the Holy Ghost, are Love and Righteousness. The Second Person of the Trinity was made man and shared the limitations of human life, the consequences of the sin of others, and the strains and temptations inherent in being a member of a particular nation at a particular time. He underwent misunderstanding, scorn, rejection, and crucifixion on our behalf, that is to say vicariously, in order to save us from the consequence of our own sin. But God did not transfer to him the punishment due to us on account of our sin, as if punishment were something impersonal. Some will feel dissatisfied with the substance of this exposition, and with them I must be resigned to differ. Others may agree with it, but add that I have expressed myself badly, maintaining that what I have said is what they mean when they apply the terms 'penal' and 'substitutionary' to the death of Christ. With them my disagreement is merely verbal.

It is possible for two modern theologians, of whom one holds a substitutionary and the other a non-substitutionary theory of the atonement, to express their different views by means of the same words. For example, the statement 'But for the death of Christ, we should all have perished' is susceptible of either interpretation, and it would have to be understood in the light of more explicit statements occurring elsewhere in the author's writings. This point is important because St. Paul uses words and phrases which can be expounded in a substitutionary sense. For instance, the word *katallassein* can be employed to express a substitutionary meaning, as it is in 2 Macc. i. 5, vii. 33, viii. 29, where the point is made quite unmistakable, whereas St. Paul's writings lack the explicit statements which would make it clear that those phrases which could bear a substitutionary meaning are intended to do so.[1]

We must now proceed to outline that theory of the atonement which I have called 'participatory'. The main positive contention of this chapter is that St. Paul understood salvation in Christ against the background of what we may term the 'presupposition of the firstfruits'.[2] In Rom. xi. 16 he writes: 'If the first portion of dough is consecrated, so is the whole lump'. He means, not that the sanctification of the first portion merely symbolizes the future sanctification of the lump, but that the sanctification of the first-portion actually accomplishes that of the lump. The conception of a substitutionary atonement, whether we accept it or no, is readily comprehensible: the presupposition of the first-portion is not, and that, I suggest, is the reason why this strand in St. Paul's theology has suffered comparative neglect; it has been distorted into substitutionary theories, or partially understood as a theory of representative salvation.

When St. Paul said: 'As in Adam all men die, so in Christ all will be brought to life' (1 Cor. xv. 22) he meant what he said in all seriousness. He did not mean that we sinned in the loins of Adam, or that we acted righteously in Christ, but that we are members of Adam who sinned, and therefore are liable to suffer the consequences of his sin. We are not, of course, members of Adam in the physical sense in which Adam's hand was a 'member of Adam' but neither are we members only in the metaphorical sense in

[1] Dom Jacques Dupont, in his short but valuable publication entitled La Réconciliation dans la Théologie de Saint Paul (*Analecta Lovaniensia Biblica et Orientalia*, ser. ii, fasc. 32, Desclée de Brouwer, Bruges–Paris, 1953), suggests that St. Paul employs the verb *katallassein* to mean neither that God changes his disposition towards us, nor that we change ours towards him, but that he takes the initative in establishing harmonious relations between us and himself.
[2] cp. J. Pedersen, *Israel: its Life and Culture* (1940), pp. 300–1.

which we can be said to be members of a college: we are members in a secondary literal sense. Christ, therefore, shared our life in order that we might share his. St. Irenaeus was fundamentally true to the thought of St. Paul when he said: *Factus est quod sumus nos, uti nos perficeret esse quod et ipse.*[3] At this point we must enter two caveats: firstly, there was one side of human life which Christ did not share, in that he *knew no sin* (2 Cor. v. 21 R.S.V.); and, secondly, as Ernest Best reminds us in his recent book *One Body in Christ*, although we share in his experience, it is he alone who creates it.[4]

St. Paul employs the language of participation in Rom. xiv. 9: 'This is why Christ died and came to life again, to establish his lord-ship over dead and living'. A similar view is expressed in 2 Cor. viii. 9: 'For you know how generous our Lord Jesus Christ has been: he was rich, yet for your sake he became poor, so that through his poverty you might become rich'. This, it is needless to say, does not exhaust his thought on the death of Christ. Firstly, the death of animals was part of the sacrificial system, which in Judaism was a means, though not the only means, of dealing with sin. Christ also died, and St. Paul in Rom. iii. 25 and elsewhere uses language with sacrificial associations in order to stress the fact that Christ died to deal with our sin. Secondly, St. Paul believed that 'For sin pays a wage, and the wage is death' (Rom. vi. 23). Death, both physical and eternal, is for St. Paul the result of sin. This general statement applies to the sin of Adam in which we are all involved: 'For if by the wrong doing of that one man death established its reign, through a single sinner . . .' (Rom. v. 17, etc.). It applies also to actual sin as what Otto Michel calls 'an eschatological possiblity remaining even for the redeemed'.[5] Under the Christian dispensation we must still endure physical death. But we undergo eternal death in a 'harmless' form, since, through baptism, our potential sharing in the death died by Christ is made actual (Rom. vi. 6–7). St. Paul never works out the implications of this teaching. He takes it for granted that man must die for sin, because God said to Adam: 'You are dust and to dust you shall return' (Gen. iii. 19). He does not say that we must die in order to satisfy the wrath of God or the claims of justice, but leaves the pre-suppositions of his belief completely unexamined. The problem

---

[3] *Adv. Haer. Omn.* V. praef. (Harvey, ii. p. 314).
[4] Op. cit. (London, 1955), p. 58.
[5] *Der Brief an die Römer*, Meyer-Kommentar, (Göttingen, 1955[10]), p. 135, n.4.

created by this belief is solved by the doctrine that we pass through death in that 'We have become incorporate with him in a death like his death'; therefore 'We shall also be one with him in a resurrection like his' (Rom. vi. 5).

But, although St. Paul's beliefs about salvation are not exhausted by a theory of participation, this strand of thought is found frequently in his Epistles. In 1 Cor. xv. 20–21 we read: 'But the truth is, Christ was raised to life—the firstfruits of the harvest of the dead. For since it was a man who brought death into the world, a man also brought resurrection of the dead'. This conception is found as early as 1 Thess., where St. Paul speaks of our Lord Jesus Christ, 'He died for us so that we, awake or asleep, might live in company with him' (1 Thess. v. 10). In *Ephesians*, which, if Pauline, is the latest of the Epistles, we find these words: 'So as to create out of the two a single new humanity in himself, thereby making peace' (Eph. ii. 15). Jew and Gentile alike participate in Christ, and in him achieve unity with each other and peace with God. It is the same thought which lies behind Rom. vi. and many other passages scattered throughout the Epistles, including those three pillars, as it has been supposed, of the substitutionary theory—Rom. viii. 3, 2 Cor. v. 21, and Gal. iii. 13. It is never easy to distinguish between a theory of the *modus operandi* of the atonement and a statement of the fact of the atonement, since the realities are beyond our grasp, with the result that, in either case, metaphors and analogies must be employed. But, if St. Paul can be said to hold a theory of the *modus operandi*, it is the 'participation' theory: his other sayings are to be regarded as statements of the fact of the atonement, expressed by means of the religious language of Judaism.

We can discern the same pattern of thought in the three famous passages which have so often been regarded as foundation stones of the substitutionary theory—Rom. viii. 3–4, 2 Cor. v. 21, and Gal. iii. 13.[6] None of these either necessitates or excludes a substitutionary explanation, and if such a theory were firmly based upon other passages in the Pauline writings it would be legitimate to intepret these three also in a similar manner.

Rom. viii. 3 includes the words: 'Sending his own son in a form like that of our own sinful nature, and as a sacrifice for sin

---

[6] E. Stauffer classifies all three as 'paradoxical incarnation formulae', *New Testament Theology* (E.T. London 1955), p. 343.

(*kai peri hamartias*) he has passed judgement against sin in that very nature.' Lagrange comments: 'Paul wished to say that the son had taken our flesh; but since the time of Adam our flesh was a flesh dominated by sin. It is in this respect that Christ could not resemble us (2 Cor. v. 21). 'The likeness of sinful flesh' means therefore 'Our flesh, but without sin'.[7] J. Bonsirven sees in Rom. viii. 3 an allusion to the incarnation and pre-existence of Christ.[8] But he goes on to say that: 'The Redeemer, without being culpable of sin, or indeed capable of it, had taken upon him the burden of the sins of men',[9] and that 'He has taken upon himself, sin and concupiscence excepted, all the weaknesses of our sinful flesh, including the ability to suffer and to die'.[10] By virtue of his solidarity with the human race, and his involvement in the human situation, Christ took upon himself three things:

1. The ability to suffer physical pain.

2. The ability to suffer, in a non-physical sense, as a result of the sins of others.

3. The strain and the agony of temptations brought upon him by the sin of others. The temptation to choose the easier path, and to win the allegiance of his contemporaries by showing them signs, was a real temptation to do wrong, and it came to Christ as a result of the sin of others, being due to their hardness of heart.

In these three respects, without himself yielding to sin, Christ took upon himself our flesh, not merely a physical body, still less a docetic, phantom body, but human nature in its entirety. It is part of the experience of all men, and we may therefore call it empirically part of human nature, to endure suffering and temptation as a result of the sin of others: all this Christ endured by sharing our life in order that we might share his; that what happened in Christ, the first-portion, might happen in the case of the human beings who constitute the lump, that is the Church, the body of which Christ is the head, the directing principle.[11]

Sanday and Headlam see in *peri hamartias* a reference to the sin-offering.[12] O. Michel briefly remarks that: 'The context gives no support to this interpretation'.[13] Such an explanation derives

[7] *Epître aux Romains* (Paris, 1950), ad loc.
[8] *L'Evangile de Paul* (Paris, 1949), p. 54.
[9] Op. cit. pp. 58–59, n.4. [10] Op. cit. p. 66.
[11] cp. S. Bedale, 'The Meaning of *kephalè* in the Pauline Epistles', *J.T.S.* N.S.v. (1954), pp. 211–15.
[12] *Romans* (I.C.C., 1895), p. 193.
[13] Op. cit. p. 161, n. 1.

L

but slender backing from the LXX. The primary function of
peri with the genitive is to denote the object or purpose about or
for which one does something.[14] This is clearly the sense of the
preposition in Lev. iv. 3, where we read that if the High Priest sin
. . . .'Then let him offer for the sin he has commited (Gk. *peri tēs
hamartias autou*, Heb, '*al ḥaṭṭa'thō*) a young bull without blemish
to the Lord for a sin offering (Gk. *peri tēs hamartias autou*, Heb,
'*al ḥaṭṭa'thō*) Thus in the LXX *peri tēs hamartias autou* can
mean either 'sin-offering' or 'to deal with sin', and in Rom. viii. 3
it is that latter explanation which fits the context.   We are to
understand that Christ took upon himself human nature like our
own except in respect of sin in order to deal with sin.

In 2 Cor. v. 21 St. Paul says: 'Christ was innocent of sin, and
yet for our sake God made him one with the sinfulness of men (*or*
and yet God made him a sin-offering for us, Greek *hamartian
epoiēsen*, lit. 'made sin'), so that in him we might be made one with
the righteousness of God.' It is only too easy to read this verse in
the light of whatever theory we may hold. It is easy to understand
it as St. Augustine does when he writes: 'Therefore God to whom
we are reconciled made him sin on our behalf, that is, the sacrifice
through which our sins are remitted'.[15] Against a different background of thought it is equally easy to view it with St. Gregory of
Nyssa as a reference to 'The changing of the Mortal to the Immortal, of the Servant to the Lord, of Sin to Righteousness (2 Cor.
v. 21), of the Curse to the Blessing (Gal. iii. 13)'.[16] Against this
interpretation Plummer[17] contends that it is excluded by the word
sin just before. Plummer means, presumably, that *hamartia* cannot refer to sin when it is said that Christ knew no sin, and then,
three words farther on, 'human nature, which in all other cases is
sinful'. But it must be said that in this paradoxical verse *hamartia*
cannot be interpreted in the same manner on both occasions. That
Christ did not know sin or, as Bultmann[18] rightly says, did not
practise sin, is obvious. St. Paul goes on to say that God made
Christ sin. 'Made sin' could mean 'Made to bear the guilt of sin,
treated in a penal substitutionary transaction as if he were a sinner'.
It could also mean that in the providence of God Christ took upon

[14] Liddell and Scott, *Lexicon*, ed. 9 s.v.

[15] *De Peccato Originali*, xxxii. (37); ed. W. Bright, *Select Anti-Pelagian
Treatises of St. Augustine* (Oxford, 1880), p. 262.

[16] *Contra Eunomium*, v. 5.

[17] 2 *Corinthians* (I.C.C., 1915), ad loc.   [18] *Theology*, vol. i, p. 264

himself human nature, which though not essentially sinful, is *de facto* sinful in all other cases. The second incarnational, participatory explanation is to be preferred, because it accords with the thought of 2 Cor. v. 14–15, 'For the love of Christ leaves us no choice, when once we have reached the conclusion that one man died for all and therefore all mankind has died. His purpose in dying for all was that men, while still in life, should cease to live for themselves, and should live for him who for their sake died and was raised to life'.

Gal. iii. 13–14, 'Christ bought us freedom from the curse of the law by becoming for our sake an accursed thing; for scripture says, 'Cursed is everyone who is hanged on a tree' (Deut. xxi. 23). And the purpose of it all was that the blessing of Abraham should in Jesus Christ be extended to the Gentiles'. This passage has already been discussed at length, (p. 84 f.) Lagrange[19] contends that the 'We' who are redeemed from the curse of the law refers to the Jews, on the ground that the Gentiles were not under the curse of the law. But Schlier,[20] followed by Bonnard,[21] points out that the 'We' implied by *labōmen* in verse 14 includes the Gentiles as well. St. Paul has described the situation of the whole human race in terms strictly applicable to the Jews alone. All human beings, then, are under a curse. Christ has completely identified himself with us. St. Paul illustrates this self-identification of the Saviour with ourselves by pointing out that he also has fallen under a curse, in that he hung on the tree. Through his identification with us Christ has delivered us from the curse: we therefore must not seek to remain in or to return to the accursed condition from which Christ came to set us free. St. Paul does not say how Christ's self-identification with mankind effected our release. The thought lying behind this verse is, I suggest, that Christ who is by nature God's son and free from sin, became what we are by nature, that is accursed, that we might achieve, by grace, the freedom from the curse which is his by nature, unless we accept the view propounded in ch. iv. pp. 83–5.

We must now consider St. Paul's use of 'purchase', 'blood', 'redemption' (*apolutrōsis*), and 'propitiation' (*hilastērion*). In four places the Apostle introduces the idea of purchase, expressing it

[19] *Saint Paul Epître aux Galates* (Paris, 1950), ad loc.
[20] *Der Brief an die Galater*, Meyer-Kommentar, (Göttingen, 1951[11]), ad loc.
[21] *L'Epître de Saint Paul aux Galates* (Neuchâtel, 1953,) ad loc.

by means of the words *agorazein* (1 Cor. vi. 20 and vii. 23, R.V. 'buy') and *exagorazein* (Gal. iii. 13 and iv. 5, R.V. 'redeem'). In all these cases the underlying thought is that of what E. G. Selwyn[22] calls 'the slave's transference from one owner to another; from man's service to Christ's'. It may be illustrated by a story, preserved in Midrash *Siphre* on Numbers, concerning a king who bought a slave. When the slave objected to the tasks assigned to him, the king produced the purchase deed, and reminded him that he was his slave.[23] In none of the relevant New Testament passages where these two words occur is there any mention of the person to whom the price is paid. In all of them the thought of service towards God is probably to be found, and in some it is positively demanded by the context. At the end of ch. vi. of 1 Cor. St. Paul urges his converts to refrain from fornication, reminds them that they were bought for a price, and exhorts them to glorify God. Likewise in vii. 23 he makes it clear that even a free man is a slave of Christ; then follows what may well have been a stock catechetical phrase, 1 Cor. vii. 23, 'You were bought at a price' and the Corinthians are forbidden to become the slaves of men, that is, as the *I.C.C.*[24] and Héring[25] correctly indicate, to allow their lives to be dominated by worldly concerns and values. In both these passages in 1 Cor. the ethical emphasis is certain and explicit. It is less obvious, although certainly present, in Gal. iv. 1–10, where St. Paul asks his converts why they return to serve their former masters, the elements (*stoicheia*), since God has sent his son and redeemed them (*exagorazein*) from slavery to the elements. Here again the meaning is practical: do not live the life from which you have been redeemed. The thought expressed in Gal. iii. 7ff. is complex. St. Paul implores his readers not to submit themselves to the demands of the law, since those who are under the law are under a curse, whereas they are free from the curse and from the law, since Christ has redeemed them. Upon this picture there is superimposed the figure of Christ, who has become a curse on our behalf. This it has been argued above, is a reference to his solidarity with us by virtue of the Incarnation.

[22] *The First Epistle of St. Peter* (London, 1947[2]), on i. 18.
[23] The parable is quoted by Leon Morris, *The Apostolic Preaching of the Cross* (London, 1955), p. 50.
[24] Robertson and Plummer, (Edinburgh, 1914[2]), ad loc.
[25] *La Première Epître de Saint Paul aux Corinthiens* (Commentaire du Nouveau Testament VII, Neuchâtel, 1949), ad loc.

St. Paul's use of the word 'blood' is clearly a matter of great moment. In the LXX *haima* (Heb. *dām*) is of frequent occurrence, and in most cases it is mentioned in connexion with violent death. The soteriological uses of this term in the Old Testament may be classified under four headings:

1. Covenant blood.
2. The blood of the Passover.
3. Sacrificial blood, including that of sin-offering.
4. The blood of the Martyrs.

The blood of the sacrifices and of the Martyrs will be considered in connexion with the word *hilastērion* below.

At least for the post-exilic Jews, the chief covenant was the one established under Moses on Mount Horeb, and recorded for us in Exod. xxiv. 3–8. On this occasion Moses used half of the blood to sprinkle the altar, and half to sprinkle the Israelites: God and his people, as they had now become, were joined together in a family relationship. In the case of a covenant between men who were equal the covenant relationship might be virtually fraternal. In the case of a covenant with God, who was superior, this could not be so, and the analogous relationship was variously conceived as that of husband and wife or father and son: by virtue of the covenant God made himself the Father of Israel and of the king of Israel, who in his own person summed up the whole people. The son owed obedience to the Father, and the Father naturally protected his son. To this family relationship, achieved by the blood of the covenant, expiation and propitiation were not essential. The 'blood of the covenant' through which the individual entered into the covenant relationship conferred upon Israel collectively at Mount Horeb was the blood of circumcision,[26] which was not in the Old Testament regarded as expiatory or propitiatory. Ideas of expiation and propitiation cannot, however, be wholly excluded from the Mosaic covenant, since before the sprinkling young men 'offered burnt offerings, and sacrificed peace offerings of oxen unto the Lord' (Exod. xxiv. 5), but they are peripheral, not central. L. Morris in *The Apostolic Preaching of the Cross* (p. 71) shows that the blood may have been sprinkled on the people to purify them. It is not necessary to argue this point, since purifying sinners is

[26] Strack-Billerbeck, vol. i, pp. 991–2.

not the same thing as atoning for their guilt by substitutionary suffering. It follows that in those Pauline references to blood which recall the covenant we are to think of the blood primarily in connexion with the relationship between God and his Israel (Gal. vi. 16) set up by the work of Christ, although the Apostle's thought may be fringed with ideas of expiation.

As for the Passover, we read in Exod. xii. how the Israelites struck the lintels of their houses with blood. This was in part, no doubt, a sign to facilitate recognition, partly an effective symbol of God's Lordship over the house and its inhabitants. Here also the covenant relatonship is to be found. It is true that the Mosaic covenant was still in the future, but Israel had already been spoken of as God's firstborn son (Exod. iv. 23), and Divine sonship was not a natural, but a covenant relationship. It may be that the Passover blood was among other things a memorial of a covenant relationship conceived of as already in existence, and that it was designed to recall this relationship, and thereby to make it effective. Be this as it may, the Passover blood was a means of salvation, and it was not regarded anywhere in the Old Testament as being expiatory or propitiatory, although such ideas would appear to have been associated with it in later Jewish thought.[27]

The right relationship between God and man, established by means of a covenant, included as one of its elements 'peace'. 'Peace' initiated through covenant blood provides the background for St. Paul's thought in Col. i. 20, 'To reconcile the whole universe to himself, making peace through the shedding of his blood upon the cross'. The Apostle means that through his death Christ constituted a relationship with all things analogous to that established in the Old Testament by means of the blood of the covenant. This interpretation also applied to Eph. ii. 13: 'You who once were far off have been brought near through the shedding of Christ's blood'. The reference to Isa. lvii. 19 is made more explicit in Eph. ii. 17, 'Peace to you who were far off, and peace to those who were near'. Christ by the blood of his cross established a relationship with God for Jew and Gentile alike which resembled but transcended that established through Moses on Mount Horeb. This explanation is rendered more probable by the likelihood that Zech. ix. 10–11 is also in the mind of the writer. According to the M.T. Zechariah says: 'And he shall command peace to the nations.

[27] e.g. in 4. Macc.

. . . As for you, because of the blood of my covenant with you, I will set your captives free from the waterless pit'.

Eph. i. 7 reads: 'For in Christ our release (*apolutrōsis*) is secured and our sins are forgiven through the shedding of his blood'. This would seem to be a doctrine of realized eschatology expressed by means of New Exodus language. In other words, St. Paul describes the victory over sin freely bestowed on us in the beloved as a redemption which fulfils the Isaianic prophecy of a New Exodus; *apolutrōsis*, as we shall see later, has New Exodus associations. In the three relevant places where it occurs in 1 Cor. *haima* refers to Eucharistic blood. The Eucharist is viewed partly as a proleptic participation in the Messianic Banquet, partly as a recalling and making effective of the death on Calvary, regarded as the new covenant. The word therefore takes its meaning from other passages, so that these three instances need not detain us. The only other references to blood in a soteriological sense are found in the Epistle to the Romans. Rom. v. 9 includes the phrase 'Since we have now been justified (*dikaiōthentes*) by Christ's sacrificial death (*haima*, lit. 'blood')'. Justification (*dikaiosunē*; Heb. *tsedhāḳāh*) is to be regarded as a regal rather than a juridical word. It means neither to make ethically righteous, which we are not, nor to account righteous by a legal fiction, but to set in a right relationship with God, a relationship by virtue of which sanctification can proceed.[28] The fact that in Rom. v. 9 the blood protects us from the future wrath of God again suggests a reference back to the original Passover. Rom. iii. 25, the sole remaining instance, must be considered after the meaning of *apolutrōsis* has been discussed.

The meanings to be assigned to *apolutrōsis* and its cognates of the *lutron* group are not easy to determine. In non-biblical Greek a *lutron* is a means of procuring freedom, primarily a price paid and is found from Aeschylus and Pindar onwards. In the LXX words of the *lutron* group represent words connected with the two Hebrew words *gā'al* and *pādhāh*. *Pādhāh* clearly has a substitutionary force in Num. iii. 40ff. and elsewhere. This is less obvious in the case of *gā'al* which means to play the part of a kinsman. Nevertheless, Morris, in *The Apostolic Preaching of the Cross*, makes a legitimate point when he reminds us that: 'Whenever the verb *gā'al* is used with a human subject the deliverance is

[28] cp. N. H. Snaith, *The Distinctive Ideas of the Old Testament* (London 1944), pp. 161–73.

always by payment of a ransom'.[29] It has frequently been noticed, for example by Westcott,[30] that in the LXX *lutrousthai* with God as the subject means redemption without any reference to the paying of a price. It describes the redemption from Egypt in Exod. vi. 6, and the redemption of the New Exodus foretold by Isaiah (xxxv. 9, xli. 14, xliii. 1 and 14). It should be noted that it represents deliverance from sin in Ps. cxxx (cxxix). 8 and from death (Hos. xiii. 14). In none of these passages is there any reference to the payment of a price, and it is surely significant that this use of the word *lutrousthai* is found in portions of the LXX which were susceptible of a Messianic interpretation and were especially familiar to the New Testament writers. Morris does not disregard these facts, and he comments in the following words: 'We saw that the idea of the price paid tends to fade away when Yahweh is the subject of the verb, but that, nevertheless, it does not disappear, for there is a reference to the price paid in the insistence that Yahweh's redemption is at the cost of the exertion of his mighty power'.[31] He appears to be overstating his case. It is certainly said that God liberates Israel by his mighty power, but the phrase 'at the cost of' is introduced by Morris. Here, as so often in the Bible, words and phrases are employed in a secondary sense, and it is difficult to determine how much of the original etymological signification has been retained. It would not be unfair to say that *lutrousthai* is used with a human subject to describe how men secure release for men by the payment of a price, but that when God is the subject the verb tells us that God secures release from sin and death by the sheer exercise of his power.

In the Greek Old Testament *apolutrōsis* is found once only, in the LXX (not Theodotion) of Dan. iv. 30. Morris comments: 'This might be interpreted as an example of simple deliverance if it did not plainly refer back to verse 24 where Daniel exhorts the king: 'Pray to him concerning thy sins and redeem (*lutrōsai*) thine iniquities with alms-giving'.[32] But it is far from certain that *apolutrōsis* does 'plainly refer back' to *lutrōsai*, which in Rahlfs's edition of the LXX occurs 36 lines earlier.

---

[29] London (1955), p. 14.
[30] *The Epistle to the Hebrews* (London, 1903³), pp. 297–9.
[31] Op. cit. p. 19.
[32] Op. cit. p. 11.

In the New Testament words belonging to this group often suggest deliverance by sheer power without any thought of the payment of a price. *Lutrōtēs* is found only at Acts vii. 35 where it is coupled with *archōn* and is applied to Moses the ruler and deliverer of his people. *Lutrōsis* occurs three times. In Luke i. 68, the first verse of the Benedictus, it is God who is said to have 'turned to his people, saved them and set them free'. In the same gospel we are told (ii. 38) that Anna spoke of Christ to all them that were looking for the redemption (*lutrōsis*) of Jerusalem. The only place in the New Testament where *lutrōsis* could possibly suggest the payment of a price in the substitutionary sense is Heb. ix. 12, 'Secured an eternal deliverance'. Héring[33] in his recent commentary appears to accept this interpretation. On the other hand, there is much to be said for the contention of Büchsel,[34] who maintains that *lutrōsis* means freeing from sin in a non-substitutionary sense, on the ground that this thought is taken up in verse 14, where we are told that the blood of Christ 'Will . . . fit us for the service of the living God'.

The verb *lutrousthai* is found three times. In Luke xxiv. 21 the two disciples whom Jesus had joined on the way to Emmaus said to Christ about himself: 'But we had hoped that he was the man to liberate (*lutrousthai*) Israel'. They had been disappointed of that hope by the fact of his crucifixion, so in this instance, any connexion of *lutrousthai* with a substitutionary death is excluded. In the case of Tit. ii. 14 and 1 Pet. i. 18ff. Büchsel[35] remarks that the connexion with the phrase 'To surrender his life as a ransom for many' recorded in Mark x. 45 and Matt. xx. 28, the only verses in the New Testament where *lutron* is found, is so obvious that *lutrousthai* must be translated by the word 'ransom' (*loskaufen*). Büchsel probably goes too far. In the two passages from Titus and 1 Peter we are told that Christ ransomed us from sinning, not from the punishment due to us on account of our sins. It is obvious that the figure of buying a man's release from a terrible condition is involved. The question at issue is whether Christ suffers a penalty instead of us, or whether he suffers on our behalf to buy us out of the terrible condition of slavery to sin. Similar considerations apply to the 'ransom for many' saying

[33] *L'Epître aux Hébreux*, Neuchâtel, 1954, ad loc.
[34] *T.W.N.T.*, iv. p. 354.
[35] Op. cit. p. 353.

preserved in Mark x. 45. It is highly probable that these words formed part of the gospel as penned by St. Mark, and it is by no means improbable that they were spoken by Christ himself. As for their meaning, two interpretations are possible:

1. Just as men are freed from slavery by the payment of a ransom, so Christ freed us from sin and from death at the cost of his own life. He died instead of (*anti*) us in the sense that but for his death we should have perished.

2. God accepted the death of Christ instead of our death in order to satisfy the demands of justice, if indeed it can be said that 'justice' is satisfied by the death of any but the sinner.

Similar problems arise in the interpretation of the parables. In the case of the Matthaean parable of the Talents, we may suppose either that Christ used a situation borrowed from the field of commerce as practised in a slave economy in order to illustrate part of his teaching or that God's dealings with men resemble the dealings of a first-century capitalist with his slaves. In the same way we may suppose that the *lutron* sayings in the gospels and the *antilutron* passage in 1 Tim. ii. 6, the only verse in the New Testament where the word occurs, are concerned with the fact of the Atonement, and describe the result of the death of Christ in terms borrowed from the Torah, but also used in connexion with slavery and with the ransoming of prisoners of war; or, alternatively, we may suppose that the sayings are concerned with the *modus operandi* of the Atonement, and that God's dealings with men are to be understood by means of analogies drawn from the spheres of war and of slavery.

The ten New Testament instances of the use of words of the *lutron* group, apart from *apolutrōsis* itself, have now been considered: in none of them is a substitutionary meaning assured, and in four of them, all drawn from Luke–Acts, it is excluded (Luke i. 68, ii. 38, *lutrōsis*; Luke xxiv. 21, *lutrousthai*; Acts viii. 35, *lutrōtēs*), while in six it is possible but unlikely (Matt. xx. 28, Mark x. 45 *lutron*; Tit. ii. 14, 1 Pet. i. 18, *lutrousthai*; Heb. ix. 12, *lutrōsis*; 1 Tim. ii. 6, *antilutron*). The only word belonging to this group which occurs in the Pauline Epistles is *apolutrōsis*. In secular Greek it means ransoming. In five of the ten places where it is found in the New Testament it refers to deliverance (Luke xxi. 28; Rom. viii. 23; Eph. i. 14, iv. 30; Heb. xi. 35), and a substitutionary signification is excluded. In Heb. ix. 15 we read: 'And therefore he is the mediator of a new covenant, or testament, ('covenant' and 'testament' are here *complementary* rendering of the one Greek word *diathēkēs*, which can mean either and may here carry overtones of both), under which, now that there has been a death to bring deliverance (*apolutrōsis*). . . .' Although there is here also a reference to a future 'New Exodus' deliverance, there is clearly a background of sacrificial thought, and on this point more must be said later. The four remaining instances of the word are found in the Pauline Epistles. Eph. i. 7 reads: 'For in Christ our release is secured and our sins are forgiven through the shedding of his blood'. This reflects Col. i. 14: 'In whom our release is secured and our sins forgiven'. The thought of Col. i. 14 is without question participatory. Christ was the agent of the original creation (*v.* 16), and he is (*v.* 18) 'moreover, the head of the body, the church. He is its origin, the first to return from the dead'. We are told in verse 13 that 'He rescued us from the domain of darkness and brought us away into the kingdom of his dear son'. This surely is the language of realized eschatology: although we are still in the world, which is ruled by the powers of darkness, we have been transferred into the future age, the kingdom of the Son of his love, in whom we already have what men look for in the future, namely redemption, *apolutrōsis*, that is to say forgiveness of our sins. In judging passages of this kind it is notoriously difficult to avoid an element of subjectivity, but to myself it seems clear that in Col. i. 14 and in Eph. i. 7 *apolutrōsis* refers to a present enjoyment of eschatological benefits rather than to redemption in the substitutionary sense of the word. Nothing can be proved from 1 Cor. i. 30, where we are told that Christ was made unto us righteousness and sanctification and *apolutrōsis*. The sole remaining passage which must be considered is Rom. iii. 23ff.: 'For all alike have sinned, and are deprived of the divine splendour, and all are justified by God's free grace alone, through his act of liberation (*apolutrōsis*) in the person of Christ Jesus. For God designed him to be the means of expiating sin (*hilastērion*) by his sacrificial death (lit. 'by his blood', *haima*) effective through faith.'

The word *hilastērion* is found at Rom. iii. 25, Heb. ix. 9, and nowhere else in the New Testament. If in the former passage St. Paul employs it to describe the work of Christ in terms of the Mercy Seat, Heb. *kappōreth*, as C. H. Dodd and

T. W. Manson have argued, I suggest that St. Paul's general meaning in Rom. iii. 19ff. is as follows. All human beings, Jews and Gentiles alike, have sinned and have incurred the wrath of God. There is no possibility that men can help themselves or win merit through works of the law or in any other way. All that we can do is to accept by that positive response of the whole personality which St. Paul describes as faith God's own solution, which depends upon him alone, and is made available to us in Jesus Christ. It is called redemption (*apolutrōsis*) a term which recalls the former redemption from the power not of sin, but of Pharaoh.

D. Daube[36] goes so far as to say: 'The Jewish—and Christian —image of redemption, "recovery", had its roots in the social laws and their miraculous application at the Exodus'. It is God's New Exodus work of salvation, looked for at the end of the ages, now already partially accomplished in Christ Jesus. God through Christ has dealt with sin, and so Christ is called the place where, or the means whereby, sin is dealt with; in him the purpose for which the Mercy Seat (Heb. *kappōreth*, Greek *hilastērion*) had been intended was perfectly fulfilled. God's new act of redemption in Christ binds us to himself as the Israelites had been bound by the blood of the Mosaic covenant, and so it is said to have taken place through the blood of Christ.

Morris contends that Dodd and T. W. Manson have not said the last word. He believes that *hilastērion* bears the same meaning as it does in 4 Macc. xvii. 21–22: '. . . they have become a ransom (*antipsuchon*) for the sin of the nation; and through the blood of these righteous men, and their propitiatory (*hilastērion*) death, the Divine Providence rescued Israel which till that time had suffered evil'.[37] But there is a great difference between this passage, where the substitutionary doctrine is explicitly stated, and Rom. iii. 23ff., where the language is allusive and ambiguous. If *hilastērion* in Rom. iii. 25 does not describe Christ as the new and greater *kappōreth*, but presupposes the thought similar to that found in 4 Macc., we must surely suppose that St. Paul employs the language of substitutionary propitiation in order to describe the result rather than the *modus operandi* of the work of Christ; the event recorded in 4 Macc. is not a parallel to, but a type of the work of Christ. Morris rightly remarks that the

---

[36] *The New Testament and Rabbinic Judaism* (Jordan Lectures, 1952; London, 1956), p 272.   [37] Op. cit. p. 170.

object of St. Paul in Rom. iii. 21ff. is to show how God dealt with the situation caused by the fact that his wrath rested upon mankind because of sin. He makes it clear that the wrath of God is not to be compared with the capricious spite of a pagan deity,[38] and he approves of Maldwyn Hughes's description of it as: 'An eternal recoil against the unholy on the part of the all-holy God'.[39] But if the notion of the wrath of God has been so transformed, the notion of propitiation must be transformed *pari passu*. The recoil of God against sin must not be quenched, or God will cease to be Holy. God's hatred of sin can be 'pro-pitiated' only by the abolition of sin. Christ deals with sin, not by throwing a cloth over the eyes of God but by setting us, at the cost of his own life, in a relationship within which sin can be done away. The New Testament speaks of Christ as a sacrifice of a transcendent nature. It is a mistake to recognize the transcendence of Christ over the old sacrifices and yet to retain the *rationale* of the old sacrifices in explaining his work. Christ was a new and greater sacrifice, and if we are to explain his work, we must invoke a new and greater theory of sacrifice. † A theory of sacrifice which can do justice to the death of Christ must transcend the theory which lies behind the substitutionary death ascribed to the seven brethren in 4 Macc. just as much as Christ himself transcends the seven brethren.[40] We are so familiar with the application to Christ of Old Testament figures like Vine, Shepherd, Son, etc., that we forget that they can be ascribed to him only in an analogical sense. It is in this way that I would understand whatever passages in St. Paul are to be interpreted on the basis of substitution. There is, of course, no passage in his writing where a substitutionary theory of Christ's death is stated explicitly and unambiguously, although there are several places where the thought of substitution cannot be excluded. On the other hand, there is a consistent strand of 'participatory' thought, and it is here, if anywhere, that we are to find St. Paul's theory of the *modus operandi* of the atonement through the death of Christ. This does not mean that the death of Our Lord is to be regarded as a 'mere' sequel to his life. Rather, the total work of God in Christ for our salvation, including the incarnation, the life, the

[38] Op. cit. p. 130.
[39] *What is the Atonement?* (London, n.d.), pp. 54f.
[40] L. Cerfaux, *Christ*, pp. 146–7 takes a similar view of the sacrificial aspect of the death of Christ.

death, the resurrection, and the heavenly session, is to be regarded as constituting a single saving act by which the Second Person of the Trinity shared all that is human, sin alone excepted, in order that we might be united with him by baptism and thereby share his life as he had shared our life and death. †

Two verses must now be examined which are not strictly relevant to St. Paul's thought on the death of Christ, but have played a large part in the history of Pauline scholarship. The first is really concerned with the church, namely Col. i. 24, 'It is now my happiness to suffer for you. This is my way of helping to complete (*antanaplērō*), in my poor human flesh, the full tale of Christ's afflictions still to be endured (*ta husterēmata tōn thlipseōn tou Christou*)'. This verse does not mean that the work of Christ was in any sense imperfect or incomplete, so that what was missing had to be made up by St. Paul or anyone else. J. A. T. Robinson[41] suggests that the *anti* (instead of) contained in the compound verb *antanaplērō* means that St. Paul suffered instead of *the Colossians*, not instead of Christ: If this plausible and attractive suggestion is true, we are still faced with the fact that the sufferings of Christ 'overflow' into His Body, the church.

C. F. D. Moule[42] distinguishes two points:

1. The reason why there are post-Calvary sufferings at all is that there is a 'quota' which must be endured before the end. This is an example of 'Blood of the Martyrs'-theology, the place of the Martyrs being taken by the Messianic community, the church.

2. No Christian still in this life has yet completed the tale of suffering which his union with the Suffering Servant implies. The two points are both necessary. The first explains why there is suffering to be borne and the second why it is the Christians who have to bear it. The reason the Christians bear it is to be understood in the light of St. Paul's 'participatory' thought: we participate with Adam in sin and death; and we participate in death and resurrection with Christ. Baptism is a once-for-all participation in the once-for-all Death and Resurrection of Jesus Christ. But if we are risen with Christ in Baptism (Col. iii. 1), we live a 'risen' 'baptized' life, that is, a life infused by the transforming power of Christ's saving acts. It would seem that

---

[41] *The Body*, S.B.T., no. 5, (London, 1952).
[42] *The Epistle to the Colossians and to Philemon* (Cambridge, 1957), pp. 74–80.

the death of Christ, just because it is once-for-all, not in spite of the fact that it is once-for-all, has lasting effects. And these include a reflection in the church of His suffering. This does not mean that the sacrifice of Christ was 'imperfect' and had to be suplemented by the Eucharist or by the sufferings of the church. The moon is not an independent source of light which makes good the shortcomings of the sun; it reflects the light of the sun. In the same way, Calvary is reflected in the Eucharist and in the suffering of the church.

Moule expresses St. Paul's theology of the Atonement and of the church by means of the Suffering Servant. This is an accurate *translation* of St. Paul's thought at Col. i. 24 into terms of language which, here at least, he does not employ. It is not legitimate to see the figure of the Servant in a passage merely because the thought of the passage can be translated into Suffering Servant-language. For example, Cullmann[43] maintains that although St. Paul's writings include few direct quotations which show that he was familiar with the applications of the '*ebed Yahweh*' concept to Christ, yet 'the idea of the vicarious suffering of the Servant of God is undoubtedly present'. This seems quite illegitimate. It is, of course, true that for St. Paul, if it had not been for the vicarious sufferings of Christ, we should all have been overwhelmed by sin and death. But because Christ and the Servant both suffered vicariously, it does not follow, in default of further evidence, that St. Paul identified them. Moule, it should be noted, does not do so, although he uses Suffering-Servant-language.

We may note at this point that although St. Paul does quote from those passages of Isaiah which Duhm isolated as 'Servant Songs', he does not himself use the figure of the Servant with reference to Our Lord's vicarious suffering. In Rom. x. 15, Isa. lii. 7, liii. 1 are quoted to account for the failure of Israel to recognize the message, and in Rom. xv. 21 St. Paul quotes Isa. lii. 15 to justify his own preaching: in neither case does St. Paul refer to Christ's vicarious sufferings, and it would seem gratuitous to read this thought into the Apostle's language merely because the Suffering Servant is mentioned in adjacent verses of Isaiah. This point has been argued by M. D. Hooker.[44]

---

[43] *Christology of the New Testament*, E.T. (London, 1959), p.76.
[44] *Jesus and the Servant* (London, 1959), pp. 116–23.

This conclusion runs counter to much recent thought, and some scholars have expressed their disagreement, but no solid evidence has been advanced to counter Miss Hooker's arguments. J. Jeremias[45] points out, truly enough, that the Jewish background is accorded a somewhat brief treatment in her book. This can not affect the main issue, which is what evidence the *New Testament* yields. Jeremias tacitly admits that Miss Hooker has made good her case in respect of the few actual quotations, but urges that she has not given a satisfactory account of the 'numerous allusions'. But he refers only to 'many' (*polloi*) and 'on behalf of' (*huper*). *Huper* is one of the commonest words in the Greek language; it is found 149 times in the New Testament. Polloi and other forms of *polus* occur 353 times in the New Testament. It is surely hazardous to suppose that St. Paul or any other writer was referring to the Servant because he uses in common with the 'Servant Songs' of Isaiah words which are so common that it would be difficult to write Greek at all without them.

Eph. v. 1–2, 'Live in love as Christ loved you, and gave himself up on your behalf (*paredōken heauton huper humōn*) as an offering and sacrifice whose fragrance is pleasing to God (*prosphoran kai thusian tō Theō eis osmēn euōdias*)' was regarded by Rashdall[46] as a substitutionary passage, though he admits in a footnote that the language is metaphorical.

If we are correct in supposing that *Ephesians* was written not by St. Paul himself but by one of his followers, this passage is not relevant. Since, however, we cannot be dogmatic concerning the authorship of this epistle, the passage must be examined. *Eis osmēn euōdias* (whose fragrance is pleasing) is a stock phrase in the LXX, being found at Gen. viii. and on about forty other occasions. 'As an offering and sacrifice (*prosphoran kai thusian*)' reflects Ps. xl. 6 (LXX, xxxix. 7), 'Sacrifice and offering (*thusian kai prosphoran*) thou dost not desire; but thou hast given me an open ear'. Since the ear was the 'organ of obedience' we can fairly paraphrase, 'Thou hast given me an obedient heart'.

It is difficult to be sure to what extent 'Paul' was referring to the whole verse. He does not quote in full, as does *Hebrews* (x. 5–9). On the other hand, both in the Psalm and in *Ephesians*

[45] In a review of the above, *J.T.S.*, N.S. xi. Pt. 1, (1960), pp. 140–44.
[46] *The Idea of Atonement in Christian Theology* (London, 1919), pp. 98–9 and p. 99 n. 1.

the context is ethical. Perhaps 'Paul' means that God does not want sacrifice but does want obedience. The kind of 'sacrifice' which He requires from the Ephesians is outlined in the second half of Ephesians iv.

It is of course certain that this verse represents Our Lord's self-sacrifice as pleasing to God. But why did it please Him? Did He want the death and pain in themselves to appease His wrath, which otherwise would have demanded the death of all men, or did God desire that all men should live, so that He was 'pleased' by the death of Christ, not for its own sake but because without this involvement and participation Christ could not have mediated life to the world? Armitage Robinson[47] warns us against pressing this verse too strongly to a doctrinal use; similar language is applied to the gifts the Philippians sent to St. Paul by the hand of Epaphroditus in Phil. iv. 19, 'It is a fragrant offering, an acceptable sacrifice, pleasing to God (osmēn euōdias, thusian dektēn, euareston tō Theō).' Similar phraseology is applied by St. Paul to his own missionary activities in 2 Cor. ii. 14–16, though the verbal parallels are not so close.

The Resurrection of Christ

St. Paul's theology of the Resurrection of Christ must be considered very briefly. This is possible, in spite of the great importance of the subject, because in St. Paul's thought the Death and Resurrection are so closely bound together that throughout this chapter we have been compelled to treat of the Resurrection of Our Lord in discussing His death. Further, the matter has been dealt with in a most admirable fashion by D. M. Stanley S.J. in *Christ's Resurrection in Pauline Soteriology.*[48]

Rom. iv. 24–5, 'It (faith) is to be "counted" in the same way to us who have faith in the God who raised Jesus our Lord from the dead; for he was delivered to death for our misdeeds, and raised to life to justify us,' puts the matter in a nutshell. First, it is God who raised Christ from the dead. 1 Thess. iv. 14, it is true, does say that 'Jesus died and rose again', but there is no other Pauline passage where we read that 'Jesus rose'. Always we are told that He 'was raised' which presupposes that God raised

---

[47] *St. Paul's Epistle to the Ephesians* (London, 1904²), pp. 114–15 and 196–7.
[48] *Analecta Biblica* no. 13, (Rome, 1961).

M

Him. (1 Cor. xv. 4 etc.), 1 Thess. i. 10, 'His Son Jesus, whom he raised from the dead', expresses the typical Pauline emphasis.[49]

Secondly, the death and resurrection are integrally united in God's purpose for our salvation. This is clear from 2 Cor. v. 15, 'His purpose in dying for all was that men, while still in life, should cease to live for themselves, and should live for him who for their sake died and was raised to life;' Rom. viii. 34, 'Christ who died, and, more than that, was raised from the dead;' 1 Thess. v. 10; 1 Cor. xv. 20; Rom. xiv. 9, already quoted in this present chapter.

That this was St. Paul's teaching is beyond dispute. Its *rationale* is less obvious. Incidentally, the Resurrection of Christ did counter the charges that He died because He was sinful, or that He could not have been the Messiah because He 'failed'. On rational grounds it might be argued that, since One had been raised from the dead, it was not impossible that others might be also. But the main explanation for the power of Christ's Resurrection to save is once again 'participation'. Because we have been made one with Christ we share in His Resurrection. This does not justify us in separating His death from His Resurrection, and saying that whereas on the one hand His death saved us from sin and death, on the other hand the Resurrection of Christ leads to our resurrection. Murdoch E. Dahl has argued this point in a convincing manner.[50]

The Ascension

St. Paul clearly believed that in some sense Christ went up into Heaven, as we can tell from Rom. x. 6, 'Who can go up to heaven, *Tis anabēsetai eis ton ouranon* (Deut. xxx. 12), that is, to bring Christ down, *katagagein*'. As Richardson points out, this does not necessarily mean that St. Paul thought in terms of the vivid symbolism used by St. Luke.[51] Phil. ii. 9, 'Therefore God raised him to the heights, *huperupsōsen*, lit. "hyper-exalted," ' may well point in the same direction. J. G. Davies[52] shows that

[49] cf. 1 Cor. vi. 14, xv. 15; 2 Cor. i. 9, iv. 14; Col. ii. 20 among other passages. But verbs passive in form, like ' he was raised ' are often virtually active in meaning, cp. *Grammar of New Testament Greek*, J. H. Moulton, iii., N. Turner, (Edinburgh, 1963), p. 57.

[50] *The Resurrection of the Body* S.B.T., no. 36, (London, 1962), Additional Note, A, pp. 96–97.

[51] *Introduction*, pp. 198–200.

[52] *He Ascended into Heaven* (London, 1958), p. 28f.

the simple verb *hupsoō* is connected with 'going up,' *anabainō*, and probably does refer to a 'lifting upwards.' Mary Magdalene could have said that on the first Easter morning the Resurrection had already taken place, but that Christ had not yet 'ascended.' Others might simply say 'Christ is risen' without limiting the Resurrection to a mere emergence from the tomb. No one believes that Christ rose from the dead and still walks the earth, so all those who say that Christ has been raised from the dead mean that He has in some sense ascended. But strictly speaking, the words *egeirō*, raise, and *anistēmi*, arise, are normally used where a simple standing on the ground is the result.[53] It is true that those who *said* 'Christ has been raised' probably *thought* something more than merely 'has been raised so as to stand erect on the ground'; this only serves to strengthen the point made by Davies, which is that in St. Paul's belief Christ had in some sense ascended.

Davies also contends that St. Paul believed in the *descensus ad inferos*[54] on the basis of Rom. x. 7, 'Who can go down to the abyss, *abusson*, to bring Christ up from the dead, *ek nekrōn*'. He points out that St. Paul changed the word 'sea', which stands in the LXX and M.T. of Deut. xxx. 13, the passage he is quoting, and substituted *abusson*, which in the LXX is normally employed to render the Hebrew *tehōm*, 'deep'. We must first ask what is meant by '*descensus ad inferos*'. St. Paul explains his own words by saying 'to bring Christ up from the dead' and he unquestionably believed that Our Lord went down among the dead. But this verse gives us no reason to suppose that he held any of the other beliefs which have later been designated by the phrase *descensus ad inferos*.

But far the most important point concerning the Ascension of Christ is to ask how it differed from the ascending into Heaven of Elijah. Elijah merely ascended: Jesus ascended and took His seat on the right hand of God (Rom. viii. 34; Col. iii. 1; Eph. i. 20). It is unnecessary to trace the history of this piece of symbolism to its pre-Israelite cultic background; we need mention only Ps. cx. 1, 'The Lord says to my lord: "Sit at my right hand. . ."' St. Paul certainly means that Christ shared in some way the sovereignty of God. On the other hand, a distinction between Father and Son is maintained in the only Pauline text which can be quoted in support of Christ's Heavenly Intercession, Rom. viii.

[53] ibid. pp. 30–33.   [54] ibid. pp. 27–28.

34, 'Christ . . . who is at God's right hand and indeed pleads our cause'.

The whole drama of Redemption is expressed in symbolic language. It is not of course mere illustrative, ornamental symbolism which he could easily have translated into 'plain language,' though it may be important for us to 'translate' his symbolism into other symbols, the better to apprehend what is expressed by both sets of symbols. In any case, St. Paul himself uses more than one set of symbols. The main consistent set of symbolism presupposes participation. Our sin and need is expressed in terms of 'participation' in Adam and his sin. Christ 'came down' to participate in human life, like someone who descends a cliff-face to rescue people trapped at the bottom by the incoming sea. Through Christ's death and our baptism participation is effected; we are linked with Christ. Here the symbolism is obscure. Christ is risen and has ascended. We are risen with Him, but our mortal bodies have not been transformed, and will not be until He returns in glory. Our human life is characterized by an undeniable element of the 'not yet' as well as by the 'already-once-for-all.'

CHAPTER SEVEN

HOW CHRIST'S WORK AFFECTS MEN

i. INTRODUCTORY

> If Christ a thousand times
> In Bethlehem were born,
> But was not born in thee,
> For thee He lived in vain.

The problem raised by these somewhat sentimental lines is a real one: how does the work of God in Christ become effective for human beings? Within the framework of St. Paul's thought the answer can be outlined by means of two phrases, 'the solidarity of man' and 'faith-baptism'.

It is not superfluous to introduce again the concept of human solidarity, solidarity in the first man Adam, and solidarity in the last Adam, since it is a basic presupposition for most of the strata of the Bible, and serves to distinguish them from the thought of the western world, which during the past few centuries has been mainly, though by no means exclusively, individualistic in tone. The collectivism typical of Biblical thought has important functions to perform in the dynamics of the Christian doctrine of salvation; and its replacement by individualism has left gaps which have often been filled in a regrettable manner. As Christian theology has relaxed its grasp upon the Biblical concept of solidarity, it has attempted to explain how Christ's work affects the Christian either by invoking a 'mechanical', 'external' theory of the imputation of Christ's merits to the believer or by distorting the theology of Baptism, so that the sacrament appears to be quasi-magical, or by laying undue emphasis upon faith, and isolating it from its true position in Christian life and theology; the result is that we appear to be saved by our own believing. St. Paul does not misrepresent either faith or baptism in this fashion, since he was not compelled to overwork them in order to fill a gap left by a loss of the presupposition of solidarity.[1]

---

[1] cf. Richardson, *Introduction* p. 236, and p. 244 and note; also Davies, *Paul and Rabbinic Judaism* (1955²), p. 273

In the twentieth century we inevitably view faith and baptism through the smoky haze left by centuries of theological battles, and it is essential by way of preliminary clarification to draw certain distinctions. First, there is no conflict in St. Paul's theology, between 'justification by faith', and 'judgement according to works': for him these 'doctrines' are not conflicting answers to the same question, but are concerned with different questions altogether. When he speaks of justification by faith, St. Paul is denying the false view that we can earn something by merits, as if we could acquire rights against God, and when he speaks of judgement according to works he is opposing a different error, the belief that conduct does not matter.

Secondly, when we moderns consider Baptism, we are haunted by the thought of infants who, it would appear, are baptized in deference to social convention alone; their parents sometimes seem devoid of all Christian convictions, so that Baptism is divorced from faith. Again, a man may have received Christian Baptism, either as an infant or as an adult; he may even give intellectual assent to the main articles of the Christian Faith; and yet his conduct is disgraceful judged not necessarily by Christian standards, but even by those of decent paganism. To us these are genuine problems, and no ready solution is available. But we must forget these contemporary questions if we are to understand the Apostle correctly, since the situation presupposed by his theology of Baptism, whether infants were then baptized or no, is one in which adult converts from Judaism or from Paganism accepted the Good News, received the renewal given in Baptism and lived henceforth a new life on the ethical plane, and thus preserved the unity of the sacramental element, the ethical element, and the element of faith.

It will be necessary to examine St. Paul's theory of Justification, to consider what he means by Faith, and finally to enquire how he conceives the relation between these two.

ii. JUSTIFICATION

The words 'justify' and 'justification' in the English Bible represent two Greek words, both of which stem from the root *dik-*, *dikaioō* and *dikaiosunē* respectively; the latter word is in some cases rendered by 'righteousness'. The meaning of these

words is not illuminated by evidence drawn from the field of
secular Greek, and for their elucidation we must have recourse to
the Hebrew Bible, which influenced the use of these Greek words
by St. Paul and other New Testament writers through the medium
of the LXX.

In the LXX *dikaioō* (justify) and its cognates *dikaios* (just),
dikaiosunē (justice or justification) and *dikaiōma* (commandment),
together with their rare cousins *dikē* (penalty; in St. Paul only at
2 Thess. i. 9), *dikaiōsis* (acquittal or vindication; in N.T. only at
Rom. iv. 25 and v. 18) and *dikaiokrisia* (righteous judgement; in
N.T. only at Rom. ii. 5 and as a variant at 2 Thess. i. 5) are
extremely common, and represent a number of Hebrew words;
but in the vast majority of cases they correspond to Hebrew words
derived from the root TSDK, notably *tsādhak*, justify or vindicate,
tsaddik, righteous, and *tsedek* or *tsedhākāh*, righteousness or
justification. It is mainly on the basis of the Old Testament meaning of this group of words that we must seek to understand the
significance of 'justification' for St. Paul. The original force of the
root is disputed. Snaith[2] maintains that it was 'to be straight', so
that a judge is one who makes things straight or restores them to
their original rectitude.

When we pass on from etymology to usage, we find such
phrases as Exod. xxiii. 7, 'For I will not acquit (M.T. *tsādhak*,
LXX *dikaioō*) the wicked,' which is reflected at Isa. v. 23. On the
basis of such passages as these Morris concludes that the main
force of this group of words is juridical,[3] although he makes it
clear that the law is inherent in God Himself, and does not control
Him *ab extra*.[4] Quell, writing in the *T.W.N.T.*, is more cautious;
he accepts the presumption that the theological meaning grew out
of the juristic, although he agrees that it is not directly demon-
strable.[5] Even this guarded statement should be accepted only
with reservations. Theological meanings do not always retain the
colour of their semantic background. Even if this language was
derived from the law courts, we must not without more ado
interpret it on a strictly legal basis. Further, in English, 'law' has
associations which are not present in Hebrew thought, so that
even if it is true to say that these words have a juridical back-

---

[2] *The Distinctive Ideas of the Old Testament* (London, 1944). p. 73.
[3] *The Apostolic Preaching of the Cross* (London, 1955²), p. 226f.
[4] ibid. p. 233.
[5] *T.W.N.T.*, ii. pp. 177-8, E.T., *Righteousness* (London, 1951), pp. 4–5.

ground, it may still be misleading. To us the law is something mechanical, which operates impersonally, or even blindly. It is something abstract, something outside and above the people whom it governs. Such a mechanical, impersonal concept is far removed from the thought of the Bible. For the Jew the Torah was no abstract system: it was based upon the will of a personal, living God, and it was binding upon the Israelites whom He had chosen and made into His own people by covenant.

There are, moreover, passages in which it is, to say the least, far from clear that the meaning of these words is juridical at all. In Judges v. 11 we read, 'There they repeat the triumphs (M.T. *tsidkōth*, the construct plural of *tsedhākāh*, literally "righteous acts", LXX *dikaiosunas*) of the Lord'. It is clear from the context that the word refers to the successful wars of the Lord against the enemies of His people, though Morris maintains that this passage shows how God's acts were thought of as acts of justice on the ground that to the Jew He was above all a judge.[6] It is fortunate that we do not have to rely upon a passage in which the Hebrew labours under such suspicion of being corrupt as it does in Judges v. Isa. xlvi. 13, 'I bring my deliverance, it is not far off', employs the same Greek and Hebrew words, and is a prophecy of the deliverance of the Jews from captivity in Babylon. Further, in Jer. xxiii. 6 we are told that 'The Lord is our righteousness'. This is not a prophecy that God will impute the merits of Christ to believers. This prophecy was fulfilled less than seventy years after it was uttered, and it foretells the 'righteous act' or 'act of vindication' performed by Yahweh when He brought back His people from the north country and put them in their proper place, in the land of Israel.

Dodd[7] is probably right when he translates Gen. xxxviii. 26, 'She is more righteous than I, "She is in the right," Heb. *tsādkāh*, Greek *dedikaiōtai*, over against me': Tamar had indeed 'put herself in the right' over against Judah, her father-in-law. This suggests what is no doubt the correct interpretation of Luke x. 29, 'But he wanted to vindicate himself, *dikaiōsai heauton*': the lawyer wished to put himself in the right by showing that the question which he had asked Jesus was not merely trivial. Dodd[8]

---

[6] *The Apostolic Preaching of the Cross* (London, 1955), p. 230.
[7] *The Bible and the Greeks* (London, 1954²), p. 46.
[8] ibid. p. 47.

further remarks: 'The Hebrew conception of the function of a judge tends to be not so much to apply with strict impartiality an abstract principle of justice, but rather to come to the assistance of the injured person and vindicate him'.

It is almost universally agreed that the word justify (*dikaioō*) does not mean 'make righteous'. Verbs ending in *-oō* are commonly found in a factitive sense when derived from adjectives with a physical, as opposed to a moral meaning; in the latter case they have the force 'to regard as', 'to treat as', not 'to make'.[9] Normal usage does not allow us to translate 'make righteous',[10] although it is difficult to avoid such rendering in Ps. lxxiii.Septuagint lxii. 13.

> 'All in vain have I kept my heart clean
> (*edikaiōsa, zikkithi*)
> and washed my hands in innocence.'

This, however, is a limiting case, and ought not to be regarded as normative[11] for the interpretation of the N.T. Morris argues that a declaratory process rather than a making righteous is intended; he does so on the basis of (M.T.) Ps. li. 4, (Septuagint) l. 6, 'So that thou art justified (*dikaiōthēs*) in thy sentence', since God already is righteous, and can not be made so, but only declared to be so. On the other hand, this does not apply with the same force in the case of men, who are by no means righteous. Morris does not, however, press his point too far; he remarks that the distinction between imputed and imparted righteousness becomes less important once we accept the fact that the righteous are those accepted by God,[12] and he quotes with approval[13] Denney's[14] saying 'When He pronounces the sinner *dikaios*, he is *dikaios*'.

It has been suggested that the justified sinner is one who has acquired a new status.[15] This could, however, be misunderstood so as to suggest that, once the status has been conferred, it becomes a 'quality' of the sinner, just as an iron bar retains, for a time at

[9] J. H. Moulton, *Grammar of N.T. Greek* ii, (Edinbugh, 1956²), p. 397.
[10] cf. *Romans* (I.C.C., Edinburgh, 1895), detached note, 'The word *dikaios* and its cognates', pp. 28–31.
[11] *The Apostolic Preaching of the Cross* (London, 1955), p. 234.
[12] Op. cit. p. 246.
[13] Op. cit. p. 247.
[14] *The Christian Doctrine of Reconciliation* (London. 1917), p. 292.
[15] Anderson Scott, *Christianity according to St. Paul* (Cambridge, 1961²), p. 55.

least, the quality of being magnetic once it has been magnetized. It is safer, therefore, to speak of justification not as a status or as a quality but as a relationship. A man may have a weight in relation to the earth, but the weight is always dependent upon the gravitational pull of the earth, and does not belong to the man as such. In the same way, a man has not righteousness in himself, even a righteousness given gratuitously by God: What God has gratuitously conferred upon men is a right relationship with Himself.

The nature of this relationship is frequently obscured for modern investigators by the fact that, when we ask who is justified and who is not, we are contrasting non-believers with believers among the Gentiles, whereas St. Paul was contrasting Jews with Gentiles. The Jew might have applied the expression 'right relationship' to the peace (shālōm) with God which he enjoyed by means of the covenant. This 'peace'[16] had been established by God on Mount Sinai with Israel as a whole, and the ancient practice of circumcision was regarded by some post-Christian Jews as the entry into the covenant of the individual. The relationship with God which the Christian enjoyed was in St. Paul's thought modelled partly upon the covenant relationship which the Jew enjoyed through the work of God on Mount Sinai and through circumcision, which was a 'sign of the covenant' (Gen. xvii. 11) between God and Abraham, and partly upon the favourable judgement which for the Jew still lay in the future. For St. Paul 'justification' has an eschatological ring; it does not belong exclusively to the sphere of realized eschatology, since a futuristic meaning is retained in Rom. ii. 13, 'It is not by hearing the law, but by doing it that men will be justified before God', and in Gal. v. 5 'For to us, our hope of attaining that righteousness which we eagerly await is the work of the Spirit through faith'. †

Finally, we shall do well to remember Davies's warning that in some contexts justification is merely one metaphor among many others employed by St. Paul to describe his deliverance through Christ, and that we are not justified in petrifying a metaphor into a dogma.[17] God, for St. Paul, is not like a Life Assurance office which 'accepts' a man because he comes up to a certain minimum standard of physical fitness. Rather, He is like a family doctor who treats a patient simply and solely because he is sick and in need of

---

[16] cf. Stauffer, *New Testament Theology*, E.T. (London, 1955), p. 143f.
[17] *Paul and Rabbinic Judiasm* (London, 1955²), pp. 221–2.

treatment. But a doctor has not finished with a man when he has accepted him as a patient; there still lies ahead the work of effecting a cure. In the same way, it is part of God's purpose for us to make us ethically pure, but this is not what St. Paul means by justification, nor does he believe that any merits whatsoever, realized or foreseen, constitute the condition of justification.

In the LXX *pistis*, faith, corresponds to Hebrew words of the *'mn* group, such as *'emeth* or *'emunāh*. The basic thought which lies behind these Hebrew words is 'truthful' or 'reliable'. The Hebrew *'āman*, make firm, means in the hiphil 'believe', as in Gen. xv. 6. In the LXX *pisteuo*, the normal Greek word for 'believe' usually corresponds to *'āman* in the hiphil, and the meaning is 'believe.' It used to be thought that such words *meant* 'unshakeable' in the case of God or 'trust in' when used of men. But this view has been effectively challenged by Barr.[18]

In the N.T. *pistis* refers to the faithfulness of God (Rom. iii. 3) or, more frequently, to human belief. St. Paul often employs words of the *pistis* group in contexts which have nothing to do with justification, and it will be convenient to clear the ground by eliminating some of these significations of the word at the outset. First, we may notice the 'faith strong enough to move mountains' of 1 Cor. xiii. 2, which is connected with the power to heal in 1 Cor. xii. 9. This is something which one Christian may possess and another lack, whereas 'justification' faith is one of the distinguishing marks of the Christian as such. Again, *pistis* can designate the content of the Christian faith, 'that which is believed', as in Gal. i. 23, 'Our former persecutor is preaching the good news of the faith which once he tried to destroy'.[19] There is another sense of the word in which faith may be said to vary in intensity from one period to another: this clearly cannot be the 'faith' through which God saves. Cases of this use are found in 1 Thess. iii. 10, where the apostle prays to be allowed to 'amend your faith where it falls short', and in 2 Cor. x. 15, where he expresses the hope that the faith of the Corinthians will grow.

That 'believe' includes an intellectual element is placed beyond dispute by Rom. x. 9, 'If on your lips is the confession, "Jesus is Lord", and in your heart the faith that God raised him from the

---

[18] *The Semantics of Biblical Language* (Oxford, 1961), pp. 161–205.
[19] This use of the word recurs in Eph. iv. 5, and possibly also in Rom. i. 5 Gal. iii. 23.

dead, then you will find salvation', by Rom. vi. 8, 'But if we thus
died with Christ, we believe that we shall also come to life with
him', and by 1 Thess. iv. 14, 'We believe that Jesus died and rose
again'.

It is Bultmann's contention that 'Paul understands faith
primarily as obedience', but the evidence which he quotes can
hardly be held to justify so sweeping an assertion.[20] He tells us
that 2 Cor. ix. 13 describes (*beschreiben*) faith as obedience in
acknowledging the Gospel of Christ. The verse reads, 'Many will
give honour to God when they see how humbly you obey (*hupo-
tagē*) him, and how faithfully ('faithfully' is not in the Greek) you
confess (*homologias*) the Gospel of Christ'. St. Paul uses the word
'obey' when he might have used the word 'faith'. But two different
words may well be used in a similar situation without our being
entitled to say that one 'describes' the other. Certainly, 'faith'
carries overtones of 'obedience', but it would be wrong to claim
more. That 'faith' does indeed bear these overtones is made
evident by other passages which Bultmann[21] mentions. Rom. i. 8,
'Because all over the world they are telling the story of your faith
(*pistis*)' is paralleled by Rom. xvi. 19, 'The fame of your obedience,
(*hupakoē*) has spread everywhere'. It might be objected that
pistis in the first case, Rom. i. 8, refers to the content of the faith.
But this objection is not valid since in that case St. Paul would not,
'Thank God for you all' (Rom. i. 8). Even better evidence is
provided by Rom. x. 16, 'But not all have responded (*hupēkousan*,
lit. 'obeyed') to the good news. For Isaiah says, 'Lord, who has
believed (*episteusen*) our message?'

It has become clear that 'faith' can refer to intellectual acceptance. It can also carry overtones of the notion of obedience. It is
hardly to be disputed that for St. Paul the justification-faith
situation included trust, intellectual acceptance, and obedience.
We shall see further that, for the Apostle, justification 'by' faith
was a gift of God. It was in no sense a work; indeed, it was
sharply contrasted with circumcision and the works of the law.
Although St. Paul does use language which suggests that faith is a
'condition' of salvation, he does not mean that it is a prior condition; rather, faith is a result of God's activity. Faith, however, is
not caused by the Spirit. On the contrary, the Spirit comes to
those who already believe.

[20] *Theology*. i., pp. 314–5.   [21] ibid.

A background factor which must not be neglected is contemporary Jewish teaching on merits.[22] This may be illustrated by Syriac Apocalypse of Baruch, xiv. 12, 'For the righteous justly hope for the end, and without fear depart from this habitation, because they have with Thee a store of works preserved in treasuries'.[23] The faith of Abraham tended to be regarded as meritorious.[24] In 1 Macc. ii. 59 Mattathias, in his farewell speech assimilates the faith of Abraham to the fidelity and endurance of his own family, saying, 'Was not Abraham found faithful in temptation (*en peirasmo heurethē pistos*) and it was reckoned to him for righteousness'. Especially interesting is *Mek*. Exod. xiv. 15 (35e),[25], 'The faith (*'emunāh*) with which your father Abraham believed in me earned this, that I divided the sea for you'; God is then made to quote Gen. xv. 6, 'And he believed the Lord, and he reckoned it to him as righteousness'. This passage makes it obvious that faith was thought of as 'earning' something. It is against such a background as this that we must understand Rom. iv. 2, 'If Abraham was justified by anything he had done, then he has a ground for pride (*kauchēma*)'. But he had no such ground before God, and Rom. iv. 16, 'The promise was made on the ground of faith, in order that it might be a matter of sheer grace (*kata charin*)', Eph. ii. 8, 'For it is by his grace you are saved, through trusting him. It is not your own doing; it is God's gift, not a reward for work done'. St. Paul's teaching on justification by faith is concerned less with how man receives the gift than how God gives it, which is simply as a gift, due to His love alone, and not to anything which we are or do.

The difference between St. Paul and his opponents was in part one of intellectual framework. Rom. iv. 3, 'Abraham put his faith in God, and that faith was reckoned (*elogisthē*) to him as righteousness (*eis dikaiosunēn*)' could be understood on the basis of a calculus of merits and demerits, according to which each deed had attached to it a corresponding 'merit' ticket and the tickets of merit and demerit were totalled up; it would be essential to 'solvency' that the merits should be greater than the demerits. Against such a background the verse would be paraphrased, 'Abraham believed; the merit of his belief was credited to his

[22] Bonsirven, *Judaisme* ii., pp. 57–60, and G. F. Moore, *Judaism*, ii. pp. 98f.
[23] Charles, ii., pp. 490–1.
[24] Strack-Billerbeck, iii, pp. 186–201.
[25] ibid. p. 200.

account, and led to his being declared solvent.' The key phrase is 'was counted for' (*elogisthē*).

A man might wish to speak to a friend and think of going to visit him on foot. He might change his mind, and decide to go on his bicycle; in this case his bicycling would be 'counted for', that is, take the place of, walking. But if he finally decided to telephone, his use of the telephone, like his use of the bicycle, could be 'counted as', that is to say replace, walking. But telephoning would not replace walking in the same sense as bicyling would have done. Bicycling and walking are co-ordinate species of the same genus, locomotion, but speaking by telephone is communication without locomotion and must be assigned to a different genus altogether. The upshot of this illustration is that faith is not 'another kind of work' which is a species of the same genus and operates in the same way: faith and works do not belong to the same genus at all. The Apostle had not available to express his thought such convenient terms as 'species' and 'genus', but he puts the point as plainly as his linguistic equipment will allow in Rom. iv. 4–5, 'Now if a man does a piece of work, his wages are not "counted" as a favour; they are paid as a debt. But if without any work to his credit he simply puts his faith in him who "acquits the guilty", then his faith is indeed counted as righteousness'.

It must be made clear that the 'calculus of merits' as we have outlined it above was not universal Jewish doctrine. It is, however, a fair caricature of a type of language which did occur in Judaism.[26] It may be regarded as a limit towards which certain elements in Judaism tended, and it is a kind of thought which we should expect to find among Gentiles who had been evangelized by Jewish Christians. We may suppose that, with typical converts' fervour, they had become more Judaistic in some respects than the Jews themselves. It is men of this sort, according to W. Manson,[27] that St. Paul had in mind when he wrote the Epistle to the Romans.

It would be superfluous to discuss any further St. Paul's attitude to the Law and to circumcision; his view of the relation of faith to them both is unambiguously disclosed in Gal. iii. 2, 'Did you receive the Spirit by keeping the law or by "believing

---

[26] cf. Bonsirven, *Judaisme*, ii., pp. 57–60.
[27] William Manson, *The Epistle to the Hebrews* (London, 1951), esp. pp. 182–3.

the gospel message"?', and in Gal. v. 6, 'If we are in union with Christ circumcision makes no difference at all, nor does the want of it'.

Bultmann[28] maintains that the condition-character of 'faith' (*Der Sinn der pistis als Bedingung*) is established by certain passages[29]; he makes it clear that faith is the renunciation of any accomplishment (*Verzicht auf die Leistung*). The passages which he points to for the support of this claim are Gal. ii. 16, 'And so we too have put our faith in Christ Jesus, in order that we might be justified through this faith (*hina dikaiōthōmen ek pisteōs Christou*)', and other passages which speak of justification from or on the basis of (*ek*) faith,[29] or through (*dia*) faith.[30] Condition (*Bedingung*) is frankly misleading, though Bultmann does not, of course, entertain the thought that faith is a prior condition or that God justifies some *because* they believe, as if faith were the criterion by which God selected those who were to be justified. St. Paul was in no position to use inverted commas. If he had been he might have said, 'We are not justified on condition that we keep the Law; the 'condition' is faith—and that is no condition at all, but acceptance'. St. Paul had to rely largely upon such prepositions as from (*ek*) or unto (*eis*), which have to be 'unpacked' and rendered 'on the basis of' or 'which leads to' if their true meaning is to be brought out.

Faith is not the reason why God justifies some and not others, but the 'response' of those who are justified; in the same way, electric current does not pass through wire because the wire is glowing and emitting light and heat; glowing is a 'response' of the wire to the current which passes through it. Rom. x. 17, 'We conclude that faith is awakened by the message (*akoē*), and the message that awakens it comes through the word of Christ', suggests such a view. That the gift of the Spirit is the result of faith, and not its cause, is made clear by Gal. iii. 14, 'So that we might receive the promised Spirit through faith'. Faith, then, is not the reason why one person is justified and another is not: it describes those who in fact are justified, and distinguishes them from those who put their trust in the works of the Law and from those who proved unfaithful (*apisteō*, Rom. iii. 3). †

[28] *Theology*, i. pp. 316–7.
[29] Rom. iii. 30, v. 1, ix. 30, x. 6; Gal. iii. 7f., 11f., 24; v. 5.
[30] Rom. iii. 22, 30; Gal. iii. 14, Phil. iii. 9.

iii. BAPTISM

(a) *The Background*

St. Paul's teaching on Baptism is an integral and vitally important element in his theology. It is in line with the thought of the earliest church, so far as we can reconstruct it, though any such reconstruction is necessarily speculative. Christian Baptism certainly has for its background the mission of John the Baptist and shares with the Baptist's thought its eschatological perspective. The Baptism of John no doubt owes something to Jewish Proselyte Baptism, but we must resist the temptation to see in John a member of the Qumran community. The latter may in general be identified with the Essenes, although we must not be uncritical about this, or assume that either the settlers of Qumran or the Essenes were entirely homogeneous throughout their history. It is true that the *Manual of Discipline* speaks of ablutions but there is no reason to suppose that the first of these was in the fullest sense a rite of initiation, like the Baptism of John or Christian Baptism; it was, after all, frequently repeated. We have no reason to suppose that the 'tanks' at Qumran were employed for initiatory submersion: they may well have been intended for purposes of storage.[31]

Baptism, as a rite of initiation, is first mentioned in the New Testament itself, but the fact that it is mentioned, without any word of explanation, suggests, although it does not prove, that it was already familiar. The schools of Hillel and Shammai debated about the immersion of Proselytes, probably in the first century A.D.[32] There are also possible references to Jewish Proselyte Baptism in Epictetus,[33] whose *Discourses* date from the end of the First Century A.D.; and in the Sibylline Oracles, Book iv, lines 65–6, we read:

'And wash your whole bodies in ever running rivers
And, stretching your hands to heaven, seek forgiveness for your former sins.[34]

[31] Rowley, 'The Baptism of John and the Qumran Sect', in *New Testament Essays, Studies in Memory of T. W. Manson* (Manchester, 1959), p. 219.

[32] Strack-Billerbeck, i., pp. 102–13; esp., Mishna, *Pesahim* (Passover) viii. 8, E .T. Danby, Oxford, 1933, p. 148; and *Eduyoth* (Testimonies), v. 2, Danby, p. 431.

[33] *Discourses*, Book II, Ch. 9, ed. and tr. Oldfather, Loeb Library (London and Cambridge, Mass., 1925), pp. 272–3. The reference may be to Christians, not Jews.   [34] Charles, i., p. 396.

Yet these verses suggest not conversion at all, but rather repeated
cleansing after the manner of the Essenes; this is actually stated
in Book iv., lines 592–3:

'Rising early from their bed, and ever cleansing their flesh
With water.'[35]

These lines from the Sybilline Oracles, which are so often
quoted in an attempt to ascertain the latest possible date for the
introduction of Proselyte Baptism are really quite irrelevant. It is
possible, however, that evidence for the observance of this rite by
Jews of the first Christian century may be derived from the
satirist Juvenal. Writing about 127 A.D., he says that it is the
custom of Jews to show the way only to those who practise the
same religion, and to lead to the fountain which they seek only the
circumcised.[36] As the context shows, Juvenal means that a Jew
will tell only a fellow-Jew where to find water, but his allegation
may be based upon a Gentile misunderstanding of the fact that, in
Proselyte Baptism, circumcision comes before immersion.[37]

The 'order' of Proselyte Baptism is preserved in the Babylonian Talmud, *Yebāmōth* (Daughters-in-law), 47[A], and in *Gerim*
(Proselytes). Gavin prints translations of these two accounts in
parallel.[38] It is clear that what these describe is no mere formality.
Stress is laid upon the keeping of the Torah, especially the tithe
for the poor and abstention from certain forms of fat; in *Gerim*
mention is made of the creation and of the fact that Israel is God's
son; in *Yebāmōth* the world to come receives emphasis. But
though the rite of Proselyte Baptism may have provided the
framework for the Christian sacrament, we must look elsewhere
for the source of the content, especially since the two accounts of
Jewish Baptism in their present form would seem to reflect the
persecution of the Jews under Hadrian in the thirties of the
second century A.D.

Our evidence for John the Baptist is derived solely from the
New Testament and from Josephus. Dodd[39] has shown that the
Mandaean documents do not provide valid evidence for the life or
teaching of the Baptist; they show no verifiable knowledge of the

---

[35] ibid. p. 389.
[36] Satire xiv, 104–5.
[37] cf. Bonsirven, Judaisme, i, pp. 29–30.
[38] Gavin, *The Jewish Antecedents of the Christian Sacraments* (London, 1928),
pp. 33–35.
[39] *The Interpretation of the Fourth Gospel* (Cambridge, 1953), pp. 115–30.

N

first century which could not have been gathered from the New Testament; and John himself is often called *Jahja*, as in the Qur'an. The evidence of Josephus, who mentions John in one passage only,[40] is not very illuminating. He omits all reference to the Baptist's Messianic doctrine and assimilates his ethical teaching to that of contemporary moralism, associating it with a suspiciously sharp distinction between soul and body. Three great developments were made by John, if we may assume that he modelled his practice upon Proselyte Baptism as performed in his own day: he baptized Jews as well as Gentiles, he laid even greater stress upon the moral element, and he strengthened the eschatological tension (Matt. iii.; Luke iii. 1–21).

(b) *Baptism depends on the Work of Christ*

Baptism in St. Paul's eyes was not a piece of 'mere' symbolism which echoed the teaching derived from a non-historical myth: it was based upon the Crucifixion and Resurrection, both of which had occurred in the world of space-time-matter during his own lifetime, and in the land of Palestine where he was presumably domiciled at the time; and it was expected to have results in the lives of its recipients which their contemporaries might observe, in addition to those consequences which would be apparent only at the end of the world. 'Was it Paul who was crucified for you? Was it in the name of Paul that you were baptized?' (1 Cor. i. 13) leaves us in no doubt concerning the close connexion between Baptism and the death of Christ. Rom. vi. 4, 'By baptism we were buried with him, and lay dead', lays further stress upon the same point; and the words which immediately follow, 'In order that, as Christ was raised from the dead in the splendour of the Father, so also we might set our feet upon the new path of life', make it clear that moral consequences were expected. This was no 'pious' hope, no expression of a polite convention in language which had grown effete. St. Paul clearly supposed that those who had been through the purifying waters would have ceased from the practice of sinning (1 Cor. vi. 11).

Obviously, the events of Good Friday and Easter Day were in no sense *repeated* when a man was baptized, but in his Baptism

---

[40]*Antiquities of the Jews*, xviii. 5, 2; (xviii. 116–19, in Niese's numbering). This passage is reproduced in *The New Testament Background: Selected Documents* (ed. C. K. Barrett, London, 1956), pp. 197–8.

those events were *reflected*, and if they had never occurred, his immersion in water would not have been Christian Baptism at all. These
events did not belong to the 'dead past' but to the 'living past'.

It is tempting to say that a past 'event' had a present effect, so
powerful is the influence of a fashionable theological word such
as 'event'. But we are saved not by the 'events' of Good Friday
and Easter Day, but by the power of God in Jesus Christ, Who
brings those events to pass. An 'event' or happening is, after all,
an abstraction, a 'verbal' abstraction of the activity from the agent,
and the agent in this case is Christ. We are not baptized into the
name of an event but into the name of Christ. When St. Paul says
that we are baptized into Christ's death he means, not that we are
baptized into an abstraction, a past event, but into Christ Himself,
Who died and was raised from the dead. When we speak of the
'living past' we mean that the living Christ has certain powers as a
result of His past Crucifixion and Resurrection. To use the
language of later theology, the Second Person of the Trinity
assumed manhood; under this term we include all the work of
God in Christ for our salvation, not the incarnation in a narrow
sense alone. Through this 'contact' with the created world, Christ
had the power to 'build into Himself' members of the human
race, and this 'incorporation' is effected through faith-baptism.

'Incorporation' is not too strong a word, as we can see from 1
Cor. i. 13–17, Rom. vi. 3–4, Eph. iv. 5 and, above all, Gal. iii. 26–7,
'For through faith you are all sons of God, in union with Christ
Jesus. Baptized into union with him, you have all put on Christ as
a garment'. This passage also suggests that St. Paul applies the
phrase 'sons of God' to those who by Baptism have been linked in
death and resurrection with the Son of God. It is probable,
although Baptism is not explicitly mentioned in the following
passages, that in this sacrament the Christian confessed Jesus as
kurios (Lord) and claimed God as his own father by calling on
Him as *Abba*. Rom. x. 9, 'If on your lips is the confession (*homo-
logēsēs*), "Jesus is Lord",' certainly seems to be a baptismal
'confession' in the technical sense. Rom. viii. 15, 'The Spirit you
have received', (presumably in Baptism) is not a spirit of slavery
leading you back into a life of fear, but a spirit that makes us sons
(*pneuma huiothesias*), enabling us to cry 'Abba! Father'. In that
cry the Spirit of God joins with our own spirit in testifying that
we are God's children; and if children, then heirs, God's heirs and

Christ's fellow-heirs if we share his sufferings now. Rom. vi. 3, 'We were baptized into his death that we may share his splendour hereafter', (cf. Rom. vi. 15), is also probably baptismal in background, and the same may be said of Gal. iv. 6, 'To prove that you are sons, God has sent into our hearts the Spirit of his Son, crying, "Abba, Father" '. It is highly probable both that the historical fact of Christ's baptism by John the Baptist had a determining influence upon Christian Baptism, and that the New Testament accounts of Christ's Baptism were affected by the liturgical *paradosis* of the church. It is clear from Matt. iii. 17; Mark i. 11; Luke iii. 22 that Christ's baptism was associated with divine sonship. We can therefore be reasonably certain that in the mind of St. Paul and other first-century Christians men could be spoken of as 'becoming sons of God' in Baptism.

It would appear, then, that the effects of Christ's work are 'communicated' to us in baptism—we should never of course say 'baptism' without also thinking 'faith'—and that this 'communication' can be described as incorporation or sonship by adoption or as sharing in the death and resurrection of Christ. In Col. ii. 11 St. Paul says that Christians are 'not circumcised physically, but divested of the lower nature', and this expression he goes on in the next verse to associate with sharing Christ's burial in baptism. Now this is not metaphorical in the sense of being 'unreal'. St. Paul's doctrine of Baptism is wholly 'realistic', but, precisely because it transcends comprehension, he can point to this mysterious reality only by means of such metaphors as circumcision, adoption, burial, and incorporation. The word 'metaphor' may raise objections, partly because adoption and incorporation have become so familiar in this application that we cease to be aware of their metaphorical character. The word 'metaphor' may also cause alarm because it can be abused, and be employed in order to deny reality to baptism. The word metaphor is here applied to St. Paul's language on the subject of baptism to express the fact that he ascribes to baptism a reality which transcends the powers of literal language and therefore compels the apostle to have recourse to the language of symbols.

iv. SACRAMENTALISM

St. Paul's teaching on Baptism may fairly be described as 'sacramental'. The word 'sacramental' strikes horror into some hearts, and this horror is due in part to a healthy and necessary reaction against the abuses of false sacramentalism. It is right to protest against such abuses where they occur under modern conditions among men whose intellectual background is dualistic, but this justifiable protest should not cause us to prejudge the entirely different problem raised by the Pauline teaching on Baptism. Argyle[41] has done well to remind us that, although the Jews did not separate the physical and the spiritual, after the manner of some of the more dualistically minded Greeks, yet they did distinguish between the 'inward' and the 'outward'. Argyle's protest is all the more salutary since a natural reaction against those who identified Christianity with a false understanding of the Sermon on the Mount has led in some circles to the opposite error, a failure to give morality its due place in a full and balanced system of theology.

Argyle draws our attention to such passages[42] as Isa. xxix. 13:

> 'Because this people draw near with their mouth
> and honor me with their lips
> while their hearts are far from me
> and their fear of me is a commandment
> of men learned by rote. . . .'

quoted by Christ Himself (Mark vi. 6–7). We must accept Argyle's contention that there is a distinction in Biblical thought between inward and outward, though this distinction must not be confused with the distinction between physical and non-physical: learning by rote includes a 'non-physical' element, yet it must still be classified as 'outward', not as 'inward'. Biblical thought does not separate the physical and the non-physical, and the distinction between outward and inward is one not of metaphysical separation, but of moral opposition.

In the case of Pauline baptism there is a distinction between the outward and the inward, but no opposition. St. Paul was well aware of the possibility that the outward and the inward might be opposed, for he writes in Rom. ii. 25, 'Circumcision has value, provided you keep the law; but if you break the law, then your circumcision is as if it had never been'. In this case he deems the

---

[41] A. W. Argyle, " 'Outward' and 'Inward' in Biblical Theology" *Exp. T.* 68., (1957), pp. 196ff.

[42] He mentions also the words of 1 Sam. xvi. 7, 'Man looks on the outward appearance, but the Lord looks on the heart', 'circumcision of the heart,' (Jer. iv. 4. etc.), and the Sermon on the Mount.

inward more important than the outward, for he continues in the next verse, 'Equally, if an uncircumcised man keeps the precepts of the law, will he not count as circumcised?' In the case of Christian Baptism, however, St. Paul gives no sign that he is aware of any opposition between the outward and the inward.

No doubt, the Apostle would have had much to say if he had lived in the twentieth century and had witnessed the spiritual deadness and the ethical insensitivity of many baptized Christians. No doubt, under those circumstances he would have contrasted baptized nominal Christians with some of the members of the Society of Friends, who do not practise Baptism at all.

It is true that St. Paul's sacramentalism was unselfconscious, whereas ours is necessarily self-conscious, since most of us start from an inherited psycho-physical dualism, with the result that when we speak of an 'outward and visible sign of an inward and spiritual grace', we are tempted to think of two realms of being, divided by a Cartesian chasm, and to suppose that they interact or are linked by some kind of psycho-physical parallelism. For St. Paul there was an unchallenged harmony between the outward and the inward in Christian Baptism.

It is certainly necessary to ask whether there was anything 'magical' about St. Paul's doctrine of baptism, but the question is less straightforward than it seems, since those who employ the term 'magic' are frequently expressing their feelings or attitudes rather than conveying information, and 'magic', quite apart from its associations and overtones, is a complex concept: it does not refer to any one feature, but to several. It is a feature which magic shares with all forms of sacramentalism and ritualism that it believes certain physical acts to have results which lie outside the sphere of normal physical causation; but to say that Pauline sacramentalism *shares* something with magic is not to say that it *is* 'magical'. The practicer of magic is normally compelling an unseen power to do something on his behalf: the candidate for baptism does not exercise compulsion, but accepts a gift. As Flemington[43] insists, St. Paul's teaching on this subject must always be viewed in the closest conjunction with his teaching on faith in Christ, and this is not typical of magical thought. Again, St. Paul does not regard baptism as something which acts mechan-

[43] W. F. Flemington, *The New Testament Doctrine of Baptism* (London, 1948) pp 81–2.

ically. The Israelites of the Exodus period had all received baptism into the fellowship of Moses in cloud and sea, yet 'most of them were not accepted by God, for the desert was strewn with their corpses' (1 Cor. x. 5). The Christians at Philippi had already been baptized, but St. Paul urged them (Phil. ii. 12–13) to 'work out their own salvation in trembling awe'. 1 Cor. ix. 27, 'For fear that after preaching to others I should find myself rejected', is a warning directed against any false sense of security, whether based upon Predestination or upon Baptism, and the same may be said about St. Paul's warning to the Gentile 'branches' who had been grafted into the true olive in Rom. xi. 20–21, 'Put away your pride and be on your guard; for if God did not spare the native branches, no more will he spare you'.

v. BAPTISM FOR THE DEAD

A special problem is raised by 1 Cor. xv. 29, 'Again, there are those who receive baptism on behalf of the dead, *huper tōn nekrōn*. Why should they do this? If the dead are not raised at all, what do they mean by being baptized on their behalf?' St. Paul's purpose in this passage is clearly to convince the Corinthians of the Resurrection of the Dead; it is generally thought that he is arguing *ad hominem*, and that he does not necessarily accept the desirability of his correspondents' practice: he may be content merely to point out the inconsistency of their practice of accepting baptism on behalf of the dead with their failure to accept the doctrine of the resurrection at all. But this point is not wholly convincing; we are surprised that St. Paul should not have counted vicarious baptism on behalf of the deceased as a charge against the Corinthians, quite apart from its inconsistency with their other beliefs, although it is true that he might have passed this 'minor' abuse over in silence because of the overriding importance of establishing belief in the resurrection of the dead. St. Paul does not appear to regard this practice as either unusual or blameworthy. Frl. Raeder[44] has again brought forward the suggestion that *huper*, rendered in our version 'on behalf of' has a final[45] sense, and means 'in order to join', that is to say, in order to join the

---

[44] Summarized by J. Jeremias, 'Flesh and Blood cannot inherit the Kingdom of God' (*N.T.S.*, ii. 1956), pp. 151–9.

[45] Blass-Debrunner-Funk, section 231, p. 121, notes this sense of 'what one wants to attain', quoting 2 Cor. i. 6, 'It is the price we pay for (*huper*, i.e. in order to achieve) your consolation'.

deceased *Christians*, on the ground that these are *hoi nekroi* (as in
1 Cor. xv. 29a, 35, 42, 52), whereas *nekroi* without the article
means dead people in general. This interpretation receives
commendation in the *I.C.C.*, but Allo rejects it because it would
be a rare, sentimental action rather than a general practice. The
same objection, if indeed it is valid, would seem to hold against his
own contention that pagans were baptized in order to accomplish
the salvation of the deceased, assuming that these were as yet
neither lost nor saved.

It is only fair to say that Allo's theory gains a measure of
support from 1 Cor. vii. 14, 'For the heathen husband now
belongs to God through his Christian wife'; this passage shows
clearly enough that a 'natural' relationship such as marriage
might have supernatural consequences. We learn from 1 Cor. xi.
30 that a number of those associated with the church at Corinth
had recently died. It may be that they were what would later
have been termed catechumens, and that their baptism was
posthumously completed on their behalf, just as a mother may
receive a military award on behalf of a son killed in action. On
the other hand, it may be that a number of those who were
already members of the Christian church had died, and their
friends and relations in Corinth who were still pagans accepted
baptism in order to join them again after death. It is clearly unwise to build much upon a passage about which we know so little.

vi. Infant Baptism

It is impossible to avoid a consideration of the place of Infant
Baptism in the teaching of St. Paul. The problem of twentieth-
century baptism is no concern of ours, but much that has been
written on it is based upon theories about the Apostle's theology.
St. Paul tells us in 1 Cor. i. 16 that he 'Did baptize the household
(*oikos*) of Stephanas'. A household would naturally include small
children, but the argument is not conclusive, since St. Paul does
not say that he baptized every single member of the household of
Stephanas, if indeed it included children at all, which it probably
would have done; it is possible that only those 'suitable' for
baptism would receive it and that children would be excluded.[46]

[46] G. R. Beasley-Murray, *Baptism in the New Testament* (London, 1962),
p. 316, points out that according to 1 Cor. xvi. 15f. the household of Stephanas
had devoted themselves to the ministry and were worthy of obedience. This
shows how dangerous it is to read too much into a passage.

The same factors must weigh with us when we consider the bearing on this matter of the 'household churches'[47] mentioned by St. Paul.

The baptism of infants is compatible with the historical evidence but is not demanded by it. It is made more probable by the fact that in Rom. iv. 11 St. Paul speaks of circumcision, which was undoubtedly administered to infants as a 'seal' (*sphragis*), while in 2 Cor. i. 22, Eph. i. 13, iv. 30 the cognate verb (*sphragizō*) may well be applied to baptism, since already about a century afterwards Hermas[48] unquestionably applies *sphragis* to baptism, but Cullmann[49] is perhaps somewhat unguarded in claiming that baptism is here intended, since St. Paul may mean only that God seals us as His own in a general way, without specific reference to any particular action. Cullmann also maintains that circumcision is spoken of as a being born again.[50] But the passages which he quotes[51] would appear to connect 'being born again' not with circumcision as such, but rather with the whole complex of conversion to Judaism. Again, the convert seems to have been likened to a new-born child in respect of freedom from sin and guilt, rather than of a newly acquired status. Further, St. Paul never speaks of 'being born again' at all, either with reference to Baptism or to anything else. Being born again or from above (*anōthen*) is mentioned nowhere in the New Testament except John iii. 3, 7 and 'being given new birth', *anagennēsas*, nowhere except 1 Pet. i. 3, 23. Indeed, Rabbinic language about 'new birth' and similar terms does not affect the issue.

More relevant is 1 Cor. vii. 14, 'For the heathen husband now belongs to God, *hēgiastai*, from *hagiazō* (lit. "is hallowed") through his Christian wife. . . . Otherwise your children would not belong to God (*akatharta*, lit. "unclean"), whereas in fact they do (*hagia*, lit. "hallowed")'. It would seem clear that the 'pureness' of the children is the basic presupposition accepted by all which underlies the whole argument. Since this 'pureness' is held to be relevant to the position of non-Christian parents, it cannot be due

[47] cf. the Baptism of the household (*oikos*) of Lydia at Philippi (Acts xvi. 15) and of the gaoler's family (*hoi autou hapantes*, literally, 'all that were his'). (Acts xvi. 33).
[48] *Similitudes* (*Parables*), ix. 16, ed. Lightfoot and Harmer, (London, 1898), pp. 386–7, and E.T., p. 472.
[49] *Baptism in the New Testament* E.T., S.B.T., no. I, (London, 1950), pp. 45–6 and p. 57.
[50] ibid. p.57.   [51] Strack-Billerbeck, ii., p. 423

to anything which the children did not share with their pagan parents. Cullmann,[52] it must be agreed, is on dangerous ground, as Craig[53] points out, when he supports the contention that such children were never baptized at all, either as infants or in adult life, but were free from any such obligation, as children born to Jews were not required to undergo proselyte baptism. However, it is clear that these children had not yet been baptized. Jeremias[54] agrees, but argues that the thought of the passage is reminiscent of Jewish discussions about whether the children of mothers converted to Judaism during pregnancy should undergo proselyte baptism or no. He further argues that Jewish boys were circumcised in spite of the fact that they were born in holiness.[55] He concludes, '*We must therefore be content with the conclusion that 1 Cor. vii. 14c bears no reference to baptism* (his italics).[56] I am personally impressed by the fact that Baptism was required both of Gentiles, who were 'unclean' by birth and of Jews who were 'clean' by birth. This reinforces the contention of Jeremias that cleanness and Baptism were independent. Beasley-Murray reaches the same general conclusion in a careful discussion of 1 Cor. vii. 14.[57] This, it should be stated to avoid confusion, is directed in part against a theory which Jeremias formerly[58] held but has now rejected,[59] namely that the Corinthian Christians baptized children born before the conversion of a parent to Christianity, but not any born after. Jeremias made known his change of mind after Beasley-Murray's book was written, but before it was published.

Far more important than any of these problems is the theology of Baptism, which St. Paul himself has expounded for us so concisely in Rom. vi. 3, 'When we were baptized into union with Christ Jesus we were baptized into his death', in Rom. vi. 5, 'For if we have become incorporate with him in a death like his, we shall also be one with him in a resurrection like his', and in Col. ii. 12, 'For in baptism you were buried with him, in baptism also you were raised to life with him'. Since we *died* with Christ, we

[52] Op. cit. p. 44.
[53] *I.B.*, x., on Cor. 1, vii. 14.
[54] *Infant Baptism in the First Four Centuries* (London, 1960), pp. 44–48.
[55] ibid. p. 47.   [56] ibid. p. 48.
[57] G. R. Beasley-Murray, *Baptism in the New Testament* (London, 1962), pp. 192–99.
[58] *Die Kindertaufe in den ersten vier Jahrhunderten* (Göttingen, 1958), pp. 54f. *Infant Baptism in the First Four Centuries* is really a new edition in English of this work (1960).
[59] *Infant Baptism in the First Four Centuries* (London, 1960), p. 47.

are freed from sin and from evil spirits. as we can see from 1 Cor. vi. 11, 'But you have been through the purifying waters' and from Col. ii. 20, 'Did you not die with Christ and pass beyond reach of the elemental spirits of the world?' Since we died *and rose* with Christ we should live the risen life, as we can see from the ethical passage which is introduced by Col. iii. 1, 'Were you not raised to life with Christ? Then aspire to the realm above'. Masson,[59a] indeed, points out that 'rising with Christ' is mentioned only in Col. ii. 12, iii. 1; Eph. ii. 6; he therefore maintains that St. Paul cannot have believed in rising with Christ, because in Rom. vi. 5 the Apostle says that we *shall* experience a resurrection like His, and because nothing in St. Paul's experience would allow him to speak of sharing Christ's resurrection, whereas baptism did allow him to speak of sharing in Christ's death. We must reply, first, that just as being immersed in the baptismal waters would suggest dying with Christ, so coming up again from the water would suggest rising with Christ, and putting on clothes would suggest putting on Christ (Rom. xiii. 14; Gal. iii. 27) or moral virtues (Col. iii. 12). Secondly, in Rom. vi. 4, 'In order that, as Christ was raised from the dead in the splendour of the Father, so also we might set our feet upon the new path of life', St. Paul connects our present moral life as Christians with the past fact of Christ's resurrection: it would be a very short step to speak of our spiritual 'resurrection' also as a past fact, even though in the 'natural' sense the resurrection of Christians still lies in the future.

We have seen that since in baptism we *died* with Christ we died to sin, and since we rose with Him we rose to newness of life. Since also in baptism we died and rose *with Christ*, we were baptized into the church and into the Holy Spirit, as we can see from 1 Cor. xii. 13, 'We were all brought into one body by baptism in the one spirit'.

Baptism was probably connected with formal ethical instruction, as will appear later; the moral teaching of the New Testament, often called Didache, contains such recurring catch-words as 'put off', 'put on' which would find a most suitable context in baptism. The 'Pauline Order of Baptism' is even more conjectural. It may be reflected in Rom. x. 8–10, which includes the words,

[59a] *L'Epître de saint Paul aux Philippiens et l'Epître de saint Paul aux Colossiens*, C.N.T., (Neuchatel, 1950) ad loc.

'If on your lips is the confession "Jesus is Lord" '. If this 'confession' (*homologeō*) refers to a baptismal response, Rom. viii. 15, 'A Spirit that makes us sons, enabling us to cry "Abba! Father!" ', may reflect a conviction on St. Paul's part that in baptism the Holy Spirit for the first time enabled the convert to call upon God as 'Father'. But this again is conjectural. Before we leave the subject of Baptism, in case we should be tempted to forget how closely St. Paul linked Baptism and faith, we should recollect that Gal. iii. 27, 'Baptized into union with him, you have all put on Christ as a garment', is immediately preceded by Gal. iii. 26, 'For through faith you are all sons of God in union with Christ Jesus'.

vii. THE LORD'S SUPPER

Before we examine the effects of the Lord's Supper, (*kuriakon deipnon*) 1 Cor. xi. 20, the only term employed by St. Paul to designate the Eucharist, we must ask why it was effective at all, and the answer to this question is that it was a 'memorial'. Needless to say, this does not mean that it was effective solely or even mainly because the Christians were stirred to virtue and to devotion by remembering the past, though this, no doubt, was a subsidiary factor. 'Remember' and similar words in our own language represent *mimnēskomai* and cognate Greek words in the N.T.; these, in turn, occur in the LXX almost without exception as renderings of the Hebrew *zākar* and its cognates, which do not suggest only thinking and feeling directed towards the past; they are used when something happens in the present because of a 'memorial' of what has already taken place in the past. 'Remember' suggests not only subjectively recalling the dead past which no longer exists, but, in the active sense, objectively *recalling* the past so that it is again present and living. In ancient ritual a past act, such as the creation of the world, might be recounted and re-enacted so that the power which had worked in the past might work again in the present and the future.[60] It may well have been the case that in pre-Biblical days, and among 'degenerate' Jews, such as those whose practices are described in Ezek. viii., such actions became quasi-magical, and were regarded as com-

---

[60] cf. Hebert in *A Theological Word Book of the Bible* (ed. Richardson, London, 1950), pp. 142–3, *s.v.* 'Memory, etc.'; Pedersen, *Israel*, i.–ii, (E.T. London, 1926), pp. 256–9, iii.–iv., (E.T. London, 1940), pp. 405–12; Frost, *Old Testament Apocalyptic* (London, 1952), esp. Ch. iii.

pelling or even creating a power which was intended to assist those who performed the ritual. Be that as it may, for normative Biblical Judaism the Passover was a 'recalling' which had to be carried out because God had so commanded.[61]

Miss Sykes has made an illuminating selection of the Old Testament passages, and concludes: 'The celebration of the Eucharist as a "memorial" is the releasing of Christ's life and personality afresh. He is vitally alive once more in the presence of his disciples.'[62] This vital starting point is really independent of whether 'Do this as a memorial of me', *eis tēn emēn anamnēsin*, means that God is to remember the Messiah, or that the Christians are to remember the Messiah: in either case the object is that the Messiah should be vitally active in the midst of the congregation, and that the purpose for which He was raised up by God should be accomplished. Jeremias[63] understands St. Paul's intention to be that *God* should remember the Messiah by bringing about His kingdom in the parousia. The more usual interpretation is that the *Corinthians* are to 'remember' or recall Christ, and the words of 1 Cor. xi. 24, 'Do this as a memorial of me', suggests that the *same people* are being commanded both to 'do this' and to 'recall' Christ. In the LXX *anamnēsis* is found at Lev. xxiv. 7, Num. x. 10, Wisd. of Sol. xvi. 6 and in the titles of Ps. (Septuagint) xxxvii. (M.T. xxxviii.) and Ps. (Septuagint) lxix. (M.T. lxx). On the other hand, *mnēmosunon*, which does not seem to differ from it in meaning, is relatively frequent. Jeremias argues that in *Lev.* and the two passages from the Psalms it is God who remembers, although he agrees that man, not God, remembers in Wisd. of Sol. xvi. 6. In the Psalm titles Greek *eis anemnēsin* and Hebrew *l'hazkir* are alike so cryptic that nothing can be built upon them. In Lev. xxiv. 7 *anamnēsin* corresponds to *'azkārāh*; this, as Jones[64] rightly maintains, is virtually a technical term, and designates the function of putting God in remembrance, a function performed by that part of the offering which is burnt; Jones explains Num. x. 10, the only other passage in the LXX where *anamnēsis* occurs, in a similar manner. We may distinguish three stages:

(1) Christ's command to repeat the rite, which, whether historical or no, is certainly part of the Pauline tradition.

[61] cf. Exod. xii. 14; xiii. 2; Deut. xvi. 1–3.
[62] *Exp. T.* lxxi. 4, (1960), pp. 115–18.
[63] *The Eucharistic Words of Jesus* (E.T. Oxford, 1955), pp. 159–65.
[64] *J.T.S.*, N.S. vi. Pt. 2 (1955,), pp. 183–91.

(2) The 'recalling' of Christ and His work, epitomized in the
Last Supper, by the Christians at their Eucharists, and

(3) God's action in completing the work of Christ by bringing
in the Parousia. This also might be described as 'remembering'
the Messiah in the sense that divine action due to a fact in the past,
for example sin, may be called a divine remembering of the past
act. Jeremias identifies the words of 1 Cor. xi. 25 with the third
stage, but Jones is probably correct in maintaining that they refer
to stage (2) which is designed to bring in stage (3). Jeremias[65]
is certainly justified in claiming that 1 Cor. xi. 26, 'Until he comes,'
achri hou elthē, does not merely specify the time during which the
Eucharist is to be celebrated: it means that obedience to this
command will hasten the end of the world, since *elthē* is in the
subjunctive, and *an* is omitted.[66] It is not unreasonable to see in
the Eucharist a proleptic sharing in the Messianic Banquet: the
Christians who take part in this service are already in contact with
the power which in the future, at the parousia, will fill the earth
as the waters cover the sea, and each Eucharist, like the miracles[67]
of Christ, may be regarded as a 'minor bridgehead', though their
effectiveness is wholly dependent upon the main and essential
bridgehead which is constituted by the life-death-resurrection of
Jesus Christ Himself.

Although the New Testament is not to be understood on the
lines of totemism, yet to share in a sacred meal with someone was
to enter a close relationship with him; it is not for nothing that
the New Testament can describe a fellow Christian as a brother
(*adelphos*). This element of communion ('vertically') with Christ
and therefore also ('horizontally') with each other is placed beyond
any reasonable doubt by 1 Cor. x. 16–17, 'When we bless the
"cup of blessing", is it not a means of sharing in the blood of
Christ? When we break the bread, is it not a means of sharing
in the body of Christ? Because there is one loaf, we, many as we
are, are one body; for it is one loaf of which we all partake'.
Bultmann points out that the unity of the celebrating congregation
is explained by the unity of the bread only if the bread is the body
of Christ.[68]

[65] *The Eucharistic Words of Jesus* (E.T. Oxfoad, 1955), p. 164.
[66] Blass-Debrunner-Funk, sect. 383, p. 193. The insertion of *an* by some of
the later scribes is due presumably to a slackening of the eschatological expectation.
[67] cf. Cullmann, 'The Proleptic Deliverance of the Body according to the
New Testament', in *The Early Church* (London, 1956), p. 170.
[68] *Theology* i., p. 147.

Two questions arise. In what sense is the congregation considered a unity, and in what sense is the bread the Body of Christ? Before the Eucharist is celebrated, the congregation already possess that unity which is due to their having been baptized into the Body of Christ. They have the unity which comes from holding, within limits, a common faith and from living the Christian life of worship and ethical practice. But each time that they share together in the Lord's Supper their unity is strengthened and renewed. A. Schweitzer roundly describes as 'mystical' the unity both of Baptism and of the Lord's Supper.[69] Mysticism is a word with many meanings and with still more overtones and associations; it is most often employed pejoratively in contemporary theological writing, on the ground that it refers to an individualistic union with God in which the 'mystic' by-passes Christ, and cuts loose from his obligations to the church and to his fellow-men; he may even 'lose' his personality in 'the Divine'. If we apply the term 'mystical' to the unity imparted by the Christian sacraments, it must be unity with a personal God achieved through Christ in the fellowship of the church; it must involve no departure from normal moral practices apart from those which depend, like celibacy, upon some special vocation; and there must be no 'loss' of personality through the transcending of the separateness of the individual: in contemporary language it may be described as a condition in which the human 'thou' is enriched by a relationship with the divine 'I'.

It is against such a background that Anderson Scott[70] approves the use of the phrase 'Real Presence' to describe St. Paul's teaching about the Eucharist. If we remember that in ancient ritual the 'celebrant' recounted and re-enacted what had taken place in the past, so that the power which had acted in the past should act again in the present and the future, we may fairly say that St. Paul regarded Christ as being active again at the Eucharist; indeed, 'Real Activity' is perhaps a helpful gloss upon 'Real Presence'. It is true that the consecrated elements are the natural focus, but St. Paul would no more separate the elements from the celebrant's recounting and re-enacting[71] of the Last Supper or

---

[69] *The Mysticism of St. Paul the Apostle* (E.T. London, 1931), p. 269.
[70] *Christianity according to St. Paul* (Cambridge, 1961[2]), p. 196.
[71] The 'breaking' of the Bread mentioned in 1 Cor. xi. 24 may well be a re-enacting of the death of Christ.

from the assembled *ekklēsia* in which the rite was performed than he would have separated Baptism from Faith or from the living of the 'Risen Life': in both cases, it is the isolation of one factor which causes legitimate Christian sacramentalism to degenerate into the semblance of magic. The 'nature' of the 'presence' of Christ at the Pauline Eucharist does not depend upon how it arose: even if Cullmann[72] is correct in his supposition that some at least of the very first Eucharists were the occasion of appearances of the Risen Christ, He was present in a different sense at the Eucharists described in St. Paul's writings. The Body and Blood of Christ in the Eucharist are not to be identified with the Body and Blood of the Risen Christ, although they are the means for the real activity of the complete Risen Personality of Christ: His 'body' and 'spirit' are not for St. Paul separated, but integral parts of the one whole.

At the Last Supper itself it was clear that the Bread and Wine were not identical with Christ's Body and Blood, so that He was able to say, 'This is my blood of the covenant', *Touto esti to haima mou tēs diathēkēs* (Mark xiv. 24; so Matt. xxvi. 28), without any danger of being misunderstood. But 1 Cor. xi. 25, 'This cup is the new covenant sealed[74] by my blood (*Touto to potērion hē kainē diathēkē estin en tō emō haimati*)', (so Luke xxii. 20), avoids a crudity which would offend Jews even more than Gentiles. It is hazardous to say which account of the Institution of the Eucharist is the earlier, the Markan or the Pauline. Jeremias[75] has recently argued the case for Markan priority, and has maintained that the Evangelist has reproduced a stylized account earlier than the Gospel as a whole; Turner[76] has replied to Jeremias. It is in any

---

[72] *Early Christian Worship* (E.T., S.B.T. no. 10, London, 1953), p. 15. pp. 7–36 of this book are the E.T. of *Urchristentum und Gottesdienst* (Zürich, 1950²).

[74] 'Sealed' is not in the Greek, but is a legitimate expansion of *en*, 'by', which is here used in the instrumental sense. cf Blass-Debrunner-Funk, sect. 195, p. 104.

[75] *The Eucharistic Words of Jesus* (Oxford, 1955), pp. 106–35. He bases his conclusion upon the 'separability' of the Institution-account from the rest of the Gospel, and upon the presence in it of twenty Semitisms.

[76] *J.T.S.*, N.S. viii, Pt. 1 (1957), pp. 108–11. He replies that the awkward connection (Mark xiv. 22) is paralleled elsewhere in this Gospel, e.g., at vii. 24, and that the style and vocabulary of these verses is not untypical of Markan usage as a whole; he quotes convincing parallels for the twenty Semitisms from other passages in Mark. It must be admitted, however, that these verses include a very high *concentration* of apparent Semitisms, and that they may embody a very early tradition indeed, even though they are not an 'erratic' in the Gospel.

case dangerous to suppose that either the Markan or the Pauline
account is older *as a whole* than the other; each may be more
primitive in some respects. We, of course, are concerned only
with the theological consequences of these enquiries; it is significant for us if St. Paul can be plausibly represented as adapting
the traditional account which he received, since it enables us to see
how he understood it. Davies maintains that St. Paul laid special
stress upon the covenantal[77] aspect of the Eucharist, as does St.
Luke, and this is certainly a valid insight into the Pauline theology
of the Lord's Supper.[78] St. Paul clearly believed that just as a
positive relationship with God was established by the Mosaic
covenant, and as this relationship was maintained by the worship
of Judaism (*latreia*), so the new relationship with God, made
possible through the work of Christ and accepted by each individual in faith-baptism, was confirmed and maintained in the
Lord's Supper.

Since the Eucharist helped to maintain a right relationship
with God, which had been the purpose of the Old Testament
sacrifices, sacrificial language could properly be applied to the new
Christian sacrament. St. Paul does not, in fact, do so explicitly.
Allo points out that in 1 Cor. x. the Eucharist is compared with
Jewish and heathen sacrifices in a manner which places it within
the same mental framework. 1 Cor. x. 20, 'The sacrifices the
heathen offer (*ha thuousin*) . . . are offered "to demons and to that
which is not God" . . . You cannot partake of the Lord's table
(*trapezēs kuriou*), and the table of demons', suggests that the
heathen sacrifices and the Christian Eucharist are *in pari materia*;
moreover, *trapeza kuriou*, the Lord's table, represents God's
altar in Mal. i. 7, 12; indeed, *trapeza* in the LXX occurs frequently
as the equivalent of Heb. *shulḥān*, table, e.g., in Num. iv. 7,
where it refers to the table of the bread of the Presence. In the

---

[77] Since St. Paul speaks of a new (*kainē*) covenant, it is clear that *diathēkē*
must mean covenant, as opposed to the old covenant recorded in Exod. xxiv,
and that it cannot mean 'will' or 'testament' as in Gal. iii. 15.

[78] *Paul and Rabbinic Judaism* (London, 1955²), esp. pp. 244–5. Jeremias is
justified in contending that the originsl words were probably 'this is my blood',
and that 'of the covenant' was added later, on the ground that in Aramaic a
noun with a pronominal suffix (my) would not govern the genitive, and 'my
covenant blood' would naturally refer to the blood of circumcision, by which
the individual was associated with the covenant on Mount Sinai, although there
is no evidence for this application of the phrase before the fourth century A.D.
The important point is that St. Paul stressed the covenantal aspect even more
definitely than St. Mark.

O

Bible ideas of 'covenant' and of 'sacrifice' are closely connected. The covenant motif is central to St. Paul's eucharistic thought, whereas sacrificial language and thought, apart from covenant language, are comparatively peripheral. To avoid possible misunderstanding, there is no question of *another* Calvary, as we can tell from Rom. vi. 10, 'For in dying as he died, he died to sin, once for all (*ephapax*)'; nor does the work of Christ require any kind of supplementation: at the Lord's Supper the power of Christ Who died and was raised from the dead becomes effective for the worshippers. If this sacrificial language may be used of the Eucharist, it reflects the sacrificial language which is applied to the death of Christ; in Eucharistic theology, as in the theology of the Atonement, the language of sacrifice may be employed only in a sense which transcends the *rationale* of the Old Testament sacrifices just as Christ Himself transcends the victims which were immolated at Jewish altars.[79]

viii. UNWORTHY PARTAKING OF THE LORD'S SUPPER

It is impossible to pass over the problem raised by 1 Cor. xi. 29–30, 'For he who eats and drinks eats and drinks judgement (*krima*) on himself if he does not discern the Body (*mē diakrinōn to sōma*). That is why many of you are feeble and sick, and a number have died'. *To sōma* must refer to the Body of Christ in the same sense as in verse 27 immediately above, not to the Body of Christ in the sense of the church. This failure to 'discern' is described in xi. 20–21, 'It is impossible for you to eat the Lord's Supper because each of you is in such a hurry to eat his own', and in xi. 27 any person who offends in this respect is said to be guilty[80] of 'desecrating the body (*enochos tou sōmatos*) and blood of the Lord'. Leenhardt[81] deprecates the suggestion that something in the elements overwhelms the guilty communicant in the same way that electricity kills anyone who touches a high-tension cable. The view which Leenhardt attacks by means of this forceful comparison had already been accepted by Allo,[82] although he was well aware of its 'terrifying realism' (*réalisme terrible*). In 1946

[79] cf. *supra*, Ch. vi. p. 147.
[80] cf. Jas. ii. 10, 'Guilty of breaking all of it, i.e., the law,' (*enochos pantōn*); in both these passages *enochos* followed by the genitive means 'guilty in respect of'. *In this context* the meaning is not 'guilty of Christ's death' but 'guilty of a desecration of the sacrament'.
[81] *Le Sacrement de la Sainte Cène* (Neuchâtel, 1948), pp. 87–8.
[82] *Première Epître aux Corinthiens* (Paris 1956²) on xi. 29, p. 282.

Cullman[83] propounded the view that the unworthy reception of the Holy Communion did not *cause* disease and death, but *impeded* the miraculous healings which would have been granted to the Corinthians if they had partaken worthily of the Lord's Supper. Cullmann's solution would appear to be rendered impossible by the words of St. Paul which follow at 1 Cor. xi. 32, 'When, however, we do fall under the Lord's judgement, he is disciplining us, to save us from being condemned with the rest of the world': the illness and death seem to have been brought upon them by God, and not to have taken place because by their sin they impeded the flow of healing power. No ingenuity can avail to make these verses fit in with twentieth-century theories about the causation of sickness and death. We should not, however, be surprised at this. Twentieth-century theories are 'disregarded' by St. Paul at 1 Cor. x. 6–13 also, where he maintains that death befell the Israelites in the desert as a symbol to warn the Christians over a thousand years later. †

I would suggest that this most difficult passage is due to two facts and one conviction. The first fact is that the Lord's Supper was observed in a scandalous manner at Corinth. The second fact is that many of the Christians at Corinth did fall sick and not a few died. St. Paul was convinced that God ruled the world, and like other Jews he took it for granted that suffering was God's chastisement for sin. He linked the two facts and explained them in the light of his conviction. We, in the present century, do not normally accept such a direct 'one-one-correspondence' between the sins and the sufferings of individuals, but St. Paul belonged to the first century, and the linking of illness and sin, no doubt, came automatically to his mind, since he accepted the presupposition of human solidarity, as was noted above, on pp. 45f.

[83] 'The Proleptic Deliverance of the Body according to the New Testament,' in *The Early Church* (London, 1956), pp. 171–2.

CHAPTER EIGHT

CHURCH AND MINISTRY

i. The Ecclesia

Ekklēsia, which generally answers to 'church' in the *EVV*, is the LXX word for the community of Israel, whether assembled or no; the evidence of the O.T. does not allow us to say more than this with certainty. *Ekklēsia* generally represents the Hebrew *ḳāhāl*, never *'ēdhāh*, whereas *sunagōgē* usually renders *'ēdhāh*, but occasionally other words, including *ḳāhāl*. In the M.T. no distinction between *ḳāhāl* and *'ēdhāh* is observed over a large enough number of books to justify us in supposing that it influenced the first generation of Christians in their choice of *ekklēsia* instead of *sunagōgē* to designate themselves; this was probably due to the fact that Judaism had staked out a prior claim to *sunagōgē*, which is applied by the N.T. to Christians only at Jas. ii. 2. It has indeed been supposed that, owing in part to the similarity in sound, *ekklēsia* suggested the Greek and Hebrew words for 'call', *kalein*, and *ḳārā*; but Schmidt[1] is surely correct when he maintains that it is unlikely, though not impossible, that St. Paul was thinking of the doctrine of election when he used the word *ekklēsia*, since 'called out', *ekklētos* and similar words are almost wholly lacking in the LXX.

St. Paul applies the word *ekklēsia* to the assembly for worship at 1 Cor. xi. 18, 22, and nine times in 1 Cor. xiv.; needless to say, we ought not to attach much weight to the frequency of this usage in a chapter which is devoted to giving directions for the proper conduct of Christian worship. On several[2] occasions the Apostle uses *ekklēsia* in a local sense, applying it to the congregation at Cenchreae (Rom. xvi. 1) or at Laodicea (Col. iv. 16) and to the congregations of Galatia (Gal. i. 2) or in Judaea (Gal. i. 22). St. Paul speaks of three 'house-churches', namely those which were accustomed to assemble at the houses of Prisca and Aquila (Rom. xvi. 5; 1 Cor. xvi. 19), Nympha or Nymphas (Col. iv. 15), and

---

[1] *T.W.N.T.* vol. iii, p. 534 (E.T. *Church*, London, 1950, p. 57).
[2] Rom. xvi. 1; 1 Cor. i. 2; xvi. i. 19; 2 Cor. i. 1, viii. 1; Gal. i. 2, 22; Col. iv. 16; 1 Thess. i. 1; ii. 14; 2 Thess. i. 1.

Philemon (Philem. 2). In fifteen[3] passages the word is plural or virtually plural, such as *en pasē ekklēsia*, 'in all our communities' (1 Cor. iv. 17) and *oudemia moi ekklēsia*, 'you were the only congregation', (Phil. iv. 15). Twice in *Colossians*[4] and nine times in *Ephesians*[5] *ekklēsia* unquestionably refers to the Catholic church.

In seven passages the meaning of *ekklēsia* may fairly be disputed. Of these the most interesting is 1 Cor. xii. 28, *Etheto ho Theos en tē ekklēsia prōton apostolous*, 'Within our community, God has appointed in the first place apostles'. Cerfaux[6] remarks that this verse is often taken to be of unquestionable clarity among those which are quoted to prove that even before the Captivity Epistles *ekklēsia* had the meaning of 'universal church'. He points out, however, that in 1 Cor. *ekklēsia* often means 'assembly' or 'gathering' and suggests that this was the meaning intended by St. Paul in the present verse also. We are naturally tempted to reply that this meaning is excluded by the use of the word 'apostles', on the ground that there would not be a plurality of apostles present in any one congregation. This is not decisive, since the Didache includes the words, 'But concerning the apostles and prophets, so do ye according to the ordinance of the gospel. Let every apostle, when he cometh to you, be received as the Lord'.[7] The phrase 'concerning apostles' is employed in spite of the fact that, as the sequel shows, there may sometimes be no apostle present. But the meaning 'universal church' though not assured for *ekklēsia* in 1 Cor. xii. 28, is certainly not excluded, and the matter must be left open.

The same must be said about Rom. xvi. 23, 'Greetings also from Gaius, my host, and host of the whole congregation'. Gaius was the host of St. Paul, and either of all the Christians in Corinth or of all who passed through that city in the course of a journey.

In 1 Cor. xv. 9; Gal. i. 13; and Phil. iii. 6, St. Paul says that he had been a persecutor of the church. According to *Acts* he had as a matter of history persecuted the Jerusalem church, and was prevented from carrying out his intention to persecute the Christians in Damascus by the vision on the road. It is impossible on the basis of these three passages to decide whether *ekklēsia*

[3] Rom. xvi. 4, 16; 1 Cor. iv. 17, vii. 17, xi. 16; 2 Cor. viii. 8, 18, 19, 23, 24; xi. 8, 28; xii. 13; Phil. iv. 15; 2 Thess. i. 4.   [4] i. 18, 24.
[5] i. 22, iii. 10, 21; v. 23, 24, 25, 27, 29, 32.   [6] *Church*, p. 192f.
[7] *Didache*, xi. 4, ed. Lightfoot and Harmer (London, 1898), p. 222., E.T. ibid. p. 233.

there refers to the church of Jerusalem or to the universal church: St. Paul was concerned with the fact that he had been a persecutor, not with the precise ecclesiastical status of his victims.

In 1 Cor. vi. 4 we read, 'How can you entrust jurisdiction to outsiders, men who count for nothing in our community (*ekklēsia*)?' Since St. Paul is urging his readers to have recourse, not to pagan law-courts but to the judgment of their fellow-Christians, it is probable that he had in mind the local community, who would be readily available; it is, however, not impossible that the Apostle is thinking of Christians as opposed to pagans, and that the Corinthian brethren are regarded as local members of the universal church. In 1 Cor. x. 32, 'Give no offence to Jews, or Greeks, or to the church of God', the balance would seem to tip slightly in the other direction: it is natural to suppose that the church is the 'third race' alongside Jews and Gentiles; but it is only fair to say that it is the members of the local Christian community who would be directly affected; and it must be agreed that the reference may be to them alone.

We have now passed under review all the passages in which St. Paul employs the word *ekklēsia*: in none of them is the notion 'People of God' inappropriate. In most of these passages a local gathering of God's people is intended. In only two passages which can be confidently attributed to the Apostle is the meaning 'universal church' completely beyond dispute. These are Col. i. 18, 'He is, moreover, the head of the body, the church (*ekklēsia*)', and Col. i. 24, 'For the sake of his body, which is the church (*ekklēsia*)'. The 'catholic' meaning is beyond doubt in the nine occurrences of *ekklēsia* in *Ephesians*.[8] If we accept the two verses in *Colossians* as Pauline, we must conclude that they alone are sufficient to show that he used *ekklēsia* in the universal sense. Since the seven[9] passages which date from before his captivity in Rome are indecisive, we cannot be sure that he did so until near the end of his life.

But, although the actual word *ekklēsia* is most frequently applied by St. Paul to a local congregation, it would be perverse to suppose that the 'universal' aspect was of small account in his theology. Indeed, the *thought of* the universal church is sometimes

[8] cf. *supra*, p. 187, n. 5.
[9] The seven indecisive passages are Rom. xvi. 23; 1 Cor. vi. 4; x. 32; xii. 8; xv. 9; Gal. i. 13; Phil. iii. 6.

conveyed by a phrase which includes the *word* in its local signification, for example in 1 Cor. iv. 17, 'I teach everywhere in all
our congregations (*en pasē ekklēsia*)'. Parallel passages are Rom.
xvi. 16, 'All Christ's congregations send you their greetings', 1 Cor.
vii. 17, 'This is what I teach in all our congregations'. A special
interest attaches to 1 Cor. xi. 16, 'However, if you insist on arguing,
let me tell you there is no such custom among us, or in any of the
congregations of God's people'. Here, 'catholic' or universal
liturgical practice is felt to carry weight, as well as the 'catholic'
doctrine which is taught in every place.

Cerfaux[10] does not go beyond the evidence when he quotes
with approval the words of Fridrichsen:[11] 'Each community
represents on the spot the one and indivisible church.' In a
similar vein, Schmidt[12] declares that: 'Each community, however
small, represents the universal community, the church' (. . . *jede,
wenn auch noch so kleine Gemeinde, die Gesamtgemeinde, die Kirche,
darstellt*). The translation given in the *Bible Key Words*[13] series
goes too far; it renders: 'The Church . . . is truly present in its
wholeness in every company of believers, however small.' But
Schmidt[14] also goes too far when he says of 1 Cor. i. 2 and of 2
Cor. i. 1, *Tē ekklēsia . . . tē ousē en Korinthō*: 'The proper translation in those verses is not 'the Corinthian congregation'—taking
its place beside the Roman, etc.—but 'the congregation, church,
gathering as it is in Corinth" '. Rigaux[15], commenting on 1
Thess. ii. 14, 'You have fared like the congregations in Judaea,
(*tōn ekklēsion tou Theou tōn ousōn en tē Ioudaia*) God's people in
Christ Jesus', says, 'The plural in the present passage is fatal to
the paraphrase proposed (by Schmidt) for 1 Cor. i. 2'. It is
possible that Rigaux may be somewhat too sweeping in his judgement, but, on balance, we do well to follow the *N.E.B.*: 'To the
congregation of God's people at Corinth.' This matter is more
important than might at first sight appear, for to say that the
whole church is present in each local congregation is a piece of
unnecessary mystification: the *whole power of Christ* is most
certainly available to every local congregation; Christ, since He

---

[10] *Church*, p. 191.
[11] '*Eglise et Sacrement dans le Nouveau Testament*' in *Revue d'Histoire et de
Philosophie religuese* xvii (1937), p. 345. I owe this reference to Cerfaux.
[12] *T.W.N.T.* vol. iii, p. 508.　　　[13] *The Church* (London, 1950), 10.
[14] *T.W.N.T.* vol. iii. p. 508.
[15] *Les Epîtres aux Thessaloniciens* (Paris, 1956).

has been raised from the dead by the power of God, has indeed become superior to the limitations imposed by locality and by other characteristics of the world of space-time-matter, but this transcendence of earthly limitations does not yet belong to the church. Beneath this somewhat obscure phraseology we may glimpse three important facts:

First, as we have just remarked, the whole power of Christ is available to every local congregation.

Secondly, each congregation has a function to perform in its own area analogous to that of the universal church in the world as a whole, and

Thirdly, the local congregation is no mere isolated group: it is in a state of 'solidarity' with Christ and with the church as a whole.

Bultmann, in his exposition of St. Paul's theology, describes the church as the 'eschatological Congregation'[16] (*eschatologische Gemeinde*)[17]; this expression also stands in need of elucidation. 'Eschatology' is a technical term which has loomed large in the theology of the present century. It means literally, 'doctrine of the end', but a strong current of Jewish thought believed that the end-time would witness the fulfilment by God of His intention to break into the world order and to transform it, redeem it and create it anew; language drawn from the biblical accounts of Israel's redemption from Egyptian bondage, and of the creation of the world was employed to sketch in God's expected intervention; the end-time was associated with the 'breaking in' of the power of God. When therefore Bultmann speaks of the church as the 'eschatological community', he means, presumably, that it is a community which has experienced, and acknowledges, the power of God. This power has already broken into the world, as it was expected to do in the last days. Therefore, the church awaits the consummation of God's new act of salvation, already begun, but not yet concluded.

ii. The Body of Christ

There are two passages only, in the acknowledged writings of St. Paul, where the church is described in so many words as the Body of Christ. They are Col. i. 18, 'He is, moreover, the head of

[16] *Theology*, vol. i, p. 308.
[17] *Theologie des Neuen Testaments* (Tübingen, 1948[1]), p. 304.

the body, the church', and Col. i. 24, 'His body which is the church'. But the same thought is expressed, although not so explicitly, in Col. i. 28, 'So as to present each one of you as a mature member of Christ's body', and in Col. ii. 19, 'From the Head the whole body, with all its joints and ligaments, receives its supplies'. From *Ephesians* we may quote i. 23, 'He . . . appointed him as supreme head to the church, which is his body', and v. 30, 'And that is how Christ treats the church, because it is his body'. The same thought lies behind seven other passages in this epistle.

In the major epistles it is never said that the *church* is the body of Christ, but we are told that *Christians* belong to the body of Christ. The two most notable cases are Rom. xii. 4–5, 'For just as in a single human body (*sōma*) there are many limbs and organs (*limbs* and *organs* together represent the one Greek word *melē*), all with different functions, so all of us, united with Christ, form one body, serving individually as limbs and organs of each other', and 1 Cor. xii. 12–27, especially xii. 12, 'For Christ is like a single body with its many limbs and organs, which, many as they are, together make up one body'. We may also notice in this connection 1 Cor. vi. 15, 'Your bodies are limbs and organs of Christ', and 1 Cor. x. 17, 'Because there is one loaf, we, many as we are, are one body; for it is one loaf of which we all partake'.

From a comparison of these passages taken from the major epistles with those which were quoted above from the epistles of the captivity, three points emerge:

(1) Although the major epistles never say that the church is the body of Christ, yet the difference is one of phraseology rather than of theological substance.

(2) According to the epistles of both periods the members of the church are not linked only with Christ individually; we are joined to Christ, and we are also joined to each other in mutual functional dependence.

(3) According to the Captivity Epistles Christ is the head of the body, the church. In 1 Cor. xii. 21 we read: 'The eye cannot say to the hand, "I do not need you"; nor the head to the feet, "I do not need you" '. In 1 Cor. the head, so far from being superior to the other members, is not distinguished from them: it is merely one organ among many. We must not imagine that this shows that there is an irreconcilable conflict between *1 Cor.* and *Col.*

There is merely a difference of language. The figures 'head' and 'body' are employed in a different manner: the doctrines which they portray are different, but not inconsistent.

When we say, 'The church is the Body of Christ', we are stating a fact by means of a metaphor. There are those who insist that the statement is 'ontological', and deprecate the use of the term 'metaphor' in this connection. Although it would be going too far to say that 'all language is decayed metaphor', there lies behind our ordinary language more metaphor than we commonly realize. But when we come to consider the statement, 'The church is the Body of Christ', unusual difficulties arise. In the first place the person and work of Christ transcend the understanding of human beings, whose minds are attuned to the commonsense-world of tables and chairs. Again, the notion of 'solidarity' is strange to the mind of Western Man in the twentieth century, just as the German ü or French u is strange to the lips of an Englishman. When we say, 'The church is the Body of Christ', we are trying to express our *solidarity* in *Christ:* both *Christ* and *solidarity* are foreign to our understanding. We are trying to express a fact which we cannot wholly understand by means of a metaphor; and the metaphor which we employ cannot be translated without remainder into non-metaphorical terms: nevertheless, the metaphor remains a metaphor.

It would, however, be extremely misleading to speak of the metaphor as a *mere* metaphor. In the words of Anderson Scott: 'The important thing is to note at how many points the symbol corresponds to the thing symbolized.'[18]

The subject has been both complicated and illuminated by J. A. T. Robinson.[19] He identifies the Risen Body of Christ with His Body which is the church as it will be after the parousia. Accordingly, when St. Paul says in 1 Cor. xv. 44, 'Sown as an animal body, it is raised as a spiritual body', he does not mean that an individual body is buried and later transformed into or replaced by a spiritual body: he means that a body in the individual sense is sown; what is raised is not a body in the individual sense at all, but a body in the communal sense, the church in glory. Needless to say, Robinson does not mean that human personality is lost or swallowed up, but he connects God's guarantee that He

[18] *Christianity according to St. Paul* (Cambridge, 1961²), p. 162.
[19] *The Body* S.B.T. no. 5, (London, 1952).

will maintain our personalities with His calling and our responsibility,[20] and not with the doctrine of the spiritual body; this, in his view, is concerned wholly with the church in the last day, and not with the individual as such. He argues that our life after death depends upon 'calling' by referring to 1 Cor. vii. 7, 'Everyone has the gift (*charisma*) God has granted him', and to 1 Cor. vii. 17: these passages are unconvincing, since they are clearly concerned with gifts for and callings to a particular state of life, such as celibacy and marriage, neither of which necessarily involves personal existence after death. More relevant are 2 Cor. v. 10 and Rom. xiv. 12 which do speak of being answerable in the future and therefore suggest existence after death. 'The resurrection body,' Robinson maintains,[21] 'signifies rather the *solidarity* of the recreated universe in Christ. It is none other than the Body of Christ in which we have a share.' The Body of Christ in the 'corporate' ecclesiological sense is to be identified not only with our own spiritual bodies, or rather spiritual body, for Robinson would presumably not regard the plural as admissible, but also with the Resurrection Body of Christ Himself. Referring to Acts xxvi. 14, ix. 4 and xxii. 7, Robinson declares[22]: '*The appearance on which Paul's whole faith and apostleship was founded wa the revelation of the resurrection body of Christ, not as an individual, but as the Christian community*' (Robinson's italics). I would agree that the term 'Body of Christ' can be applied both to the Resurrection body of Christ and to the church, and that the Resurrection body of Christ is closely associated with the Christian community; the latter could never have come into existence at all if Christ had not died and been raised from the dead, and a very close link exists between Christ and those who are baptized into Him. A man could never have come into existence if it had not been for his mother, and a good mother does not give birth to a son and desert him, but loves him and tends him; yet this close, enduring connection does not constitute *identity*: nor does the close, indeed even closer, connection between Christ and the church constitute identity; and although the same phrase, *Body of Christ*, is applied to both by St. Paul, we must still maintain that he employs the same phrase with two distinct but closely related meanings.

Robinson's book has been widely influential. Its treatment of Pauline theology is invariably illuminating and sometimes original.

[20] Op. cit. pp. 78–9.　　[21] Op. cit. p. 79.　　[22] Op. cit. p. 58.

It lays great emphasis upon 'solidarity', which is still necessary, and it has important practical implications for the 'problem how to "find oneself in community instead of recoiling back from true community into either authoritarianism or individualism".'[23] But the sheer excellence of the work as a whole should not blind our eyes to particular instances of doubtful exegesis. That St. Paul should have been led to apply the term 'Body of Christ' to the church because of his experience upon the road to Damascus is of course highly speculative, but not inherently impossible, although it might have been imagined that, if this were the case, the expression would have been applied to the Christian community more explicitly in his earliest epistles. But it is one matter to suppose that the words of Acts ix. 4, 'Saul, Saul, why do you persecute me?' suggested to the Apostle a close connexion between the 'body' and its 'Head', as they did to St. Augustine[24]; it is quite another matter to maintain that they could have lead St. Paul to *identify* the Resurrection Body of Christ with the church. It is indeed quite impossible to imagine how the vision could possibly have taken a form which might have led to identification. If St. Paul had received merely a 'mystical intimation' that the two were in fact identical, he could scarcely have claimed that the Risen Lord had appeared to him as to the other apostles. Let us suppose, on the other hand, that he was aware of a 'risen body'; this is suggested by the fact that he saw a light, even if he did not actually see a 'shape'. In that case it is only natural to conclude that he would have been led to think of the Resurrection Body of Christ as distinct from His Body which is the church, though this would not preclude a close relationship between the two.

More important is the question whether the 'spiritual body' (*sōma pneumatikon*) of 1 Cor. xv. 44 refers to the manner in which individuals are to exist as individuals after the parousia, or whether it attests the solidarity of all in Christ. The word *sōma* in the Homeric writings[25] is applied exclusively to a corpse. In later Greek it is applied more usually to a living body, although 'corpse'

---

[23] C. F. D. Moule in a review of Robinson's *The Body*, *J.T.S.*, N.S. iv. Pt. I., (1953). p. 74.
[24] St. Augustine, on the basis of Acts ix. 9, applied to the church passages which might have seemed to be applicable to Christ if they had not been unworthy of Him. cf. Pontet, *L'Exégèse de St. Augustin Prédicateur* (Paris, 1944), pp. 397–8.
[25] *Iliad*, iii, 23.

is still a possible meaning in the fifth century B.C.[26] After this the
meaning of 'corpse' 'goes underground'; it disappears from
'respectable' Greek, though it may well have remained current in
the spoken tongue, since we find it in Biblical Greek, and in the
papyri. Moulton and Milligan quote the case of a public physician,
who had been sent (173 A.D.) to 'inspect the dead body' (*sōma
nekron*) of a man found hanged. More usually in classical Greek
after the time of Homer it refers to the living body.[27] When we
turn to the LXX we find that Hatch and Redpath list 141 occurrences of the word *sōma*. It corresponds to fourteen different
Hebrew words. The only one which can claim to be 'common' is
bāsār, flesh, and this it renders almost exclusively in the Pentateuch, especially *Leviticus* in verses concerned with ritual purifica-
tion; it is impossible to maintain that any but the obvious meaning
may be ascribed to *sōma* on the basis of its use to render technical
terms in the Hebrew. In 139 of the 141 cases where it is found
in the LXX *sōma* refers to the human body, dead or alive; the
exceptions are Gen. xv. 11, where it is applied to the carcases of
sacrificial beasts and birds, and Job xl. 32, where it describes the
body of Behemoth.

Morgenthaler[27a] notes 142 instances of the use of *sōma* in the
New Testament. Of these fifty-one are found in the non-Pauline
writings, and in every case but three it refers to the human body
alive or dead, except for Mark xiv. 22 (=Matt. xxvi. 26=Luke
xxii. 19), and in these three cases *sōma* represents the Eucharistic
Body of Christ. Since we are concerned with the exegesis of 1 Cor.
xv. 35, 'How are the dead raised (*egeirō*)? In what kind of body
(*sōma*)?' it is useful to notice Matt. xxvii. 52, 'And many of God's
people arose from sleep [lit., many bodies (*sōma*) of those belonging
to God who slept were raised (*egeirō*)']. The author of *Matthew*
presumably regards this event as a foretaste of the general resurrection due to Christ's victory on Calvary, and it is significant
that he describes this in terms of the raising of bodies in the plural,
using much the same language as St. Paul had done in 1 Cor. xv.
35.

The word *sōma* is absent from the Pastorals, but it is found
ninety-one times in the Paulines and *Ephesians* together, nine

[26] Sophocles, *Electra*, 758. The *sōma* is here strictly a corpse.
[27] In Luke xvii. 37 it probably refers to an animal's carcase, while in Jas. iii.
3 it certainly refers to the living bodies of horses.
[27a] *Statistik des Neutestamentlichen Wortschatzes* (Zürich, 1958), *sub voce*.

times in *Ephesians* and on eighty-two occasions in the admittedly Pauline epistles. Once, in Col. ii. 17, it means 'substance', being explicitly contrasted with 'shadow' (*skia*). There are five Eucharistic applications at 1 Cor. x. 16, 17; xi. 24, 27, 29. In a number of instances the word denotes the church.[28] But in the vast majority of cases the reference is to the human individual, indeed, in the opinion of the majority of scholars, Robinson and Ellis[29] being notable exceptions, this is the meaning of *sōma* in every other case where it is found in the Pauline Epistles. Sometimes the human individual is meant in an apparently straightforward, physical sense, for example in Gal. vi. 17, 'For I bear the marks of Jesus branded on my body'; sometimes *sōma* designates the entire human personality, as in Rom. viii. 10, where the physical body is not literally dead, but the whole personality is 'dead' (*nekron*) in the sense that it is overwhelmed by sin; in two places the word serves to describe a man as being in the grip of sin or of death, though it is not clear whether in these two passages, Rom. vi. 6 and vii. 24 the 'body of sin' and 'body of death' respectively are the 'sinful self' and the 'body doomed to death', as in the N.E.B., or 'solidarity' with sin and death respectively, as Robinson would no doubt maintain.

The upshot of this summary examination is that in the Bible *sōma* is applied to the individual human being, alive or dead, except where some other meaning is demanded by the context.

It is difficult to see how the context of 1 Cor. xv. 35 demands any but an individual meaning. The question asked by the Corinthians would seem to move within the same field of interest as we find in the Syriac Apocalypse of Baruch (compiled after 70 A.D., but not much later), i. 1–ii. 5, 'For the earth shall then assuredly restore the dead. . . . But as it has received them, so it shall restore them. . . . For then it will be necessary to show to the living that the dead have come to life again . . . they shall respectively be transformed, the latter (i.e. the righteous) into the splendour of angels'.[30] In 1 Cor. xv. 38, St. Paul illustrates his thesis with parallels drawn from the vegetable realm; speaking of wheat and other grains he says: 'God clothes it with the body (*sōma*) of his own choice, each (*hekastō*) seed with its own (*idion*) body'. It would certainly appear that the Apostle is thinking of the

[28] cf. *supra*, pp. 187ff. and notes.
[29] cf. *supra*, pp. 192ff. and *infra*, pp. 225–8.
[30] Charles, vol. ii. p. 508.

outward appearance of wheat, barley and other grains, rather than of the 'solidarities' into which they might be subsequently incorporated. Rabbi Eliezer (c. 90 A.D.) used a similar figure to show that the dead would rise with their clothes[31]; a difficulty is raised for Robinson's theory by 1 Cor. xv. 44, 'Sown as an animal body, it is raised as a spiritual body'. It is not, of course, certain that the subject of the two verbs 'sown' (*speiretai*) and 'raised' (*egeiretai*) is the same. It would be possible to translate: 'An animal organ of individuality is sown; a spiritual organ of corporate existence is raised'. But this does not really sound at all convincing.

Although the matter is clearly not beyond dispute, it seems more probable that 'body' in 1 Cor. xv. refers to individuals, and not to the church. We must summarize our consideration of the word body. This word can be applied to

(a) the body of Christ in His earthly life,

(b) the Resurrection Body of Christ,

(c) the Church, and

(d) the Eucharistic body.

(a) The earthly body of Christ belonged to the natural order and was described in straightforward literal language.

(b) The Resurrection body belongs to the supernatural order, but the language used to describe it is nonetheless literal.

(c) The church is both 'natural' and 'supernatural'; the term 'Body of Christ' is a metaphorical manner of describing a fact which cannot be adequately described without the use of metaphor: there is thus no question of calling it a 'mere' metaphor, because the use of metaphor is inevitable, and because, as will appear later, there is more than one point of correspondence.

(d) The consecrated elements in the Eucharist cannot be ascribed exclusively to either the 'natural' or the 'supernatural' realm. The elements remain 'natural' after consecration: but God employs them for a 'supernatural' purpose. The reality of the Eucharist, like that of the church, can be expressed only by the use of metaphor, and the same metaphor or figure, namely that of the Body of Christ, is used to express two different realities. Here again, and for similar reasons, there is no question of 'mere' metaphor.

The realities denoted by the word 'body' are closely connected. St. Paul almost certainly believed that (a) the earthly body of

---

[31] Strack-Billerbeck, vol. iii. p. 475.

Christ was identical with (b) the Resurrection body, and that the change from the one to the other, through the Crucifixion and Resurrection, was essential to our salvation, with the corollary that apart from this change the church and the Eucharistic Body would have been pointless and ineffectual.

On the other hand (c), Christ's Body which is the church, is not identical with (a) and (b), but is very closely connected. It is primarily through the church that Christ continues to accomplish the final purpose for which He assumed human nature, and the link between Christ and His church is not mechanical or external: though there is no swallowing up of human personality, there is for St. Paul a general transcending of the separateness of normal human individuality in the case of those who are baptized into Christ.

Again, (d) the Eucharistic body of Christ is not to be identified either with the church or with the Resurrection Body; but it is a link between the two: it is a means of continuing the purpose of the Incarnation, and it is most clearly a point at which we are linked both with Christ in His 'Resurrection body' and, through Him, with other members of His Body, which is the church.

Those who speak of 'identity' between the different realities expressed by the term 'Body of Christ' are probably employing the word 'identity' not strictly, but in a suggestive, evocative sense.

To employ a familiar illustration, the moon is not identical with the sun, but reflects its light, having none of its own. Christ's Eucharistic Body and His Body the church are not identical with the Glorified Body, but they reflect and diffuse the power of the Risen and Glorified Christ.

Although the reality cannot be expressed without metaphor, or translated without remainder into purely literal language, there is more than one metaphor used by St. Paul to describe the church. It is not only the Body of Christ, but the Israel of God (Gal. vi. 16), the Bride betrothed to God (2 Cor. xi. 2).

Concerning these metaphors three points must be made. First, all the metaphorical expressions used by St. Paul to describe the church are connected either with Christ or with Israel: since Christ and Israel were the individual and the group respectively, in whom God had acted supremely, all these metaphors describe the church as the sphere of God's activity, and to be more precise, as the sphere of God's activity in Christ. St. Paul's *doctrine* of the church is not complicated. It fails to be easily comprehensible because God and His activity are beyond our understanding, but St. Paul does not make a large number of complicated statements about the church. On the contrary, he says in effect that the church is the chief sphere of the activity of God in Christ, but he expresses this simple truth through a variety of metaphors which lend to his doctrine the appearance of complexity.

The expression 'Israel of God', applied by St. Paul to the church in Gal. vi. 16, cannot reasonably be described as a metaphor, since the Apostle's contention was precisely this, that the function of being 'Israel', the People of God, had passed to the church from 'Israel according to the flesh'. The expression 'New Israel' is found nowhere in the New Testament; it is well known to be a piece of contemporary theological jargon which is perfectly legitimate, provided that it does not lure us into adopting an unjustifiably schematic view of salvation-history, and into accepting the view that there was for St. Paul a one-one correspondence between the events of the old and the new dispensations.

When we come to examine St. Paul's use of language derived from building to describe the church, it becomes clear to us that 'building' was not a 'standard title' for the church, as 'Lord' was for Christ, or as 'body' had become for the church at least in the Epistle to the Ephesians. St. Paul never calls the church a building, although he does apply the verb 'build' metaphorically to the church. The word *oikos*, house, is invariably used by St. Paul of a dwelling place, although it is the place where the local congregation met for worship. The same must be said of *oikia*, house, except in 2 Cor. v. 1, where it refers to the spiritual body.

iii. THE APOSTOLATE

St. Luke's understanding of the qualifications which were necessary to be reckoned as one of the twelve apostles is clear from Acts i. 21–25, 'Therefore one of those who bore us company all the while we had the Lord Jesus with us, coming and going, from John's ministry of baptism until the day when he was taken up from us—one of those must now join us as a witness of his resurrection. . . . Then they prayed and said, "Thou Lord who knowest the hearts of all men, declare which of these two thou hast chosen to receive this office of ministry (*diakonias*) and apostleship (*apostolē*)".' To be a member of the twelve it was necessary

P

(1) to have been with Jesus from the beginning,

(2) to have been a witness of the Resurrection, and specially

(3) to have been chosen for the purpose by Christ (Luke vi. 13 = Mark iii. 16 = Matt. x. 1) or by God, as in the present passage.

St. Paul's teaching was similar, as we can see from the fundamental passage, 1 Cor. xv. 5–8, 'He appeared (1) to Cephas, and afterwards to (2) the Twelve. Then he appeared (3) to over five hundred of our brothers at once, most of whom are still alive, though some have died. Then he appeared to (4) James, and afterwards to (5) all the apostles. In the end he appeared (6) even to me'. It would appear that a distinction is intended between the Twelve, who witnessed the second of the six appearances here recorded by St. Paul, and 'all the apostles', who were witnesses of the fifth such appearance.

All scholars agree that St. Paul regarded himself as an apostle along with the Twelve, but many doubt whether he extended the apostolate much further. Most scholars also agree that he regarded James the brother of the Lord as an apostle, since he says in Gal. i. 18–19, 'I stayed with him (Cephas) for a fortnight without seeing any other of the apostles except (*ei mē*) James the Lord's brother'. It is, of course, quite possible that *ei mē* in this verse means 'but only', as in Matt. xii. 14 and in Rom. xiv. 14, 'Nothing is impure in itself; only (*ei mē*) if a man considers a particular thing impure, then to him it is impure'.

There is good reason to hold that St. Paul regarded others as apostles of Christ besides the Twelve, St. James, and himself. First, in 1 Cor. xv. the fifth recorded appearance, the appearance to all the apostles, would naturally suggest persons other than the Twelve, St. James and St. Paul, who witnessed the second, fourth and sixth appearances respectively. This point is not conclusive, since the first appearance was a 'private' one to St. Peter, who was also, we may suppose, included in the appearance to the Twelve. Again, the fact that St. Paul mentions in 2 Cor. xi. 13, 'Sham-apostles . . . masquerading as apostles of Christ', suggests that there were genuine apostles of Christ apart from a small fixed number.

2 Cor. viii. 23 speaks of the 'delegates of our congregations' (*apostoloi ekklēsiōn*) and the same use is found in Phil. ii. 25, 'Epaphroditus . . . whom you commissioned', lit. 'your *apostolos*'. These 'delegates of congregations' may have been persons endowed with the regular status of 'representative', or they may have been

individuals who on one or more occasions were commissioned to carry out a particular task. Since there were both 'apostles of Christ' and also 'delegates' (*apostoloi*) of congregations, in cases where the word *apostolos* is not so defined we must decide from the context which St. Paul intended.

1 Thess. ii. 6, 'Although as Christ's own envoys (*apostoloi*) we might have made our weight felt', is applied by A. T. Hanson[32] to Paul, Silvanus, and Timothy, in whose names the epistle was written. To the objection that the 'we' is an epistolary plural, referring to St. Paul alone, Hanson replies that the plural *apostoloi* makes it impossible, and that our hearts (*kardias*) in v. 4 and our very selves (*psuchas*) in v. 8 would make it unlikely. Hanson's argument is extremely probable, but is not quite conclusive, because much variation in number can occur. Milligan[33] quotes from a papyrus of the third century B.C., 'We wrote . . . seeing (plural participle) . . . I thought, *egrapsamen* . . . *horōntes* . . . *ōimēn*, all three plural'. However, it would be contrary to the evidence to reject Hanson's conclusion, above all since the plural is found in St. Paul's letters *only* when others are associated with him as joint-authors; whereas in *Romans*, written by St. Paul alone, the singular is found throughout.

In 1 Cor. iv. 9, 'Us apostles' may well refer back to Paul and Apollos in iv. 6, but this is an open question. 1 Cor. ix. 1–6 claims that St. Paul himself is an apostle, points out that apostolic rights are accorded to the rest of the apostles and the Lord's brothers and Cephas, and goes on to claim rights for Barnabas and Paul; the natural inference is that Barnabas also was regarded as an apostle, though this is not quite conclusive, since a man who was not an apostle, but was doing the work of an apostle, might claim the maintenance due to an apostle.

Rom. xvi. 7, 'Greet Andronicus and Junias. . . . They are eminent among the apostles (*episēmoi en tois apostolois*)', would appear to add two more to the list of apostles. The accusative *Iounian* may come from the nominative masculine *Iounias*, in which case it must be accented perispomenon, *Iouniân*, which is the accentuation followed in the text of Nestle-Kilpatrick. It may, however, come from the nominative feminine *Iounia*, in which case it must be accented paroxytone, *Iounian*. Since accentuation was

[32] A. T. Hanson, *The Pioneer Ministry* (London, 1961), p. 48.
[33] This example and several others are quoted in *St. Paul's Epistle to the Thessalonians* (London, 1908), Additional Note B, pp. 131–2.

not used until long after the time of St. Paul, it was impossible in his own day to show whether Junian was a feminine or a masculine accusative. Some authorities, however, including the early third-century Chester Beatty Papyrus 46 read *Ioulian*, Julia, which is unquestionably feminine. That a woman should be an apostle is surprising, although Chrysostom accepted this understanding of Rom. xvi. 7. On the principle that the harder reading is to be preferred, we ought not lightly to reject the reading of Papyrus 46: it would be natural for a scribe in all good faith to 'correct the obvious error', as it would appear to him, of a female apostle; but what scribe would turn a masculine name for an apostle into the feminine? According to Arndt-Gringrich the possibility that a feminine name is here intended is unlikely, because of the context. If we adopt a fixed view of the apostolate, we can fairly say that it is unlikely that a woman would have been an apostle. But the question we must ask is this: was the word *apostolos* applied to a woman? The answer must surely be that it may have been. We know from the Gospels that women saw the risen Lord, and it is not impossible that, though all the twelve were men, a woman who had seen the Lord may also have received a call to be an apostle.

It is probable then that there were other apostles besides the Twelve, St. Paul, the Lord's brother and Barnabas. It is possible that at least one woman was an apostle. It is only fair to add that the wider we draw the circle, the more we see the apostle in functional terms. He ceases to be a member of a fixed group with a peculiar status and becomes a person who had witnessed the Resurrection and received a call to be an apostle, that is, a person 'sent'.

What matters about the Apostles is not so much the fact that they were *sent*, but the fact that they were sent by *God*. 1 Cor. xii. 28, 'Within our community God has appointed, in the first place apostles', shows this in the case of apostles in general.[34] So does Gal. i. 1, 'From Paul, an apostle, not by human appointment or human commission, but by commission from Jesus Christ and God the Father . . .', in the case of St. Paul himself. The apostle enjoyed pre-eminence and authority, as we can see from 1 Thess. ii. 6, 'As Christ's own envoys, *apostoloi*, lit. "apostles", we might have made our weight felt'.

The problem of Apostolic Succession has been the focus of

---

[34] The divine source of the apostolate is shown also in Eph. iv. 11, 'And these were his gifts: some to be apostles. . .'

much difficulty in reunion consultations. It is clear that there can be no succession *to* the Apostolate as such: no one can 'succeed' to having seen the Risen Christ. But there may be succession *from* the Apostles, though this is a controversial matter concerning the difficult 'tunnel'-period; in any case, the dispute centres round the significance as well as the 'fact' of Apostolic Succession. But in any body of Christians worthy of the name the functions performed by the Apostles in the First-Century church must be carried out. Our contemporary problems concern the ministry and jurisdiction. To see the Pauline apostle in true perspective, we must remember that he was above all the link between Christ and the Christians with respect to God's self-revelation. In our own day these functions are carried out in part by the New Testament, in the Liturgy and in many cases by the sermon which is a proclamation of the message committed in the First Century to the Apostles. Nevertheless, there does remain an essential place for the ministry, and this has become the focus of controversies which are outside the scope of this book.

iv. OTHER MINISTRIES

Priests, *presbuteroi*, are never mentioned in the Paulines or in *Ephesians*. *Episkopoi* and *diakonoi*, overseers and servants, are mentioned at Phil. i. 1 only. 'Serving' and 'overseeing' were certainly functions; it is not clear whether in St. Paul's day they had hardened into 'offices'. We are told in Acts xx. 18 that St. Paul at Miletus sent to Ephesus and summoned *tous presbuterous tēs ekklēsias*; since St. Luke speaks of *presbuteroi* as men in charge of charitable gifts at Acts xi. 30, refers to the appointment of presbuteroi at Acts xiv. 23, and associates them with the Apostles in his account of the Council of Jerusalem, it is surely justifiable to regard them as 'office holders', elders, and not simply 'old men' as at Acts ii. 17. When he speaks to these elders St. Paul says in Acts xx. 28, 'The flock of which the Holy Spirit has given you charge, *etheto episkopous*', which could be rendered 'appointed you bishops'. In so far as this passage reflects Pauline, and not exclusively Lucan phraseology, it confirms the Pauline stress on divine appointment of Christian ministers. It shows that there were those who exercised oversight, but does not make it clear whether or no the '*episkopos*' held an office of *episkopos* or merely carried out the function of oversight.

Prophecy, *prophēteia* is recognized as a gift of God in Rom. xii 6, while the Thessalonians are forbidden to despise it in 1 Thess. v. 20. Apart from these two passages the subject is mentioned in the Pauline Epistles, excluding *Eph.*, only in *1 Cor.* There are in St. Paul's Epistles three lists of spiritual gifts:

(1) Rom. xii. 6-8.
(2) 1 Cor. xii. 8-10.
(3) 1 Cor. xii. 28-30. We may add
(4) Eph. iv. 11.

In each of these it is made clear that the gift in question is due to God or the Spirit. In the three Pauline lists it is obvious from the context that the gifts are to be employed for the good of the whole church: in each case the 'body' is mentioned, at Rom. xii. 4; 1 Cor. xii. 12, 27, while in Eph. iv. 11-12 we are told in so many words that these gifts were given by God 'for work in his service, to the building up of the body of Christ'.

In the passages where apostles are mentioned at all, 1 Cor. xii. 28, Eph. iv. 11, they are mentioned first. In both cases the prophets come next. In Rom. xii. 6f., where apostles are not mentioned, the prophets come first. In 1 Cor. xii. 8f. prophecy is mentioned sixth in a list of nine gifts. 1 Cor. xiv. 4-5 makes it clear that prophecy, inspired speaking, is superior to incoherent 'talking with tongues' because it builds up the church. An examination of the other gifts, teaching, healing, administrative ability, etc., belongs to the exegesis of the individual passages and to a study of Christian life and institutions rather than to the theology of St. Paul. Two points, however, are significant theologically. First, for St. Paul the activity of the Spirit is vital. It has often been said that the Third Person of the Trinity has been neglected in books on New Testament theology. This may be because so much of His importance lies in the sphere of 'Life and Work', not of 'Faith and Order' in so far as they can legitimately be distinguished. Secondly, we must resist any temptation to regard the mention of healing as a sign of a Jewish, as opposed to Greek, view of matter: the healing cult of Asclepius was one of the most popular in the Graeco-Roman world. To conclude, the cardinal point about 'spiritual' gifts is that these were not due to the inherent capacity of the individual but were given by God for the building up of the church.

CHAPTER NINE

MORALITY

i. Morality Integral to St. Paul's Theology

It has become fashionable in recent years to regard ethics as a very trivial part of theology. This is a comprehensible, but nevertheless thoroughly regrettable reaction against the tendency which formerly obtained in some quarters to limit Christianity to the Sermon on the Mount, incorrectly interpreted. Christianity according to St. Paul is not mere *morality*, but for him morality itself is not *mere* morality: it is an essential and inseparable part of his entire corpus of thought, and its status is not diminished but enchanced by its integration with his 'dogmatic' theology. In this St. Paul is showing himself to be a true Biblical Jew, for, as Dodd remarks,[1] whereas Greek teachers attempted to develop systems of ethics which were self-contained and self-justifying, the Old Testament based its moral precepts firmly upon the Nature of God and His saving acts.

Many of St. Paul's fundamental utterances, essential pillars of Christian theology, are occasioned by the need to drive home some ethical point. Among those we may note 1 Cor. v. 7, 'The sacrifice is offered—Christ himself,' which is introduced to urge more stringent moral standards. 1 Cor. viii. 6, 'There is one Lord, Jesus Christ, through whom all things came to be, and we through him,' is introduced in the course of teaching about food consecrated to heathen deities; and 2 Cor. viii. 9, 'You know how generous our Lord Jesus Christ has been: he was rich, yet for your sake he became poor, so that through his poverty you might become rich,' is introduced in order to show the need for generous giving.

Indeed, every 'article'[2] of the *kerygma* is connected by St. Paul with moral exhortation.

1. *The fulfilment of Scripture.* 1 Cor. x. 11. cf. Rom. xv. 4.
2. *The coming of the Messiah.* In the 'Incarnation hymn' of Phil. ii. 5–11, the Incarnation, Death, Resurrection, and Heavenly

---

[1] *Gospel and Law* (Cambridge, 1951), pp. 10–11.
[2] cf. *supra* p. 9ff.

Session of Christ are all employed to the end that the Philippians may have the right bearing towards one another.

3. *The Crucifixion.* Rom. xiv. 15, 'Do not by your eating bring disaster to a man for whom Christ died!'

4. *The Burial.* Rom. vi. 4, 'By baptism we were buried with him, and lay dead, in order that, as Christ was raised from the dead in the splendour of the Father, so also we might set our feet upon the new path of life.'

5. and 6. *The Resurrection and Heavenly Session.* Col. iii. 1–2, 'Were you not raised to life with Christ? Then aspire to the realm above, where Christ is, seated at the right hand of God.'

7. *The sending of the Spirit.* Gal. v. 25, 'If the spirit is the source of our life, let the spirit also direct our course.'

8. *The Judgement.* 2 Cor. v. 10, 'For we must all have our lives laid open before the tribunal of Christ, where each must receive what is due to him for his conduct in the body, good or bad.'

Needless to say, this list is merely illustrative, and is far from being exhaustive. It is intended to show how uncharacteristic of St. Paul is any dichotomy between *Heilsgeschichte* and morality.

St. Paul never suggests that morality is in any sense a prior condition necessary for justification,[3] but he insists that to live an immoral life is inconsistent with being a Christian, as appears from the passages cited under 4, 5, 6, and 7 above.[4] God's moral demands upon the Christian are linked by St. Paul with His Saving Acts, and especially with Baptism, with the Imitation of Christ, which may be regarded as the ethical aspect of 'being' in Christ, and with eschatology.

Morality is closely connected with Baptism, through which we share in the Death and Resurrection of Christ. In answer to the question raised in Rom. vi. 1, 'Shall we persist in sin, so that there may be all the more grace?' St. Paul replies: 'Have you forgotten that when we were baptized into union with Christ Jesus we were baptized into his death? . . . We know that the man we once were has been crucified with Christ, for the destruction of the sinful self'. (Rom. vi. 3, 6.)[5] The imitation of Christ is not to be conceived 'externally'; rather, when we 'imitate' Christ, we 'reflect' His manner of living. It is because we are 'in' Christ, and our lives are 'continuous' with His that they bear the imprint

---

[3] cf. *supra* p. 156ff.

[4] cf. Anderson Scott, *Christianity according to St. Paul* (Cambridge, 1961²), pp. 207–8.   [5] cf. Gal. ii. 20; iii. 27; Col. ii. 12; iii. 3.

of His example. Sometimes the command to follow Christ's example is direct, as in Rom. xv. 7, 'Accept one another as Christ accepted us, to the Glory of God'.[6] More frequently the Christians are urged to imitate St. Paul, who was himself an imitator of Christ, as in 1 Thess. i. 6, 'And you, in your turn, followed the example set by us and by the Lord,' and in 1 Cor. xi. 1, 'Follow my example, as I follow Christ's.'[7] Tinsley has examined the Pauline passages where the imitation of Christ is mentioned, and has shown how they are paralleled in the Gospels.[8]

It is primarily because of the relation between morality and baptism that the hypothesis of the moral *didache* or teaching is relevant to our purpose. According to this hypothesis the apostolic *paradosis*, or tradition comprised, in addition to kerygmatic[9] and liturgical elements, standard moral instruction, expressed in similar words and arranged under certain standard themes; this moral teaching, it is held, was imparted at baptism; and similar passages in different epistles are to be accounted for on the basis of common dependence upon the oral *didache*, not by a theory of literary dependence, e.g. by 1 *Peter* upon *Ephesians* or *Romans*. This theory owes its origin to Alfred Seeberg[10] and has been developed by Hunter,[11] Carrington,[12] Selwyn,[13] and Dodd.[14]

The theory has been attacked by Beare. The first edition of his book *The First Epistle of Peter*[15] was written before the publication of Selwyn's commentary, which he was therefore unable to consider, but in the second edition,[16] he includes for the first time a brief critique[17] of the *didache*-theory. This is an important issue for the critical study of the New Testament but its solution is not necessary for an understanding of the ethical teaching of St. Paul. It is in any case beyond dispute that his epistles include ethical teaching which is connected with baptism and expounded with authority. It is not necessary to decide whether St. Paul and 1 *Peter* reproduced common catechetical

---

[6] cf. Phil. ii. 5f; Eph. iv. 32f.   [7] cf. 1 Cor. iv. 17; Gal. iv. 12.
[8] E. J. Tinsley, *The Imitation of God in Christ* (London, 1960), pp. 134–65.
[9] cf. *supra*, pp. 9ff.
[10] *Der Katechismus der Urchristenheit* (Leipzig, 1903).
[11] A. M. Hunter, *Paul and his Predecessors* (London, 1961²).
[12] P. Carrington. *The Primitive Christian Catechism* (Cambridge, 1940).
[13] E. G. Selwyn, *The First Epistle of St. Peter* (London, 1947²), Essay II, pp. 365–466, including some valuable tables.
[14] *Gospel and Law* (Cambridge, 1951).
[15] F. W. Beare (Oxford, 1947).   [16] (Oxford, 1958²).
[17] Op. cit. pp. 194–6, with short but useful bibliographical footnotes.

material or whether 1 *Peter* derived material from *Ephesians*, and through *Ephesians* from *Colossians*.

Baptism, however, although an *essential*[18] beginning, is only a *beginning*.[19] This supplies the clue to the apparent conflict between St. Paul's indicatives, such as Rom. v. 1, 'We have been justified through faith,' 2 Cor. v. 17, 'When anyone is united to Christ, there is a new world,' and Col. i. 13, 'He rescued us from the domain of darkness and transferred us into the kingdom of his dear Son,'[20] and on the other hand his imperatives such as Gal. v. 13, 'Be servants to one another in love.' The indicative describes what God has already done, and provides the basis for the imperative, which tells the Christian what each one must still do.[21] The indicatives speak of something which is independent of human initiative and of human merit, but they do not preclude human obedience, though human merit and 'boasting' have, of course, no place in the thought of St. Paul.

The apparent contradiction is due partly to the fact that morality is not a prior condition for justification, whereas it is an aspect of sanctification, partly to the fact that St. Paul is dealing with different problems in different passages, and that confusion is the inevitable result if we pit against each other sayings which do not really deal with the same problems. Gal. v. 24, 'And those who belong to Christ Jesus have crucified the lower nature with its passions and desires,' does not contradict Gal. vi. 7, 'God is not to be fooled; a man reaps what he sows.' The former shows that in Baptism[22] the Christian, by faith in Christ, has renounced evil: the latter that if the Christian practises the gross sins which he has already renounced, he cannot rely complacently upon Baptism.[23] The doctrine of the two verses is not contradictory and is indeed combined in Gal. v. 13, 'You, my friends, were called to be free men, only do not turn your freedom into licence for your lower nature, but be servants to one another in love.'

The Christian must face temptation, and will be judged in

[18] Remembering always that Baptism is for St. Paul inseparable from Faith and newness of life. cf. *supra*, p. 170 ff.

[19] So Bonsirven, *L'Evangile de Paul* (Paris, 1948). p. 286.

[20] Among other such 'indicative' passages are Gal. v. 24, Eph. ii. 5, 18.

[21] cf. Bultmann, *Theology*, vol. i. p. 333.

[22] Baptism, though not explicitly mentioned, is clearly presupposed.

[23] The incompatibility of gross sin with possession of the Kingdom of God is also made clear in 1 Cor. vi. 9–11, Gal. v. 21.

accordance with his works; the outcome must not be taken for granted. By 'putting on Christ' he has accepted the *possibility* of possessing the Kingdom of God; apart from Christ, this would have been wholly impossible. That there is nothing automatic about being in Christ is apparent from 1 Thess. iii. 5, 'When I could bear it no longer I sent to find out about your faith, fearing lest the tempter might have tempted you and my labour might be lost'.[24] St. Paul's name is so closely connected with 'salvation by faith' that it is frequently forgotten how strongly he expresses the doctrine of judgement according to works. It is true that Rom. ii. 5, 'You are laying up for yourself a store of retribution,' applies to 'the critic' who *may* be a Jew and not, as is more probable, a Jewish Christian, but Rom. xiv. 10, 'We shall all stand before God's tribunal,' includes all Christians by virtue of their solidarity with Christ. 2 Cor. xi. 15 refers to false apostles, and 1 Cor. iii. 17 is addressed primarily to those who are quarrelsome and have schismatic tendencies, but 2 Cor. v. 10 applies to Christians in general, while we read in 1 Cor. iv. 4, 'I have nothing on my conscience; but that does not mean that I stand acquitted. My judge is the Lord.' The Apostle here makes it perfectly obvious that he himself stands under judgement.

All these considerations make it certain that ethics was not peripheral for St. Paul, but an integral and essential part of the fabric of his thought. Contemporary discussion on this matter has been bedevilled by two facts. First, we are living in an age of 'residual Christianity' when many who do not attend public worship nevertheless acknowledge moral standards which in content can fairly be described as Christian. Churchmen who argue that the position of these 'semi-christians' is not satisfactory can easily fall into the error of belittling the vital importance of morality as part of the total Christian life, whereas what in most cases they wish to attack is the contention that morality is sufficient by itself, divorced from other aspects of the whole Christian life. Secondly, we are familiar with the view that there are moral systems independent of God. To St. Paul this would have been unthinkable. God had made His will known to all men, who therefore stood under judgement. For St. Paul the sinner was not merely guilty of an offence against an impersonal code: he was in a state of deliberate rebellion against a personal God.

[24] cf. 1 Cor. vii. 5; 2 Cor. ii. 11.

ii. THE CRITERIA OF MORALITY

(a) 'Conscience' only negative

We must now consider how St. Paul thought that we can know what is right and what is wrong.

We may first clear the ground by saying that 'conscience' is a correct answer only in a negative sense, if by 'conscience' we refer to the word *suneidēsis* which it normally renders in the English version of the Greek Testament. C. A. Pierce[25] has shown that this word, taken over by St. Paul from the popular language of his time, meant simply 'remorse' or, when modified by some such word as 'good', 'freedom from remorse.' 'Conscience' then shows us what is right only in the sense that when we feel 'remorse' we know that we have already done wrong. In later Christian writers, from the third century onward, 'conscience' came to bear the meaning 'good' conscience and came to be thought of as a positive, selective power enabling us to know what is right before we do it, like the *phronēsis*, 'practical wisdom', of Aristotle instead of merely telling us that something is wrong after we have done it. The latter is the sole meaning of the word in all the fourteen[26] Pauline occurrences. In Rom. xiii. 5, 'It is an obligation imposed not merely by fear of retribution but by conscience,' the 'positive' obligation to submit is backed by two 'negative' sanctions, fear of retribution and remorse. In 1 Cor. viii. 10, 'Will not his conscience be emboldened (*oikodomēthēsetai*, lit. built up, edified) to eat food consecrated to the heathen deity?,' the meaning is that the 'weak character's' sense of remorse will be so distorted that he feels no remorse even after taking part in heathen sacrifices; the word *oikodomeō* is probably used sarcastically.

(b) Ground, motive, and criterion

The criterion, the means by which we know what is right or wrong, must be distinguished both from the motive, the reason for which we do it, and from the 'ground'; the 'ground' is what makes something right or wrong as opposed both to the motive, the reason for which we do it, and to the criterion. In the case

---

[25] *Conscience in the New Testament* S.B.T., 15, (London, 1955).
[26] Rom. ii. 15; ix. 1; xiii. 5; 1 Cor. viii. 7, 10, 12; x. 25, 27, 28, 29 (twice); 2 Cor. i. 12; iv. 2; v. 11. The word is absent from *Ephesians*, and is found six times in the Pastorals.

of the 'ordinary' Christian (it is not intended to use this word in a bad sense) we may say that his motive is the hope of being with Christ in Heaven, that his criterion is his conscience, in the modern, not the Pauline sense, and that he believes the 'ground' which makes an act right, to be the fact that it is in accordance with the will of God. St. Paul did not consciously use these distinctions, and it can be urged that 'unity with Christ as a member of His body the church' could be all three; it could be the reason why we should be long-suffering with our fellow-Christians, the means by which we know that we ought to be, end the reason why we are.

(c) *God's Commandments*

St. Paul would have agreed that the Will of God is the ultimate ground of all true morality. 1 Thess. iv. 9, 'You yourselves are taught by God to love one another,' shows that God directly supplies the means of knowing what is right. Though a considerable proportion of St. Paul's epistles are devoted to ethical matters, he is for the most part not consciously aware of how he knows what is right. When he speaks of the duties of wives, children, slaves and other members of families he is unconsciously taking for granted what is really traditional teaching. Most of it in fact he probably did derive from Judaism: some of it he could have taken from Gentile sources. In Rom. xiii. 9 he accepts as binding prohibitions of adultery, murder, theft, and covetousness included in the Decalogue. Although he drew no conscious distinction between the moral and the ceremonial law, he clearly took over much of the content of the moral teaching of the Old Testament.

1 Cor. viii. 25, 'I give my judgement as one who by God's mercy is fit to be trusted,' links the Apostle's own awareness of right and wrong with the first Person of the Trinity as do other passages with the Second and Third; though it is unlikely that he was consciously aware of the Trinitarian issue in this verse.

(d) *The teaching and example of Christ and St. Paul*

In 1 Cor. ix. 14 St. Paul produces as a criterion the teaching of Christ. He ascribes to the Lord the instruction that those who preach the Gospel should earn their living by the Gospel; he evidently has in mind the saying preserved in Matt. x. 10=Luke x. 7. Another reference to Christ's teaching is 1 Cor. vii. 10, 'To

the married I give this ruling, which is not mine but the Lord's. . .'
St. Paul clearly has in mind the dominical teaching embodied in
Mark x. 1–12. These are two cases of the teaching of Christ
when on earth being used as a moral criterion. They can be
matched by others in which the Risen Christ is represented as
speaking through St. Paul. These are 1 Cor. ii. 16, 'We, however,
possess the mind of Christ,' and 2 Cor. xiii. 3, 'The Christ who
speaks through me'; it is significant that in the very next verse
St. Paul stresses the fact that he shares the weakness and life of
Christ. It should be admitted that the point at issue in both these
cases is ecclesiastical authority rather than the power to distinguish between right and wrong in a narrowly ethical sense.

It may seem strange that St. Paul should make such sparing
use of Christ's ethical teaching. E. J. Tinsley[27] points out that
this was due to an unwillingness to separate the teaching from
the life. He quotes a number of Pauline passages which may be
paraphrases of Christ's teaching.

The teaching of Christ was for St. Paul mediated less through
His words than through His life, and His life also was mediated
through that of the church, including especially St. Paul himself.
This becomes abundantly clear from 1 Thess. i. 6, 'You, in your
turn, followed the example set by us and by the Lord; the welcome
you gave the message meant grave suffering for you.' Sometimes
the example of Paul alone is mentioned, as in 1 Cor. iv. 16 and in
2 Thess. iii. 7, and Phil. iii. 17. Rom. xv. 7, 'In a word, accept
one another, as Christ accepted us,' mentions the example of
Christ alone.

St. Paul would have been horrified at the thought that his
example should be accorded any weight at all as that of a second
authority *independent* of Christ. The Apostle's example had value
only because 'The life I now live is not my life, but the life which
Christ lives in me' (Gal. ii. 20). At the risk of understanding
St. Paul too much in the light of the conditions which obtain in
the middle of our own century, we may venture upon a partial
explanation for the emphasis which St. Paul lays upon his own
example, that is, upon the example of a life in which Christ lived.
St. Paul, being a missionary to the Gentiles, was continually
meeting new situations for which precedents drawn from the
past were of limited value. Under such conditions, abstract

[27] *The Imitation of God in Christ* (London, 1960), pp. 148–50.

theoretical reasoning, which was not St. Paul's way, is also insufficient, though it has its place. What is needed is an actual decision in a concrete situation by the 'right kind of man.' St. Paul was 'the right kind of man' in the sense that Christ lived in him. This is unavoidably speculative, but we may suggest that for St. Paul Christ taught not only by word but by example, not only by the example of His incarnate life, but through the example of His continued life in His body the church.

(e) *Guidance by the Holy Spirit*

In the case of Jesus Christ, Who was at one time Incarnate, there is a distinction between the teaching given in the days of His flesh and that delivered through others after His Resurrection. No such distinction arises in the case of the Holy Spirit, Who was never incarnate.

We distinguish between knowledge of what is right and the power to carry it out. St. Paul ascribes both gifts to the Spirit in Gal. v. 25, 'Let the spirit also direct our course.' Gal. v. 16, 'If you are guided by the spirit, you will not fulfil the desires of your lower nature,' certainly refers to the power to do what is right and probably also to the ability to know what is right.

It is important to add that 'ability to know' what is right is not a specialized gift of the Spirit, like prophecy, which is confined to some Christians only. All Christians, just because they are Christians, are 'in Christ', and all are led by the Spirit. It is true that there are, and were, 'bad' Christians, but St. Paul never worked out a theology of the 'bad' Christians, though he was not unaware of the problem, as we can tell from 1 Cor. v. †

iii. Marriage

(a) *Fornication*

The gross 'sexual immorality' which St. Paul castigates in 1 Cor. v. 1f. was probably the union of a man with his stepmother. The Greek word *porneia* covered a wider range than the English 'fornication.' It is probably fornication in our limited sense which he condemns in 2 Cor. xii. 21; 1 Thess. iv. 3, and also, along with other vices, in Gal. v. 19; Col. iii. 5.

Far more significant, however, is the attack which he launches upon it in 1 Cor. vi. 9-20. He maintains that sexual intercourse is not something indifferent, a mere satisfying of a natural need, like eating food; eating is something which belongs only to the present age; God will one day put an end to it. 1 Cor. vi. 18, 'Every other sin that a man can commit is outside the body; but the fornicator sins against his own body,' appears at first sight to be untrue. A man who is guilty of gluttony does sin against his body. The point is probably this: St. Paul means that such sins as gluttony affect only the temporary state of the 'body' considered as a merely physical organism. They do not have a profound effect on the total, integrated personality which St. Paul calls the 'body' (sōma). We might say, 'Gluttony harms only the body: fornication the whole personality'. But if St. Paul had said anything of the kind, if for example, he had said that gluttony harms the body, but fornication harms the soul, then he would have given a foot-hold to the dangerous tendency to separate the body from the 'higher self' which it was essential for him to combat. What he seeks to do is to show that the body is not a mere unimportant husk, but that it has a genuine theological significance.

First, we are to be raised by God's power, as Christ was. We shall consider later[28] how St. Paul thought that this would work out in the case of those who died before the Second Coming. But even if we are at death given 'another' body in which we appear at the Last Day, to replace the body 'lost' at death, at least, according to 2 Cor. v. 10, 'Each must receive what is due to him for his conduct in the body, good or bad': even if the actual physical particles which constitute our bodies here on earth are no longer 'part of us', we shall not be able to disclaim responsibility for the deeds we did in the bodies which comprised them.

Secondly, fornication is a 'sin against the doctrine of the church' as well as against the doctrine of the resurrection of Christians. A Christian is a member of the body of Christ. This is a literal fact, though 'metaphysical,' not physical, which is nonetheless 'true' because St. Paul expresses it by means of a metaphor. But a man who 'links himself with a harlot becomes physically one with her' (1 Cor. vi. 16). It may appear that St. Paul is taking an almost 'magical' view of the power of sexual intercourse to bind people together. But there is a sense in which it can be said that a man and woman who have sexual intercourse together

[28] cf. infra, pp. 248 ff.

do become 'one flesh,' that is one person, simply through sharing
something which is so intimate. There is clearly something wrong
in having *both* an intimate relationship with Christ as a member
of His body and also a relationship which is intimate in another
sense with a prostitute, especially if she is a temple prostitute.
A temple prostitute, for example one attached to the temple of
Venus at Corinth, was supposed to put her 'client' into touch
with the goddess.[29]

(b) *Marriage and remarriage*

It is popularly believed that St. Paul's attitude to marriage
was 'morbidly ascetic.' The word 'ascetic' is justified, 'morbid'
is not. In favour of the popular view it is usual to quote 1 Cor.
vii. 1, 'It is a good thing for a man to have nothing to do with
women,' (lit. 'not to touch a woman'). It is by no means certain
that the Apostle was here stating his own view; he may well have
been quoting a passage from the Corinthians' letter to him. Even
if the sentence did express his own view, we must take it in
conjunction with his later statement that celibacy is a vocation
which God has given to a few; this does not mean that marriage
is sinful or even a second-best. We are accustomed to pray in
our churches for the increase of the clergy, and to say 'it is a good
thing for a young man to offer himself as a candidate for the
sacred ministry' without for one moment suggesting that there
is anything 'wrong' or 'unclean' about being a layman. But it
must be confessed that the choice of 'touch a woman' instead of
'to be married,' always assuming that the words do represent
his own thought, suggests that his attitude to marriage was in
some ways rather negative. Again, there is an ascetic flavour
about 1 Cor. vii. 2, 'Because there is so much immorality let
each man have his own wife,' and about 1 Cor. vii. 9, 'Better be
married than burn with vain desire'. Further, as we shall see
later, St. Paul had a high regard for celibacy.

On the other hand, this was due in part to his belief that the
return of Christ was at hand; such a belief would account for
his failure to mention the procreation of children as an end of
marriage, which for a Jew was a really astonishing omission. A
second point which tells against the contention that St. Paul's

[29] J. Héring, *The First Epistle of St. Paul to the Corinthians* (E.T. London, 1962), p. 45.

Q

view of sex was morbid is the stress which he lays upon vocation. Even in the modern world there are circumstances in which a man may believe that it is God's will for him to be celibate, not on the ground that marriage is inferior but because he has responsibilities which are not compatible with marriage. In 1 Cor. vii. 32–35 this point is put forward. It is urged that for many it is not bad to marry, but that it is better to be single, so that the whole life may be devoted to God's service. Those who lose their partners by death receive the same advice in 1 Cor. vii. 39–40: it is better to remain as a widow, but there is nothing wrong in her marrying again, provided always that she marries a Christian. There is no reason to suppose that St. Paul would ever have approved of a marriage between a non-Christian and one who was already a Christian, though if one party only to a marriage became a Christian, the marriage could not be broken except at the initiative of the partner who had remained a non-Christian. Thirdly, we may instance his 'sensible' attitude to sexual intercourse as expounded in 1 Cor. vii. 3–5, based upon the 'healthy' view of sex which is typical of Judaism. We find it in Exod. xxi. 10, where it is laid down that a man who takes a second wife must not diminish the food, clothing or marital rights of the first. St. Paul makes it quite clear that each partner has the same claim upon the other in this respect.

(c) *Divorce*

St. Paul forbids divorce, not on his own authority, but on that of the Lord, in the case of those who are Christians (1 Cor. vii. 10–11). He certainly had in mind those who married after they had become Christians and probably also the case where a couple, married as pagans or as Jews, both accepted Christianity. Rom. vii. 2–3, where St. Paul employs the figure of marriage to illustrate his views about the Law, would seem to take it for granted that death alone makes it possible to remarry: to marry again during the life of the marriage partner is to commit adultery. We should remark that in Rom. vii. 2–3 St. Paul talks in general terms, and does not limit himself to those who are Christian. J. J. von Allmen[30] makes the point that death is regarded as an act of God, so that those who are parted by death have been put asunder by God Himself.

[30] E.T. *Pauline Teaching on Marriage* (London, 1963), p. 53.

In 1 Cor. vii. 12–16 St. Paul considers the case of a non-Christian married couple of which one partner only has become a Christian. A non-Christian partner who wishes to continue the marriage is not to be divorced, and may even be won over: marriage, like parenthood, is a sanctifying relationship. Nothing that St. Paul says here could be held to justify Christians in marrying non-Christians with the hope of winning them over. This he would almost certainly have condemned. He is concerned solely with the case of a marriage in being when one partner only accepts Christianity. If on the other hand the heathen partner wishes for a separation, let him have it (lit. if he separates himself, *chōrizetai*, let him separate himself, *chōrizesthō*). In such cases the Christian husband or wife is under no compulsion, (*ou dedoulō-tai*), lit. is not 'enslaved' or 'bound' (1 Cor. vii. 15). It is quite clear that the Christian partner must permit the marriage to break up if this is the desire of the non-Christian. There is, of course, nothing to suggest that the *Christian* partner may take the initiative in breaking up the marriage. It is not clear whether the Christian partner who has been deserted is allowed to remarry or no; Rom. vii. 2–3 would suggest not. The question in 1 Cor. vii. is whether *chōrizetai* refers to separation or divorce in our modern sense, that is, whether it refers to a loosing from the bond of bed and board (Latin *a mensa ac toro*) or from the bond of marriage (Latin *a vinculo matrimonii*); this would include freedom to remarry. *Chōrizesthai*[31] in secular Greek is often used in this context in a quasi-technical sense, meaning 'divorce' and in the Greek world this did include freedom to remarry. Again, what is the meaning of *ou dedoulōtai*, lit. 'is not enslaved', which the *N.E.B.* renders 'is under no compulsion'? It could of itself mean 'is not bound to continue to live with an unbeliever', or it could mean 'is not tied by the marriage bond'. It should be noted that in this section, 1 Cor. vii. 12–16, the problem of remarriage after divorce is never raised: the problem of whether a Christian should insist upon living in marriage with an unwilling non-Christian partner has been raised in so many words. The only real argument in favour of the view that St. Paul here, in this particular case, allows remarriage is the 'technical' use of *chōrizes-thai* in secular Greek. On balance, it would seem more probable that remarriage is not here permitted.

[31] cf. Arndt and Gringrich and Moulton and Milligan, *sub voce.*

(d) *Partners in celibacy?*

1 Cor. vii. 36, 'But if a man has a partner in celibacy (*parthenos*, lit. virgin) and feels that he is not behaving properly towards her, that is if his instincts are too strong for him (*ean ē huperakmos*, otherwise rendered, "if she be past the flower of her age"), and something must be done, he may do as he pleases; there is nothing wrong in it; let them marry (*gameitōsan*)', has caused much difficulty to commentators.

The 'traditional' view is that St. Paul was advising the fathers of marriageable girls. He says that it is better for them to remain celibate, but if the daughters are getting too old, or finding it difficult to control their natural instincts, then their fathers can marry them off without fear of blame.[32] An alternative explanation, first suggested by Grafe and Achelis and developed by Lietzmann, has now been most conveniently expounded by Héring.[33]

This alternative theory is that St. Paul was giving advice to keen young Christian men and women who had formed 'spiritual alliances', living, not necessarily in the same house, as spiritual companions. If the young man finds that his physical instincts are becoming too strong (*ean ē huperakmos*) then it is no sin for them to convert their relationship into a full, normal marriage, though it is even better for them to stay as they are.

The suggestion is in fact that St. Paul is dealing with the practice which later grew into the 'institution' of *virgines subintroductae*. It has been supposed that there is evidence for this custom in Hermas' work *The Shepherd* which dates from the second century, probably from about 140 A.D. In that work, Similitude ix. 11, the virgins make Hermas pass the night with them 'as a brother, not as a husband'. But in the explanation of this Similitude (ix. 13) it is said 'these virgins are powers of the Son of God'. It would appear wholly gratuitous to imagine that Hermas is making an oblique reference to customs at Rome in his own day. This is very natural imagery and reminds us of the interpretations which had then already been given to the Song of Songs. The custom did however exist early in the third century

---

[32] This 'traditional' theory was propounded by St. John Chrysostom. It is defended by Goudge and Robertson-Plummer in the Westminster and I.C.C. commentaries ad loc., and, above all, by Allo, *Première Epître aux Corinthiens* (Paris, 1956), excursus VII, pp. 189–94.

[33] *The First Epistle to St. Paul to the Corinthians* (E.T. London, 1962), ad loc. pp. 63–4.

as we know from Tertullian, *Concerning the Veiling of Virgins*, xiv. and *On Fasting*, xvii.

Against the traditional explanation Héring[34] makes the following points:

1. *Parthenos* means 'virgin', not 'daughter', and does not refer to daughters unless the context makes it clear.

2. *Huperakmos*, can be either feminine, in which case it would mean 'over age', or masculine in which case *huper* is intensive and the word means 'endowed with excessive vigour'. Héring says it is strange that it should be thought improper behaviour for a father to bar his daughter's marriage because she is getting too old. It is however quite natural that a woman should abstain from marriage in the belief that the world will soon end, and then, when life continues as before, wish to marry after all, since time is going on. 'Past age' or 'of full age' is easier to defend from the point of view of parallels than 'endowed with instincts that are too strong'. But in favour of Héring's view we must make two points. First, the fact that a woman was getting old would naturally make her wish to marry, instead of continuing in 'spiritual companionship', while she could still have children, as soon as the expectation of the end of the world became less vivid. Secondly *huperakmos* could very well mean, as the *N.E.B.* suggests in a footnote, 'ripe for marriage'. An enthusiastic young male convert might well have a romantic attachment for a girl which was closely associated with the emotional upheaval and renewal which they both experienced when they became Christians. Such a shared experience might suitably lead to marriage with the important proviso that the girl was old enough.[35]

3. *Gameitōsan*, 'let them marry' would be most unsuitable coming between two sentences in each of which the subject was the girl's father. It is quite in place if the subject in the singular is the male partner in a 'spiritual companionship'.

4. A father does not sin in letting his daughter marry, nor

5. is he to be praised for keeping her celibate, since it is she who would make the sacrifice. But, granted that asceticism was strong in some circles at Corinth, it might be imagined that a man did do wrong in letting his daughter marry. Further, a man

---

[34] ibid.

[35] The two chief protagonists of the traditional view, Robertson-Plummer, op. cit. ad loc., and Allo, op. cit. p. 192, both, take the view, I think correctly, that *huperakmos* means 'old enough for marriage'.

might be praised for keeping his daughter single if it were thought
to be right. A general may be praised for 'sacrificing' the lives of
men under his control if the circumstances demand it.

6. Col. iii. 21, 'Fathers do not exasperate your children', is
thought by Héring to be hardly compatible with praising a father
for keeping his daughter unmarried. But this would not be so
if father and daughter both believed that celibacy is better than
marriage. In pious Roman Catholic circles a father might well
be praised for furthering his daughter's wish to become a nun.

Héring's arguments, then, are of unequal weight. Some of
them fail to take into account the fact that certain people really
do believe that celibacy is in itself superior to marriage.

On the other hand, it should be made clear that the 'new'
view does not necessarily mean that St. Paul found and approved
at Corinth the full-blown system of *virgines subintroductae* which
the church in the third century so rightly condemned. It is quite
suitable for young men and women to have warm friendships in
which a shared religious faith plays a large part. But such a
situation is not always stable. If, as so often occurs, the man
discovers that physical desires are stirring, real moral danger may
lie ahead. Marriage may well be the right course; in other cases
the best solution is to end the relationship. But if physical desires
are under control, such relationships may, for a time at least, be
innocent and may enrich both parties. Since St. Paul did appreciate
the advantages of celibacy, he might well approve such relationships. In a word, it is here suggested that St. Paul approved an
innocent but precarious state of affairs and proposed a safeguard
for lack of which the abuse of *virgines subintroductae* later arose.

Allo's[36] arguments against this interpretation may be summarized as follows:

1. There is no evidence for *virgines subintroductae*, apart from
the heretics mentioned by Irenaeus, *Adversus Haereses*, i. 6, 3,
until Tertullian early in the third century. Allo's facts are correct,
and his inference has some weight, though it is not conclusive,
against the view that St. Paul found in Corinth *virgines subintroductae* as a regular institution of the later type. It weighs much less
heavily against the theory that the virgins of 1 Cor. vii. were not
part of a 'regular institution' of any kind, but that they were part
of a temporary movement, consisting possibly of no more than a

[36] Op. cit. excursus VII, pp. 189–94.

dozen couples, who lived for some time, it may only be for a matter of months, in a manner which was in itself innocent though inherently dangerous. The dangers, thanks to St. Paul, probably never materialized.

2. *Huperakmos*, says Allo, ought to mean 'nubile'. So it probably does. On the 'new' hypothesis St. Paul was guarding his flock against under-age marriage.

3. *Gamizō*, Allo maintains, 'ought' to mean 'give in marriage' (French *marier*), not 'contract a marriage with' (French *épouser*). So it ought, but does it? Allo, with his invariable honesty and thoroughness, mentions the fact that in parts of the French-speaking world *marier* is used in the sense of *épouser*. The word *gamizō* is extremely rare. According to Moulton and Milligan *sub voce* it is not found outside the New Testament apart from a single passage in Apollonius Dyscolos, to which we shall return. I have not been able to discover that Moulton and Milligan are wrong. No evidence to the contrary is quoted in the latest, ninth, edition of Liddell and Scott, and the word *gamizō* is not even mentioned in *A Patristic Greek Lexicon*.[37]

It is said the *gameō* means 'contract a marriage' and that *gamizō* means 'give a woman in marriage' by Apollonius Dyscolos, an Alexandrian grammarian of the second century A.D. Though it must be confessed that we are indebted to him for much valuable information, he was a pedant by nature. His whole cast of mind was theoretical, rationalistic and *a priori* rather than descriptive. For example on theoretical grounds, he insisted upon the spelling *imi* instead of *eimi* ('I shall go', properispomenon, distinguished by the accent from the oxytone *eimi*, 'I am') by false analogy with the plural and dual. It is only natural that such a man should tell us what meanings *gamizō* might be *expected* to bear merely on the grounds of its formation. We should hardly take him as a reliable witness for usage.[38] On the other hand, there is no certain case at all where *gamizō* means 'marry with' as opposed to 'give in marriage' and no place apart from the present passage where such a meaning is even plausible.[39]

---

[37] ed. G. W. H. Lampe, Fascicle 2 (Oxford, 1962).
[38] cf. *The Oxford Classical Dictionary* (Oxford, 1949), p. 72, *sub voce* 'Apollonius' (15).
[39] Greek words ending in *eō* and *izō* do vary in manuscripts in Hellenistic Greek. For example, *apologeō* and *apologizō* are confused. cf. Moulton and Milligan *sub voce gamizō* and Blass-Debrunner-Funk, section 100, p. 51, *sub voce ameō*.

On balance, the 'traditional' view is less likely; its strongest point is, of course, the meaning of *gamizō*. We are in the difficult position of trying to understand the middle of a conversation when we have not heard the beginning, since we have to guess the meaning of the question from the answer which St. Paul gave to it.

iv. EQUALITY AND SUBORDINATION

(a) *The Problem*

Gal. iii. 28, 'There is no such thing as Jew and Greek, slave and freeman, male and female; for you are all one person in Christ Jesus,' finds a parallel in Col. iii. 11, 'There is no question here of Greek and Jew, circumcised and uncircumcised, barbarian, Scythian, freeman, slave; but Christ is all, and is in all'. The passage from *Colossians* is followed by Col. iii. 18, 'Wives, subject to your husbands', and Col. iii. 22, 'Slaves, give entire obedience to your earthly masters.' This latter command is qualified by Col. iv. 1, 'Masters, be just and fair to your slaves, knowing that you too have a Master in heaven'. Again, the subjection of wives is modified by Col. iii. 19, 'Husbands, love your wives and do not be harsh with them'.

The practical significance of these problems is enormous. Perhaps the greatest single secular problem of the world today is the rise to power of those previously underprivileged because of race, social or economic status, or sex. Within the Christian church, race is a burning problem for South Africa and for the U.S.A. Englishmen are tempted to be smug about the difficulties caused by the race problem, which has only just begun to exist in England, and has not yet assumed large proportions; we need to remember that the analogous problem in England is excessive privilege attached to social stratification. In Sweden the matter of female ministers has led to considerable heartburning. On these matters we all have something to be ashamed of, and we are all tempted to concentrate upon the faults of others as a counter-irritant to the sting of our own conscience. Above all, the anti-Christian may claim that in allowing all men equality in the right to become Christians, we are giving them a mere 'spiritual shadow', while we withold the substance of economic and social opportunity. Because of these problems we may be tempted either to twist St. Paul's thought to make him into a twentieth century egalitarian or to magnify the elements of subordination in his thought in order to justify ourselves. Again, precisely because St. Paul was a practical man, his teaching was adapted to his own age. It is always difficult to say whether a particular element is eternally valid or due to the passing conditions of a former century. I myself have no doubt that the subordination of women is socially conditioned. 1 Cor. xi. 2–16 and Eph. v. 22f. compare the subordination of woman to man and wife to husband with the relation of Christ to God and the church to the Lord. I suggest that St. Paul would have employed different analogies if he had lived in a different civilization. But many scholars will of course disagree.

(b) *Women and Children*

Col. iii. 20, 'Children, obey your parents in everything, for that is pleasing to God and is the Christian way. Fathers, do not exasperate your children, for fear they grow disheartened,' is a passage which presents no problems. As a general ordinance it is unexceptionable: it is in the detailed, practical working out that difficulties arise. The only point that should be noted is the stress that St. Paul lays upon the integration of ethics and theology. The obedience of children is no mere 'ethical commonplace' in the eyes of St. Paul: it is the 'will of God', and 'the Christian way'.

It can be argued that St. Paul is saying in Col. iii. 18f. not that males are superior to females in *status*, but that husbands have the *function* of giving rather than taking orders, and wives the function of obeying rather than of ordering.

But although the subordination of women may be primarily or wholly functional in *Colossians*, it is more difficult to sustain this theory in the case of 1 *Corinthians*. Commenting on 1 Cor. xi. 3, Grosheide maintains that *the man*, not the husband of a woman, but every man, is in question. 'Of every man it can be said that he is above the woman'.[40]

1 Cor. xiv. 34, 'As in all congregations (*ekklēsiais*) of God's people, women should not address the meeting. They have no licence to speak (*lalein*), but should keep their place (*hupotasses-thōsan*, lit., 'let them be subject') as the law directs', would appear to ban all talking by women in church. On the other hand, 1 Cor.

---

[40] *Commentary on the First Epistle to the Corinthians*, London N.T.C. (London, 1954²), p. 250.

xi. 5, 'Any woman who prays or prophesies with her head unveiled dishonours her head', (*R.S.V.*) would seem to suggest that women did prophesy.

To this difficulty the following solutions have been suggested, none being wholly satisfactory:

1. According to Anderson Scott,[41] who follows Bousset and J. Weiss, the 'anti-feminist' verses, 1 Cor. xiv. 34–5 are an interpolation. The verses are transposed to the end of xiv. 40 by several manuscripts, including the sixth century uncial, *Codex Claromontanus*. Further, they break the connexion between verses thirty-three and thirty-six. On the other hand, it may be precisely *because* they break the connexion that later scribes transposed them to the end of the chapter. It is further urged that they resemble 1 Tim. ii. 11 and that St. Paul would hardly appeal to the Torah. But 1 Tim. ii. 11 may be based upon 1 Cor. xiv. 34, not the other way round, and St. Paul appealed to the Torah literally in Rom. xii 9, where he approves of the substance of the Decalogue.

2. Grosheide[42] maintains that women were allowed to prophesy publicly, but not in church. It is clear that prophecy was known among women in the apostolic church, for we are told in Acts xxi. 9 of Philip the evangelist that he had four unmarried daughters who had the gift of prophecy (*prophētuousai:* this present participle shows that they had the gift, not , as the *A.V.* might suggest, that they exercised it on any particular occasion). But there is no passage in the N.T. where we are told in so many words that women prophesied *in church*. On the other hand, it is difficult to suppose that the men in 1 Cor. xi. 4 are praying or prophesying in church and the women, contrasted with them in respect of head-gear, are prophesying elsewhere when we consider that the same participial construction (praying or prophesying, *proseuchōn —ousa, propheteuōn—ousa*) is used for both men and women. Since, moreover, the whole subject of 1 Cor. xi. 2–16 is public worship, 1 Cor. xi. 16, 'There is no such custom among us, or in any of the congregations of God's people,' naturally refers to 'congregations' (*ekklēsiai*) in the sense of 'assemblies for worship'. Again, the non-existent custom would naturally, though not inevitably, be for a woman to pray or prophesy without a veil.

---

[41] *Christianity according to St. Paul* (Cambridge, 1961²). pp. 227–8.
[42] *Commentary on the First Epistle to the Corinthians*, London N.T.C. (London, 1954²), pp. 252 and 342.

3. Héring[43] believes that 1 Cor. xi. 2f. allows women to prophesy and pray in church, provided that they are veiled, and that 1 Cor. xiv. 34–5 means that women are not to take part in questions or discussions afterwards. In Classical Greek *lalein* means 'chatter', though it often means 'speak with authority' as in 1 Cor. ii. 6, 7, etc. The following point may be made against Héring: in 1 Cor. xiv. *lalein* occurs with great frequency, and refers to speaking with tongues or to prophecy, not to asking questions. In the context of 1 Cor. xiv. 34–5 *lalein* in church seems to be contrasted with asking questions at home. But, as Héring could reply, St. Paul probably had *lalein* so much on the tip of his tongue when dictating 1 Cor. xiv that he used it again in xiv. 34 in a different though perfectly possible sense. Héring's theory is probably the least unsatisfactory. It is not inconsistent that women should be allowed to *pray* and *prophesy* in church, since it would be the Holy Spirit that spoke through them. It is surely legitimate to compare Matt. x. 20, 'For it is not you who will be speaking: it will be the Spirit of your Father speaking in you,' and Rom. viii. 26, 'Through our inarticulate groans the Spirit himself is pleading for us'. When on the other hand the women were not inspired by the Holy Spirit, for example, when they asked questions afterwards, they were merely speaking for themselves and this was forbidden, because they were to be in subjection.

It would appear that, according to even the least anti-feminist interpretation of 1 *Cor.* which is at all plausible, St. Paul did believe that women were inferior in status because of their sex, in addition to being functionally subordinate in marriage. Though the sex distinction no longer existed in Christ (Gal. iii. 28) it was still important as part of the 'natural order'.

(c) *Slaves*

1 Cor. xii. 13, 'We were all brought into one body by baptism in the one Spirit, whether we are Jews or Greeks, whether slaves (*douloi*) or free men', might suggest that slavery is to be abolished; still more does this apply to Gal. iii. 28 and Col. iii. 11, quoted above. But slaves are commanded to be good slaves in Col. iii. 22, and *Philemon* was a 'covering letter' in which St. Paul returned Onesimus to his master.

The only Pauline passage apart from *Philemon* in which

[43] *The First Epistle of St. Paul to the Corinthians* (E.T. London, 1962), p. 154.

emancipation may have been taught is 1 Cor. vii. 21, 'Were you
a slave when you were called? Do not let that trouble you; but if
a chance of liberty should come, take it (*all' ei kai dunasai eleu-
theros genesthai, mallon chrēsai*),' the alternative translation being,
'But even if a chance of liberty should come, choose rather to
make good use of your servitude.' Grosheide[44] puts forward what
he regards as a third solution, 'If you can be free, make a better
use of your vocation,' which is really a variation of the second
view.

In favour of the theory that the slave is advised to make a
better use of his slavery it has been argued:

1. *Ei kai* is normally concessive.[45] This, of course, is in general
correct, but J. B. Lightfoot[46] points out that in Luke xi. 18, 'If
(*ei kai*) Satan is divided against himself,' the words *ei kai* mean
simply 'if', without any concessive force, while the same applies
to *ean kai* at 1 Cor. vii. 11; Gal. vi. 1.

2. The Greek Fathers take the view that the slave should make
the best of his slavery. To this some weight must be accorded,
but Lightfoot[47] reminds us that slavery still continued in the
Patristic period. Under pagan emperors the Fathers would not
wish to give the impression that they were dangerous social and
economic reformers. Under Christian emperors they would
hardly desire to charge the government with being false to St.
Paul's teaching. This is true, but it hardly explains why they
should be influenced to suppose that St. Paul discouraged a
Christian from accepting emancipation if it lay open to him.

3. Much the most powerful argument against the emancipation
theory is this: St. Paul is urging all the time that a man should
stay as he is. Lightfoot[48] correctly explains that if we accept the
'emancipation' theory we must suppose that the words 'But if a
chance of liberty should come, take it' are in parenthesis. This is
possible. The ancients did not use brackets, so that St. Paul's
manner of speaking the words has not been recorded. This leaves
the emancipation theory possible.

[44] *Commentary on the First Epistle to the Corinthians*, London N.T.C.(London,
1954²), p. 170.
[45] Blass-Debrunner-Funk, section 374, p. 190.
[46] *Notes on Epistles of St. Paul from unpublished commentaries* (London, 1895),
on 1 Cor. vii. 21, p. 229.
[47] ibid.
[48] ibid.

Positive arguments in favour of the emancipation theory are:

1. A slave should be far more use if he were free, according to Lightfoot.[49] But would he? If his master were a Christian, it would make little difference. If the master were a pagan, it would depend on the terms of his manumission. We cannot say that emancipation would *always* give a man a better chance.

2. The aorist imperative *chrēsai* suggests, it is alleged, a change. This is not necessarily correct. The aorist imperative would be usual in peremptory or formal commands.[50] In any case, the aorist often takes the place of the perfective present, which does not exist in Greek.[51]

Philem. 15, 'For perhaps this is why you lost him for a time that you might have him back for good, no longer as a slave (*ouketi hōs doulon*)' seems to leave the question of emancipation open. Lightfoot[52] points out that St. Paul says 'no longer *as* (*hōs*) a slave', not 'no longer a slave'. That is to say, whether Onesimus is to remain a slave or no, he is to be regarded, not as a slave, but as a fellow Christian. Further, the negative is *ouketi*, not *mēketi*, and therefore refers to a fact already accomplished. Onesimus is already a 'brother in Christ', whether he is to become in law a free man or no.

v. FOOD LAWS

To us the discussion of food laws can appear trivial and remote. In the teaching of St. Paul this matter was integrally connected with each of the great commandments of the Law, love of God and love of our neightbour.

The main passages which illustrate this are Rom. xiv.; 1 Cor. viii. and x. 18–32, and Col. ii. 21.

Four different issues are involved.

1. Meals in a heathen temple (1 Cor. viii. 10, x. 21). These are simply condemned. An 'enlightened' Corinthian might as part of some 'civic' function take his share in a heathen sacrifice. To him it would be a mere empty form. But another Christian who was led on to do the same might still more than half believe in

[49] ibid.
[50] Blass-Debrunner-Funk, section 337(4), p. 174.
[51] Op. cit. section 333, p. 171.
[52] *St. Paul's Epistle to the Colossians and to Philemon* (London, 1876²), pp. 323f., and 342–3.

heathen gods as well as in God; this situation is naturally common enough among recent converts living in a heathen environment. The 'weaker brother' would not of course be put into communion with 'other gods', since there are none, but he would be disloyal to God, so that the first great commandment would be violated.

2. A Christian might be invited to a private meal at the house of a heathen friend. Possibly he might be offered food which had already been presented in a heathen temple. St. Paul did not, of course, believe in any kind of transmutation of food offered to idols, so no harm would be done if it were eaten. If, on the other hand, the host volunteered the information that the food had been presented to an idol, then as an act of witness the Christian must decline to eat.

3. In the case of meat offered for sale in the meat-market (1 Cor. x. 25-6) the Christian may buy and eat without question, since the issue of bearing witness does not arise. St. Paul does not consider what would happen if the butcher remarked in a pointed manner to a known Christian, 'This joint has been offered to such and such an idol'. By analogy with the case of the private meal, we can only suppose that the Christian must refuse to purchase it.

4. Christian asceticism. Col. ii. 16, 'Allow no one therefore to take you to task about what you eat or drink,' is addressed to a situation in which a false asceticism, including non-Jewish elements, was a danger. For this 'Colossian Heresy' Lightfoot's[53] essay is still indispensable. It is probable that Hellenistic dualism and astrology had become combined with Jewish calendrical and dietetic regulations. As in the case envisaged in Gal. iv. 9f. this involved returning to a non-Christian security based upon the Law or even upon dualistic and quasi-magical beliefs, and so was grossly disloyal to Christ.[54]

In Rom. xiv. St. Paul's emphasis is completely different, and this no doubt reflects a different situation. Some of the Roman Christians were 'enlightened' and believed that they were not bound by certain food regulations, which are not specified. On the other hand, there were Christians who felt that they would

---

[53] St. Paul's Epistle to the Colossians and to Philemon (London, 1876²), pp. 73–113.
[54] cf. Bruce in Epistle to the Ephesians and Colossians, London N.T.C. (London, 1957), pp. 243f., on Col. ii. 16.

be doing wrong if they availed themselves of this liberty. Since their eating would be due not to faith but to a disregard for what they believed to be the will of God, they would be sinful if they did so. Further, the 'enlightened' would be guilty of a lack of love if by their eating they outraged their more scrupulous brethren (Rom. xiv. 15).

It is most important to note that what for us might be matters of 'mere ritualistic taboos' have a genuine theological concern for St. Paul. Rom. xiv. 15, 'Do not by your eating bring disaster to a man for whom Christ died,' places food laws in the context of the basic doctrines of the Incarnation and the Atonement, and by implication of the church also. †

vi. THE STATE

The passages in St. Paul's epistles that would appear to shed light on his thought about the State include 1 Cor. ii. 8, vi. 1, and 2 Thess. ii. 3–12 which have already been examined with reference to the Apostle's demonology and, in addition, 1 Cor. v. 10, vii. 12–16, 20–24, and x. 27. These make it clear that St. Paul did not enjoin any rupturing of existing natural relationships. 1 Cor. v. 10, 'To avoid them (i.e. grossly immoral pagans) you would have to get right out of the world', makes it obvious that St. Paul regarded it as unthinkable that the Christians should do what the Qumran sectaries had done already. Since he can hardly have been ignorant of them, it is possible that he was led to envisage and reject this course for the Christians of Corinth precisely because he knew that at Qumran it had already been followed; on the other hand, it is possible that he was rejecting a solution, namely withdrawal from the world, which is always a 'live option' since in all ages there are a few who would wish to adopt it. But it is worthy of serious consideration that St. Paul's incidental references to withdrawal, as in this passage and also to celibacy (1 Cor. vii. 25) may be due to the fact that the Qumran sectaries had already taken a stand on these matters.

It is beyond dispute that St. Paul in Rom. xiii. 1, 'Every person must submit to the supreme authorities (*exousiais huperechousais*)' enjoins universal obedience to the civil authorities. Cullmann and others[55] have maintained that the *exousiai* were not merely civil

[55] The connection between spiritual powers and the state was first developed by Dibelius in *Die Geisterwelt im Glauben des Paulus* (Göttingen, 1909).

powers as such, but also 'invisible powers and forces' of which the earthly rulers, the Roman administrators of Palestine, are the effective agents.[56] Cullmann also maintains that the reason why all must obey the *exousiai* is that Christ has conquered them, so that disobedience to the *exousiai* is defiance of Christ. In fact 'the Pauline explanation of the State is not based in some way on natural law, but on *Heilsgeschichte*'.[57]

Considerable confusion is liable to occur when a writer discusses not only St. Paul but theories about St. Paul, and the reader patiently pursues the scent through a forest of pros and cons. To aid understanding, the conclusions which we shall reach are these:

1. Dibelius and Cullmann are correct in believing that for St. Paul the *exousia* is *both* the 'invisible power' *and* its earthly agent, just as for *Daniel* the Princes of Persia and Greece were invisible powers inextricably connected with the peoples whom they ruled (Dan. x. 20).

2. Morrison[58] is right in denying Cullmann's contention that the subjection of the *exousiai* is due to the Work of Christ. On the contrary, the powers are subject to God because He made them, although they have behaved like rebellious satraps in the Persian Empire. There is, however, this to be said for Cullmann's thesis: Christ has already to some extent re-established *de facto* God's sovereignty *de jure* over the *exousiai*, and will in the end complete this work.

It is essential to be clear what issues we have to determine at this juncture. That invisible forces lie behind the power of the state we have already argued.[59] In the next chapter we shall maintain that in 1 Thess. ii. 3–22 St. Paul thinks of 'the restrainer' etc. as the Roman Empire and the invisible forces with which it is associated. As all agree, in Rom. xiii. St. Paul's meaning is that the state must be obeyed; therefore *exousia* does in fact refer to the state. The point at issue is really how *exousia* in Rom. xiii. 1 comes to refer to the state. Does *exousia* as such mean 'state' or does it really mean 'invisible power' and come to mean 'state' derivatively because the 'state' is controlled by invisible powers? We should

[56] Cullmann, *The State in the New Testament* (E.T. London, 1957). p. 63.
[57] ibid. p. 99 (excursus).
[58] C. D. Morrison, *The Powers that Be* S.B.T. 29, (London, 1960).
[59] cf. Ch. II, pp. 26–27.

note that St. Paul speaks in the plural about 'supreme authorities', that is, presumably, provincial governors and others who, collectively, might be held to constitute the state.

Rom. ix. 21, 'Surely the potter can do what he likes (lit. has *exousia*) with the clay,' is a good case of *exousia* meaning simply authority and power. It occurs, for example, in 1 Cor. vii. 37, ix. 4, 5, 6; 2 Cor. xiii. 10. On the other hand, *exousia* means invisible power at Col. i. 16, ii. 15; Eph. iii. 10, vi. 12.

The *exousiai* of Rom. xiii. 1 would seem to be the *archontes* (*N.E.B.* 'government') of xiii. 3. This word also is ambiguous and *might* refer to invisible rulers as in Eph. ii. 2, but in Rom. xiii, where we are concerned with taxes (*phoron*, Rom. xiii. 7), than which nothing could be more mundane, this is hardly to be maintained.

The positive value of Cullmann's thesis, however *exousiai* may come to refer to the state in Rom. xiii., is that it accounts for the ambivalence of St. Paul's attitude to the state and does so in terms of the Jewish doctrine of 'angels of the nations'.

vii. LOVE

It may seem strange that no *long* separate section should be devoted to the subject of *agapē*, love. In fact, no long *separate* section ought to be devoted to it: love is all-pervasive in Pauline ethics and integral to his theology.

It is misleading to say that *agapē* is a specifically Christian word. The noun *agapē* is found about nineteen times in the LXX;[60] in Eccles. ix. 6 there is a variant. Philologically speaking, the noun *agapē* is a back-formation from the verb *agapaō*, which is found about 200[61] times in the LXX. *Agapē* is also found in Philo and almost certainly in pre-Christian pagan sources.[63] It is not possible to base any theology upon the philological origin of the word.

Far more important is St. Paul's usage. He says that love transcends all other virtues (1 Cor. xiii.) and links it with faith and hope there and at 1 Thess. v. 8. Typically, *agapē* is God's attitude to us, but for that very reason it is also ours to Him (Rom.

---

[60] e.g. LXX. 2 Kingdoms, M.T. 2 Sam. xiii. 15; eleven times in *Song of Sol.*

[61] e.g. Gen. xxii. 2.

[63] Arndt and Gringrich, *sub voce.*

R

viii. 28). The subject is one of supreme importance, and must be treated either at great length[64] or very briefly. Here it must suffice merely to show how important it is by quoting Gal. v. 13-14, 'Be servants to one another in love. For the whole law can be summed up in a single commandment: "Love your neighbour as yourself".'

[64] Ceslas Spicq, *Agapé dans le Nouveau Testament* (Paris, i., (1958); ii. and iii., (1959). St. Paul's writings are treated i., p. 208–ii., p. 305. cf. also Spicq, *Agapé, prologomènes à une étude de théologie néotestamentaire* (Louvain, 1955).

For a briefer treatment, cf. E. Stauffer, *T.W.N.T.* i. pp. 20–55, E.T. *Love* (London, 1949).

CHAPTER TEN

ESCHATOLOGY

i. INTRODUCTORY

In current theological usage the word 'eschatology' has two distinct but closely related meanings. First, it is employed to designate teaching about the 'end-things', and includes both doctrine concerning the end of the whole world, or the coming of the Messiah, and also beliefs relating to the fate of individuals who die before the end of the world, such as beliefs in Heaven, Hell and Purgatory.

It has, however, acquired in recent years a second meaning, due to the basic Christian conviction that: 'the Messiah who should come at the end of the age has in fact come, though the end of history is still delayed'.[1] Since what God has done in Christ is described in terms of what the Jews expected God to do in the future, that is, in terms of eschatology, eschatological language suggests not only futurity, but also the *quality* of the event. 'This is an eschatological event' thus comes to mean that the event is in a very special sense the work of *God*. When we say, for example, that the sacraments are 'eschatological events', we are above all concerned to maintain that in the sacraments God is at work.

In this sense of the word, virtually all St. Paul's teaching about Christ can be described as eschatological; and, in this sense of the word, Albert Schweitzer[2] is correct when he maintains that eschatology should not be left to the final chapter, since it pervades the whole of the Apostle's thinking. In previous chapters dealing with the Person and Work of Christ etc., we have really been treating of Pauline eschatology in the second sense. In this last chapter we shall examine those aspects of his thought which are eschatological in both senses; they are concerned with the end of the world and with the 'last things', and they are also transmuted by the Christian conviction that in Christ God had brought in the beginning at least of the final consummation.

It has been customary to ask whether St. Paul's eschatology

[1] Schoeps, *Paul* (E.T. London, 1961), p. 88.
[2] *Paul and his Interpreters* (E.T. London, 1912), pp. 52ff.

developed as he grew older; in particular, R. H. Charles[3] has expounded St. Paul's teaching on this matter in four stages. Before examining the numerous important problems involved, we shall present the broad sweep of the Apostle's eschatology in four stages, just as Charles did, but without prejudice to the question whether his thought on this matter did in fact undergo any change or no: that is one of the problems which will call for subsequent examination. But first it will be necessary to consider the teaching found in 2 *Thessalonians* about the events which must come to pass before the end begins.

ii. TEACHING PECULIAR TO 2 THESSALONIANS

The main passage (ii. 3–7) reads as follows, 'That day cannot come before the final rebellion against God, when wickedness will be revealed in human form, the man doomed to perdition. . . . You cannot but remember that I told you this while I was still with you; you must now be aware of the restraining hand . . . until the Restrainer disappears from the scene'. Three questions have vexed the brains of scholars: What is the *apostasia* (final rebellion against God)? Who is *ho anthrōpos tēs anomias* (wickedness in human form)?, and What is the nature and identity of *ho katechōn* (the Restrainer)? It is not hard to discern the general drift of the passage, and we can say much about the sources from which St. Paul derives these puzzling phrases and about their actual meaning; it is their application, rather than their meaning which eludes us.

St. Paul is here concerned not to convey instruction about eschatology, but rather to damp down the unhealthy interest which the Thessalonians seemed to be showing in that subject. He is anxious that they should not lose their heads or alarm themselves through imagining that the Day of the Lord was already upon them. He knew that they would accept the belief that the Day of the Lord could not possibly come until after the *apostasia*, since He had told them so Himself. It would have been superfluous to tell them once again what the *apostasia* was; it was only necessary to remind them that it had not yet occurred. It was part of the 'eschatological programme' which the writer and first recipients of the Epistle accepted in common, and which

[3] *Eschatology, Hebrew, Jewish and Christian* (London, 1963[2]), Ch. XI.

therefore he used as a basis for moral exhortation. It would be dangerous for us to attempt to give St. Paul's thought at this point a precision which would have been superfluous for his argument.

The word *apostasia*, like the earlier form *apostasis*, originally meant 'rebellion' in a political sense. Apart from the present passage it occurs in the N.T. only at Acts xxi. 21, where it clearly refers to St. Paul's alleged *religious* rebellion against the Law of Moses. The cognate verb *aphistēmi* is found fourteen times in the N.T. Of these, four refer to apostasy in a technical sense,[4] and the revolt organized by Judas of Galilee as recorded in Acts v. 37-8, where the word occurs twice, was as much religious as political; in the remaining cases it bears the neutral meaning 'depart'. In the LXX *apostasia* is found six times; it is closely related to *apostasis*, and indeed the MSS vary in some passages between the two words. The basic philological sense of 'departing from' is applied to moral evil in 1 Kings xx. (M.T. xxi.) 13 (A) and in Jer. ii. 19. In 2 Chron. xxix. 19, and xxxiii. 19 it refers to religious, indeed to cultic offences and in Joshua xxii. 22 it is not clear either from the context or from the Hebrew (*merer*) whether the 'rebellion' is moral or cultic or both. In 1 Macc. ii. 15 *apostasia* clearly refers to rebellion in the religious sense, to a formal apostasy from Judaism.

Apostasy became in fact a regular part of the 'birthpangs of the Messiah', that is the woes which were destined to herald the dawn of the Messianic age. The reason, presumably, is that the Jews, looking back upon their past, saw the hand of Yahweh above all in the major crises of their national history, such as the return from Exile, the Exodus and the Creation. In Isaiah li. 9-11, the Creation, the Exodus and the Future Deliverance are spoken of in language which suggests that each had affected the prophet's thought about the other. The Jews, when they had to speculate about God's acts in the future, were compelled to take as their model His mighty acts performed in the past. It is clear that this tendency was already operative in Old Testament days. Jeremiah[5] speaks of the return from Exile as something similar to, but greater than the Exodus. Ezekiel[6] speaks of monsters, Gog and Magog,

---

[4] Luke, viii. 13; 1 Tim. iv. 1; 2 Tim. ii. 19; Heb. iii. 12.
[5] Jer. xxiii. 5-8.
[6] Ezek. xxxviii–xxxix.

who are to be overthrown in the future, just as Leviathan, according to Ps. lxxiv,[7] was overthrown in the past. In Deutero-Isaiah the Return is described in language reminiscent of the Exodus story. It would have been surprising if this had not been the case among people whose regular worship consisted very largely in recounting and re-enacting the mighty works of God which He had performed on their behalf in the distant past.

The age of the Maccabees also had been a time of deliverance for Israel; it is possible that the apostasy of the Hellenizing Jews recorded in 1 Macc. ii. 15 became added to the stock features of an 'age of deliverance' which would naturally recur, raised, as it were, to the nth power, at the time of the final deliverance. In any case the apostasy of the many was a suitable back-cloth to the fidelity of the chosen few, the remnant; and indifference or even hostility to religion was a feature of actual experience which the Jews were too realistic to omit from their theology. St. Paul clearly believed that *some* kind of rebellion in the religious sphere was to occur before the end came. There is no reason at all to suppose that he had any clear picture in his own mind as to what form that rebellion was to take. A theological student may be convinced that in two years time he will begin his first pastoral work without knowing the location or the specific nature of that work. I would suggest that St. Paul, when he wrote 2 *Thess.*, was certain that events which he described as the *apostasia* would occur, but that he did not know what specific form it would take.

Much the same may be said about 'wickedness. . . in human form' (*ho anthrōpos tēs anomias*). St. Paul certainly believed that this being would appear before the end came and it is possible for us to analyse the background of ideas from which he derived this figure, but we have no reason to suppose that he ascribed a specific value to it. A mathematician may do a great deal of work in which he uses an indeterminate quantity which he designates 'x'. He may know what part 'x' plays without knowing what value 'x' has. At a later stage he may discover that the value of 'x' is, for example, 317. It is possible that 'wickedness . . . in human form' was an 'indeterminate quantity' for St. Paul when he wrote 2 *Thess.*, but that during his last days in Rome he ascribed to it the determinate value '*Nero*'. It is hardly necessary to say

[7] Frost, *Old Testament Apocalyptic* (London, 1952), esp. Ch. I.

that for St. Paul he was not an 'abstract principle of evil', but a concrete, though indeterminate, human being.

It is only too easy to become so closely involved in details and in the highly speculative origins of St. Paul's language that we allow the main structure of his thought to be obscured. The close examination of such details is an essential part of Biblical scholarship, and a full, concise, and judicious examination of this subject has been carried out by Rigaux, who includes in his study a fully adequate survey of the literature.[8] We must above all remember that the evil forces are described in terms which suggest that they are analogous to Christ, and almost amount to a blasphemous caricature. Secondly, this whole passage would be nonsense if it did not presuppose the conviction that all will happen in accordance with a programme which is in the hands of God; He will bring in the end through Jesus Christ. This belief in the sovereignty of God, which extends over 'Antichrist'[9] as well as over human beings, is so much a part of the structure of St. Paul's thinking that he fails to express it in words, although it is inevitably presupposed by what he actually says. Thirdly, the Apostle's thought is related to the practical situation: the end is not yet; the Thessalonians must carry on in a sober and disciplined fashion. It is not possible, however, to omit a discussion of the 'restraining hand' (*to katechon*, neuter) and of the 'Restrainer' (*ho katechōn*, masculine), especially since important work has been published on this matter in recent years. We already have concluded that the 'final rebellion' and 'wickedness revealed in human form' (ii. 3) refer in St. Paul's mind to an event and to a person which are to be expected in the near future, not to abstract 'principles' of evil, although the reference is indefinite, not specific; this is hardly surprising, because the Apostle here speaks of what still lies in the future. Since the 'restraining hand' and the 'Restrainer' were already in operation at the time when 2 *Thess.* was written, it is difficult to suppose that they did not refer to specific, concrete beings.

Milligan[10] indeed suggests that the 'restraining hand' is a principle; but the logic of his own exposition would be better served by saying that the restraining hand (neuter) is an institution,

---

[8] *Les Epîtres aux Thessaloniciens* (Paris, 1956), pp. 195–280.

[9] The actual word 'antichrist' is found in the N.T. only at 1 John. ii 18, 22; iv. 3; 2 John 7, but in 2 Thess. ii. 3 'wickedness . . . in human form' is a figure of the Antichrist-type.

[10] *St. Paul's Epistle to the Thessalonians* (London, 1908).

that is, the Roman Empire, and that the 'Restrainer' is the Emperor himself. Morris,[11] with the rest of whose exposition of this passage I find myself in general agreement, suggests that it is the 'principle of order which restrains the working of evil. . . . It might be illustrated by the system of law in the Roman Empire, or in other systems of law which have succeeded to that'. This interpretation is hard to reconcile with the words of ii. 7, 'Until the Restrainer disappears from the scene'; St. Paul could hardly be referring both to the Roman Empire and also to such analogous institutions as the League of Nations and U.N.O., since the whole passage suggests that the end is imminent.

The most favoured interpretation was formerly that propounded by Tertullian, who identified the restraining hand with the Roman Empire. Dibelius, in the early years of this century, developed the theory that St. Paul was referring to an act like the 'binding', 'restraining' or 'keeping' of Satan (Rev. xx) or Behemoth and Leviathan (2 Esdras vi. 49–52). It is certain that ideas of this kind form the ultimate source of St. Paul's thought-forms, but the Apostle actually refers to something far more concrete. Again, as Masson remarks,[12] it is not easy on this theory to distinguish between the 'restraining hand' and the 'Restrainer'.

Cullmann,[13] followed by Munck,[14] has given fruitful development to an idea which had already been suggested in germinal form by Theodoret of Cyr.[15] Cullmann's theory is based upon the view expressed in Mark. xiii. 10, 'But before the end the Gospel must first be proclaimed to all nations'. That this view enjoyed wide acceptance in the apostolic church is clear from a number of passages.[16] Cullmann suggests that the 'restraining hand' is the preaching of the Gospel, and that the 'Restrainer' is St. Paul himself: in accordance with God's plan, it is impossible for wickedness to be revealed in human form until St. Paul has accomplished his task of preaching the Gospel throughout the world.[17]

[11] *Epistle to the Thessalonians*, London N.T.C. (London, 1959), p. 226.
[12] *Les Deux Epîtres de Saint Paul aux Thessaloniciens* (Neuchâtel, 1957), p. 99.
[13] *Revue d'histoire et de philosophie réligieuse* (1936), p. 210f., *Christ and Time* (E.T. London, 1951), pp. 165 ff.
[14] *Paul and the Salvation of Mankind* (E.T. London, 1959), p. 36f.
[15] P.G. 82, 665A.
[16] e.g., Matt. xxiv. 14; Acts i. 6f., x. 42, Rev. vi. 1–8; cited by Munck, op. cit., p. 39.
[17] *Christ and Time* (E.T. London, 1962² revised), p. 165.

This attractive theory lies open to some weighty objections:

1. It is extremely hard to suppose that St. Paul thinks of a time when, in accordance with God's plan, he himself 'disappears from the scene' (*ek mesou genētai*). Such phraseology would be more appropriate to an enemy of God.[18]

2. The natural interpretation of 1 Thess. iv. 15, 'We who are left alive until the Lord comes,' etc. is that St. Paul expects to live until the Parousia, not to disappear from the scene beforehand.

3. It has been urged that if St. Paul had wished to make such an important point as Cullmann suggests, he would have done so more clearly[19] in other passages in his epistles. But it is only fair to say that as Rigaux suggests,[20] St. Paul is probably saying something new to the Thessalonians when he speaks about the 'Restrainer', whereas he had already told them about the 'rebellion' and 'wickedness in human form' when he was with them. Writing to Thessalonica in haste, he might well fail to give specific information about the 'Restrainer': it was only necessary to his purpose to insist that the 'Restrainer' was still at work, so that the end was not to be expected at once.

4. It has also been urged that the Thessalonians, if they knew that it was God's plan for St. Paul to complete his task of evangelization before the end, would hardly imagine that he could have done so already in a matter of a few months. If, of course, St. Paul had not told them about the 'Restrainer' during his visit to Thessalonica, this fourth point does not arise at all. Even if he had told them, it would still have been possible for them to have drifted away from the moorings of their instruction: it is common Christian experience that we need to be reminded about matters which we are already supposed to know.

Although points 3 and 4 above are weak, 1 and 2 are strong. Accordingly, Cullmann's theory cannot be regarded as certainly established; neither, of course, can we claim that it has been refuted. Under these circumstances it is worth looking once more at the 'traditional' explanation which claims that the 'restraining hand' is the Roman Empire. This explanation is a serious rival to the Cullmann-Munck theory, and it is not wholly at variance

[18] So Rigaux, *Les Epîtres aux Thessaloniciens* (Paris, 1956), p. 275.

[19] Masson, *Les Deux Epîtres de Saint Paul aux Thessaloniciens* (Neuchâtel, 1957), p. 100.

[20] *Les Epîtres aux Thessaloniciens* (Paris, 1956), p. 665.

with the 'mythological' explanation propounded by Dibelius. It may well be the case that St. Paul has resorted to historization (*Historisierung*); that is, he has referred to a reality of contemporary history, the Roman Empire, in language derived from mythology.

Rigaux[21] insists that the tradition does not go back far, since the Fathers give so many interpretations and since Tertullian (died c. 220 A.D.) is our earliest witness for it. Rigaux's latter point would be more convincing if he had quoted an alternative explanation from some source earlier than Tertullian. The fact that the Fathers give such varied accounts proves nothing, since St. Paul's language is in any case so obscure. We conclude that Tertullian *may* be preserving a first-century tradition, although to regard this as certain would be foolhardy.

Again, Masson contends that St. Paul would be unlikely to introduce an historical entity into a passage which otherwise speaks of apocalyptic concepts, not of historical realities. To this criticism two objections must be raised. First, the 'restraining hand' is active when St. Paul is writing; such apocalyptic preliminaries to the 'parousia' as the rebellion and the revelation of wickedness in human form had not yet come to pass. We might paraphrase St. Paul as follows: 'apocalyptic' or 'metahistory' cannot begin yet because history, which includes the 'restraining hand' of the Roman Empire, is still in possession of the field.

Further, it has been maintained that a mere political organization could not hold back the forces of Satan. This is certainly true, but neither could St. Paul in his own strength. If either St. Paul's duty to complete his task or the Roman Empire could hold back the course of history, it was only because God had so ordained.

Fourthly, it has been argued that St. Paul had not enjoyed only good from the Empire; in fact his experience has been decidedly mixed, so that he would not have thought of the Empire as holding back the forces of evil. But St. Paul's language in this passage is just as 'mixed' as his experience had been: the Empire, if this interpretation is correct, was to play a part in God's plan and to restrain the forces of Satan; but as soon as its task was over, the Empire was to be removed from the scene in a manner which reminds us of the function and fate of Assyria in Isaiah x. †

---

[21] *Les Epîtres aux Thessaloniciens* (Paris, 1956), p. 274.

iii. Did St. Paul think the End was at Hand?

When we come to examine the teaching of 1 *Thess.* we immediately encounter a problem. 1 Thess. iv. 15, 'We who are left alive until the Lord comes shall not forestall those who have died,' would appear to suggest that St. Paul, at least when he wrote this letter, expected that the end would come soon, indeed that he himself would live to see it. This 'natural' interpretation is strongly attacked by some scholars, and would have been examined at a later stage among the 'problems' if it were not for the fact that it has to be considered before we proceed to such other matters as whether St. Paul's thought developed. The question is important because it trenches upon the infallibility of the Apostles. As a point of history, St. Paul did not live until the second coming. In 1915 the Biblical Commission[23] laid down the ruling that St. Paul did not teach either that he himself would survive until the second coming or that it would take place soon. On the contrary, he did not know whether the end would come on the next day or countless years after.

Chrysostom,[24] followed by Bonsirven[25] and Morris[26], maintains that St. Paul 'identifies' himself with the last generation without supposing that he himself would necessarily belong to it. We may note that this 'identification' would be more likely to occur if he thought that at least some of the Thessalonians would live till the Parousia, and would be somewhat unnatural if he had envisaged the possibility that centuries, if not millenia, were to elapse before the return of Christ. However, Chrysostom's theory is not formally impossible. There are, of course, many passages in which St. Paul identifies himself with the recipients of his letters. Morris[27] draws our attention to 1 Cor. vi. 14, 'God not only raised our Lord from the dead; he will also raise us by his power,' suggesting that St. Paul 'identified' himself with his fellow-Christians as a figure of speech, but did not necessarily include himself in the class with which he identified himself.

Since Morris, a conservative evangelical Protestant, and the Roman Catholics hold these views partly because of a belief in the inerrancy of Scripture, it is fair to remark that they would appear

---

[23] Denziger-Schönmetzer, *Enchiridion symbolorum, definitionum ac declarationum*, ed. xxxii (Freiburg-im-Breisgau, 1963), c. 3630.
[24] P.G. 62, c. 436.   [25] *L'Evangile de Paul* (Paris, 1948), pp. 338ff.
[26] *Epistles to the Thessalonians* London N.T.C. (London, 1959), pp. 141–2.
[27] ibid.

to be sacrificing the clarity of the Apostle to his inerrancy, and that it is doubtful whether they have really safeguarded the reality of revelation, since they make it less clear, and in that sense, less revealing.

We may add that when St. Paul says in 1 Cor. vi. 14, 'He will raise us by his power', he may be employing the word 'raise' (*egeirein*; the tense of the verb varies in different MSS.) in a general sense, which would cover both the 'raising' or 'awakening' which is presupposed and also the 'changing' which is mentioned in 1 Cor. xv. 51, 'We shall not all die, but we shall all be changed'. In 1 Cor. vi. 14 St. Paul is not distinguishing between those who are to be alive at Christ's appearing and those who are not. The whole point of 1 Thess. iv 15 and 17 is to compare and contrast the fate of those who are and those who are not to be alive at the second coming: and it is in this context that St. Paul 'identifies' himself with those who are to be still alive, speaking of them in the first person plural, whereas in the preceding two verses he had spoken of those who would be dead by the time the end came in the *third* person plural. It is certainly *possible* that Bonsirven and Morris are correct, so that this passage *by itself* is not fatal to the hypothesis of apostolic inerrancy, but I find it difficult not to accept the conclusion of Frame[28] when he quotes with approval the judgement of Denney: 'Is it not better to recognise the obvious fact that Paul was mistaken as to the nearness of the second advent than to torture his words to secure infallibility?'

We must pass from the question whether St. Paul expected to survive until the second advent when he wrote the Thessalonian Epistles and 1 *Corinthians*, to the wider problem which includes it. Did St. Paul believe that the end of the world was coming soon, that is, in the life-time of men already living, or was he completely open on this point? That St. Paul did expect an early parousia is strongly suggested by Rom. xiii. 12, 'It is far on in the night; day is near,' Phil. iv. 6, 'The Lord is near,' and 1 Cor. vii. 29, 'The time we live in will not last long,' and the bias given in that chapter to St. Paul's ethical teaching by the expectation of the end. Bonsirven explains Rom. xiii. 12 as an exhortation to moral vigilance[29] and Phil. iv. 6 as a prayer.[30] In 1 Cor. vii. he finds no

[28] *The Epistle of St. Paul to the Thessalonians* (I.C.C. Edinburgh, 1912), p. 173.
[29] *L'Evangile de Paul* (Paris, 1948), p. 342.
[30] ibid.

reference to the second coming but only the influence of Christian ascetic teaching. Bonsirven does however frankly agree[31] that many Christians did believe that the end was near. It is perhaps not unfair to remark that the Thessalonians seem to have believed that only those who were alive at the parousia would share in its blessings. Who had taught them this? St. Paul does not lay the blame on any strange teacher. It seems probable that St. Paul's teaching during his few weeks[32] in Thessalonica had at least been capable of being misunderstood to mean that the end was very near indeed. Again, when he wrote to Corinth he spoke of death as a punishment for sin connected with the Eucharist,[33] as if it were 'unnatural' for a Christian to die before the return of Christ (1 Cor. xi. 27–30). On these and similar grounds I would maintain that St. Paul expected the return of Christ to take place in the life-time of his own generation, and that at least when he wrote 1 and 2 *Thessalonians* and 1 *Corinthians* he thought that he himself would live to witness the end; but on this point there is no general agreement.

It is, however, quite certain that 1 Thess. iv. 15, 'We who are left alive until the Lord comes shall not forestall those who have died,' means that all Christians will share in the blessings of the final generation. This is a deliberate counter to the view propounded in 2 Esdras xiii. 24, 'Understand therefore that those who are left are more blessed than those who have died.'

The verses which follow, 1 Thess. iv. 16, 17, 'Because at the word of command, at the sound of the archangel's voice and God's trumpet-call, the Lord himself will descend from heaven; first the Christian dead will rise, then we who are left alive shall join them, caught up in the clouds to meet the Lord in the air,' are probably more illuminating because of the indirect light which they shed upon St. Paul's Christology than they are for the direct information which they afford us concerning his eschatology. The whole passage suggests the Day of Yahweh, and Jesus is associated with Yahweh by the mere fact that he is described as Lord (*kurios*). The meaning of 'the archangel's voice' is obscure; it may be the voice of St. Michael, since *archangelos* occurs elsewhere in the N.T. only at Jude 9 in the phrase 'the archangel Michael', but in any

---

[31] *L'Evangile de Paul* (Paris, 1948), p. 342.
[32] This is a reasonable inference from Acts xvii 2, 'For the next three Sabbaths he argued with them. . . .'
[33] cf. *supra*, p. 184 f.

case the purpose of the phrase is not to give detailed information concerning sounds which will be audible but to build up the mass effects. God's trumpet-call (*salpinx*), according to Dodd[34] 'has passed into the standing symbolism of Christian eschatology'; it recalls many events in the O.T.,[35] and is frequently employed for that purpose in the N.T.[36] Much the same may be said about the 'clouds'; this word looks back to Dan. vii. 13f. The phrase 'to meet' (*eis apantēsin*) suggests going out of a city to meet some great personage, as Dupont has shown,[37] and the same background of thought lies behind 'until the Lord comes' (*eis tēn parousian tou kuriou*) in *v.* 15, since *parousia*, to draw once again upon the researches of Dupont,[38] is used of the 'appearing' of a royal personage.

iv. Did St. Paul's Eschatology Develop? †

Dodd[39] has argued that St. Paul's eschatology shows signs of development; he sees a difference of emphasis between the later epistles, that is, *Romans*, 2 Cor. i–ix. and the Captivity Epistles on the one hand, and on the other hand, the earlier epistles, that is 1 and 2 *Thess.*, 1 *Cor.*, 2 Cor. vi. 14–vii. 1, and 2 Cor. x.1–xiii. 10. He suggests that 2 Cor. vi. 14–vii.1 is a fragment from the possibly harsh, puritanical letter mentioned by St. Paul in 1 Cor. v. 19. Dodd puts forward the hypothesis that this 'puritanical' letter caused the Corinthians to send St. Paul a letter containing questions which St. Paul answered in a non-puritanical sense in 1 *Cor.* St. Paul then heard that the Corinthians had defied his apostolic authority, and replied with an epistolary broad-side which included 2 Cor. x. 1–xiii. 10. This led to the capitulation of the Corinthians, and in a mood of thanksgiving the Apostle wrote 2 Cor. i–ix, the first of his writings which reflects a new attitude. Dodd suggests that in all the epistles assigned to the period before the capitulation of the Corinthians St. Paul showed signs of a certain pride which

---

[34] *According to the Scriptures* (London, 1952), pp. 62–3.

[35] e.g. Joel ii. 1, Isa. xxvii. 13.

[36] e.g. 1 Cor. xv. 52, Rev. i. 10, iv. 1, etc.

[37] *L'Union avec le Christ suivant Saint Paul*, première partie, '*Avec le Christ*' *dans la vie future* (Louvain and Paris, 1952), pp. 64ff.

[38] ibid. pp. 49ff.

[39] In 'The Mind of Paul' I. and II. These two articles first appeared in the *B.J.R.L.* for 1933 and 1934 respectively, and were reprinted in a book entitled *New Testament Studies*, (Manchester, 1953), which must be distinguished from the periodical of the same name. References will be given to the page numbers in *New Testament Studies*.

remained from his days as a Pharisee, and that he tended to be world-denying and puritanical. After the humiliating experience of being defied, and after his thankfulness for victory, he achieved more humility and became more inclined to accept the world, or rather to claim it for Christ, instead of denying it. To ask such questions at all is to enter the realm of speculation, and any answer which we may give must, because of the nature of the question, be somewhat precarious. But quite apart from the *reasons* which, he suggests, may account for this change, Dodd would appear to have given evidence for the fact of a change of emphasis, which justify us in accepting his thesis with some degree of confidence.

Dodd's case is as follows:

1. In 1 Thess. iv. 15, 17, St. Paul would appear to think[40] that he himself would remain in the body on earth until the return of Christ, but in 2 Cor. iv. 12; v. 4 he faces the possibility that he will die before the Lord's return.[41] Although it is not *certain* either that St. Paul expected to live until the parousia in 1 Thess. or that he expected to die before it in 2 Cor. yet Dodd's point has some weight: an argument is not wholly nullified by the mere *possibility* that it may not be soundly based, though naturally its force is diminished.

2. In the earlier epistles St. Paul would seem to teach that the Second Coming is near at hand. Again, Dodd may have been somewhat too definite in stating his case, but the main weight of the evidence on this matter would appear to favour his contention. In the later epistles, on the other hand, Dodd maintains that emphasis upon the Second Coming is lacking, apart from Rom. xiii. 11–14. It is worth noting that this passage presents a close parallel with 1 Thess. v. 4–8; both speak of the soldiers or children of light and of armour. It may well be that St. Paul here has recourse to a stock theme[42] of Christian teaching, in which case its significance as evidence against Dodd is to some extent diminished.

Lowe[43] contends that the eschatological element appears also in a 'late' epistle, Rom. v. 9–10, 'Since we have now been justified

[40] *New Testament Studies* (Manchester, 1953), p. 110.
[41] ibid.
[42] cf. Selwyn, *The First Epistle of St. Peter* (London, 1947²), Essay ii, pp 375–82, esp. Table II, pp. 376–8.
[43] *J.T.S.* xlii. (1941) pp. 129–142.

by Christ's sacrificial death, we shall all the more certainly be saved through him from final retribution . . . much more, now that we are reconciled, shall we be saved by his life.' It is true that soteriology, the main theme of the passage, is set within a framework of eschatology, but there is no suggestion that the end is at hand; indeed, the point which St. Paul here presses home is that God's love is not exhausted by the initial phase of 'justification' or 'reconciliation', but continues until its purpose is achieved. Much the same must be said about three passages which Lowe quotes from *Philippians*, i. 6, 'The One who started the good work in you will bring it to completion by the Day of Christ Jesus'; i. 10, 'Then on the Day of Christ you will be flawless and without blame; and ii. 16, 'Thus you will be my pride on the Day of Christ.' All these passages are directly concerned with the progress of the Philippians during the remainder of the present age, rather than with the nearness of the end as such. But it is surely significant that the end of the age should be so much in evidence as the background to the Apostle's thought.

Lowe also mentions Phil. iv. 6, 'The Lord is near (*ho kurios engus*)', which he understands to mean that the return of the Lord is to occur in the immediate future. Dodd[44] has argued that this phrase is to be interpreted in the light of Ps. cxlv. (LXX, cxliv) 18, 'The Lord is near to all who call upon him,' understanding 'near' to mean 'ready to hear' without any reference to time. But the use of *engus* in the N.T. and LXX, when used without any such qualifying phrase is against[45] this, although it is not impossible that the phrase is an abbreviated quotation from the psalm. It may represent the *Maranatha* of 1 Cor. xvi. 22.[46]

We must also notice Phil. iii. 20, 'From heaven we expect our deliverer to come, the Lord Jesus Christ.' From these five[47] passages it is clear that when[48] he wrote *Philippians* St. Paul had the Second Coming very much in the foreground of his mind. The recognition of this fact is not incompatible with holding the belief that St. Paul's eschatological thought developed. Development

---

[44] *New Testament Studies* (Manchester, 1953), p. 112.
[45] cf. J. Y. Campbell, *Exp.T.*, xlviii, p. 91f., and R. H. Fuller, *The Mission and Achievement of Jesus*, S.B.T., no. 12, (London, 1954), pp. 20–5.
[46] So E. F. Scott, *I.B.* on Phil. iv. 5.
[47] Phil. i. 6, 10; ii. 16; iii. 20; iv. 5.
[48] We disregard for the moment the possibility that *Philippians* may consist of more than one letter.

does not always occur in a uniform manner. It is possible to suppose that his thought changed as he grew older, and all the same to accept the fact that *Philippians* in this matter represents a return in the direction of the doctrine found in the Thessalonian Epistles and in 1 *Corinthians*.

We must also bear in mind the possibility that *Philippians* is an early epistle, and was not written from prison at all. T. W. Manson has argued plausibly that *Philippians* was written soon after the foundation of the church of Philippi.[49]

The only evidence in *Philippians* that it was written from prison is provided by the words *desmous*, bonds, and *praitōriō*, 'headquarters', in i. 13. Manson sees in this Paul's appearance in the Praetorium or 'Government House' at Corinth, under arrest but not sentenced, as recorded in Acts xviii. 12-17.

3. In 1 Cor. vi. 1-11, Dodd continues, St. Paul takes a low view of the Roman law-courts, and says that Christians should not have recourse to them for private disputes, whereas in Rom. xiii. 1-11 a more positive evulation of the Roman state is put forward. It is true that these two contrasted passages are not concerned with the same matter, since 1 Cor. vi deals with private disputes between Christians, while Rom. xiii. 1-11 enjoins obedience to the public law of the Roman State, but Dodd is surely correct with regard to the atmosphere, which is one of approval in Romans and of disapproval in 1 *Corinthians*.

4. In 2 Cor. vi. 14-vii. 1 St. Paul urges the Corinthians to have nothing to do with unbelievers. Yet, in Rom. ii. 14 he says, not merely that the pagans have knowledge of the contents of the law, but they sometimes obey it (*ta tou nomou poiōsi*). The force of this argument is weakened by the fact that in *Romans* St. Paul is concerned to show the faults of the Jews, and does this by pointing to the actual virtues of the Gentiles, while in 2 Cor. vi. 14-vii. 1 he is anxious to warn the Corinthians against allowing themselves to be corrupted. It is possible both to warn converts that pagans are for them a dangerous influence and also to do justice to the fact that pagans are not devoid of righteous deeds.

5. In 1 Cor. vii. St. Paul would appear to think of marriage as a 'second-best'. It is not evil in itself, but under the actual circumstances celibacy is better. On the other hand, in *Colossians* a

---

[49] 'The Date of the Epistle to the Philippians', *B.J.R.L.* (1939), reprinted in *Studies in the Gospels and Epistles* (Manchester, 1962), pp. 150–167.

S

high value is ascribed to marriage. Lowe[51] replies that 1 *Pet.* includes both positive teaching on marriage (1 Pet. iii. 1–7) and also a belief in the imminence of the end, as in iv. 17. 'The time has come for the judgement to begin.' Even if 1 *Pet.* as we have it does derive from more than one source, we find a belief in the imminence of the end combined with a concern for morality in a single verse at 1 Pet. iv. 7, 'The end of all things is upon us, so you must lead an ordered and sober life, given to prayer'. But this does not really affect Dodd's point which is, not that belief in the imminence of the end is incompatible with a concern for morality and for family life, but that in *1 Cor.* as a matter of plain fact, St. Paul did take a somewhat negative view of marriage while in *Colossians* he accords it a higher valuation. It is difficult to avoid the conclusion that subsequent criticism has weakened Dodd's case, but has not destroyed it.

v. The Resurrection of the Faithful

We pass to a consideration of St. Paul's teaching about the resurrection of Christians. This includes his thought concerning the nature of the resurrection body and the manner of its bestowal upon those who survive until the Second Coming and of those who die beforehand; these will be referred to as 'the survivors' and 'the deceased' respectively. From this discussion the following conclusions emerge.

1. There is no reason to suppose that St. Paul's thought on the resurrection developed, whatever may be said about his teaching on other matters of eschatology. In his various epistles he did not give different answers to the same questions, but addressed himself to different problems.

2. St. Paul does not propound definite answers to all the questions raised: in some cases he teaches that God will accomplish His purpose for those who are in Christ, without being at all specific about precisely how He will do so.

3. Eschatology, anthropology, and soteriology are closely interwoven. 1 Cor. xv. 50, 'Flesh and blood can never possess the kingdom of God,' is probably soteriological in its emphasis, as Jeremias suggests,[52] while 2 Cor. v. 3, 'In the hope, that, being thus clothed, we shall not find ourselves naked', is primarily,

[51] *J.T.S.* xlii. (1941), p. 139.
[52] *N.T.S.* ii. (1955–6). pp. 151–9.

pace Ellis,[53] eschatological rather than soteriological, though it is true that the eschatological hope of the Christian is founded upon a soteriological basis.

For the sake of convenience we shall reserve for a later section such closely related subjects as the question whether St. Paul taught the sleep of the soul and whether he believed that all men would be raised from the dead or only Christians.

In the light of these questions we must now carry out a brief review of the most important passages.

1 Thess. iv. 13–18 tells us only that the final state of both the survivors and the deceased will be the same. It tells us nothing about such problems as the nature of the resurrection body etc., and is compatible with almost any answer to them which may be proposed.

Phil. iii. 20–21, 'From heaven we expect our deliverer to come, the Lord Jesus Christ. He will transfigure the body belonging to our humble estate. . . .', refers solely to the survivors, and tells us nothing at all about the deceased, though indirect light is shed upon this problem by Phil. i. 21–5.

Rom. viii. 11, 'The God who raised Christ Jesus from the dead will also give new life to your mortal bodies through his indwelling spirit,' almost certainly refers to the survivors, not to the deceased, and it speaks of soteriology just as much as it does of eschatology: it is concerned not only with the fact that God will give us the gift of life after death, but with the quality of the state into which Christians are to be transformed.

We must now examine these passages in greater detail, and it will be convenient to take first, because the issues which it raises are comparatively simple, Phil. iii. 20–21, 'From heaven we expect our deliverer (*sotēra*) to come, the Lord Jesus Christ. He will transfigure (*metaschēmatisei*) the body belonging to our humble estate, and give it a form like (*summorphon*) that of his own resplendent (*doxēs*) body'. It will not be superfluous to stress the fact that St. Paul is speaking about a change, not about an exchange. He says, not that Christ will give the survivors a new body to replace the old one, but that the old body will be transformed. It will be as if a block of ice were transformed into steam. The 'atoms' will be the same, but they will be in the gaseous, not the solid state, it may be suggested. This analogy does justice to the element of

[53] *N.T.S.* vi. (1959–60), pp. 211–24. cf. *infra*, pp. 255–8.

continuity; it will be the same body. But no metaphor can do justice to the change. This act of transformation is analogous to the transformation of the physical world spoken of by St. Paul in Rom. viii. 19–23. This links the eschatological change with its soteriological cause, as does the word *doxēs*, which probably does not refer only to the resplendent nature of Christ's Resurrection Body, but to the fact that, as St. Paul tells us in Rom. vi. 4, 'Christ was raised from the dead in the splendour (*dia tēs doxēs*) of the Father'; I would suggest that *doxēs*[54] means God's display of power, and that *dia* expresses the efficient cause, not the attendant circumstances, although both uses are found.[55]

In 1 Cor. xv. 35, 'How are the dead raised? In what kind of body?' St. Paul would appear to be speaking about the resurrection of the deceased. Reasons have been adduced in a previous chapter[56] for rejecting the contention that he is concerned in this passage not with the resurrection of individual Christians, but with their solidarity in the Body of Christ.

St. Paul is bound from the nature of the case to make use of illustrations and to speak, for example, of sowing seeds. It is difficult to be certain how far we are justified in pressing the analogy. No one would seriously argue that there is a complete parallel between the seed and the grain on the one hand and the corpse and the resurrection body of Christians on the other; but St. Paul's choice of illustrations was obviously not completely arbitrary, and we are entitled to attach some significance to the fact that he employed one analogy rather than another, even if he did take it over from Jewish or Christian tradition, e.g. that preserved in John xii. 24.

It will here be maintained that we are on dangerous ground if we press the metaphor very far, and that the Apostle is concerned to make clear the fact that God, the sovereign Lord of the Old Creation, who on the third day, according to Gen. i. 9–13, commanded the earth to put forth 'plants yielding seed', is able to give to the deceased Christians a body suited to their state of glory in the New Creation. There is not however enough verbal resemblance between *1 Cor.* and Gen. i. and ii. to justify us in

---

[54] cf. Brockington, 'The Septuagintal Background to the New Testament Use of *doxa*' in *Studies in the Gospels* (Oxford, 1955), pp. 5–6.

[55] cf. Arndt and Gringrich *sub voce* '*dia*'.

[56] cf. *supra*, pp. 184–7.

supposing that St. Paul had the Creation narrative consciously in mind. However, there is a real parallel of content in the sovereign power of God over every possible form of 'body'. We suggested in a previous chapter (vi) that it is incorrect to press the analogies which St. Paul employs in order to stress the fact of the Atonement and to construct out of them a theory of the *modus operandi* of the Atonement.[57] It is almost equally misleading to build a theory of the *modus operandi* of the resurrection of Christians upon the metaphors used by St. Paul to emphasize the fact.

We return to 1 Cor. xv. 35, 'How are the dead raised? In what kind of body? A senseless question!' These last three words represent the single Greek word *aphrōn*, 'foolish', and the *R.S.V.* renders 'You foolish man!' The words of the *N.E.B.* are not an exact translation, but a paraphrase based upon what is no doubt the correct interpretation. When St. Paul says in 1 Cor. xv. 36, 'The seed you sow does not come to life unless it has first died,' he is *not* 'answering a fool according to his folly', that is, he is not speaking within the false framework of ideas presupposed by the 'foolish question'. He avoids the unanswerable questions of the nature of the resurrection body, and speaks about the power of God, for there is no thought of any 'natural law' operating in a kind of quasi-independence of God, to give to the 'dead' seed, by miraculous means, a 'resurrection body'. There is here no 'argument', no parallel. St. Paul is not 'explaining' one fact by adducing a parallel example. Rather he invites us to accept the miracle of the resurrection body by pointing to the lesser miracle of the harvest, which to us is not as 'miraculous' as it was to St. Paul, because of our greater knowledge of botany. There is probably a genuine parallel of attitude in Rom. ix. 19–20, 'You will say "Then why does God blame a man? For who can resist his will?" Who are you, sir, to answer God back? Can the pot speak to the potter and say, "Why did you make me like this?"' It is possible to accept something which we do not understand, and in *1 Cor.* St. Paul is not trying to explain the resurrection of the deceased: he expresses his conviction that they will be raised, although he does not know how.

Since, however, St. Paul says in 1 Cor. xv. 42, 'What is sown in the earth as a perishable thing is raised imperishable,'[58] we are

[57] cf. *supra*, p. 147.
[58] cf. *supra*, p. 196 f.

to understand that there is continuity between the deceased and those raised in glory, but Clavier[59] is right when he maintains that we cannot speak in this case of numerical identity if we follow out the analogy of the seed. St. Paul continues in 1 Cor. xv. 44, 'Sown as an animal (*psuchikon*) body, it is raised as a spiritual (*pneumatikon*) body.' Adjectives ending with the suffix—*ikos* mean 'like', whereas those ending in -*inos* mean 'made of.'[60] Accordingly, we may follow *Arndt and Gringrich* when they render *pneumatikos* 'belonging to the supernatural order'; it does not *mean* 'made of spiritual matter', although such a meaning is consistent with the thought of these verses as a whole. We need not ask whether he was thinking of the substance or the orientation of the 'spiritual body' as if the two explanations were mutually exclusive: each involves the other. As in the healing miracles of Christ, 'spiritual renewal' and 'physical healing' go together. St. Paul's thought includes both the eschatological transformation of the body and the soteriological transformation of the whole personality; and both these changes are made possible by the work of Jesus Christ; this is made clear in the next few verses which are summarized in 1 Cor. xv. 49. 'As we have worn the likeness of the man made of dust, so shall we wear the likeness of the heavenly man.'

Jeremias in an important article[61] to which reference has already been made on a related subject[62] maintains that 1 Cor. xv. 50, 'What I mean, my brothers, is this: flesh and blood can never possess the kingdom of God', is to be understood as follows: 'Flesh and blood' does not refer to the corrupted human corpse but to human nature as such, with an emphasis upon its frailty.[63] This phrase occurs in Ecclus. xiv. 18, where it renders the Hebrew *bāsār wādhām*, which occurs frequently with this meaning in Rabbinic sources.[64] It is found with this meaning at Gal. i. 17, 'Without consulting any human being (lit., "flesh and blood")', at Matt xvi. 17, and Eph. vi. 12; at Heb. ii. 14 the meaning is only slightly different. Jeremias argues that neither the living nor

---

[59] 'Brèves remarques sur la notion de *sōma pneumatikon*' in *The Background of the New Testament and its Eschatology* (Cambridge, 1956), p. 347.

[60] Moulton and Howard, *A Grammar of New Testament Greek* (ii, Edinburgh, 1956²), pp. 378–9.

[61] *N.T.S.* ii (1955–6), pp. 151–9, 'Flesh and Blood cannot inherit the Kingdom of God'.

[62] cf. *supra*, pp. 173f.

[63] cf. *supra*, p. 35.

[64] Strack-Billerbeck, i, pp. 730–1, on Matt. xvi. 17.

the dead can take part in the kingdom of God as they are, and that St. Paul is referring to the change of the survivors when he speaks of 'flesh and blood', while 'The perishable (*phthora*) cannot possess immortality (*aphtharsian*)' refers to the changing of the deceased. Allo[65] accuses Robertson and Plummer,[66] who had made much the same point as Jeremias, of being unduly subtle, but adduces no reason to substantiate his judgement. In fact, the solution put forward by Jeremias would seem to be correct, both because it ascribes to 'flesh and blood' its normal meaning and because it fits in with St. Paul's exposition of his thought in 1 Cor. xv., where he goes on to speak about the change which must come to both survivors and deceased at the parousia.

He continues in 1 Cor. xv. 51–2, 'We shall not[67] all die, but we shall all be changed . . . the dead will rise immortal, and we shall be changed.' It is perfectly clear that here, as in *1 Thess.*, St. Paul ascribes to survivors and deceased the same ultimate fate. His teaching about seeds and about the splendour (*doxa*) of sun and stars (1 Cor. xv. 44) has this main end in view: it makes it quite clear that God has power to make the deceased share the triumph of the survivors. It is not so clear how this is to happen; such precision was not necessary for the Apostle's purpose, and it is possible that he had no clear opinion on the *modus operandi* of the resurrection of the faithful.

Nor does he make it clear in 1 Cor. xv. 51–2 what the fate of the deceased is to be during the time which is to elapse between their death and the Second Coming, and the same ambiguity is found in 1 Thess. iv. 17, 'First the Christian dead will rise (*anastēsontai*)'. What does 'rise' mean, and what was their state to be before the parousia? In 1 Thess. iv. 13, 14, St. Paul uses the verb *koimaomai*, lit., 'sleep', to designate the dead. The deceased are certainly 'asleep' in the metaphorical sense that they are dead, but are they also asleep in the literal sense of being unconscious? That the dead, according to St. Paul and other N.T. writers, are asleep, in the sense of being unconscious until the parousia is the opinion

---

[65] *Première Epître aux Corinthiens* (Paris, 1956²), p. 431 on xv. 50.

[66] *First Epistle to the Corinthians* (Edinburgh, 1914²), pp. 375–6. They understand the words to mean 'our present mortal nature', not 'our evil propensities', which would be *sarx*, 'flesh', without *haima*, 'blood'.

[67] The MSS. here include some most important variants but they concern the question *who* is to suffer various changes, not the nature of the change. cf. *infra*, p. 273.

of many leading scholars, including Cullmann.[68] We shall later give reasons for holding that this interpretation of the N.T. is, on balance, improbable. It is only necessary at this point to note that I Thess. iv. 13f. is consistent with either hypothesis. We are not told whether the dead, literally those who had fallen asleep (*koimēthentas*) are unconscious or no. We are told that they will rise, which must surely mean that they will be given resurrection bodies, but we are not told whether they will first be roused to consciousness or not.

The same ambiguity is found in 1 Cor. xv. 52, 'The dead will rise immortal and we shall be changed.' At the end all will be in the same condition, both the survivors and the deceased. The survivors, as in Phil. iii. 20f., 1 Thess. iv. 15f., and, in all probability, Rom. viii. 11, are to be transformed. About the deceased we are told that they are to be raised, but no information is accorded to us about their previous condition.

Rom. viii. 11, 'The God who raised Christ Jesus from the dead will also give new life (*zōopoiēsei*) to your mortal (*thnēta*) bodies through his indwelling spirit,' probably refers to the transformation of the survivors, in so far as it is eschatological at all, rather than to the raising up of the deceased. *Thnētos* (mortal) means 'capable of dying', not 'dead'. Again, the whole subject of Rom. viii. 1–17 is the present, not the future state of the Christian. Indeed, the meaning is probably soteriological, not eschatological, as we can see from Rom. viii. 10, 'Although the body is a dead thing (*nekron*) because you sinned, yet the spirit is life because you have been justified'.

In 2 Cor. St. Paul states once more his familiar teaching about the survivors, and adds some further material concerning the deceased. He first says that in this present life we groan because we have our existence as 'personality-involved-in-perishable body',[69] and because we are faced with the prospect of death. It would be best of all to pass straight to the condition of 'personality-glorified-by-spiritual-body',[70] that is, to survive until the parousia, so that our physical bodies are not lost, but swallowed up by the resurrection body. It would be as if an overcoat[71] (the spiritual

[68] O. Cullmann, *Immortality of the Soul or Resurrection of the Dead?* (E.T. London, 1958).
[69] I owe this phrase to R. P. C. Hanson, 2 *Corinthians* (Torch ser., London, 1954), p. 46.
[70] This phrase also is due to R. P. C. Hanson, ibid.
[71] This illustration of the 'overcoat' is intended to illuminate one point only. It is not an attempt to read into St. Paul a full-blown 'dualistic' view of man.

body) were put on over our ordinary clothes (the physical body), so that it was never necessary to have them stripped off. But, as he had already said in 2 Cor. v. 1, 'If the earthly frame that houses us today should be demolished, we possess a building (*oikodomē*) which God has provided—a house (*oikia*) not made by human hands, eternal, and in heaven.' For this reason it would really be better to have passed through death, since then we shall not be naked, but can look forward to a closer union with Christ; indeed, St. Paul says in 2 Cor. v. 8, 'We . . . would rather leave our home in the body and go to live with the Lord'.

The view sketched in above may be regarded as the normal interpretation of 2 Cor. v., but it has been challenged in an important article by Ellis.[72] He points out that according to this explanation:

1. The 'building' which God has provided' (v. 1f.) is the resurrection body of Christians.

2. 'Naked' (v. 2) means disembodied and

3. *Ekdēmeō* (v. 8) really does mean 'leaving our home in the body'.

Ellis maintain that the 'heavenly habitation' is not an individual 'spiritual body', though it has its 'individual perspective', but refers rather to corporate solidarity in Christ. 'Naked', according to Ellis, does not refer to a soul stripped of its body; it does not refer to 'parts' of a divided human being at all, but to judgement, and means being found 'naked in guilt and shame' at the Second Coming. The opposite of being 'naked' is not 'having a body', but 'having a wedding garment' (Matt. xxii. 11) and being welcomed to the Messianic Banquet. 2 Cor. v. 8, 'Leave our home in the body and go to live with the Lord,' means to cast off 'the solidarities and securities of earthly existence' and to gain 'the solidarities of the new aeon'. The thesis advanced by Ellis appears at first sight to be more probable than it really is, largely because the main interest of St. Paul is in soteriology, not in anthropology for its own sake, or in the details of life after death; also, for St. Paul, soteriology is not at all sharply distinguished from eschatology. The result is that in this passage, the only one in all his surviving letters where he would appear to cast more than a passing glance

---

[72] E. Earle Ellis, '2 Corinthians v. 1–10 in Pauline Eschatology' *N.T.S.* iii. (1959–60), pp. 211–24. This has been reprinted in Ellis, *Paul and His Recent Interpreters* (Grand Rapids, Michigan, 1961), pp. 35–48. References will here be made to the original article in *N.T.S.*

upon the problem presented by the state of the deceased between their own death and the general judgement, the Apostle naturally employs language elsewhere applied to matters of soteriology.

The first point made by Ellis is that the 'habitation' is not an individual spiritual body. He remarks that *oikodomē*, in all its other Pauline occurrences,[73] refers to edification or to the church. This is true, but the reason may well be that *oikdomē* can mean the process of constructing as well as the result of constructing, whereas 'result of constructing' is the only literal meaning of *oikia*, and a process word is generally required by the context. Again, 2 Cor. v. 1, 'A building (*oikodomē*) which God has provided, a house (*oikia*) not made by human hands' would suggest that St. Paul is using *oikodomē* in the same sense as *oikia*. This latter word is never used in the N.T. in connection with edification, and as Ellis points out, *oikia* means 'physical body' in Philo, and 'frame' (*skēnos*) is used in this sense in Wisd. of Sol. ix. 15. It should be remembered that *oikodomē* in the plural refers to the buildings of the Temple in Mark. iii. 1-2.

The second point made by Ellis is that 'naked' (*gumnos*) does not refer to a soul separated from its body, but to the state of condemnation experienced by the unrighteous. Ellis urges that the 'Greek trail' has been a false detour. But Hebrew and Greek ideas do overlap at some points. By the time of St. Paul, Hebrew thought was not unfamiliar with the belief that the soul was separated from the body at death,[74] although such ideas are not to be found in the canonical books of the Old Testament. Ellis argues that the 'normal' interpretation presupposes an anthropological dualism absent from St. Paul elsewhere. But 2 Cor. xii. 2 and 3, 'Whether in the body (*en sōmati*) or out of it (*ektos tou sōmatos*) I do not know—God knows,' would also appear to presuppose something very much like 'anthropological dualism'; it is not asserted, but is envisaged as possible. Much the same applies to Phil. i. 23, 'I should like to depart (*analusai*) and be with Christ . . . but for your sake there is greater need to stay on in the body (*epimenein tē sarki*). This 'anthropological dualism' is thus contemplated in two other passages, and there are really no other places in St. Paul's writings where it would be natural to consider it. It should be noted that such dualism is never

[73] *N.T.S.* vi. p. 217.
[74] *v. supra*, pp. 36f.

asserted. The 'usual' interpretation does not saddle the Apostle with the 'Greek' doctrine of desiring to be a 'naked soul'. According to the usual interpretation St. Paul rejoices in the fact that 'we shall NOT find ourselves naked'. St. Paul differs from dualism in that he looks forward to being provided by God with another body.

The word *gumnos* (naked) occurs twice in St. Paul, the other passage being 1 Cor. xv. 37. In all of the remaining thirteen N.T. passages it could mean 'naked' in a straightforward literal sense. In some it may be connected with defeat or desolation. In the LXX *gumnos* occurs thirty-three times, normally as a rendering of *'ārōm*. It is connected in some passages with poverty or captivity or with 'shame' in a sexual sense. But although in certain contexts it is connected with those upon whom God's judgement has fallen, it is not true to say that the *word itself* comes to mean anything approaching 'liable to God's judgement'. Such 'moral' interpretations as 'devoid of good works' were suggested by Theodoret, and others, (cp. Allo[75]) and a 'religious' interpretation was put forward by Calvin.[76] But Allo is surely correct when he maintains that although St. Paul could have said all this, he does not appear to have done so in the passage under discussion.

The third contention advanced by Ellis[77] is that, as Robinson[78] had previously argued, 'At home in the body' means 'in the solidarities and securities of earthly existence'. But, as we have already[79] stated, 'body' (*sōma*) normally refers to the physical body of men or animals alive or dead, and this natural meaning ought to be accepted unless there is good reason to the contrary. Ellis would here understand *sōma* on the analogy of Rom. vi. 6, 'The sinful self,' arguing, quite correctly, that 'on a number of occasions Paul uses *sōma* to refer to the self in its solidarity with sin. There is usually a qualifying phrase such as the mortal body (Rom. vi. 12), the body of sin (Rom. vi. 6), of death (Rom. vii. 24), of humility (Phil. iii. 21), of dishonour (1 Cor. xv. 43) or the natural body (1 Cor. xv. 44f.). But this is not always the case; and even the immediate context speaks of deeds done 'in the body', i.e.,

[75] *Seconde Epître aux Corinthiens* (Paris, 1956²), p. 145. This passage occurs in excursus ix: 'Les diverses théories explicatives de v. 2–10 et leur valeur', op. cit. pp. 137–55, which is one of the best treatments of the problem.
[76] ibid.
[77] *N.T.S.* vi. (1960) p. 222.
[78] *Body*, p. 69.
[79] *v. supra*, pp. 194–6.

in the mortal earthly life.'[80] A footnote (4) reads ' 2 Cor. v. 10; cf.
Robinson, *Body*, p, 29; Rom. viii. 13, Col. ii. 11, Heb. xiii. 3.'
The words 'in the body', i.e. 'in the mortal earthly life' are misleading. Deeds done (2 Cor. v. 10) in the physical body are in
fact done 'in the mortal earthly life'. But this does not justify
us in claiming that 'in the body' *means* 'in the mortal earthly life'
any more than 'in a diving suit' *means* 'under the sea', although
most deeds done in a diving suit are in fact done under the sea,
and all deeds done in the human body are in fact done in the
mortal, earthly life. More important, Ellis makes it clear that
'there is usually a qualifying phrase' and claims that 'this is not
always the case', but fails to show that there are any exceptions.
Of the passages to which he gives a reference, Rom. viii. 13, 'But
if by the Spirit you *put to death* all the base pursuits of the body',
includes a most powerful qualifying phrase, which we have
italicized, and the same applies, in a less degree, to Col. ii. 11,
Divested of the *lower* nature (*tou sōmatos tēs sarkos*) since *sarx*,
flesh, has acquired a connotation of weakness which does not
attach to *sōma*, body, alone. As for Heb. xiii. 3, 'Remember . . .
those who are being maltreated, for you like them are still in the
world (*en sōmati*)', the literal meaning of '*en sōmati*' is 'in the body'
and 'in the world' is an inference from the meaning rather than
the meaning itself; it has presumably been adopted in the *N.E.B.*
because the idea of 'in the body', and therefore all the natural
phrases which might have been used to express it, is archaic and
therefore excluded. †

vi. THE RESURRECTION BODY

The whole problem of 2 Cor. v. is placed in its proper perspective by v. 5, 'God himself has shaped us for this very end;
and as pledge of it he has given us the Spirit'. St. Paul is primarily
concerned with the fact that God will not leave us in the 'naked'
condition of disembodied spirits, but will provide a body: he is
much less concerned with the nature of the body which God will
give us. The same emphasis was already apparent in 2 Cor. v. 1,
'We possess a building which God has provided—a house not
made by human hands (*acheiropoiēton*) eternal (*aiōnion*) and in
heaven'. These words which qualify the 'house' describe not so

much its nature as its origin and its 'order'. It is a body of a 'higher', supernatural order, as appears from the two other passages in the N.T. where *acheiropoiēton* occurs, Mark. xiv. 58, and Col. ii.11. Much the same can be said about 'eternal' (*aiōnion*) which suggests 'of a higher order' in addition to meaning 'everlasting'. We are reminded of 1 Cor. xv. 38, 'God clothes it (i.e. the grain of wheat etc.) with the body of his choice'. St. Paul is quite definite that God's purpose for us will be accomplished. He is less definite about the specific nature of that purpose.

Unnecessary speculation has been raised about the word 'we possess', *echomen*, in 2 Cor. v. 1. Winer[81] is surely correct when he says, in a section devoted to the discussion of passages where the present tense is employed although the future might have been expected: 'The words are designed to indicate the instantaneous acquisition of a new habitation as soon as the *kataluesthai* (be demolished) has taken place'. Whether this means that the body is pre-existent, and is already waiting for us or that God will create it for us at the moment of death is a 'curious' question which St. Paul would not appear to have considered, and it is reading too much into his words to suggest what answer he would have given. It is more important to underline the connection between the new body and the pledge which is the Holy Spirit (2 Cor. v. 5). It must also be noted that in 2 Cor. v. 6–10, as in Phil. i. 19–26, St. Paul stresses the positive advantages of leaving our home in the body and going to live with the Lord.[82] More must be said on this point when we come to examine Cullmann's opinions on the 'sleep of the soul'.[83]

We must now enquire how St. Paul's teaching in 2 Cor. v. 1f. and in Phil. i. 23, 4 is related to the earlier teaching found in 1 Cor. xv. 51, 'We shall not all die but we shall all be changed.' Some scholars have argued that the Apostle's thought on this matter has developed, others that it has not. Clearly, there is no contradiction between the earlier and the later teaching, but the later teaching includes features which are not found in 1 Cor. and St. Paul has not shown how the teaching of 1 Cor. xv. is to be integrated with that of 2 Cor. v. and Phil. i. 19–26. It is obviously

---

[81] *Grammar of New Testament Greek* (E.T. Edinburgh, 1882⁹), p. 333.
[82] So L. S. Thornton, *The Common Life in the Body of Christ* (London, 1950³), p. 285. Additional Note A, 'St. Paul on the Resurrection of the Body', pp. 284–6, is brief but valuable.
[83] cf. *infra*, pp. 262–9.

not possible to be certain whether at the time when he wrote 1 Cor.
xv. St. Paul already thought, but did not yet commit to paper,
the views concerning the 'spiritual bodies' of the deceased which
he later expounded in 2 Cor. v., or whether he excogitated these
views for the first time after *1 Cor.* had already been completed
and dispatched, perhaps as a result of illness, which caused him
to think more closely about life after death; these are legitimate
speculations, but the evidence does not permit of any definitive
solution. As for St. Paul's 'failure' to integrate his teaching, it
must be realized that it is more apparent to us than it was to him,
since we unconsciously compare his thought with that of the
systematic theologians of medieval and later times. It may well
be that if St. Paul had been questioned on this matter he would
have said that, when Christ comes again, *all* bodies will be transformed, both the 'physical' bodies of the survivors (1 Cor. xv. 51;
2 Cor. v. 4; Phil. iii. 21) and the building which God is to provide
for the deceased (2 Cor. v. 1). 1 Cor. xv. 52, 'The dead will rise
immortal, and we shall be changed', seems to raise a difficulty,
since it might suggest that only the survivors will be changed,
and the dead will merely 'rise immortal', and not be changed.
But 1 Cor. xv. 51, 'We shall not all die (i.e. the survivors, as opposed
to the deceased will not die) but we shall all (i.e. both survivors
and deceased) be changed in a flash, in the twinkling of an eye
at the last trumpet-call,' leads us to suppose that all will be
changed at the last day, and this could well include those who had
already received at death the building provided by God. This
does not mean that the deceased receive at death a 'temporary'
body: the 'house not made by human hands' is a temporary phase
of the eternal body of the deceased, just as the physical body
is a temporary phase of the eternal body of the survivors.

vii. Purgatory

Whether we conclude that St. Paul believed in an 'intermediate
state' or no is largely a matter of words. Davies,[84] for example,
contends that he did not, but he seems to mean by this that St.
Paul did not believe that Christians would exist after death in a
disembodied state. Since 2 Cor. v., the only passage where the
subject is raised at all, asserts, so we believe, that God does give

[84] *Paul and Rabbinic Judaism* (London, 1955²) p. 318.

Christians a body after death, we cannot but agree with Davies. But I should describe the state indicated in 2 Cor. v. as an embodied intermediate state, believing myself to be holding the same opinion as Davies, but expressing it in different words.

When we go to ask whether St. Paul taught a doctrine of Purgatory, we must be careful not to confuse questions which are different. It is an important problem for the systematic theologian whether there is 'cleansing after death', it being always assumed that the final fate of the individual is already decided at the moment of dissolution. There is also the quite different question whether there is any change of direction after death; this would involve acts of will after death, and is contrary to the official teaching of the Roman church. These questions, though very important and perfectly legitimate in their own sphere, do not concern us here. We are to consider only the teaching of St. Paul. The important verses are 1 Cor. iii. 14–15, 'If a man's building stands, he will be rewarded; if it burns, he will have to bear the loss; and yet he will escape with his life, as one might from a fire (*hōs dia puros*)'. This verse has been taken to refer to Purgatory because *dia* with the genitive has been given an instrumental force, which is just as likely, grammatically speaking, as the local sense ascribed to it by the *N.E.B.* But, as the Roman Catholic Allo justly remarks,[85] the fire in question burns on earth and destroys earthly works; Grosheide[86] also reminds us that the fire attacks things, not people, and is not therefore purgatorial fire. Allo, however, goes on to say[87] that although the doctrine of purgatory is not taught in this passage, it is merely an application to life after death of a principle recognized by St. Paul with regard to life on earth. Clearly, we are not concerned with speculations, legitimate though they may be in their own branch of theology, which involve an application to one question of a principle which St. Paul applied in another. Allo adds further that 2 Cor. v. 10, 'For we must all have our lives laid open before the tribunal of Christ,'[88] cannot apply to the final judgement, since in this very chapter St. Paul speaks of being with Christ immediately after death and of being sure, long before the

[85] *Première Epître aux Corinthiens* (Paris, 1956²), p. 61, on 1 Cor. iii. 13.
[86] F. W. Grosheide, *The First Epistle to the Corinthians* London N.T.C., (London, 1954²), p. 88.
[87] Op. cit. excursus iii., pp. 66–7.
[88] cf. Rom. xiv. 10, 'We shall all stand before God's tribunal'.

Parousia, that he will be with Christ forever. This, Allo suggests, presupposes a 'particular judgement'. But although a form of particular judgement is connected with the doctrine of purgatory, the particular judgement doctrine and the purgatory doctrine are logically independent, and each can be held without the other. Again, it is unlikely that any particular judgement is thought of in 2 Cor. v. 10 and Rom. xiv. 10. 2 Esdras vii. thinks of the righteous being with the Messiah in the 'millenial 'kingdom, which for this writer lasts 400 years, before the end. So in the thought of St. Paul, who does not believe in a 'millenial' kingdom[89] it is possible to be with Christ before the judgement.

viii. The 'Sleep of the Soul'

The doctrine of the 'sleep of the soul' which in previous centuries was held mainly by sectaries, has now received the support of some highly competent N.T. scholars including Cullmann.[90] His views, as he points out, have been greeted with storms of protest.[91] This is due in part to the fact that he has stressed the difference between the N.T. view, which regards death as an enemy and the belief held by some Greeks and some moderns that death is a friend. For the N.T., Cullmann reminds us,[92] 'Deliverance consists not in a release of soul from body, but in a release of both from flesh'. He also points out that Socrates, according to Plato's description in the *Phaedo*, faced death with sublime heroism, whereas Christ is portrayed as 'weeping and crying'.[93] 'The Evangelists, who none the less intended to present Jesus as the Son of God, have not tried to soften the terribleness of His thoroughly human death'.[94] Such words as these, understandably, have given an uncomfortable jolt to many pious Christians. We have mentioned these facts only because they should be brought into the open to prevent them from weighing with us. Cullmann has caused horror by pointing to forgotten truths. We are concerned only with his belief in the sleep of the soul in the thought of St. Paul, and this belief, we hold, is not supported by the evidence.

[89] cf. *infra*, pp. 270–1
[90] *Immortality of the Soul or Resurrection of the Dead?* (E.T. London, 1958). From now on this work will be referred to as *Immortality or Resurrection?*
[91] *Immortality or Resurrection?*, p. 5.   [92] ibid. p. 36.
[93] ibid. p. 24.   [94] ibid. p. 26.

Cullmann really offers very little to support his contention. He takes it for granted that *koimaomai* means both 'die 'and 'be unconscious' at the same time, and he deals with certain difficulties. We maintain on the other hand that:

1. *koimaomai* means literally 'sleep' and metaphorically either 'die' or 'have sexual intercourse' but that no N.T. occurrence of it need bear more than one of these three possible meanings, although it is possible to say both that a man has died and that he is unconscious.

2. In some contemporary Jewish writings those who are said to 'sleep' in the sense of being 'dead' appear also to be conscious and active.

3. In non-Pauline N.T. passages the dead appear at times to be conscious, and there is no passage where the meaning 'unconscious' is certain.

4. In some Pauline passages for the dead to be unconscious would be inapposite, although not impossible.

1. The word *koimaomai* is found frequently in the LXX and normally renders the Hebrew *shākab*. In many passages it bears its literal meaning, but its two euphemistic senses of 'death' and 'sexual intercourse' are also very frequent, and are clear from the context since such phrases as 'with my fathers' (Gen. xlvii. 30) are added. No difficulty arises with the second euphemism, since it is not possible to do both at once, but confusion can arise with the first since it is clearly possible to be dead and to be unconscious. In the N.T. excluding St. Paul *koimaomai* is found seven times, apart from two occurrences in the account of the raising of Lazarus: in Matt. xxviii. 13, 'His disciples came by night and stole the body while we were asleep', the word is obviously used of natural sleep, as it is in Luke xxii. 45; Acts xii. 6. In Acts vii. 60, 'And with that he (Stephen) died' *ekoimēthē*, lit. 'fell asleep', the reference is to death, as it is in Acts xiii. 36; 2 Pet. iii. 4. Of the non-Pauline instances there remains only Matt. xvii. 52, 'Many of God's people arose from sleep; and coming out of their graves after his resurrection they entered the Holy City, where many saw them,' reads literally, 'And many bodies (*sōmata*) of those of God's people (*hagiōn*) who had fallen asleep (*kekoimēmenōn*, the perfect participle) were raised.' This might be held to tell against Cullmann on the ground that 'to have fallen asleep' is clearly compatible with being active and with being

T

recognized. But it is surely the intention of the Evangelist to show that the Crucifixion of Jesus Christ would lead to the resurrection of all Christians; this verse is therefore an anticipation of the Last Day, and does not tell one way or the other. Each of these passages means that those concerned had died. There is nothing to show whether or no the dead were unconscious.

2. The question of what St. Paul's Jewish contemporaries and immediate predecessors believed is made more difficult by the fact that beliefs which do not 'belong together' may be included in the same book, because the author, or authors, made use of sources or oral tradition. It is very difficult to be sure how much the thought of an author in one passage is to be understood in the light of what is found elsewhere. Jubilees xxiii. 1, for example, states that Jacob 'slept the sleep of eternity'.[95] This may mean that he died and became unconscious as in sleep, or that he slept the permanent sleep of death, as opposed to the temporary sleep from which a man awakes next morning. In xxiii. 31 we read:

And their bones shall rest in the earth,
And their spirits shall have much joy,
And they shall know that it is the Lord
who executes judgement.[96]

Again, 2 Esdras vii. 32 reads, 'And the earth shall give up those who are asleep' (*dormiunt*), yet in vii. 76f. we find accounts of the joy of the righteous in their habitations. It should be remembered that 2 Esdras vii. 32, 'The chambers shall give up the souls that have been committed to them,' is parallel to the clause which speaks of the earth giving up those that sleep. No scholar could maintain that *2 Esdras* presents us with a coherent and carefully articulated system of eschatology, but at least it is clear that in such writings, when the word 'sleep' is applied to the dead, it is most hazardous to conclude that they are not conscious simply on the ground that the word 'sleep' is employed euphemistically for death. It is in any case beyond question that whatever meaning, or meanings, St. Paul's contemporaries applied to the concept 'sleep' when used in this context, they held no uniform view of death as a state of unconsciousness, though this view probably inspired 1 Enoch c. 5,[97] 'And though the righteous sleep a long sleep, they have nought to fear.'

[95] Charles, ii., p. 47.   [96] ibid. p. 49.
[97] Charles, ii., p. 272

3. Mark xii. 23, 'At the resurrection, when they come back to life (*hotan anastōsin*)[98] whose wife will she be?' is most illuminating. It suggests, though it does not prove, that the Sadducees are familiar with and are attacking a doctrine not unlike that propounded by Cullmann: the question whose wife she will be does not arise until the resurrection (because all eight will be unconscious). It is possible, though on balance less likely, that the Sadducees thought that, in the opinion of Christ, the reason why the question did not arise until the resurrection was that although the dead were not unconscious, they had not yet been re-embodied. It is therefore probable that the Sadducees attacked the theory, which they ascribed to Christ, that the 'sleep' of the dead, which they would accept, understanding 'sleep' to be annihilation, was to be terminated by the resurrection, and that Christ replied in language which suggested that the dead were already alive with God, thus asserting a theory even more 'advanced' than that which was ascribed to Him. Christ said in Mark. xii. 27, 'God is not God of the dead, but of the living.' Since the patriarchs were already dead in the Sadducean view which Christ was concerned to deny, we are probably justified in supposing that in His own view they were 'already' alive, and although they had died, yet God had never ceased to hold them in life. A similar movement of thought would seem to lie behind Ezra's question in 2 Esdras vii. 75, 'O Lord, show this also to thy servant: whether after death, as soon as every one of us yields up his soul, we shall be kept in rest until those times come when thou wilt renew the creation, or whether we shall be tormented at once?' The answer is that torments and rewards will begin at once. Through reaction against earlier tendencies we are perhaps too unwilling to see stages of development in the thought of the Bible, but probably the late-biblical view that there was no significant life after death was followed by the conviction expressed in Dan. xii. 2 that at the last day some (or all in later writings) would be raised or recreated, and this belief developed in its turn to the faith that rewards and punishments would follow immediately upon death. This would appear to be virtually certain in 2 Esdras vii. 75f. and probable in Mark xii. 18f. and parallels. This means

---

[98] 'When they come back to life' is probably to be regarded as a gloss, since different groups of MSS. give this same explanation in slightly different language which suggests that they are trying to clarify the passage independently.

that the theology of the Jews was moving from (1) Annihilation, as in *Ecclesiastes* to (2) Unconscious sleep followed by resurrection to joy or sorrow as in *Daniel* and thence to (3) Rewards and punishments immediately after death, followed by the final allocation to heaven or hell. This movement was taking place in Judaism, although there was no uniform development. In Christianity it received a powerful impetus from the Resurrection of Christ. It would therefore be natural for 'sleep' in its euphemistic meaning 'death' to be still used without the further meaning of 'unconscious' which it probably carried in Dan. xii. 2 and 1 Enoch c. 5.

The Parable of the Sheep and the Goats (Matt. xxv. 31–46) is clearly irrelevant since it draws its imagery from the Day of Judgement, and tells us nothing at all about the matter at present under discussion, which is whether the deceased were thought to be unconscious between their death and the Last Day; and this applies also to the Transfiguration, which may well be regarded as an anticipation of the Last Day, not as a description of the normal state of the dead, above all as Elijah at least had not died. The same must be said about the enigmatic fragment Luke xii. 47, 48. We are told that the severity of the flogging will depend upon whether or no the servant knew his master's will, but the context is not defined. How Christ Himself employed this analogy we do not know. St. Luke, who may be correct, understands it to refer to life after death, or at any rate to the time after the Judgement, as we may infer from the context in which he has placed it, but it would be hazardous to suppose that it refers to 'purgatory' in which case it would provide evidence for consciousness between death and the end. The whole passage would appear to be oriented towards the survivors rather than the deceased, though Allo rightly[99] claims that the doctrine of purgatory is an application to a particular problem of the principle embodied in these two verses.

At this point, before we come to those N.T. passages which really are important, we must examine more carefully the thesis propounded by Cullmann. He claims,[100] quite correctly, that the passages which naturally spring to mind in this connection, Luke xvi. 22 ('Dives' and Lazarus), xxiii. 43 (the Penitent Thief); Phil.

[99] cf. *supra*, pp. 261–2.
[100] *Immortality or Resurrection?*, p. 50.

i. 23, 'What I should like is to depart and be with Christ'; Rev.
vi. 11. (the cry of the Martyrs under the altar) do not prove that
the resurrection of the body takes place immediately after the
individual death. 'In none of these texts is there so much as a
word about the resurrection of the body',[101] he declares. He understands the N.T. teaching that it is a blessed fate to die in the Lord
in the sense that the deceased Christian 'continues to live with
Christ in this transformed state in the condition of sleep'.[102] If by
sleep Cullmann does not mean 'unconsciousness', then the view
which he propounds does not differ from that of much Greek and
modern thought; and to use 'sleep' as a blanket-term for 'an unknown condition'[103] is misleading. If, however, by 'sleep'
Cullmann really does mean 'unconsciousness' then we must reply
that the passages mentioned above, though they do not suggest that
the resurrection of the body takes place at the moment of physical
death, are at least unfavourable to the theory that the deceased
remain in a state of unconsciousness between their death and the
resurrection.

The view of the deceased presupposed by the Parable of
'Dives' and Lazarus (Luke. xvi. 19–31) is that during the life-
time of 'Dives's' five brothers, that is, before any Final Judgement,
Dives and Lazarus, so far from being unconscious, are aware of
their own torment and joy, while Dives at least is aware of Lazarus'
blessedness. The significance of these facts is lessened because
the purpose of the parable is not to give instruction concerning
life after death. As in the Parable of the Sheep and the Goats,[104]
an account of the 'next world' is employed to convey teaching about
life in this world. The pericope of the Penitent Thief is more
important for the thought of the N.T. Cullmann is almost
certainly correct in rejecting the view that 'today' (sēmeron)
qualifies 'I tell you this', not 'you shall be with me in Paradise'
(Luke. xxiii. 43)'.[105] He is probably right also when he understands the cry of the criminal to mean that he wants Jesus to

---

[101] ibid. pp. 50–51.   [102] ibid. p. 56.
[103] ibid. p. 57. Cullmann here equates 'sleep' with 'another time-conscious-
ness'. Since in sleep we are *not* conscious of time, unless we are dreaming,
Cullmann's phraseology is misleading. It is most unlikely that the N.T. writers
held the somewhat sophisticated modern notion of different kinds of time-
consciousness.
[104] cf. J. A. T. Robinson, 'The "Parable" of the Sheep and the Goats'
N.T.S. ii. (1956), pp. 225–37, reprinted in *Twelve New Testament Studies*
S.B.T. no. 34, (London, 1962), pp. 76–93.
[105] *Immortality or Resurrection?* p. 50, n. 5.

remember him at the end of the world when He comes in His glory. The reply: 'I tell you this: today you shall be *unconscious* with me in Paradise' would be a lame and evasive reply, whereas according to the 'conventional' interpretation Our Lord's words could be paraphrased 'You ask me to remember you in the future, when I return in glory; I grant you more: this very day you shall have the (conscious) joy with me of being in Paradise'.[106]

Rev. vi. 10, They gave a great cry: 'How long, sovereign Lord, holy and true, must it be before thou wilt vindicate us and avenge our blood on the inhabitants of the earth?' does not suggest that the martyrs are unconscious, though Cullmann[107] describes them as 'sleeping under the altar'. Since he gives the reference vi. 11, he is clearly basing himself upon *anapausōntai*, but this word seldom[108] occurs in the N.T. in a passage where the context requires the notion of unconsciousness, and in some it would be most unsuitable, for example in Matt. xi. 28, 'Come to me, all whose work is hard, whose yoke is heavy; and I will give you relief (*anapausō*)', and Philem. 7, 'Through you, my brother, God's people have been much refreshed (*anapepautai*)'. As Rev. xiv. 13 would suggest, the martyrs are to rest from labour, sorrow and worry, not from consciousness.

4. In the writings of St. Paul the word *koimaomai* occurs nine times in all, five times in the aorist (1 Cor. vii. 39, xv. 6, 18; 1 Thess. iv. 14, 15), twice in the present (1 Cor. ix. 30; 1 Thess. iv. 13), and once each in the perfect (1 Cor. xv. 20) and in the future (1 Cor. xv. 51). In none of these passages is natural sleep in question; in each case the Apostle refers to death. There is no passage where the sense requires that 'sleep' should mean 'be unconscious' as well as 'die'. It might be argued that the use of the present in 1 Cor. xi. 30 (*koimōntai*) and in 1 Thess. iv. 13 (*koimōmenōn*)[109] suggested that the word refers to the continued state of being unconscious rather than to the fact of having died. It could be replied that the continued fact of 'being dead' is

---

[106] Cullmann himself (*Immortality or Resurrection?*, p. 50, n. 5) gives virtually the same explanation of Luke xxii. 40, but claims that 'Understood *according to their intention* these words do not constitute a difficulty' for his theory (cf. n. 105). He means, presumably, that the case of the Penitent Thief was an exceptional boon contrary to all normal happenings, granted on one occasion only.

[107] ibid. p. 50.

[108] The meaning 'sleep' is certain only at Mark xiv. 41 = Matt. xxvi. 45

[109] The perfect is read by some MSS. at 1 Thess. iv. 13.

at issue, since *koimaomai*, literally 'sleep', has so completely taken over the sense of 'death', but Grosheide[110] is probably correct when he maintains that in 1 Cor. xi. 30 the force of the present tense is that a large number of deaths keep on occurring. Morris[111] understands the present tense at 1 Thess. iv. 13 in the same way. All in all, it cannot be maintained that the support afforded to Cullmann's theory by the use of the present tense is very strong.

Although there is no passage in St. Paul's writings which lends any positive weight to Cullmann's contention, there is none which makes it impossible. There are, however, two passages for which Cullmann's explanation would appear to be forced. 2 Cor. v. 8, 'We . . . would rather leave our home in the body and go to live with the Lord,' *might* be understood to mean that the Apostle thought he would lapse into a state of unconsciousness so profound that, however long it might last, be it months or years, the 'leaving the body' and 'going to live with the Lord' would seem to have taken place in two successive moments of time, although in fact they were separated by what might prove to be a considerable interval. Such an explanation is not impossible, but it does seem frankly artificial. The same may be said about Phil. i. 23, 'What I should like is to depart and be with Christ'. It is possible that the verse is to be understood on the lines mentioned above in the case of 2 Cor. v. 8, but here again such an interpretation is extremely forced. It is not impossible that St. Paul may have regarded 'being unconscious in the presence of Christ' as preferable to being conscious in the world, above all in captivity. Such an understanding would be possible if there were any strong ground for accepting it. But in point of fact there is no reason at all to accept it apart from the assumption that when *koimaomai* is employed in the metaphorical sense of death, it must *also* carry with it the meaning of being unconscious, and for this assumption there is no warrant. It is altogether more natural to suppose that, in the thought of St. Paul, God would give the Christian a body as soon as he died; in that body he could be with Christ, although, no doubt this body 'not made with hands' would be transformed, like the physical bodies of the survivors, at the last day.

---

[110] F. W. Grosheide, *The First Epistle to the Corinthians*, London N.T.C. (London, 1954²), pp. 275–6.

[111] L. Morris, *Epistle to the Thessalonians*, London N.T.C. (London, 1959), pp. 136–7, n. 39.

ix. The Millenium not Pauline

The remaining topics of Pauline eschatology may be considered, for the sake of convenience, as they arise from a consideration of 1 Cor. xv. 20–28. 1 Cor. xv. 25, 'For he is destined to reign until God has put all enemies under his feet,' has appeared to some to mean that St. Paul believed in a 'millenial' kingdom of Christ. The only passage in the canonical scriptures where this doctrine can be found with certainty is Rev. xx. It occurs also in 2 Esdras vii. 28, 'For my son the Messiah[112] shall be revealed and those who are with him, and those who remain shall rejoice four hundred years'. This verse like Rev. xx. suggests an unchallenged reign of bliss, although it is to be temporary. The picture presented by 1 Cor. xv. differs so much that it is really misleading to describe both by the same phrase. According to St. Paul, Christ is to 'reign (*basileuein*) until God has put all enemies under his feet' (1 Cor. xv. 25). In fact Christ is like a general whose command lasts only during the period of the military emergency. As soon as victory is won he must hand over to the civil ruler. Here is no doctrine of the millenial kingdom. This verse is really more significant for Christology,[113] since it might appear to suggest subordinationist thought, than it is for Eschatology.

The quotation from Ps. viii, 'He has put all things in subjection under his feet,' and the saying 'The last enemy to be abolished is death,' reminds us of Rom. viii. 21, 'The universe itself is to be freed from the shackles of mortality' and of Rom. viii. 38, 39, 'There is nothing in death or life . . . that can separate us from the love of God in Christ Jesus our Lord.' Perhaps the thought which originally lay behind the words employed in this latter passage comes from the same syncretistic background which produced Gnosticism.[114] We are here concerned not with the origin of the words used by St. Paul but with the thought which he intended to convey. Freeing the universe from the shackles of mortality is clearly a reversal of the disaster caused by Adam's fall. St. Paul uses these concepts derived from *Genesis* and perhaps also from 'proto-gnostic' sources as 'stage-furniture' to portray the completeness of God's future victory in Christ. The same is probably true about the cosmic victory of Col. i. 20. St. Paul is

---

[112] The uncertainty of the text at this point does not affect the present issue.
[113] cf. *supra*, pp. 120–2.   [114] cf. *supra*, p. 7.

concerned to teach us not about those who are to be defeated, but about God Who is to be victor. It would be hazardous to speculate about the future of the physical universe on the basis of Rom. viii. 18–25; the physical universe is 'used' by St. Paul to show the completeness of God's future victory, just as oxen are 'used' by God, according to 1 Cor. ix. 10 in order to show His will for men on a moral issue. This does not of course mean that for St. Paul the physical universe was not important: St. Paul was too good a Hebrew for that. He merely means that God's will for the physical universe, like His will for mankind, is to be victorious in spite of Adam's sin. St. Paul gives us no specific information about what God's will is for the physical universe.

x. WILL ALL BE SAVED?

1 Cor. xv. 22–24 reads, 'As in Adam all men die, so in Christ all will be brought to life, but each in his own proper place: Christ the firstfruits, and afterwards, at his coming, those who belong to Christ. Then comes the end'. It has been urged that all human beings die in Adam, and that all therefore will rise in Christ. But 'in Adam all' would naturally mean 'all that are in Adam'. In the same way, *en tō Christō pantes* would appear to mean 'all that are in Christ' rather than 'in Christ all will be brought to life'.[115] Again, the passage suggests that there are three stages, first Christ alone, then secondly, those that are Christ's (*v.* 23), thirdly the end (*v.* 24), no room being left for the resurrection of those who are not in Christ. Lietzmann has suggested that *telos* here means not 'the end', but 'the remainder'. For this rare meaning of *telos* which normally means 'end' reference is made to Isa. xix. 25, which is so obscure that it is dangerous to build anything upon it,[116] and to a few other passages listed in *Arndt and Gringrich*. This interpretation cannot be ruled out as impossible, but it is certainly less probable than the normally accepted rendering.

A powerful plea has been made for the resurrection of *the unjust* and those who are not in Christ as well as of those who are by Sevenster.[117] He argues that St. Paul must believe in the

---

[115] This 'limiting' explanation is supported by R. H. Charles, *Eschatology, Hebrew, Jewish and Christian* (London, 1963²), p. 449, quoting as parallels for the construction 1 Cor. xv. 18; 1 Thess. iv. 16; Col. i. 4; Rom. ix. 3.

[116] J. Héring points out, correctly, that there is nothing equally clear which tells in the opposite direction, *Le Royaume de Dieu et sa venue* (Neuchâtel, 1959²), addition III, pp. 250–3.

[117] *Studia Paulina* (Haarlem, 1953), pp. 205–6.

resurrection of unbelievers because in certain passages he presupposes the judgement of all men, believers and unbelievers
alike. These passages must be examined carefully. They are not
conclusive, which is hardly surprising in view of the fact that St.
Paul was not writing to unbelievers but to Christians; on the other
hand, they cannot be simply dismissed. Sevenster's passages fall
into two classes. The first comprises those which speak of judgement to be meted out on all who have done evil. He refers to
2 Cor. v. 10; 1 Thess. iv. 6; Rom. xiv. 10, 12. But all these
verses may refer exclusively to those who are in Christ. Sevenster's
second class consists of the passages which teach that the believers
too may lose their salvation in the day of judgement, Gal. v.
19–21; 1 Cor. vi. 9f.; 2 Cor. xi. 14f.; Rom. vi. 21; Phil. iii. 19.
But because Christians are summoned to the judgement and may
lose salvation, it does not necessarily follow that non-Christians
are raised from the dead or summoned to the judgement at all.

The truth is that St. Paul has simply not told us what will
happen to those who are not Christians: he has not even told us
for certain whether in the end there will be any such. He did
of course speak clear words in 2 Thess. i. 8, 9, 'Then he will
do justice upon those who refuse to acknowledge God, and upon
those who will not obey the gospel of our Lord Jesus. They will
suffer the punishment (*dikē*) of eternal ruin (*olethron aiōnion*)
cut off from the presence of the Lord'. This passage makes it
clear that when he wrote *2 Thess.* St. Paul did believe that some
would be 'condemned'. It is true that *hoitines*, 'who' speaks of a
'class', not of definite individuals. But it is most unlikely that St.
Paul thought of this as a 'null'-class. Is damnation to be annihilation or 'eternal torment'? Nothing is said about positive torment.
'Ruin' and banishment from the presence of God is what St. Paul
has in mind. But even if there is not positive torment, St. Paul
would not regard loss of God's presence, the loss of all that made
existence worth-while, as a *light* punishment. The distinction
between positive and negative is not very illuminating.

Is it possible that 'ruin', *olethron*, means annihilation? It is
rather less probable than the alternative. Morris[118] argues that in
1 Cor. v. 5 the destruction (*olethron*) of the flesh (*sarx*) does not
refer to annihilation. St. Paul may, however, quite well mean that

---

[118] *Epistles to the Thessalonians*, London N.T.C. (London, 1959), on 2 Thess.
i. 9. He refers condemnation to those who are culpably ignorant, not to people
who have never heard of the true God.

the *sarx* or flesh, that is the evil in us, is to be annihilated so that
the spirit may be saved in the day of the Lord. The fact that the
'lost' are not mentioned in 1 Thess. iv. 17 or in 1 Cor. xv. 20–8
is negative evidence against punishment; this is compatible with
either the annihilation of the lost or universal salvation, whatever
may be said about 2 Thess. i. 8–9, where eternal punishment is
the most probable interpretation if we take the passage by itself
as it stands. Further, 2 Cor. v. 10; Gal. v. 19–21 etc., whether
they refer only to Christians or to others as well, undoubtedly
speak of judgement to come, though this does not necessarily
mean eternal torment. In some passages St. Paul is more concerned
with the present warning than with the exact nature of the future
fate. The annihilation of the lost is supported by a variant in
1 Cor. xv. 51, *pantes koimēthēsometha, ou pantes de allagēsometha,*
'We shall all sleep, but we shall not all be changed.' This suggests
that at the end all will be dead and only the saved will be restored
to life. This reading has the support of *Codex Sinaiticus* from the
fourth century and of *Codex Alexandrinus* and the *Codex Ephraemi
Rescriptus* from the fifth as well as the minuscule 33 from the
tenth. The thought fits St. Paul's day better than that of later
centuries, so the reading must be taken seriously.[119]

Finally, if we take Rom. xi. 25–32 by itself as it stands, we
must suppose that St. Paul speaks in favour of universal salvation
almost as clearly as he had spoken against it in 2 Thess. i. 8–9.
The passage from *Romans* is later and forms part of a sustained
and considered argument. Further it is just possible that *2 Thess.*
is not by the Apostle at all. Col. i. 20, 'Through him God chose
to reconcile the whole universe to himself making peace through
the shedding of his blood upon the cross—to reconcile all things
(*ta panta*), whether on earth or in heaven, through him alone,'
suggests universal salvation, as does 2 Cor. v. 19, 'Reconciling the
world (*ton kosmon*) to himself'. But in neither of these passages
was St. Paul asking himself the question which we are now posing.

We may put the matter in visual terms. We look at the place
where the 'lost' stood, but we see only darkness. We do not know
whether they are in torment or whether they have been annihilated
or whether the love of God has snatched them to the centre of
the stage: on this centre alone the light now shines, where God
is all in all.

[119] cf. Kenneth W. Clark in *Studia Paulina*, (Haarlem, 1953), pp. 63–4.

LIST OF ABBREVIATIONS

B	Arndt and Gringrich, *A Greek-English Lexicon of the New Testament*
A.V.	*Authorized (King James) Version*
P *B.A.S.O.R.*	*Bulletin of the American Schools of Oriental Research*
P *B.J.R.L.*	*Bulletin of the John Rylands Library* (Manchester)
Black N.T.C.	Black New Testament Commentary (London)
B	Blass-Debrunner-Funk, *A Greek Grammar of the New Testament* (E.T., R. W. Funk, 1961)
B *The Body*	J. A. T. Robinson *The Body*, S.B.T., no. 5, (London, 1952)
Charles (ed.)	*The Apocrypha and Pseudepigrapha of the Old Testament*, 2 vols. (Oxford, 1963²)
Christ	L. Cerfaux, *Christ in the Theology of St. Paul* (E.T. New York and Edinburgh, 1959)
Church	L. Cerfaux, *The Church in the Theology of St. Paul* (E.T., New York and Edinburgh, 1959)
C.N.T.	*Commentaire de Nouveau Testament* (Neuchâtel)
Danby	*The Mishnah*, E.T., H. Danby (Oxford, 1933¹, often reprinted)
E.T.	English Translation
E.VV.	English Versions
P *Exp.T.*	*Expository Times* (Edinburgh)
I.B.	*The Interpreter's Bible* (Nashville, Tennessee)
I.C.C.	International Critical Commentary (Edinburgh)
Introduction	A. Richardson, *An Introduction to the Theology of the New Testament* (London, 1958)
P *J.B.L.*	*Journal of Biblical Literature* (Philadelphia)
P *J.T.S.*	*Journal of Theological Studies* (Oxford). The New Series (N.S.) began in 1950
B *Judaism*	G. F. Moore, *Judaism in the Early Centuries*, etc.
Judaisme	J. Bonsirven, *Le Judaisme Palestinien au temps de Jésus-Christ* (2 vols., Paris, 1935)
London N.T.C.	London New Testament Commentary
LXX	Septuagint
Moffatt N.T.C.	Moffatt New Testament Commentary
M.T.	Massoretic Text
N.E.B.	New English Bible
P *N.T.S.*	*New Testament Studies* (Cambridge, England)
P *R.B.*	*Revue biblique* (Jerusalem)
R.V.	*Revised Version*
R.S.V.	*Revised Standard Version*
S.B.T.	Studies in Biblical Theology (London)
Strack-Billerbeck	H. L. Strack and P. Billerbeck, *Kommentar zum Neuen Testament aus Talmud und Midrasch* (Munich, 1922 f.)
Theology	R. Bultmann, *Theology of the New Testament* (E.T. London, vol. 1, 1952, vol. 2, 1955)
T.W.N.T.	*Theologisches Wörterbuch zum Neuen Testament*, ed. Kittel and Friedrich (Stuttgart, 1933 f.)

P = Periodical
B = see also *Bibliography*, pp. 315–22

POSTSCRIPT

I undertook to say more about the Atonement, and in particular about its treatment by D. Hill.[1]

I must first make it clear that during the past fifteen years my theological thinking has been more and more influenced by the theory of 'models'. This has been expounded most notably by the late I. T. Ramsey in *Religious Language*,[2] and in *Models and Mystery*[3] (the easiest and simplest exposition). It is also applied in *Freedom and Immortality*.[4] In addition to reading Ramsey's books, I was for many years his neighbour, and he was my friend. We discussed theological subjects together, although I must stress the fact that anything I say in this postscript is something for which I alone must bear the responsibility.

Since 1964 I have come even more to regard what the Bible says about Salvation as a series of disclosure models rather than one single scale model. I do not object to 'substitution' as a description of Christ's work *provided* that we regard it as one model among many, not as the sole explanation within the framework of a legalistic system which was totally foreign to Paul. I must again stress the fact that 'substitutionary' language lends itself most readily to abuse in the pulpit, though it has a natural and useful place in the devotional life of some people.

'Models', as the term is used in the Natural Sciences and in Theology, are of two kinds, 'scale' models and 'disclosure' models:

(a) *Scale Models*. Perhaps the best-known examples of scale models are the complex constructions which depict D.N.A. and R.N.A. The model corresponds to the substances in question as regards both the constituents of which they are composed and the spatial relation between them. In other words, the scale model is isomorphic with what it portrays.

(b) *Disclosure models*. These do not correspond with what they are intended to illuminate. Light, for example, is not a 'wave' in the ether, as was supposed in the nineteenth century, nor is it a series of corpuscles travelling through space like peas shot out of

[1] Additional note, p. 303ff.
[2] (London, 1957).
[3] (London, New York and Toronto, 1964).
[4] I. T. Ramsey (London, 1960).

a pea-shooter. But both the corpuscular model and the wave model are disclosure models: they do not tell us what light 'is', but they are useful to disclose certain facts about light, such as the photo-electric effect and the interference phenomenon respectively. In the same way, the planetary representation of the atom is a disclosure model. The atom is not 'like' the solar system with planets rotating round the sun, but this disclosure model enables us to understand and to carry out research in a manner which otherwise would probably be impossible. It should be said that the contemporary theory of disclosure models roughly corresponds to the traditional teaching on analogy.

Every writer has much to learn from competent reviewers. The Introduction to the first edition of this book was largely concerned with a review by the Presbyterian E. Best. This postscript will deal largely with one by the Roman Catholic P. Benoit.[1]

His review is penetrating and charitable. I shall not waste time in recounting its favourable comments, which allege that I have succeeded in attaining my primary objectives, but I shall draw attention to his criticisms, especially because they illustrate the differences between British, Anglican theology on the one hand, and Roman Catholic theology on the other.

Benoit makes the following criticisms, all of which are fully justified in view of his background. Some of them are not justified in view of my own. I lay stress upon them in the hope that the Roman Catholic and Reformed traditions may understand each other more clearly.

Benoit says, quite correctly, that the following subjects are accorded either too much or too little space:

(a) *Virgines subintroductae* (1 Cor. vii. 36ff.). Benoit says I devote too much space (4 pages) to this subject. Before I was appointed to an academic post, which, in accordance with the British, 'Oxford' tradition, is combined with pastoral responsibilities, I spent seven years, mostly during the 1939–45 World War, in parochial work. In my first parish, I found that 1 Cor. vii. 36 was widely misunderstood as a justification for fornication, of which, I am sure, Benoit disapproves as strongly as I do myself. If one is to consider this subject at all, and to do even the scantiest justice to it, one must devote at least four pages to it.

[1] *Revue Biblique*, January 1972, pp. 141f.

(b) Benoit points out that I devote seven out of 273 pages to the 'sleep' of the soul and to the intermediate state. This has become an important issue in English-speaking Christianity, especially among the 'sects', who are making far greater progress, especially in the 'Third World', than such 'established' branches of the Church as the Roman Catholics and the Anglicans. It is for this reason that I gave it more attention than it would otherwise deserve in Benoit's opinion (or in my own).

(c) We both regret that I cannot accept *Ephesians* as directly Pauline: it would make life much easier for me if I could. It is true I make some use of it, but, as I said on p. xiii of the first (and p. xix in this) edition, I did so *only* when *Ephesians* seemed to run contrary to my own fallible opinion.

(d) Benoit says that on p. 94f. I fail to understand the meaning of *proorisas*, in Eph. i.5 ('destined' in *N.E.B.*). In my view we both understand *Ephesians* correctly, but fail to understand each other. Benoit says that 'destined' applies 'Not to certain individuals (*hēmas*, we), . . . but to the form God chooses to give to the salvation of the elect.' On this point we are agreed, and on re-reading p. 94f. I believe that this is the meaning of what I said in 1964.

Benoit rightly points out that in 1964 I did insufficient justice to the Targum tradition which lies behind the Christian *Testimonia*. I can now refer the student to an article by E. Earle Ellis,[2] which points out that Christian *testimonia* probably had a targum tradition behind them.

Benoit says that 'Whiteley cannot accept (*recule devant*) the idea of "substitution" ', about which I have spoken above, 'and prefers to speak of "participation", in a manner which suggests a moral rather than a real union (*une union Morale plutôt que physique*).' Now I am an Anglican, and am unable to remember a time when I did not accept God, Christ and the Church as the three dominating factors in the Universe. I have always accepted that in my Baptism, reaffirmed in Confirmation, I was made a *member* of Christ in a sense which is made clear both in the admitted and the questioned epistles of Paul. When I speak of 'participation' in Christ, I do so in a 'realistic' sense, whether it is called 'moral', 'physical', or 'metaphysical'. I feel that here

[2] Midrash, Targum and New Testament. *Neotestamentica et Semitica*, Festschrift for M. Black (Edinburgh, 1969).

again Benoit and I differ less in our apprehension of truth than in our use of language. I agree that my treatment of the Spirit is too brief. If I had had more space at my disposal I should certainly have devoted some of it to 2 Cor. iii.17, '*Ho de Kurios to Pneuma estin*', which, literally translated, means 'Now the Lord is the Spirit.' Actually I favour the interpretation (hardly a translation) of the *N.E.B.*, 'Now the Lord of whom this passage speaks is the Spirit'. In other words, I believe that this verse speaks of the Lordship of the Spirit, not of the relation between Son and Spirit as such.

Finally, I should like to thank Benoit and my other fellow-workers in the field of Pauline studies. I have learned from their writings and been encouraged when I found that we are in agreement. Equally, when there is disagreement, I have been spurred on to re-examine the evidence and sometimes to modify or to refine my opinions.

ADDITIONAL NOTES

Page 3, after section (a)

Since the first edition of this book (1964) important new evidence has been published. I still deny the popular view that the Christian sacraments are borrowed from the later and more decadent stages of the Pagan mysteries. Already in 1964 I felt, although I did not put it on paper, that Christianity and the Mystery Religions had a degree of common background. This new evidence strengthens me in the conviction that there may well have been some mutual borrowing even in N.T. times, at least in the case of Mithra.

Günter Wagner[1] indeed has shown that the attested resemblances between the Mystery Religions and Christianity post-date the N.T. For example, we first hear of the resurrection of Adonis in Lucian of Samosata's *De dea Syria* 6, III, p. 342f., ed. Iacobitz; and Lucian was not born until *c.* A.D. 120. The passage is quoted in full (in Greek) by Wagner, op. cit., p. 198, n. 132. The other alleged borrowings are treated in a like manner, and the work is scholarly and well documented. But R. H. Fuller[2] points out that the existence of many of these deities is attested in their homelands before the Christian era, and that Paul himself may give indirect evidence for this in 1 Cor. viii.5, 'that there were "gods many and lords many".' It remain true, however, that close links between the N.T. and the Mystery Cults have not yet been discovered.

John R. Hinnells, writing in *Theology*,[3] points out that the existence of Mithra is attested in the Bogaz Khoi tablets, dating from 1380 B.C. Mithra was worshipped by Darius I, king of Persia from 521 to 486 B.C. The feast day of Mithra was the only day of the year on which the king was allowed to drink to excess! Again, it was under the banner of Mithra that Mithridates Eupator caused great military difficulties to Rome in Asia Minor between 88 and 68 B.C. Hinnells has presented his case and quoted his

---

[1] *Pauline Baptism and the Pagan Mysteries* (Edinburgh and London, 1967). This E.T. is virtually a 2nd edition of the original *Das Religionsgeschichtliche Problem von Römer* 6, 1–11, (Zürich, 1962).

[2] *The Foundations of New Testament Christology*, (London, 1965), p. 92.

[3] Vol. LXXI No. 571, Jan., 1968, pp. 20–25.

U

evidence in a convincing manner, and has persuaded me that the Apostolic Church could well have been familiar with Mithra as a kind of military messiah. It is perfectly possible that the formulation of N.T. Christianity may owe something to Mithra and *vice versa*, but there is no real proof.

Edward Yarnold[1] has made some interesting points. He suggests that the more objectionable features of the Mystery Cults developed during the fourth century A.D. as a last desperate attempt to quell the advance of Christianity, and that Christianity also cheapened itself in opposition to the Mystery Cults. It is a familiar fact that in war atrocities are most frequently committed on both sides when both sides feel themselves threatened. In the Apostolic Age both Christianity and the Mystery Cults, which shared a common intellectual milieu (or perhaps it would be more true to say that their backgrounds of ideas overlapped), were free from the abuses they developed in the fourth century after Christ.

Page 14, after first paragraph

A substantial contribution to the question of Testimonia has recently been made by Fitzmyer.[2] He examines the evidence from Qumran and concludes (*op. cit.*, p. 88f.), though with less confidence than Allegro, that the Jews probably did have testimony books in pre-Christian times. He agrees, however, that this is not inconsistent with Dodd's main contention that the early Christians were especially devoted to certain blocks of the O.T.

Page 29, after section (g)

For many centuries the Scriptures were largely understood in a way which showed no awareness of any distinction between 'What Paul meant in his own day' and 'What Paul means for us'. Still less was any distinction thought permissible between 'What Paul meant', and 'What is true'. Thirdly, in those days, before the advent of scientific exegesis, scholars were confessionalists, reading *into* Scripture, all too often, what they already believed, instead of reading *out of* Scripture something which might have challenged and corrected what they already held to be true. To be confessionally minded is not necessarily to be wrong. The whole

---

[1] *The Heythrop Journal*, Vol. xiii, No. 3, July 1972, pp. 247–67, 'Pagan Mysteries in the Fourth Century'.

[2] Joseph A. Fitzmyer, *Essays on the Semitic Background of the New Testament* (London and Blackrock, County Dublin, 1971), pp. 3–89.

of the N.T. is written from faith to faith, and a man who does not take part in living under God as a member of the People of God in his own day must inevitably be deaf to many of the overtones of Scripture. But the fact remains that for many centuries the ordinary beliefs of the Church, irrespective of which branch of the Church was in question, were simply read into the Bible.

It is not surprising that the 'scientific' approach to the Bible, with its cleansing concentration on what the Biblical writers meant when they wrote or dictated, came as a mighty rush of fresh air. This 'scientific' approach had the additional merit of cutting across denominational barriers. To speak only of the dead, I am seldom aware when reading Cerfaux that he was a bishop of the Latin Obedience or that Vincent Taylor was a Methodist: for me they are simply first rate scholars.

Literal, historical exegesis has a certain primacy as well as a permanent place in Theology, but it is not the whole of Theology; I am somewhat suspicious of *sensus pleniores*. I would agree that the author of Isaiah liii. was speaking truer than he knew, even though I follow Dr. Morna Hooker[1] on the question of the Suffering Servant. I would not quarrel with Our Lord's 'Scriptural Proof', as recorded in Mark xii, of the life after death: the authority behind this teaching comes from God through Christ himself and not through Exodus iii.6. When the N.T. re-uses the O.T., the resultant doctrine has the authority of the N.T., and that is all we need. But if we ourselves read a new meaning into Scripture, unless there is good reason to suppose it was intended from the beginning, the authority is our own. What is even worse, we may unconsciously appear to be trying to drape our own human thoughts with the authority of the Bible. For example, I myself believe in artificial contraception, but I base my belief on reason, adducing such evidence as the decline in death among infants, and would not attempt to claim scriptural warrant for views reached on other grounds. We must be prepared, both in moral and in systematic theology, to face the fact that non-Biblical evidence must be considered, and that the framework of thought of the Biblical writers, like our own, may well be wrong. At the end of Romans viii. Paul appears to be speaking in terms of the mental

---

[1] *Jesus and the Servant* (London, 1959), in which she shows, that though the N.T. does quote from Isa. liii. in a 'suffering sense', neither the thought of Jesus himself, nor that of the N.T. as a whole was dominated by the concept of the suffering servant.

framework of astrology. If he did, what he said in terms of this framework was nevertheless correct, since it is true that astrological forces, whether they exist or no, cannot cut us off from the love of God in Christ Jesus.

This lengthy preamble means simply this: if we take Romans viii. 18–39 as Paul meant it to be taken, is it true? An immediate defence presents itself. If Paul is not asserting facts, but expressing feelings, aspirations, etc., these cannot be either true or false, so the question does not arise. This defence is legitimate up to a point, but should not be pressed too far. Feelings and aspirations, I agree, cannot be true or false; but they are ridiculous or plain escapism unless they are closely related to truth. A prayer to God can be neither true nor false, but it is ridiculous if there is no God to pray to. Again, if we understand the Bible in a way which is so 'religious' that it is wholly removed from this world, we rob it of all value and incidentally fail to take account of the doctrines of the Creation and of the Incarnation. It is true that we may believe something we do not know, but though belief may well go beyond the facts it should never go against them. It is, I think, misleading to say that 'On the cross Christ conquered sin' when one recalls the history of the Christian centuries and the appalling state of the world today. I do however believe, on the basis of Scripture, that in the life, death and resurrection of Christ God did something necessary for the abolition of sin; but the abolition of sin, which, in concrete terms, means the sanctification of human beings, lies still in the future.

In the light of this introduction we now proceed to examine some of the topics treated in Rom. viii. 18–39, asking in each case if what Paul says is factual and, if so, if it is true or false.

I should like to ask in the first place whether in Rom. viii. 18–22 Paul means that the physical universe will be transformed, so that matter becomes divinized, or whether he means this: the physical universe is the arena in which men ought to honour God but in fact disobey Him. By disobeying God we dishonour the physical universe which is what *ktisis*, 'creation', must here refer to. *Phthora*, 'decay', though it often has a moral sense, refers here, I believe, like *mataiotēs*, 'frustration', to 'coming into being and passing away'. A well-known Christian scholar, it is said, was horrified to hear from a professor of Geology that dinosaurs already in the Jurassic Age, long before man appeared on the scene, suffered from cancer and from osteoarthritis: to him it seemed impossible that grave disease should occur before Adam sinned. We must here pose starkly the questions: (1) What did Paul mean? and (2) What is true? I suggest that Paul meant that the physical created order would share in man's glory, and would be transformed at the last day like our own bodies. I would further suggest that this belief was part of the poetic background he shared with contemporary Judaism, and indeed with many of the Fathers. I think we underestimate the non-literal nature of much of the background of Scripture, and fail to do justice to the central foreground. According to *Acts*, St. Peter on the first Pentecost Sunday saw the fulfilment of Joel's cosmological prophecy in the activity of the Spirit. I believe that when Paul was raised by God after his martyrdom he must have recognized in the glory of Christ into which he had entered the fulfilment not only of Phil. i. 23, but also of our present passage.

I have mentioned this problem because the question I wish to raise is this: is God merely the focus-point of our prayers, our hopes and our aspirations, or does He act in the 'real' world?

By the 'real' world I mean both the world of space-time-matter we now inhabit, and whatever states of being we may enter after death. Since the important topic of the Spirit would take us too far afield, I shall raise this question of God's real activity in relation to three topics:

(1) Providence, as seen in viii. 28.

(2) Predestination, or, according to my own understanding of the passage, assurance, viii. 29–30.

(3) Above all, the demonic (?astrological) which partly overlaps, I believe, with Luther's 'Hidden God' and corresponds to many of the problems which face us today on the boundaries of Theology and other disciplines. To make my meaning clear I have in mind such problems as whether senile and schizophrenic dementia cut us off from God. What 'personality' (*sōma*) is left to be raised up, and what real continuity exists?

As for the first passage 'He cooperates for good with those who love God and are called according to his purpose', the general sense is the same whether *Theos*, 'God', is the subject[1] expressed,

---

[1] *Theos* is the reading of Papyrus 46, *Codex Vaticanus* and *Codex Alexandrinus*. This reading also is in accordance with the normal personal theism of the Bible and the common transitive use of *Sunergei* (work together).

depending on the text, or whether the grammatical subject is *panta*, 'everything'. In either case Paul means that everything is made to work out right for the Christians, in spite of the fact that he lays so much stress upon our *koinōnia*, 'sharing', in the *pathēmata*, 'sufferings' of Christ.

It is clearly wrong to imagine that this passage is to be understood magically. The more elderly of us have been involved in one way or another, and on one side or the other, in one or both of the World Wars. We can therefore feel for the couple who, on the evening before their only child joined the Army, recited over him the words from Psalm xci. 7, 'A thousand may fall at your side, ten thousand at your right hand; but it will not come near you'. We must neither condemn their anxiety nor condone their superstition. I would add in passing that to understand the so-called predestinarian verses, Rom. viii. 29–30, as if they meant that some are to be picked out and saved, whether before or after the Fall, and others to be left to their well deserved fate in the *massa perditionis* 'mass of perdition', is an error of the same type.

On the other hand, it is clearly right to say that 'He cooperates for good with those who love God' means that we should have attitudes and feelings of being at peace with the supreme power, viewed not impersonally as *to ontōs on*, 'that which really is', the view of God held by some Greeks, but as the living God. It is clearly right, but is it enough? If it is an unchangeable attitude, a 'policy statement' of what we intend to do and feel whatever may happen in this or any other world, the philosophers of the school of linguistic analysis will say that it is in principle incapable of verification and therefore devoid of meaning. Moreover, to put what is essentially the same point in another way, it would be possible to maintain this attitude in our devotional life and in our aspirations whether there were a God or no. It could fit into a framework of atheism or of an Epicurean system like that of Lucretius. It might be an exclusively subjective form of autosuggestion. St. Paul's theology presupposed a framework and background based on the O.T. as seen through Pharisaic eyes. The foreground was occupied by actual events in this present world of space-time-matter: the death and resurrection of Christ and his own experience on the road to Damascus.

To approach the problem from another angle, I imagine that most of us from time to time have felt that some higher power has been guiding us. In the case of an individual occurrence it is impossible in principle to prove one way or the other whether it is due to some outside influence or to coincidence. In the present age, when materialism has become the unconscious background of most minds, it is usual to imagine that an event is due to 'coincidence' unless the contrary is proved, which in principle is impossible. The cases of this sense of guidance may be subjectively convincing to the person in question, but because they can not be standardized, and because so many factors are involved, it is, I believe, also impossible to reach a decision in either direction by invoking the aid of statistical analysis.

St. Paul seems to have understood *panta*, 'all things', in an adverbial sense: God cooperates in all sorts of ways with those who love him; this alone is consistent with his frank admissions of failure and disaster. I conclude then that in our modern systematics we can not 'see the hand of God in history' or draw up the laws of providence, but when someone tells me that he has been conscious as he looks back over his life of a purpose of which he was unaware, especially if it is *not* a matter of marvellous hairbreadth escapes, then unless there is good reason to do so, I am not disposed to maintain that he is wrong.

We now come to Rom. viii. 29-30, which has been held to support predestination. For predestination in the old sense, the belief that some human beings, whether before or after the Fall, were consigned by God to salvation or alternatively, either allowed to perish by default or, as Gottschalk[1] and Calvin had the courage, honesty and mental clarity to admit, consigned by God to Hell, I shall employ the term 'allocation'. For 'predestination' as it is taught in Rom. viii. I shall use the word 'assurance'.

If we look at the *New English Bible* we find that St. Paul begins the paragraph in which these verses occur with, 'In the same way the Spirit comes to the aid of our weakness'. The next paragraph, vv. 31-39, is well summed up by the words of the opening verse: 'If God is on our side, who is against us?' The belief that Rom. viii. 29-30, supports the to me repugnant doctrine of allocation is an example of 'framework error'. In Britain there was a T.V. show with which tired clergy used to refresh themselves. In one episode of this series, 'Dr. Finlay's Casebook', an undertaker

---

[1] An extreme Predestinarian, who seems to have taught that God predestined some to salvation and some to damnation. He lived *c.* A.D. 805-*c.* 68.

orders his own coffin because on his medical report, at the top of
the second page, he had read the words 'heart will not last a
week'. The complete sentence that started on the previous page,
which the undertaker had never seen, ran 'This man is perfectly
fit and the muscular pain around his heart will not last a week'.
If we have already in our minds a theological framework which
includes the doctrine of allocation by God to salvation, we naturally find strong support for it in Rom. viii. 29–30.

But if we do so we are disregarding the context. St. Paul is not
concerned directly with the human race as a whole, although what
he says presupposes a doctrine of God which is of supreme
importance for all mankind. Paul is here concerned simply and
solely with 'us' with *hēmeis*, 'we', that is with those who are
Christians. He has primarily in mind the Christian recipients of
his letter to Rome, but no doubt he would have said the same
about the Christian communities scattered round the North East
coast of the Mediterranean. He assures them that they are safe,
safe not because of what they are or have been, but because of
what God is and has done. We ask from what are they safe? I
think it is clear that they are safe from sin, from the Jewish Law
and from demonic forces. The point of the verses is that they are
safe because they rely not upon their unreliable selves, upon any
sort of merit or upon their own feelings, but solely and exclusively
upon God. He is not concerned with the delimitations of *hēmeis*
'we', with sheep and goats or with 'them and us'.

Normally St. Paul teaches a doctrine of *justification* by faith and
judgement according to works: we are accepted not because of
ourselves, but because of the free unmerited graciousness of God,
and the name given to our acceptance of that free gift is faith.
Being freely accepted by God is not at all inconsistent with judgement according to works. In this present passage, though there
is no suggesting of any divine picking and choosing, we come very
near to a doctrine of final perseverance: rather, what Paul says
here bears the same relation to a doctrine of final perseverance as
a living human being does to a corpse preserved in formalin for
students to dissect. I must confess that I am a universalist at
heart, believing in the ultimate salvation of all men. This can only
be a hope and not an article of faith since the evidence of Scripture
is inconclusive, and because God may choose so to limit his

omnipotence that he does not finally beat down the resistance of those who refuse salvation.

There is still something to be said about allocation, that is predestination, if we use the old language. It is said that it does justice to the initiative of God. By all means let us do justice to the initiative of God, but this does not necessarily involve us in accepting the doctrine of allocation. It is said also that allocation stresses our absolute dependence on God. It is the case that a truth can be expressed by means of an error. But the truth can be expressed without the error. By all means let us stress the truth of our dependence upon God, but we need not do so by means of the doctrine of allocation. It has, however, been suggested, that allocation, including failure to allocate to salvation, which in practice comes to the same as allocation to damnation, is due to the *Deus Absconditus*, the Hidden God. I believe, however, that the realities referred to in the doctrine of the *Deus Absconditus* are the same realities St. Paul refers to in Rom. viii. 35–39.

I should like to approach this problem from two widely divergent angles, that of popular anti-Christian humanist propaganda and secondly that of the Bible itself. The humanist will tell us that it is not fair for men to be judged according to works, as Paul claims in 2 Cor. v. 10, Gal. vi. 7. A man may sin because of causes for which he is not responsible, such as the additional chromosome said to be associated with psychopathic behaviour; he may be 'depraved on account he's deprived', as in *West Side Story*. It is true that much of this language is the language of excuse, but the fact remains that human behaviour is profoundly influenced for the worse by physical, economic and social conditions over which individuals have no control.

From popular humanist propaganda, with its bitter core of truth, we turn to the pages of Scripture and find in Isaiah xlv. 7. the words 'I (God) . . . create woe',=*uvōrē rāᶜ*. My pupils told me a story by the late C. A. Simpson, then Dean of Christ Church, Oxford, when he was doing pastoral work in one of the least savoury parts of New York. He went to visit a woman whose husband had just died and assured her that she must not regard God as the author of her husband's death. The widow rounded on him and said, 'If I did not believe my husband's death was the will of God I just could not bear it'. The picture-language of principalities and powers, and of the demonic and (?) astrological forces mentioned in this section of *Romans* have the function of recognizing the fact of evil and yet asserting the faith that all evil is somehow under the control of God.

Luther with his doctrine of the Hiddenness of God was pointing out to us, or rather, warning us not to disregard, a number of important matters. These include the fact that things do not work together for good for those who love God in an obvious manner which all can see. They also include the fact that human beings are distorted and kept from Christ by physical, social, political and economic factors so far as we can see in this world. It is well known that the finest men can degenerate through senile decay into a mere wreckage of their former selves. I know of one such man who had gained the respect and affection of innumerable people in his neighbourhood. In his dotage he degenerated into a cantankerous old man and the young nurses could not understand why some people still came to visit him. In the Church overseas the tie-up of Christianity with colonialism is still a great barrier to identification with the church visible. In many English parishes the Church has become associated so exclusively with the middle-aged and the middle-class that the poor, or ex-poor, and the young just do not feel that they belong. Along the Russo-Chinese border there are millions for whom Christianity has never been a live option. I suggest in all seriousness that in our contemporary world it is realities such as these which correspond to the *dunameis, hupsōma, bathos* etc. of Rom. viii.

Yet we believe that we are conquerors in spite of all this, and that nothing can separate us from the love of God which is in Christ Jesus. Why do we believe? Many would explain this on purely psychological and social grounds. But if a lucky few through an occasional rift in the clouds can see the stars, even though their ability to do so is due to the absence of cloud-cover, it does not justify us in concluding that the stars are not there. I believe that these occasional glimpses are due to the Holy Spirit, but it is clearly never possible to produce a natural history of the Spirit. I take it that 'Christians' and 'Those who have the *aparchē* (first fruits) of the Spirit' are the same people.

There is clearly here an eschatological tension: we who have the spirit are in bondage to social pressures, psychological pressures, and physical, medical and pathological conditions which in various ways cut us off from God and turn us at the end, if our physical health survives, into senile delinquents.

The word 'eschatological' has become a theological *oubliette* into which unexamined problems can be cast. I suggest that the fundamental eschatological tension is the tension between human existence as God wishes it to be and human existence as we actually experience it. To St. Paul in *Romans* this 'theological' tension was connected with a tension in time, the tension between this present age and the age to come.

I personally believe that Paul was right in his theology when he said that nothing at all, whether medical, psychological, social, astrological or demonic can cut us from God. If he believed that God would transform the world within a century or even in his own lifetime, as the epistles would suggest, then he was wrong, wrong not about *what* God will do, but about *when* He will do it. It is still perfectly possible that Christ will return in glory as Paul thought, but not when he thought it would happen. Even if this is so, the second coming will, in a sense, concern only the last Christian generation, and not the one-and-only Christian generation as Paul would appear to have thought. I must confess that I do not believe the doctrine of the Second Coming in its traditional form. But the N.T. doctrine of the Second Coming was the N.T. method of expressing belief in the final victory of God, and if we cease to believe in the final victory of God, I would stop bothering to be a Christian at all.

Many prefer to adopt at this point an attitude of 'reverent' agnosticism. In a sense, we must do so since this is a sphere in which knowledge is impossible. Nevertheless, I venture to speculate about a *possible* form that God's final victory *may* take. It is difficult to believe in what is clearly impossible.

The problem is that in this world, so far as we can observe, it is not possible to see God's providence ordering all things or keeping guard over his elect, whatever our attitude in prayer may be, and whatever personal convictions we may have about God's guidance in our own lives. Also, it seems clear that many people are kept away from God, and separated from the love of God which is in Christ Jesus, by social and medical factors etc.; I quote as an instance the well-known case of the devout officer in the Salvation Army who lost her faith in God following an operation on her brain.

I have spoken about what we can observe, and about this world. I now propose to pass on to the next world and to what we cannot observe, or do not normally observe. At this point many English clergy would cry out:

‘ “Pie in the sky when you die

It’s a lie.”

The laity would never swallow it.’ At the moment we are not concerned with what the laity will swallow, but with what is true. I believe that we have been too much afraid of what people will think of us in this age when materialism has become so much a part of the mental background of most of the world that any evidence or theory which appears to conflict with it is automatically dismissed.

I suggest that the theological tension between human existence as God would have it be and as we actually experience it, is connected with, and ultimately solved through, a tension between, on the one hand, human life now on this planet and, on the other hand, certainly human life after death, and possibly a better social order in this world, though I reserve my efforts for this world and my hopes for the next. This is hardly a novel solution. It is a return to something very much like the medieval theology of the Western Church. It differs in two ways: firstly, I envisage a Purgatory, or as many British Christians prefer to say, an Intermediate State, or series of states, not confined to those who die in a state of grace, but including all human beings. Secondly, whereas the medieval doctrine presupposed a legal framework, the framework I would suggest is not legal but psychological or personal. It is not a question of ‘paying off’ our debts, but of growing into the kind of person who would not have sinned. This framework is consistent with, but does not necessitate, a belief in universalism, the eventual salvation of all human beings.

But here another question arises. If human beings live after death, what is it that lives on? This problem is especially acute in the case of those who have suffered any kind of degeneration in later life, whether physical or, so far as we can judge, moral and spiritual. A similar problem arises in the case of those children born with some congenital defect, such as mongolism.

Purgatory rouses strong feelings, but there is one word even dirtier —I mean ‘soul’. I am not of course using the word soul in the way it is normally used in the Bible, but as in medieval and modern times. I recognize the unity between body and soul in this present life, a unity comparable to that between the elements oxygen and hydrogen when they combine to form water. I do not for one moment suggest that matter is in itself evil: the deadliest sins could clearly be committed by sexless Archangels.

When we visit an idiot child or a case of senile dementia, is what we can see all that there is to see, or is there an invisible pianist who can no longer express himself through his shattered piano? The gradual and intermittent nature of the onset of arterio-sclerosis, from which some of us must already be suffering, suggests to me the latter explanation. The existentialist plea that we make ourselves, or our souls if you prefer that language, strengthens me in that conviction. I do not deny the *possibility* that body and 'soul', i.e. the whole personality, may die completely, and that God may reconstitute us. That, however, is not how I understand 2 Cor. v. 1–10, and the reconstitution view raises problems connected with the continuity of personality.

It may be felt that I have wandered far from St. Paul, but I believe I have good reasons for doing so. Serious theologians do not study St. Paul as a mere academic game, or even as they might study Seneca. We are studying St. Paul because we believe that through him we can learn something about man and God which no Seneca can teach us.

Paul tells us that our present existence is one of woe, and that is clearly true for most human beings. He speaks of demonic powers, etc. We probably do not believe in them quite as he did, but we can recognize in our own experience forces just as evil and just as powerful. Paul promises us that these evil forces can not separate us from the love of God. He suggests that this evil will be overthrown by the second coming of Christ. The manner of God's victory has clearly not taken the form the Apostle expected. I believe that God's victory *will* be achieved, and I have ventured to suggest a possible manner in which it *may* be achieved. However, when we finally know the truth, my speculations will probably seem far more naïve than St. Paul's doctrine of the Second Coming. What matters to us all is not the *manner* of God's victory, but the *fact*.

For further consideration of this problem, see, among many others, John C. Gibbs, *Creation and Redemption, a study in*

Pauline Theology, Supplements to *Novum Testamentum*, Volume XXVI (Leiden, 1971), especially pp. 154–60, and *Sociology, Theology and Conflict*, ed. Whiteley, D. E. H. and Martin, R. (Oxford, 1969), especially, pp. 48–94.

Page 46, after section (a)

When I wrote the preceding paragraphs ten years ago, I already had some misgivings about solidarity in the O.T., simply because I did not find so much evidence for it in reading the O.T. myself as O.T. scholars appeared to do. One unfortunate result of my somewhat uncritical acceptance of this popular theory was that I did not pay proper attention to Paul's own doctrine of being 'in Christ' (*en Christō*).

In 1965 J. R. Porter[1] showed that most of the O.T. passages adduced to support 'corporate personality' proved on examination to support instead 'corporate legal responsibility'. J. W. Rogerson[2] has pointed out that Wheeler Robinson was led astray by some earlier writers. Maine, e.g., showed, not that man in primitive society had no consciousness that he was an individual, but that he had no individual rights. Rogerson does not deny that certain primitive societies were dominated by ideas of identity of substance between the clan and the eponymous totem, but he claims that these ideas do not apply to the Hebrews.

I agree that we can no longer accept ideas of corporate personality in the O.T. as uncritically as we used to, but we need not ascribe to the O.T. the extreme individualism which we find in modern western countries. No doubt, as Rogerson suggests, there was a certain oscillation between 'identification' with one's nation and assertion of one's own individuality, just as there is in modern times.

I have not changed my mind concerning the dominance of the presupposition of corporate personality in St. Paul, but I now realize that he derived this idea less than I had supposed from the O.T. and more from his sense of being in Christ.

[1] 'The legal Aspects of the Concept of "Corporate Personality" in the Old Testament', *Vetus Testamentum*, xv (1965), pp. 361–80.
[2] 'The Hebrew Conception of Corporate Personality: A Re-examination', *J.T.S.*, N.S., Vol. xxi, Pt. 1, April 1970, pp. 1–16.

Page 69, after section (c)

Cranfield[1] rejects Barrett's[2] contention that the wrath of God and the righteousness of God are *both* being revealed and that the wrath takes the form of the 'observable situation', i.e. the prevalence of idolatry and sin on the ground that Paul is hardly likely to have entertained the view that the wickedness and corruption of his own times were something new. I would defend Barrett on the ground that it was a widespread belief that the 'Birth Pangs of the Messiah', would precede the end. This is clear from 2 Thess. ii and Mk. xiii, and even if Paul did not write the one and had not read the other, the belief is clear in *Daniel* and indeed in the Gog and Magog section of *Ezekiel*. We must surely agree with Anders Nygren's[3] comment on this passage when he says that 'God's wrath is His holy displeasure at sin . . . more than a passive discountenancing of sin . . . a terrifying reality' (p. 97).

I would suggest that Dodd's theory of the wrath of God, which he identifies with the evidence of sin and of the 'escalation' of sin which Paul saw around him, is true as far as it goes: the phenomena it refers to overlap in large measure with the work of the Lutheran *Deus Absconditus* (Hidden God). But Cranfield is surely correct when he says (op. cit., p. 334) that '*orgē Theou* (wrath of God) is also being revealed *in the gospel* (italics Cranfield's), that is, in the on-going proclamation of the gospel'. The situation is partially —but only partially—parallel to what happens when a human physician is horrified at a disease: the progress of the disease continues, just as sin grows and escalates, but a remedy, parallel to the Gospel, is prescribed and the patient is cured. The difference is that any deterioration in the patient takes place in spite of the doctor's will, or is accepted by him as an inevitable 'side-effect' of the treatment, whereas the self-destroying power of sin and the work of God in Christ, which finally conquers sin, are each the result both of the love and of the wrath of God, if, indeed, it is possible to disentangle them.

Cranfield also writes some golden words (op. cit., p. 333) about the wrath of God: 'Even the very highest and purest human

---

[1] C. E. B. Cranfield, 'Romans 1.18', *Scottish Journal of Theology*, vol. 21, No. 3, Sept. 1968, pp. 330–35.
[2] C. K. Barrett, *The Epistle to the Romans* (London, 1957). There is a corrected edition of 1962 but none since.
[3] *Commentary on Romans* (London, 1952), being the E.T. of *Romarbrevet* (Sweden, 1944).

wrath can at the best afford but a distorted and twisted reflection
of the wrath of God. . .'. Now if we accept this view it means to
say that the wrath of God affords no basis at all for crude penal
and substitutionary theories of the death of Christ. Much preaching of the Gospel is not the necessary anthropomorphism by
which alone the nature and work of God can be hinted at, but a
crude, distorted anthropomorphism which degrades—uninten-
tionally—the God whose glory it seeks to proclaim.

Again, Leon Morris[1] writes: 'Perhaps the difficulty arises
because we are making a false antithesis between the divine wrath
and the divine love. We are handicapped by the fact that we must
necessarily use terms properly applicable to human affairs, and
for us it is very difficult to be simultaneously wrathful and loving.
But, upon analysis, this seems to be largely because our anger is
such a selfish passion, usually involving a large element of
irrationality together with a lack of self-control. . . .
Those who object to the conception of the wrath of God. . . .'.
I myself have no objection at all to the conception of the wrath of
God—indeed, I regard it as an essential part of Paul's soteriology
if it is expressed in the refined manner employed by Morris. But
if God's wrath is so refined, then 'propitiation', if that is indeed
the true interpretation of *hilastērion* at Rom. iii. 25, must also be
used in a refined sense. Further, 'substitutionary',[2] though it is
Biblical in the sense that it corresponds to the Hebrew *kōpher* in
the sense of 'equivalent' must also be understood in a refined sense.
That Christ paid a price, which I should term 'vicarious', for
human salvation is a proposition which no reader of the Bible can
reasonably deny, but that Christ paid this price to God, or to the
Devil, a theory never explicitly stated in Scripture, appears to me
wholly inconsistent with the admirable description of the wrath of
God, penned by Morris, which I have quoted above. Morris
himself is quite aware of this point when he says: 'This averting
(i.e. of God's wrath, which he has just mentioned) we may
properly term "propitiation", if that word is understood as
excluding the pagan idea of a process of celestial bribery' (italics
mine) (op. cit. p. 178). When I reject the substitutionary theory of

[1] *The Apostolic Preaching of the Cross* (London, 1965[3]), p. 208f.
[2] For a definition of the terms 'substitutionary' and 'vicarious' see pp. 130–32.

the Atonement, my meaning is precisely that expressed by Morris in the words I have italicized. In other words, Morris and I agree about the theological fact but differ in our use of the term 'substitutionary'. My chief criticism of Morris is that he still speaks of 'averting' God's wrath, whereas I believe that God's wrath, in the refined form Morris and I alike ascribe to it, should not be 'averted' but allowed to fulfil its cleansing function.

Page 86, to follow section (e).

GALATIANS: THEN AND NOW

What was it that enabled Israel to keep together as a people before the first destruction of the Temple? In alphabetical order: a common God, a common land and a common way of life. The common land, it was true, had shifting boundaries. It also had shrines which grew and waned in importance, shrines and sacred places which were connected with traditions about God and their ancestors. The common way of life from our modern analytic point of view appears to be composed of:

(a) Religious rituals, especially feasts and sacrifices.
(b) Moral laws such as the prohibition of murder, adultery and theft.
(c) Folk customs such as abstention from certain articles of diet and various positive customs including male circumcision.

But to the average Israelite of the 10th century B.C., this tripartite division might well have sounded somewhat artificial. Isaiah lviii. insists that liturgy alone is not enough, as if the point required to be made. All these aspects of the Life of Israel, which kept them together as a people, and gave them a sense of belonging, their land, their traditions, whether written or oral, and their way of life (in spite of the fact that they all fell within the horizon of the Ancient Near East, the land geographically, the traditions and the way of life from the point of view of culture) were linked with each other, and distinguished from the heritage of the surrounding peoples, by their relation to Yahweh. It was Yahweh, as the traditions were primarily concerned to recount, who had made them a people and had given them their land on condition that they continued to live the Israelite way of life, both in moral and ceremonial matters, which was the content of the

x

covenant. It was the covenant above all which made them the people of Yahweh. Apart from the covenant you could not join yourself to the people of the God of Abraham.

We are not here concerned about the date when monotheism or the covenant became effectively part of the Israelite tradition. The tragedy was that, although Yahweh was the only God, the God of all peoples of the earth, He had a covenant with Israel alone. I disregard for the moment the strand of tradition which spoke of the covenant with Noah and all Noah's descendants, who included all the inhabitants of the earth, so that Israel alone was the people of God. You could not belong to God's people or have access to Him unless you lived the Israelite way of life.

This unfortunate fact, the fact that the God of all the earth was alleged to acknowledge as his people only those who followed certain customs, was perpetuated by the disaster of the exile. This disaster brought it about that Israel kept together as a people, indeed as the peculiar people of the one true God, by adhering with greater fidelity to the Israelite way of life, the content of the covenant. The fact that they suffered meant that they either ceased to belong to Israel at all, and became part of the surrounding peoples, or else adhered to the covenant with a zeal that bordered on fanaticism.

We must ask ourselves, not how Israel tried to make converts, but how they tried to maintain their religious and national identity, and prevent their children from drifting away from it. They no longer had their land or their sacred shrines, but it is likely that in many places they had their community who met together at what we may call a proto-synagogue to read and expound their traditions, now committed to writing. Also, they had their micro-environment, the family, in which the Israelite way of life could be preserved. It would be possible to observe dietary laws and taboos without too much hardship in one's own home. The sabbath could be observed by peasants and small traders without great difficulty. The Babylonians had not universalized mass production on modern factory lines which force all workmen to work to a common time-table.

Further, the ancient Palestinian folk-custom of male circumcision must suddenly have become significant. In the old country it can have meant little, since it was observed by the surrounding nations. But in the Babylonian Diaspora, and later in the Diaspora of the Greeks, where it was strange, it helped to keep Israel a peculiar people. It was an outward and normally invisible sign of membership of the people of Yahweh. You could observe one sabbath and not observe the next, but once you were circumcised you were circumcised, though at a later date a reverse operation which would evade all but close inspection was introduced. It was a rite closely connected with marriage and the family, and, if practised in infancy, it avoided the adolescent rebellion problem which dogs confirmation. In a word, infant male circumcision was an excellent practice for keeping the people of Yahweh together and keeping them apart from other people. It was a sign ('ōth) of the covenant between God and His people (Gen. xvii. 11).

But although infant circumcision was probably a real help in keeping God's people together, adult circumcision was a terrible liability for those who tried to proselytize Gentiles, especially in areas where circumcision was not familiar. Indeed, many of the commandments of the Law must have been a barrier. It might be possible for a Gentile interested in Judaism to adopt a token part of the Torah, e.g. to observe the sabbath, but to keep the whole of the Torah would have been a burden in areas where the dietary parts of the Law were not, as they were in Palestine, largely a formalization of the customs of the country. We must, of course, remember that many of the stricter and more precise points of the Law were probably not enforced in St. Paul's day, but introduced by the School of Jamnia to keep the Jews together after the destruction of the Temple in A.D. 71. But circumcision was in force, and even a comparatively liberal Jew such as Philo was not prepared to waive it. In an age when so many of us were ourselves circumcised as infants under modern conditions, it is hard to realize what a traumatic experience this operation must have been before the days of anaesthetics and of aseptic and antiseptic surgery.

Paul's basic vision was that the God of the whole earth was not bound by the customary manner of life of any nation, not even that of the Jews, although it was this customary way of life, crystallized together with the traditions of the Exodus and other events of salvation-history in the Torah, which had kept a remnant of Israel faithful to Israel's God. But Paul had to face Genesis xvii. 14: '. . . Any uncircumcised male who is not circumcised in the flesh of his foreskin shall be cut off from his people; he has broken my covenant'. This custom was reinforced by centuries of tradition and by the fact that circumcision had been a rallying point during the successful war of liberation in the time of the Maccabees (168 B.C. onwards).

What was St. Paul to do? He could not say that the Bible was wrong or take refuge in a theory of progressive revelation, although he came very near to doing just that when he said that the promise made to Abraham could not be invalidated by a law made four hundred and thirty years later: this was almost 'progressive revelation' in reverse. The *N.E.B.* says that the law was a 'temporary measure', an over-free translation, but a sound explanation of the Greek *achris hou* of Gal. iii. 19: in this case Paul was ascribing different values to different parts of the Torah.

In *Galatians* the word 'law' has two main applications: it refers to the content of the covenant, and is relevant to the question of how human beings can 'belong' to the people of God; secondly it has an application by which wrong action becomes 'sin'. It may be likened to a police speed-trap by which the wrong action of driving too fast becomes a legal offence. For convenience I shall refer to these two applications of the word *nomos* (law) as the 'covenant' use and the 'speed-trap' use respectively. The word *nomos* has thirty-two occurrences in Galatians, of which sixteen[1] are 'covenant' use, four[2] are 'speed-trap' use, eight[3] partake of the nature of both, that is they are 'mixed' uses, and four[4] are anomalous.

The four cases of the 'speed-trap' use of *nomos* all have one thing in common: they declare Paul's conviction that it is not possible to be justified by the Law. In other words, all the Law can do is to make a man aware of his own failure and the failure of the Law itself. This is clear from ii. 19: 'Through the law (speed-trap) I died to law' (covenant). That is, the law showed up Paul's failure and its own failure, with the result that Paul ceased to live for the Law and began to live for God. This is likewise apparent from iii. 10, 'Those who rely on obedience to the law are under a curse; for Scripture says, "Cursed are all who do not persevere in doing everything that is written in the Book of the Law" '; and

---

[1] ii. 16 (a) (b), ii. 19 (b), iii. 2, iii. 5, iii. 11, iii. 12, iii. 13, iii. 17, iii. 18, iv. 5 (a) (b), iv. 21 (a), v. 3, v. 4, v. 18.
[2] ii. 19 (a), iii. 10 (a) (b), iii. 19.
[3] ii. 17, ii. 21, iii. 21 (a) (b) (c), iii. 23, iii. 24, vi. 13.
[4] iv. 21 (b), v. 14, v. 23, vi. 2.

from iii. 19, 'Then what of the law? It was added to make wrong-doing a legal offence'.

The same applies to the eight 'mixed' cases where the word *nomos* suggests both that the law is a speed-trap, an indicator of sin, and that it is not, as Paul's opponents believed, a means of justification. This becomes clear from ii. 17, 'We ourselves no less than the Gentiles turn out to be sinners against the law'; iii. 21, 'Does the law, then, contradict the promises? No, never! If a law had been given . . . to bestow life, then indeed righteousness would have come from keeping the law'; iii, 23, 24, 'We were close prisoners in the custody of law, pending the revelation of faith. Thus the law was a kind of tutor in charge of us till Christ should come'; and finally from vi. 13, 'Even those who do receive circumcision are not thoroughgoing observers of the law', that is, the Law quâ speed-trap shows that those who trust in the law regarded as the content of the covenant, prove in fact to be violators of that same covenant.

As for the four 'anomalous' cases, in iv. 21 *nomos* is the canon of Scripture, v. 23 is purely negative, saying that certain virtues are outside the scope of *nomos*, and vi.2 refers to the *nomos* of Christ, which, whatever it may mean, is not relevant to our present purpose. The fourth, v. 14, will be treated later.

What does concern our present purpose is that in none of the fifteen uses of *nomos* so far considered is there any suggestion that Christ saves us from sin or from our offences against the Law. Indeed, there is only one passage in the whole epistle to the Galatians where it is said that Christ saves us from our sins, namely, i. 4 'Who sacrificed himself for our sins, to rescue us out of this present age of wickedness'. This, of course, is typical Pauline teaching, but my contention is that it is only incidental to this particular epistle.

If we carry out a gross dissection of *Galatians*, which is not to condemn those who legitimately divide it more finely, we discover that it falls into three main divisions:

(1) Paul asserts his apostolic authority (i. 1– ii. 14).
(2) He maintains that no one, Jew or Gentile, can be justified by the law (ii. 15– v. 12).
(3) Paul reminds us that though we are not under the law, we are bound to act in accordance with love, which is the essence of the law (v. 13– vi. 10).

It is unnecessary to say anything more in this chapter about section (1). It is in section (2) that references to *nomos* begin and that the three references to *diathēkē* (covenant) are found. In iii. 15 and iii. 17 *diathēkē* means not 'covenant' as usual, but 'will' in the sense of testamentary disposition. The point is made that the promise to Abraham (the testamentary disposition, a play being made on two meanings of *diathēkē*), could not be set aside, once ratified, by the *nomos* which was promulgated 430 years later. At this point a Jewish objector would have gasped with rage and surprise and would have said: 'The brazen impertinence of the man! Has he forgotten that the *diathēkē* with Abraham was in fact sealed with the blood of circumcision?' We may speculate that someone did make this supremely obvious point and that this led Paul to make the reply expounded in Rom. iv. that it is recorded that Abraham put his faith (Hebrew *'āman*) in God (Gen. xv. 6, and here only), while his circumcision was not recorded until Gen. xvii. In Gal. iv. 24 the word *diathēkē* is again found and means covenant, as usual. The point is made that the new (Christian) covenant is superior to the old (Jewish) covenant, just as Isaac was superior to Ishmael and Sarah to Hagar.

This may seem tortuous logic, and indeed there is no logic at all in the ordinary sense of the word. I have already given a defence of male infant circumcision for Jews and have shown the disadvantages of forcing circumcision on adult male converts. I have done so avowedly and explicitly on grounds which are drawn from the study now known as sociology of religion. I could make a similar defence on sociological grounds of Paul's rejection of other Jewish observances which also formed part of the content of the covenant. It may be objected (correctly!) that Paul did not wish to do away with the whole of the covenant since, in the third of the three sections into which we have divided his epistle by gross dissection, he makes it clear that idolatry, for example, which is certainly forbidden in the Jewish Law, cannot be tolerated among Christians (v. 20). It is not very illuminating to say that Paul retained the moral law and rejected the ceremonial law. It is better to say that he rejected explicitly the obligation to observe specifically Jewish national customs such as the dietary regulations, which had in practice caused difficulty in the 'Mission Field'. The principle at issue was this: membership of the kingdom of God is not dependent upon any specifically national or class *mores*, Jewish or, we may add, British, German or American.

This concludes our treatment of section (2). In the final section Paul urges the Galatians not to abuse their freedom. During most of the 20th century N.T. scholars have spoken much about 'the Christian community', but it has always seemed to me that this 'community' has been thought of in a very abstract manner. Also, scholars have written as if the concerns of the *Urgemeinde* (the primitive Christian community in the Apostolic Age) to dignify it with its German title, were purely theological. I should like to supplement this by making a sociological approach to the Christian community in Galatia. It is clear that such an approach is bound to be highly speculative.

Why was it necessary for Paul to put his ethical point so strongly? Why should he think it likely that the Galatians might live according to their 'lower nature' (v. 19), to quote the *N.E.B.* rendering of *sarx*? When a new religion begins in any locality, it is natural that it should attract the 'misfits', those who do not 'belong' in their previous religion, if any. This seems to have been Paul's experience at Corinth, as we can tell from 1 Cor. i. 26–28.f. Again, if people leave their old community and abandon its customs, they abandon the moral equivalent of corsets so that they are liable to suffer from the moral equivalent of middle-age spread: or rather, their lack of true morality becomes obvious because they are no longer lulled into moral conformity by sheer force of habit. It is not surprising that the early Christians, for these two reasons, were liable to moral scandals.

On the other hand it is clear that the Christian converts were capable of great devotion, as we can tell from Gal. iv. 15, 'You would have torn out your very eyes, and given them to me, had that been possible!' Again, we read, 'If you are guided by the Spirit you will not fulfil the desires of your lower nature', (Gal. v. 16) and, 'The harvest of the spirit is love, joy, peace, patience, kindness, goodness, fidelity, gentleness, and self-control'. This passage ought to be read in the light of Rom. viii. 14, 'For all who are moved by the Spirit of God are sons of God', and Gal. iv. 6, 'To prove that you are sons, God has sent into our hearts the Spirit of his Son', which suggest that all Christians were led by the Spirit of God, and that the kind of behaviour described in Gal. v. 22 as 'The harvest of the Spirit' was not seldom attained in the Christian communities of the Apostolic Age. How are we to account for the moral excellence of which the N.T. speaks? A sociologist who kept religion out of his mind would probably say that a small new community might well enjoy a 'honeymoon' period of relatively short duration. I am sure that this is right as far as it goes. A Christian might go further and say that during this 'honeymoon' period it was easier for the Christians to be influenced by the Holy Spirit.

Paul's attack on the Jewish Law, like that of Jesus Christ, was a corrective, and not the whole truth. They both presupposed the truth of the O.T. and regarded it as infallible if understood correctly. For this reason Paul was compelled to bring back much of the content of the law in Gal. v. 14, 'for the whole law can be summed up in a single commandment: "Love your neighbour as yourself",' which is the last of the four anomalous occurrences of the word *nomos*.

My contention is that, apart from this ethical section, the necessity for which I have tried to explain, Paul's main purpose in writing, or rather in dictating, *Galatians* was not to set forth Christ as a redeemer who saved men from the result of their sins. Gal. i. 4 is the sole exception. Gal. iii. 13, has been taken to be another exception, but I have argued[1] that this is not so. His purpose, I believe, was to set forth Christ as one who saved us from the fate resultant on not being a member of the right trades union. He did not raise the question of whether it is necessary to belong to the right religion, though he tacitly assumed it was necessary to be a Christian. He maintained that, 'There is no such thing as Jew and Greek, slave and freeman, male and female; for you are all one person in Christ Jesus' (Gal. iii. 28). This unity was no doubt a reality in the early 'honeymoon' period of Galatian church history, but we are told that this period came to an end almost at once (Gal. i. 6), so that even Barnabas fell away (Gal. ii. 13), not to mention Peter (Gal. ii, 11f.).

Are we to say then that Paul was a failure? He laid down the principle, which has now become a platitude, and fought hard for its realization. Paul did his work. Others, including ourselves, have not yet done ours. The Pauline platitude is that human beings should not be divided race against race, class against class, sex against sex or colour against colour. In order to put this

[1] pp. 83ff.

principle into practice we must do other things in addition to studying the Bible. Hard economic and social facts, as well as the facts of religion, must be the concern of this generation if we are to put St. Paul's platitude into practice: if we fail to do so, we are heading for destruction.

Page 105, at end of first paragraph

I have been confirmed in my opinion by Langevin's[1] careful study of 1 Thess. i. 9–10, v. 2, 1 Cor. xvi. 22, and less importantly, Rev. xxii. 20, and *Didache* x. 6. He avoids arguing in circles, and employs five criteria for pre-Pauline origin:

(1) An explicit claim to this effect, as in 1 Cor. xv. 3.

(2) The recurrence of stereotyped formulae. This is important, though every formula *must* have been used for the first time, and some *may* have been coined by St. Paul.

(3) The use in the immediate vicininity of such 'tradition technical terms' as *paradidonai*, and *paralambanein*, i.e. 'hand on', as in 1 Cor. xi. 23, and 'received', as in 1 Cor. xv.

(4) Loose connexion of the formulaic passage with its context, and

(5) The use of technical terms like *Kurios*, 'Lord', without explanation.

For our purposes, of course, it is for his examination of the three Pauline passages that Langevin's work is most important. This examination is scholarly and the conclusion that their Christology is pre-Pauline must be judged probable. I have drawn attention to this work, both because of its intrinsic importance and because it is a model in method for young research workers.

Page 147, line 19 after 'a new and greater theory of sacrifice.'

In the light of this belief I should like to make a few comments on the work of David Hill.[2] He gives a careful summary of the theory of T. W. Manson[3] and of the work of L. Morris.[4] I do not wish to plagiarize either Morris or Hill, who have given what I

[1] Langevin, E. L., *Jésus Seigneur et l'Eschatologie. Exégèse de Textes Prépauliniens*, Studia, Travaux de recherche, Universities of Montréal and Sudbury, No. 21, (Bruges–Paris, 1967).

[2] *Greek Words and Hebrew Meanings*, (Cambridge, 1967), pp. 38–48.

[3] *J.T.S.* (Old Series), 1945, pp. 1–10.

[4] *The Apostolic Preaching of the Cross* (London, 1957), pp. 125–85.

believe to be the best defence in English of the 'substitutionary' theory of the Atonement, so I must be content with few words. On p. 42 Hill says that in 4 Macc. and Rom. iii. 25 death was 'vicarious'. In a footnote to this word (p. 42, n. 2) he quotes Büchsel as saying: 'Only through substitutionary suffering, through personal self-offering, is the community atoned' (*T.W.N.T.*, III, 323). Morris[1] makes his understanding of the words of the 'substitution' group clear (*op. cit.*, pp. 34 ff.) when he adds to a statement that the paying of a 'ransom price' is substitutionary in character a reference to J. H. Moulton[2] that in the N.T. the word denotes equivalence or substitution.[3] It is worth remembering the often repeated fact that *anti* is applied to the death of Christ in the N.T. *only* at Mk. x. 45, and its parallel in Matt. xx. 28. At Heb. xii. 2, it bears a sense of purpose and should be rendered 'for the sake of'. I must confess that I find it hard to see how the suffering and death of the sinless Jesus, human and divine, is 'equivalent' to the sins of human beings *unless* we presuppose the 'celestial bribery' so rightly rejected by Morris.

Hill like T. W. Manson before him, employs calendrical considerations. T. W. Manson, it will be remembered, had suggested that Paul wrote Romans around the Passover season and that the ritual of Passover reminded him of the ritual of the Day of Atonement, and suggested to his mind the word *kappōreth* =*hilastērion*=mercy seat used on the Day of Atonement. Hill (op. cit., p. 47) suggests that *Romans* was written during the winter (Acts xx. 2 ff.) and that Paul was thinking of the Winter Feast of the Dedication, and that the martyr-theology of 4 Maccabees *may well have been* (italics mine) associated with the Feast of Dedication. About both these calendrical theories, those of T. W. Manson and of Hill alike, I can say only that they are most ingenious but that the nature of the evidence does not enable us to regard them as more than plausible (though legitimate) speculations.

At the risk of seeming to cavil, I must challenge one of Hill's contentions. He says:[4] 'The idea of propitiation is unmistakably

---

[1] *Apostolic Preaching of the Cross* (London, 1965[3]).

[2] *op. cit.*, p. 178.

[3] *A Grammar of New Testament Greek*, vol. i, *Prolegomena*, (Edinburgh, 1903, often reprinted), p. 100.

[4] Op. cit., p. 39. Hill deals with this point far more thoroughly than I have space to do.

present in *exilaskesthai*, (a word of the *hilastērion?*=propitiation group) at Zech. 7:2; 8:22, Mal. 1:9'. In Zech. vii. 2f., men were sent to *exilaskesthai* the Lord, reminding him that the due sacrifices had been carried out. *Exilaskesthai* certainly means 'render gracious'. The Lord replies after the manner of Isa. lviii, saying that the people had fasted and feasted for the wrong motives: the people are in effect told to improve their motives, and in the next section to reform their morals. There is no suggestion of making amends by means of an equivalent. In Zech. viii. 22 many gentiles, it is said, will approach the Lord and seek to make him gracious (*hilaskesthai*) to them. They seek to 'propitiate' him in the sense of winning his favour, and perhaps acknowledging themselves to have been in the wrong by persecuting the Lord's own people, though this is not explicitly stated. There is no mention of winning his favour by means of any kind of offering. Mal. i. 9 is probably a better passage for Hill's thesis. The Jews are told *'exilaskesthe'* ('propitiate', in the imperative mood) the Lord and to make supplications to him. Certainly Israel had sinned in that the priests had acted from the wrong motives. There is no question of any sort of 'equivalent'. Israel is told that they have lost God's favour because of their sins. In English 'propitiate' generally means 'win the favour of someone ill-disposed to you by means of an equivalent'. In Greek, words of the *hilastērion* group mean 'win the favour of'. 'By means of an equivalent' is not necessarily included. (N.B. See also Postscript, p. 275 ff.)

Page 148, after first paragraph

In this context it is worth noticing the powerful words of Markus Barth[1] of Basle, son of Karl Barth. He equates 'blood' with 'life', but does not think it is a magic potion or a substitute (*Ersatz*), p. 164. His main contention is: 'That does not mean that he died in the place (*an Stelle*) of Israel. It is rather that with the crucified king of Israel every servant of the king has been "crucified along with him" . . . then the Israel represented through Jesus Christ is for its part representative of "all flesh" . . . the whole world is "crucified with" Christ . . . whether all men know of his death or not, whether they believe in God and the Messiah and witnesses sent by him or not—they are in a legal sense dead'.[2]

[1] *Foi et Salut selon S. Paul*, Analecta Biblica, No. 42 (Rome, 1970).
[2] Op. cit., p. 167.

Page 160, after second paragraph

D. Hill[1] (op. cit., p. 160) says that: 'The verb (*dikaioō*, justify) is primarily and predominantly a forensic term, a word of the law court. . . .' I would offer two comments. First, in making this statement he is, I feel, doing insufficient justice to his own account of the use of words of this group in the LXX of Deutero-Isaiah. Secondly, and more importantly, though I agree that words of this group have 'forensic' overtones in St. Paul, the very word 'forensic' has entirely different associations in the Bible and in modern England. There was nothing in the Bible like the Old Bailey, the Assize Courts or the Crown Courts, with their formal, impersonal atmosphere, even though the Judge is a representative of the Sovereign. In O.T. times the king of Israel administered justice at the gate of the city, among members of a 'primary community' of people who had known each other as persons since their childhood. Hill says that the word (justify) describes: 'a relation to or a status before God, the judge of all men" '. Hill does not in this passage say anything about a price or a ransom. If he means by the term 'forensic' that God, the King of all men, not because of any merits, actual or foreseen, but solely of his own volition, accepts us, in spite of our sins, though without in any way condoning them, then I am in full agreement with him. The reason why I have laboured this obvious but fundamental point is that words like 'forensic', read in and remembered from a book like Hill's, when their Biblical background is forgotten and replaced by that of our depersonalized modern society, are apt to be profoundly misleading.

Meanwhile there has appeared in the sky a cloud no bigger than a man's hand. In the realm of secular studies much work has been published on semantic fields, etc. This makes a great deal of Biblical word-study appear amateurish in comparison. Now John F. A. Sawyer[2] has applied some of these new techniques to O.T. Hebrew. He maintains (op. cit., p. 54) that many of the key words used in the Biblical teaching on salvation are examples of metaphorical transference from the forensic sphere. This is what in an amateurish, intuitive way, I had always supposed. It would be hazardous to place much weight upon one book in a new sphere,

---

[1] *Greek Words and Hebrew Meanings, studies in the Semantics of soteriological terms, S.N.T.S.* Monograph Series, No. 5 (Cambridge, 1967).

[2] *Semantics in Biblical Research: New Methods of Defining Hebrew Words for Salvation,* S.B.T., *Second Series,* No. 24 (London, 1972).

but I suspect that this new line of approach will be of great importance in the next ten years.

Page 165, after last paragraph

It is most important to realize that we are saved by God's objective initiative which we 'subjectively' accept by faith: We are NOT saved by our own 'subjective' believing. This is made very clear by C. K. Barrett and by Markus Barth. Barrett[1,2] maintains that 'I am not ashamed of the Gospel', is not a statement about the Apostle's own psychological state but an expression of solidarity with the early communities which framed their discipline in terms of loyalty to Jesus'. Markus Barth contends[3] that *diakrinomai*, in Rom. iv. 20 does not mean that Abraham was free from psychological doubt about God, but that he was free from disloyalty.

Page 185, after first paragraph

Käsemann[4] believes that a communicant is 'guilty of "the body and blood of the Lord"—which can have no other meaning than "the death of Jesus",' if he eats and drinks unworthily, in the sense that he ranges himself with the 'world', which was responsible for the death of Christ. This sensible suggestion has much to commend it.[5]

Page 213, after section (e)

A reply to J. C. O'Neill's proposed excision of the main moral teaching in Galatians.

J. C. O'Neill[6] has recently argued, following many predecessors, to whom he makes due acknowledgment, that a considerable portion of *Galatians* was not written by Paul, but added later. His excisions fall into three classes:

---

[1] *Foi et Salut selon S. Paul*, Analecta Biblica, No. 42, (Rome, 1970), p. 19.
[2] Barrett's contribution is reprinted verbatim in *New Testament Essays*, (London, 1972), pp. 116–43. The quotation is found on p. 116.
[3] *Foi et Salut selon S. Paul*, Analecta Biblica, No. 42. (Rome, 1970), pp. 59–60.
[4] 'The Pauline Doctrine of the Lord's Supper', *Essays on New Testament Themes*, S.B.T. No. 41, pp. 108–35 (London, 1964) being the E.T. by W. J. Montague of selections from *Exegetische Versuche und Besinnungen*, Erster Band, Vandenhoeck und Ruprecht, Göttingen (1960²).
[5] Op. cit., p. 123.
[6] *The Recovery of Paul's Letter to the Galatians* (London, 1972).

(1) As an example of the first class we may cite Gal. ii. 3, 'Yet even my companion Titus, Greek though he is, was not compelled to be circumcised.' O'Neill proposes to omit the word 'Titus' for two reasons, which command respect. First, several manuscripts omit 'Titus',[1] and, secondly, the inclusion of the word 'Titus' makes this extremely difficult passage easier to understand. Where these two conditions, variation of manuscripts and difficulty of the presumed original, are found, O'Neill's omissions must be regarded as plausible, especially where different manuscipts preserve different readings which seem intended to clarify an obscure passage.

(2) In the second class we place his omission of such passages as Gal. iv. 1–3, 8–10, where he[2] argues that it would not have been necessary to warn Jews against astrology and indeed idolatry. It is true that, as he says, such beliefs were more typical of later Jewish syncretistic gnosticism, but, because this phenomenon *did* occur after Paul's day, it does not follow that it did not exist in a milder form when the Apostle wrote *Galatians*. Few aberrations are confined to a single age, and, as E. P. Sanders has shown us in his magnificent book *The Tendencies of the Synoptic Tradition*,[3] the progress of Christian and near-Christian thought did not follow a regular pattern, in which one stage succeeded another like the layers of an enormous sandwich, but rather resembled a series of turbulent whirl-pools in which re-Judaization took place as well as de-Judaization. For these reasons I am most sceptical about the second class of O'Neill's omission.

(3) The third class contains a single member, the ethical teaching of Gal. v. 13–vi. 10. By this supposition I remain utterly unconvinced, and this for two reasons:

(I) O'Neill notes the theory of W. Lütgert,[4] followed by J. H. Ropes,[5] that Paul was fighting on two fronts, but contends that 'There is no discernible trace in *Galatians* that Paul is fighting on two fronts'.[6] But there *is* evidence that Paul in *Galatians* is

---

[1] op. cit., p. 30.
[2] op. cit., p. 56ff.
[3] Monograph Series 9 (Cambridge, 1969).
[4] *Gesetz und Geist: Eine Untersuchung zur Vorgeschichte des Galatesbriefes* (Gütersloh, 1919).
[5] *The Singular Problem of the Epistle to the Galatians* (Cambridge, Mass., 1929).
[6] O'Neill, J. C., *The Recovery of Paul's Letter to the Galatians*, (London, 1972).

fighting on two fronts—the trouble is that O'Neill has removed the evidence himself! His argument is in fact circular.

(II) It is not unusual for Paul to end his epistles with moral teaching. He clearly does so in *Romans*. In the Corinthian epistles, it is true, the moral teaching is interspersed. The example of *Romans* is followed in the Thessalonian epistles, *Philippians* and *Colossians*, but their Pauline authenticity has been disputed. I much regret having to take such a negative view about a well-written book. I am glad that it has been published, because it saves us from the mistake of regarding all 'radical criticism' as something to be disregarded. Positions like those taken up by O'Neill should be re-examined from time to time, and judged on their merits.

Page 229, after section v

The relevance of Paul's moral teaching to our own day.

It may seem capricious in the extreme to treat so vital a matter as a mere tail-piece to the Apostle's teaching on food laws. The reason I have chosen to do so is that Rom. xiv, mainly concerned with food laws, is especially relevant to our own day.

Since the publication of the first edition of this book in 1964, I have asked my colleagues who have used it what changes they would most desire in a possible later edition; some of them have consulted their pupils on this point. One change which almost all teachers and students would desire above all is a treatment of the relevance of Paul's teaching to the moral problems of our own day.

I suspect that some at least of the pupils are asking for the impossible: consciously or otherwise, they would like to use the N.T. as a slide-rule and read off its answers to their moral problems in a purely mechanical manner. This, of course, cannot be done. The main contribution of Paul's writings to our present practical difficulties is that they help us to 'possess the mind of Christ' (1 Cor. ii. 16), and to judge for ourselves, becoming imitators of Christ, as I contended in 1964 (cp. above, pp. 211 ff.). At that time I had overlooked a fuller treatment of the subject by D. M. Stanley.[1]

Much the same point is made by Rudolf Schnackenburg in *The Moral teaching of the New Testament*,[2] pp. 268–77.

[1] " 'Become imitators of me': The Pauline conception of Apostolic Tradition", *Biblica* 40 (1959), pp. 859–77.
[2] (Freiburg and London, 1965).

Page 240, after section (ii)

Charles H. Giblin[1] suggests that 'Wickedness in human form' =Greek *ho anthrōpos tēs anomias* is a false prophet, trying to replace God. *To katechon*, the 'restraining hand' of 2 Thess. ii. 6, sometimes personalized as *ho katechōn* (masculine) 'the Restrainer' of v. 7 is not a restrainer, but a concrete expression of a demonic pseudo-prophetic movement already active in Thessalonica. In v. 8 Paul refers to the revelation, *apokalypsis*, of this force, which is not its full flowering, but its exposure, that will lead to its destruction by the Lord at his advent. This is a plausible suggestion, but I must confess that I still adhere to the traditionalist position of Tertullian.

Page 244, insert new opening paragraph to section iv

Did St. Paul's Eschatology Develop?

This problem is dogged from the start by two inherent and insoluble difficulties.

(1) *If* we knew the absolute dates of all the Pauline writings an observable change (a word which I employ to avoid the question -begging term 'development') would then lead to two possibilities:

Either (a) Paul had changed his mind, or at least the emphasis and relative importance of his theories.

Or (b) Paul's thought had not developed at all, but the needs of the recipients of his letters had altered, so that Paul brought out different weapons from his theological armoury, and employed them in a different manner. It is in fact not possible to be certain whether the change took place in Paul's thought or in the needs of his flock, or in both.

(2) We cannot be certain of the authenticity or otherwise of all the Pauline writings. For these reasons it is not possible to be sure whether Paul's doctrine of eschatology developed or no. My personal opinion is that his doctrine did develop and that the needs of his congregations also changed.

We may note in passing the appearance of two new books on Pauline Chronology, *Saint Paul, a Study of the Development of his Thought*,[2] by C. Buck and G. Taylor, and *The Chronology of the*

---

[1] *The Threat to Faith: An Exegetical and Theological Re-examination of* 2 *Thessalonians* 2, Analecta Biblica, No. 31 (Rome, 1967).

[2] (New York, 1969).

Life of St. Paul,[1] by G. Ogg. The publication dates were so close that neither book could be expected to take account of the other. Buck and Taylor date both the Corinthian letters and *Romans* to 47, and say that the Apostle was sent to Rome in 55, (p. 215). Ogg adheres more closely to the accepted chronology. The reason I have mentioned these books is that Buck and Taylor believe Paul's eschatology did develop, cp. pp. 12ff., 115ff., 142f., 226ff. Though it would be out of place to examine their chronology here,[2] I am inclined on balance to agree with them that Paul's eschatology did develop.

Page 258, at end of section v

Since 1964 the 'traditionalist' view, to which I still adhere, has lost ground to the 'corporate' view propounded by J. A. T. Robinson[3] and Earle Ellis.[4] The problem has been discussed and the literature reviewed by J-F. Collange,[5] who strongly, though fairly, supports the 'corporate' interpretation.

It is important to remember just what is at issue. The supporters of the corporate view do not suggest that individuality is lost! Indeed, Collange[6] seems to think less of incorporation into the body of Christ than of the courage given to the deceased by the presence of the risen Lord. We 'traditionalists', on the other hand, would stress the fact that the Christian is already in this present life a member of the body of Christ, a point which the evidence forbids anyone to dispute, and I personally would hazard the guess that this union with Christ will be even closer after death, though this will lead to an enrichment, not to an impoverishment of personality.

What is at issue is the 'mechanics' of the matter. Does the passage refer to death, an intermediate state, a temporary body, as I maintain, or to sin, and solidarity with Christ, quite apart from

---

[1] (London, 1968).
[2] For a brief outline and bibliography of the problems of Pauline chronology, cp. W. G. Kümmel, *Introduction to the New Testament* (London, 1966), pp. 179–81. This book is the E.T. of the 14th revised edition of *Einleitung in das neue Testament*, founded by P. Feine and J. Behm (Heidelberg, 1965[14]).
[3] *The Body*, S.B.T., No. 5 (London, 1952). He hints at this view (p. 78) but does not develop it with specific reference to 2 Cor. v. as Ellis does.
[4] *op. cit.*
[5] *Énigmes de la deuxième Épître de Paul aux Corinthiens.* Etude exégétique de 2 Cor. 2.14–7.4. *S.N.T.S.* Monograph Series, No. 18 (Cambridge, 1972). esp. pp. 179–243.
[6] *op. cit.*, pp. 190–91.

Y

death, which is a main thrust of the 'corporate' argument, though this victory over sin becomes especially important after death?

C. F. D. Moule[1] has produced a careful and balanced defence of the traditionalist position. He makes four main points:

(1) The 'dualism' which means most to St. Paul is moral dualism, not metaphysical or anthropological dualism (p. 121).

(2) 'If transformation is to take place at all, it is because God, by his glorious power, raised up Christ from among the dead, and, therefore, is able to raise up our mortal bodies also' (p. 108).

(3) Moule lays great stress upon the language of clothing. He agrees that this concept is employed metaphorically, as in Ps. cxxxii. 9, 'Let thy priests be clothed with righteousness . . .' (p. 117) but argues that *ependuesthai*, which in 1964 I had explained by means of the analogy of an overcoat (2 Cor. v. 2, 4), probably does refer to an 'additional garment', e.g. a pullover, since *ependutēs*, in John xxi. 7, a fact I had forgotten, actually does mean 'overcoat'. He points out that the metaphor of clothing is applied to a dualistic doctrine of the soul in *The Gospel of Truth*, xx. 29ff., *The Gospel of Philip*, lxiii, 16–21, and other similar literature (p. 117f.).

(4) Moule maintains, as I do, that: 'Whereas I Cor. xv. implies that the new is *added to* the old and *superimposed* upon it, II Cor. v. 4 implies that the new is received only *in exchange for* the old' (p. 116). Moule 'would like to believe that Paul actually conceived of the matter which is progressively surrendered by the Christian in the process of living, dangerously and laboriously, in the service of God, as being used, and used up in the creation of the life, as fuel is used up to produce energy' (p. 121f.). I am basically in agreement with Moule, though I feel he thinks that anthropological dualism in Paul's theology is even more peripheral than I do. I hope that by means of a 'scissors and paste' technique of direct quotation I have succeeded in conveying Moule's thought without distortion.

I have three comments to offer:

(1) I agree that growth in maturity of personality is normally accompanied by physical decay. This, indeed, is in line with Paul's thought in 2 Cor. iv. But I have reservations about the analogy of the healthy physical body being transformed into the

---

[1] 'St. Paul and Dualism: The Pauline Conception of Resurrection', *N.T.S.*, vol. 12, No. 2, Jan. 1966, pp. 106–23.

body that shall be, as fuel into energy. I suggest that we grow in maturity and are built up as members of the body of Christ, after justification, and without any question of human merit being entertained, as a result of struggle and 'creative decisions' in novel situations, and through sharing in the sufferings of Christ. I suggest that physical decay is not the cause of spiritual growth but a normal by-product of the true cause.

(2) If Moule is correct, either as he himself has stated his view or as I have amended it, then we must agree that it is in accordance with what we see going on all around us. But a problem arises: What about those who die young? They are few in contemporary industrial society, but early death was almost the norm until the nineteenth century A.D., and is still far too common in the 'Third World'. What happens to those who die young? Do they continue their growth in Christ elsewhere, in Purgatory or Paradise or what are we to say?

It is no discredit to Moule that his exegesis of Scripture gives rise to these problems. It is indeed the duty of the Biblical theologian to expound just what the Biblical writers say, and leave the problems so generated to systematic theologians or moralists as the case may be.

Apostolic Preaching of the Cross by L. Morris

Comparison of the pagination in (1953[1]) and (1965[3])

Most students who read *The Apostolic Preaching of the Cross* by L. Morris, London, Tyndale Press, will possess either the first edition of 1955 or the third edition of 1965, reprinted in 1972. This last edition is longer than the first, and I feel that Morris has refined his views, as I have mine, and that we are coming near to agreement. I therefore drew up this table, putting in italics those pages of the third edition which appear to have no parallel in the first edition.

1955 *pages*	1965 *pages*
14	21
50	54
	178
	208
226	253
230	256
234	260
270f.	294f.

The Rev. A. E. Harvey's article 'Elders' will appear, it is confidently expected, in the J.T.S. for October 1974, N.S. vol. xxv, part 2.

BIBLIOGRAPHY TO FIRST EDITION

(see also Contents, pp. vii–xi)

ALLMEN, J. J. VON, *Pauline Teaching on Marriage* (E.T. London, 1963).
ALLO, E.-B., *Première Epître aux Corinthiens* (Paris, 1956²).
   Seconde Epître aux Corinthiens (Paris, 1956²).
AMSLER, S., *L'Ancien Testament dans l'Eglise* (Neuchâtel, 1960).
ARGYLE, A. W., ' "Outward" and "Inward" in Biblical Theology.' *Expository Times*, LXVIII, 1957, pp. 196 ff.
ARNDT, WILLIAM F. and F. WILBUR GRINGRICH, *A Greek-English Lexicon of the New Testament and Other Early Christian Literature* (Chicago and Cambridge, 1957) being a translation and adaptation of W. Bauer's *Wörterbuch* (1952⁴).
BARR, J., *The Semantics of Biblical Language* (Oxford, 1961).
BARRETT, C. K., *The Epistle to the Romans*, Black N.T.C. (London, 1957).
   Review of O. Cullmann, *Die Christologie des Neuen Testaments*, *J.T.S.*, N.S. x, (1959), pp. 376–9.
   'The Background of Mark x. 45' in *New Testament Essays, Studies in Memory of T. W. Manson*, pp. 1–18 (Manchester, 1959).
   Luke the Historian in Recent Study (London, 1961).
BEARE, F. W., *The First Epistle of Peter* (Oxford, 1958²).
   The Epistle to the Philippians, Black N.T.C., with appended note on 'The "kenotic" Christology' by Eugene R. Fairweather, pp. 159–74 (London, 1959).
BEASLEY-MURRAY, G. R., *Baptism in the New Testament* (London, 1962).
BEDALE, S., 'The Meaning of *kephalē* in the Pauline Epistles', *J.T.S.*, N.S. vii (1954), pp. 211–15.
BENOIT, P., Review of O. Cullmann, *Die Christologie des Neuen Testaments*, *R.B.* (1958), pp. 268–75.
BEST, E., *One Body in Christ* (London, 1955).
BICKNELL, E. J., *The First and Second Epistles to the Thessalonians*, Westminster Commentary (London, 1932).
BLASS, F. and A. DEBRUNNER, *A Greek Grammar of the New Testament and other Early Christian Literature*, E.T. by Robert W. Funk (Chicago and Cambridge, 1961).
BONNARD, P., *L'Epître de Saint Paul aux Galates*, *C.N.T.*, vol. 9, (Neuchâtel, 1953).
BONSIRVEN, J., *Le Judaisme Palestinien au temps de Jésus-Christ* (2 vols., Paris, 1935).
   Exégèse rabbinique et Exégèse paulinienne (Paris, 1939).
   L'Evangile de Paul (Paris, 1948).
BOUSSET, W., *Kyrios Christos* (Göttingen, 1921²).
BROCKINGTON, L., 'The Septuagintal Background to the New Testament use of *Doxa*', *Studies in the Gospels*, ed. D.E. Nineham (Oxford, 1955), pp. 1–8.
BRUCE, F. F., *Commentary on the Epistles to the Ephesians and the Colossians*, London N.T.C. (London, 1957).
BÜCHSEL, F., *Apolutrōsis*, *T.W.N.T.* iv, (Stuttgart, 1942), pp. 354–9.
BURNEY, C. F., 'Christ as the *Archē* of "Creation" ', *J.T.S.*, xxvii (1926), pp. 160 ff.
BULTMANN, R., *Theology of the New Testament* (E.T. London, vol. i, 1952, vol. ii, 1955).
CAIRD, G. B., *Principalities and Powers* (Oxford, 1956).
CAMPBELL, J. Y., 'The Kingdom of God has come', *Exp.T.*, xlviii (1936), pp. 91–4.

CARRINGTON, P., *The Primitive Christian Catechism* (Cambridge, 1940).
CERFAUX, L., *Recueil Lucien Cerfaux*, Bibliotheca Ephemeridum Theologicarum Lovaniensium, vols. vi.–vii. (Gembloux, 1954).
  Christ in the Theology of St. Paul (E.T. New York and Edinburgh, 1959).
  The Church in the Theology of St. Paul (E.T. New York and Edinburgh, 1959).
CHARLES, R. H., *Eschatology, Hebrew, Jewish, and Christian* (London, 1963²).
CLARK, K. W., 'Textual Criticism and Doctrine' in *Studia Paulina* (Haarlem, 1953,) pp. 52–65.
CLAVIER, H., 'Brèves remarques sur la notion de *sōma pneumatikon*' in *The Background of the New Testament and its Eschatology* (Cambridge, 1956), pp. 342–67.
CONZELMANN, H., *The Theology of St. Luke* (E.T. London, 1960).
CRAIG, CLARENCE T., '1 Corinthians' in *I.B.* vol. 10 (Nashville, 1953).
CULLMANN, O., *Baptism in the New Testament* (E.T., S.B.T., no. 1, London, 1950).
  Christ and Time (E.T. London, 1962² revised).
  'The Proleptic Deliverance of the Body according to the New Testament' in *The Early Church* (E.T. London, 1956), pp. 165–73.
  The State in the New Testament (E.T. London, 1957).
  Immortality of the Soul or Resurrection of the Dead? (E.T. London, 1958).
  Peter, Disciple, Apostle, and Martyr, E.T. (revised) London 1962².
DAHL, MURDOCH E., *The Resurrection of the Body*, S.B.T. no. 36 (London, 1962).
DAUBE, D., *The New Testament and Rabbinic Judaism* (London, 1956).
DAVIES, J. G., *He ascended into Heaven* (London, 1958).
DAVIES, W. D., *Paul and Rabbinic Judaism* (London, 1955²), cf. p. 4, n. 12.
  Christian Origins and Judaism (London, 1962).
DENZIGER-SCHÖNMETZER, *Enchiridion symbolosum, definitionum et declarationum*, ed xxxii, Freiburg-im-Bresgau, 1963.
DIBELIUS, M., *Die Geisterwelt im Glauben des Paulus* (Göttingen, 1909).
  From Tradition to Gospel (E.T. London, 1934).
  Studies in the Acts of the Apostles (E.T. London, 1956).
DODD, C. H., *The Epistle to the Romans*, Moffatt N.T.C. (London, 1932).
  Gospel and Law (Cambridge, 1951).
  According to the Scriptures (London, 1952).
  'The Mind of Paul: I and II' in *New Testament Studies* (Manchester, 1953). [Reprinted from *B.J.R.L.*, vols. 17 and 18, 1932 and 1933.]
  The Interpretation of the Fourth Gospel (Cambridge, 1953).
DODD, C. H., *The Bible and the Greeks* (London, 1954²).
DUPONT, J., *L'Union avec le Christ suivant Saint Paul* (Louvain-Paris, 1952).
  La Réconciliation dans la théologie de Saint Paul, Analecta Lovaniensia Biblica et Orientalia, ser. II, fasc. 32 (Bruges-Paris, 1953).
EICHRODT, W., *Man in the Old Testament* (E.T., S.B.T. no. 4, London, 1951).
ELLIS, E. EARLE, *St. Paul's Use of the Old Testament* (Edinburgh, 1957).
  '2 Corinthians V, 1–10 in Pauline Eschatology', *N.T.S.*, 3 (1959–60), pp. 211–24, reprinted in *Paul and His Recent Interpreters* (Grand Rapids, Michigan, 1961).
EVANS, C. F., 'The Kerygma', *J.T.S.*, N.S. vii (1956), pp. 25–41.
FAIRWEATHER, EUGENE R., cp. Beare, F.W.
FLEMINGTON, W. F., *The New Testament Doctrine of Baptism* (London, 1948).
FRAME, J. E., *The Epistles of St. Paul to the Thessalonians*, I.C.C. (Edinburgh, 1912).
FRIDRICHSEN, A., *The Apostle and his Message* (Uppsala, 1947).
  'Eglise et sacrement dans le Nouveau Testament' in *Revue d'histoire et de philosophie religieuse*, 17 (1937), pp. 337–56.

FROST, STANLEY, B., *Old Testament Apocalyptic* (London, 1952).

FULLER, R. H., *The Mission and Achievement of Jesus*, S.B.T., no. 12 (London, 1954).

FUNK, ROBERT W., cp. Blass, A.

GAVIN, F., *The Jewish Background of the Christian Sacraments* (London, 1928).

GLASSON, T. FRANCIS, *Greek Influence in Jewish Eschatology* (London, 1961).

  The Second Advent. The origin of the New Testament Doctrine (London, 1963³).

GOODENOUGH, E. R., *Jewish Symbolism in the Greco-Roman Period* (New York, 1953).

GOODRICK, A. T. S., *The Book of Wisdom* (London, 1913).

GORDON, CYRUS H., *Before the Bible* (London, 1962).

GOUDGE, H. L., *The First Epistle to the Corinthians*, Westminster Commentaries (London, 1909²).

GRANT, FREDERICK C., *Roman Hellenism and the New Testament* (Edinburgh and London, 1962).

GRANT, R. M., *Gnosticism and Early Christianity* (Oxford, 1959).

GROSHEIDE, F. W., *Commentary on the First Epistle to the Corinthians*, London N.T.C. (London, 1954²).

GUIGNEBERT, C. A. H., *The Jewish World in the Time of Jesus* (E.T., London, 1939).

GUTBROD, W., *Nomos*, *T.W.N.T.*, iv (Stuttgart, 1942), pp. 1029–1084, E.T. *Law*, Bible Key Words (London, 1962).

HANSON, A. T., *The Wrath of the Lamb* (London, 1957).

  The Pioneer Ministry (London, 1961).

HANSON, R. P. C., *II Corinthians*, Torch ser. (London, 1954).

HARNACK, A. VON, *The Expansion of Christianity in the First Three Centuries* (E.T. London and New York, vol. i, 1904, vol. ii, 1905).

HATCH, E. and REDPATH, H. A., *A Concordance to the Septuagint*, 2 vols., (Graz, 1954²).

HEBERT, A. G., *The Authority of the Old Testament* (London, 1947).

HARRIS, J. RENDELL, *Testimonies* (Cambridge, vol. 1, 1916, vol. 2, 1920).

HÉRING, J., *La Seconde Epître de Saint Paul aux Corinthiens*, C.N.T., vol. 8 (Neuchâtel, 1958).

  L'Epître aux Hébreux, C.N.T., vol. 12 (Neuchâtel, 1954).

  Le Royaume de Dieu et sa venue (Neuchâtel, 1959²).

  The First Epistle of Saint Paul to the Corinthians (E.T. London, 1962).

HOOKER, MISS MORNA D., *Jesus and the Servant* (London, 1959).

  'Adam in Romans 1', *N.T.S.*, 6 (1960), pp. 297–306.

HUGHES, MALDWYN, *What is atonement?* (London, n.d.)

HUNT, B. P. W. STATHER, *Primitive Gospel Sources* (London, 1951).

HUNTER, A. M., *St. Paul and his Predecessors* (London, 1961²).

JEREMIAS, J., *The Eucharistic Words of Jesus* (E.T. Oxford, 1955).

  'Flesh and Blood cannot Inherit the Kingdom of God', *N.T.S.*, 2 (1956), pp. 151–9.

  Infant Baptism in the First Four Centuries (E.T. London, 1960). This translation is equivalent to a fifth German edition.

JOHNSON, A. R., *The Vitality of the Individual in the thought of Ancient Israel* (Cardiff, 1949).

JOHNSON, A. R., *The One and the Many in the Israelite Conception of God* (Cardiff, 1961²).

JONES, D. R. 'Anamnēsis in the LXX and the Interpretation of 1 Cor. xi, 25', *J.T.S.* N.S. vol. vi, Pt. 2 (October 1955), pp. 183–91.

KELLY, J. N. D., *Early Christian Creeds* (London, 1960²).

KLAUSNER, J., *From Jesus to Paul* (E.T. London, 1942).
KLEIN, G., *Studien über Paulus* (Stockholm, 1918).
KNOX, J., 'Romans', *I.B.*, vol. 9 (Nashville, 1954).
KNOX, W. L., *St. Paul and the Church of Jerusalem* (Cambridge, 1925).
    Some Hellenistic Elements in Primitive Christianity (London, 1924).
    St. Paul and the Church of the Gentiles (Cambridge, 1961²).
KRAUSS, S., *Griechische und lateinische Lehnwörter im Talmud, Midrasch und Targum* (Berlin, 1898).
KUHN, K. G., *Maranatha, T.W. N.T.*, iv, pp. 470–5.
LAGRANGE, M.-J., *Epître aux Galates* (Paris, 1925²).
    Epître aux Romains (Paris, 1950).
LAMPE, G. W. H. (*ed.*) *A Patristic Greek Lexicon* (Oxford, 1961–).
LEENHARDT, F. J., *Le Sacrement de la Sainte Cène* (Neuchâtel, 1948).
    The Epistle to the Romans, C.N.T. (E.T. London, 1961).
LIDDELL, H. G. and SCOTT, R. (*edd.*) *A Greek-English Lexicon*, revised Stuart Jones, H. and McKenzie, R., 2 vols. (Oxford, 1940)
LIETZMANN, H., *An die Römer*, Handbuch zum N.T. (Tübingen, 1938²).
LIGHTFOOT, J. B., *St. Paul's Epistles to the Colossians and to Philemon* (London, 1876²).
    St. Paul's Epistle to the Galatians (London, 1881⁷).
    Notes on Epistles of St. Paul from unpublished commentaries (London, 1895).
LINDARS, B., *New Testament Apologetic* (London, 1961).
LING, T., *The Significance of Satan* (London, 1961).
LOWE, J., 'An examination of attempts to detect development in St. Paul's Theology', *J.T.S.*, vol. 42, July 1941, 129–42.
MACHEN, J. GRESHAM, *The Origin of St. Paul's Religion* (Grand Rapids, Michigan, 1947²).
McCOWN, C. C. (*ed.*), *Testament of Solomon* (Leipzig, 1922).
MACGREGOR, G. H. C., 'Principalities and Powers', *N.T.S.*, 1, (1954), pp. 17–28.
MANSON, T. W., 'The Date of the Epistle of the Philippians', *B.J.R.L.* (1939), reprinted in *Studies in the Gospels and Epistles* (Manchester, 1962), pp. 150–67.
MANSON, W., *The Epistle to the Hebrews* (London, 1951).
MASCALL, E. L., *Christian Theology and Natural Science* (London, 1956).
MASSON, C., *Les deux Epîtres de Saint Paul aux Thessaloniciens, C.N.T.* (Neuchâtel, 1957).
MENOUD, PH. H., 'L'Echarde et l'Ange satanique', in *Studia Paulina* (Haarlem, 1953), pp. 163–71.
MICHEL, O., *Der Brief an die Römer*, Meyer-Kommentar, (Göttingen, 1955¹⁰).
MILDERT, W. VAN, Bampton Lectures (Oxford, 1815).
MILLIGAN, G., *St. Paul's Epistle to the Thessalonians* (London, 1908).
MOORE, G. F., *Judaism in the first centuries of the Christian Era* (Cambridge, Mass., vols. 1 and 2, 1927, vol. 3 [notes] 1930).
MORGENTHALER, R., *Statistik des Neutestamentlichen Wortschatzes* (Zürich, 1958).
MORRIS, L., *The Apostolic Preaching of the Cross* (London, 1955).
    The First and Second Epistles to the Thessalonians, London N.T.C. (London, 1959).
MORRISON, C. D., *The Powers that Be*, S.B.T. no. 29 (London, 1960).
MOULE, C. F. D., *The Epistles of Paul the Apostle to the Colossians and to Philemon* (Cambridge, 1957).
MOULTON, J. H. and E. HOWARD, *A Grammar of New Testament Greek* (Edinburgh, vol. i, *Prologomena*, 1949,² vol. ii, *Accidence and Word Formation*, 1956², vol. iii, *Syntax*, ed. Nigel Turner, 1963).

MOULTON, J. H. and G. MILLIGAN, *The Vocubulary of the Greek New Testament, illustrated from the Papyri and other non-literary sources* (London, 1952²).

MOWINCKEL, S., *He that Cometh* (E.T. Oxford, 1956).

MUNCK, J., 'Israel and the Gentiles in the New Testament, *J.T.S.*, N.S. ii (1951), pp. 3–16.

Paul and the Salvation of Mankind (E.T. London, 1959).

MURRAY, J., *The Epistle to the Romans, vol. 1, Chs. 1–8*, London N.T.C. (London, 1960).

NEIL, W., *Thessalonians*, Moffat N.T.C. (London, 1950).

NYGREN, A., *Commentary on Romans* (E.T. London, 1952).

Oxford Classical Dictionary (Oxford, 1949).

O'NEILL, J. C., *The Theology of Acts in its Historical Setting* (London, 1961).

OWEN, H. P., 'The Scope of Natural Revelation in Rom. i and Acts xvii, *N.T.S.* 5 (1959), pp. 133–43.

PEDERSEN, J., *Israel, its Life and Culture* (E.T. London and Copenhagen, i–ii, 1946²; iii.iv., 1947²).

PIERCE, C. A., *Conscience in the New Testament*, S.B.T. no. 15 (London, 1955).

PLUMMER, A., *2 Corinthians*, I.C.C. (Edinburgh, 1915).

PONTET, M., *L'Exégèse de St. Augustin Prédicateur* (Paris, 1944).

PRAT, F., *Theology of St. Paul* (E.T. 2 vols. in 1, London, 1959).

PUECH, H. C., G. QUISPEL and W. C. VAN UNNIK, *The Jung Codex*, (E.T. London, 1955).

QUELL, G., 'Justice in the O.T.', *T.W.N.T.*, ii (Stuttgart, 1950²), pp. 176–80, E.T. *Righteousness* (London, 1951), 1–8.

QUISPEL, G., cp. Puech, H.C.

RASHDALL, H., *The Idea of Atonement in Christian Theology* (London, 1919).

RAWLINSON, A. E. J., *The New Testament Doctrine of the Christ* (London, 1929²).

REICKE, B., 'The Law and this World according to Paul', *J.B.L.*, 71 (1950), pp. 259–76, translated from *Svensk Exegetisk Årsbok* (Uppsala, 1942).

REICKE, B., 'Traces of Gnosticism in the Dead Sea Scrolls?' *N.T.S.*, 1 (1954), pp. 137–41.

RICHARDSON, A., *An Introduction to the Theology of the New Testament* (London, 1958).

ed. *A Theological Word Book of the Bible* (London, 1950).

RIDDERBOS, H. N., *Epistle to the Galatians*, London N.T.C. (London, 1961²).

RIESENFELD, H., 'The Mythological Background of the New Testament Christology' in *The Background of the New Testament and its Eschatology* (Cambridge, 1956).

RIGAUX, B., *Les Epîtres aux Thessaloniciens* (Paris, 1956).

ROBERTSON, A. and A. PLUMMER, *1 Corinthians*, I.C.C. (Edinburgh, 1914²).

ROBINSON, H. WHEELER, *The Christian Doctrine of Man* (London, 1926³).

ROBINSON, J. ARMITAGE, *St. Paul's Epistle to the Ephesians* (London, 1904²).

ROBINSON, J. A. T., *The Body*, S.B.T. no. 5 (London, 1952).

'The "Parable" of the Sheep and the Goats', *N.T.S.* 2 (1956), pp. 225–37, reprinted in *Twelve New Testament Studies*, S.B.T. no. 34 (London, 1962), pp. 76–93.

ROWLEY, H. H., 'The Baptism of John and the Qumran Sect' in *New Testament Essays, Studies in Memory of T. W. Manson* (Manchester, 1959), pp. 218–29.

RYLE, G., *The Concept of Mind*, London (1949).

SANDAY, W., and A. C. HEADLAM, *Romans*, I.C.C. (Edinburgh, 1902⁵).

SCHLIER, H., *Der Brief an die Galater*, Meyer-Kommentar, (Göttingen, 1951¹¹).

Principalities and Powers in the New Testament, Quaestiones Disputatae no. 3 (E.T. Freiburg and Edinburgh—London, 1961).

SCHMIDT, K. L., *ekklēsia*, *T.W.N.T.*, iii (Stuttgart, 1950²), pp. 502-39, E.T., *The Church* (London, 1957²).

SCHNEIDER, J., *homoiōma*, *T.W.N.T.*, v (Stuttgart, 1954), pp. 191-197.

SCHOEPS, H. J., *Paul, The Theology of the Apostle in the Light of Jewish History* (E.T. London, 1961).

SCHWEITZER, ALBERT, *Paul and his Interpreters* (E.T. London, 1912).

     The Mysticism of St. Paul the Apostle (E.T. London, 1931).

SCOTT, C. A. ANDERSON, *Christianity according to St. Paul* (Cambridge, 1961²).

SCOTT, E. F, The Epistle to the Philippians, *I.B.*, vol. 11 (Nashville, 1955).

SEEBERG, ALFRED, *Der Katechismus der Urchristenheit* (Leipzig, 1903).

SELWYN, E. G., *The First Epistle of St. Peter* (London, 1947²).

SEVENSTER, J. N., 'Some Remarks on the *Gumnos* in 2 Cor. v. 3,' in *Studia Paulina* (Haarlem, 1953), pp. 202-14.

SHEDD, R. P., *Man in Community. A Study of St. Paul's Teaching* (London, 1958).

SKEHAN, P. W., 'A Fragment of the "Song of Moses" (Deut. 32) from Qumran,' *Bulletin of the American Schools of Oriental Research*, No. 136, Dec. 1954.

SMITH, C. RYDER, *The Bible Doctrine of Man* (London, 1951).

SMITH, MORTON, 'What is implied by the variety of Messianic Figures?' *J.B.L.* 78 (1959), pp. 66-72.

SNAITH, N. H., *The Distinctive Ideas of the Old Testament* (London, 1944).

SPICQ, B., *Agapé, prologomènes à une étude de théologie néotestamentaire* (Louvain, 1955).

     Agapé dans le Nouveau Testament (Paris, vol. i. 1958, ii. and iii. 1959).

STACEY, W. D., *The Pauline View of Man* (London, 1956).

STANLEY, D. M., *Christ's Resurrection in Pauline Soteriology*, Analecta Biblica no. 13 (Rome, 1961).

STAUFFER, E., *New Testament Theology* (E.T. London, 1955).

STENDAHL, K., *The School of St. Matthew* (Uppsala, 1954).

     'Matthew' in *Peake's Commentary on the Bible* (London, 1962).

SYKES, MISS MARJORIE H., 'The Eucharist as Anamnesis', *Exp. T.* 71 (1960), pp. 115-8.

TASKER, R. V. G., *The Biblical Doctrine of the Wrath of God*, Tyndale Lecture for 1951 (London, 1957²).

TAYLOR, VINCENT, *The Atonement in New Testament Teaching* (London, 1946²).

     The Names of Jesus (London, 1953).

     The Person of Christ (London, 1958).

THACKERAY, H. ST. J., *St. Paul and Contemporary Jewish Theology* (London, 1900).

TILLICH, P., *The Interpretation of History* (E.T. New York, 1936).

TINSLEY, E. J., *The Imitation of God in Christ* (London, 1960).

THORNTON, L. S., *The Common Life in the Body of Christ* (London, 1950³).

TURNER, NIGEL, 'The Style of St. Mark's Eucharistic Words', *J.T.S.*, N.S. 8, (April, 1957), pp. 108-11. cp. also Moulton, J. H.

UNNIK, W. C. VAN, *Tarsus or Jerusalem?* (E.T. London, 1962). cp. also Puech, H. C.

WAINWRIGHT, A. W., *The Trinity in the New Testament* (London, 1962).

WESTCOTT, B. F., *The Epistle to the Hebrews* (London, 1903³).

WILSON, R. McL., *The Gnostic Problem* (London, 1958).

WINER, G. B., Grammar of New Testament Greek (E.T. Edinburgh, 1882⁹).

YADIN, Y., 'More Discoveries in the Judaean Desert'. *Biblical Archaeologist*, 24, (May, 1961), pp. 34-50.

     'More on the Letters of Bar Kochba'. *Biblical Archaeologist*, 24, (Sept. 1961), pp. 86-95.

BIBLIOGRAPHY TO SECOND EDITION

BARRETT, C. K., *A Commentary on the First Epistle to the Corinthians*, Black N.T.C, (Ed. 1, London 1968, ed. 3, embodying a number of minor but important corrections, 1973).

BARRETT, C. K., 'I am not ashamed of the Gospel', *Foi et Salut selon S. Paul, Analecta Biblica* no. 42, (Rome, 1970) pp. 19—50, reproduced in *New Testament Essays* (London, 1972), pp. 116—143.

BARTH, Markus, ' Rechfertigung,' *Foi et Salut selon S. Paul, Analecta Biblica* no. 42 (Rome, 1970) pp. 137-209, and 59-60.

BORNKAMM, GÜNTHER, *Paul* (New York and London, 1971), E.T. by Stalker, D. G. M. of *Paulus* (Stuttgart, 1969).

BUCK, C. and TAYLOR, G., *Saint Paul: A Study of the development of his thought* (New York, 1969).

COLLANGE, J-F., *Enigmes de la deuxième épître de Paul aux Corinthiens*. Etude exégétique de 2 Cor. 2.14-7.4 S.N.T.S. Monograph Series 18 (Cambridge, 1972).

CRANFIELD, C. E. B., ' Romans 1.18 ', *Scottish Journal of Theology*, Vol. 21, no. 3, Sept. 1968, pp. 330-35.

DANIÉLOU, J., *The Theology of Jewish Christianity* (London, 1964), E. T. by Baker, J.A.
Gospel Message and Hellenistic Culture (London, 1973), E.T. with concluding evaluative postscript by Baker, J. A.

FITZMYER, Joseph A., *Essays on the Semitic Background of the New Testament* (London and Blackrock, County Dublin, 1971).

FULLER, R. H., *The Foundations of New Testament Christology* (London, 1965).

GIBBS, J. C., *Creation and Redemption, a Study in Pauline Theology*, Supplements to *Novum Testamentum*, vol. xxvi (Leiden, 1971).

GIBLIN, Charles H., *The Threat to Faith: An Exegetical and Theological Reexamination of 2 Thessalonians 2, Analecta Biblica*, no. 31 (Rome, 1967).

HAENCHEN, E., *The Acts of the Apostles* (E.T., Oxford, 1971) from the German original (Göttingen, 1965). This is the 14th edition of the Meyer Commentary.

HILL, D., *Greek Words and Hebrew Meanings: Studies in the Semantics of Soteriological Terms*, S.N.T.S. Monograph Series no. 5 (Cambridge, 1967).

HINNELLS, John R., Christianity and the Mystery Cults, *Theology*, vol. lxxi no. 571, Jan. 1968, pp. 20—25.

HUNT, E. W., *Portrait of Paul* (London, 1968).

HURD, JOHN C., JR, *The Origin of 1 Corinthians* (London, 1965).

JONES, C. P. M., *Christ and Christianity in the light of St. Paul*, being the Bampton Lectures for 1970. Date of publication not yet known.

KÄSEMANN, E., ' The Pauline Doctrine of the Lord's Supper', *Essays on New Testament Themes*, S.B.T. no. 41, (London, 1964) pp. 108—135. This is an E.T. by W. J. Montague of selections from *Exegetische Versuche und Besinnungen*, Erster Band, Vandenhoeck und Ruprecht, Göttingen 1960[2].
Perspectives on Paul (London, 1971), E. T. by Kohl, M. of *Paulinische Perspectiven* (Tübingen, 1969).

KÜMMEL, W. G., *Introduction to the New Testament* (London, 1966), being the E.T. of *Einleitung in das neue Testament*, founded by P. Feine and J. Behm (Heidelberg, 1965[14]).

LANGEVIN, Paul-Émile, S.J., *Jésus Seigneur et l'Eschatologie. Exégèse de Textes Prépauliniens, Studia*, Travaux de recherche, Universities of Montréal and Sudbury, no. 21 (Bruges-Paris, 1967).

LÜTGERT, W., *Gesetz und Geist: Eine Untersuchung zur Vorgeschichte des Galaterbriefes* (Gütersloh, 1919).

MANSON, T. W., *J.T.S.*, Old Series 1945, pp. 1-10.

MORGENTHALER, R., *Statistik des Neutestamentichen Wortschatzes* (Zürich and Frankfurt am Main, 1958).

MORRIS, L., *The Apostolic Preaching of the Cross* (London, 1955. Third, enlarged edition, London, 1965, reprinted 1972).

MOULE, C. F. D., ' St. Paul and Dualism: The Pauline Conception of Resurrection,' *N.T.S.* vol. 12, no. 2, Jan. 1966, pp. 106-23.

MOULTON, J. H., *A Grammar of New Testament Greek* vol. i, *Prolegomena* (Edinburgh, 1908³, often reprinted) p. 100.

NEUFELD, V. H., *The Earliest Christian Confessions* (Leiden, 1963).

NYGREN, Anders, *Romarbrevet* (Sweden, 1944; E.T. *Commentary on Romans* London, 1952).

O'CONNOR, J. M. ed., *Paul and Qumran* (London, Dublin, and Melbourne, 1968).

OGG, G., *The Chronology of the Life of St. Paul* (London, 1968).

O'NEIL, J. C. *The Recovery of Paul's Letter to the Galatians* (London, 1972).

PORTER, J. R., ' The Legal Aspects of the Concept of "Corporate Personality" in the Old Testament', *Vetus Testamentum*, xv (1965), pp. 360-380.

RAD, G. von, *Old Testament Theology*, vol. ii, E.T., D. G. M. Stalker, (Edinburgh and London, 1965). This is the E.T. of *Theologie des Alten Testaments* Bd. ii, *Die Theologie der prophetischen Überlieferungen Israels* (Munich, 1960).

ROGERSON, J. W., 'The Hebrew Conception of Corporate Personality: A Re-examination ', *J.T.S.*, N.S., vol. xxi, Pt. 1, April, 1970, pp. 1-16.

ROPES, J. H., *The Singular Problem of the Epistle to the Galatians* (Cambridge, Mass., 1929).

SAWYER, John F. A., *Semantics in Biblical Research: New Methods of Defining Hebrew Words for Salvation*, S.B.T., Second Series, no. 24 (London, 1972).

SCHMITALS, W., *Paul and James* (London, 1965), S.B.T. no. 46, E.T. by Barton, D. M. of *Paulus und Jacobus* (Göttingen, 1963), Forschungen zur Religion und Literatur des Alten und Neuen Testaments 85.

The Office of Apostle in the Early Church (London, 1971), E. T. by Steely, J. E., of *Das kirchliche Apostelamt* (Göttingen, n.d.). The E.T. was revised and brought to date under the direction of Schmitals.

Paul and the Gnostics (New York, 1972), E.T. by Steely, J. E. of *Paulus und die Gnostiker* (Hamburg, 1965).

Gnosticism in Corinth (New York, 1972), E.T. by Steely, J. E. of *Gnosis in Korinth* (1969³).

SCHNACKENBURG, R., Original edition, *Die Sittliche Botschaft des Neuen Testaments* (E. T. *The Moral Teaching of the New Testament* from revised German edition 1962ª, Freiburg and London, 1962).

SEVENSTER, J. N., *Do you know Greek? How much Greek could the first Jewish Christians have known? Novum Testamentum*, Supplement xix (Leiden, 1968).

STANLEY, D. M., " 'Become imitators of me ': The Pauline conception of Apostolic Tradition ", *Biblica*, 40 (1959) pp. 859-77.

STENDAHL, K. ed., *The Scrolls and the New Testament* (New York, 1957).

WAGNER, G., *Das Religionsgeschichtliche Problem von Römer 6, 1-11* (Zürich, 1962). The E.T., *Pauline Baptism and the Pagan Mysteries* (Edinburgh and London, 1967), is virtually a second edition.

WHITELEY, D. E. H., and MARTIN, R., *Sociology, Theology and Conflict* (Oxford 1969).

YARNOLD, Edward, ' Pagan Mysteries, in the Fourth Century ', *The Heythrop Journal*, vol. xiii, no. 3, July 1972, pp. 247-67. This Journal is a quarterly issued by Heythrop College (University of London) and distributed by them in association with B. H. Blackwell, Oxford, England.

ZIESLER, J. A., *The Meaning of Righteousness in Paul. A Linguistic and Theological Enquiry*, S.N.T.S. Monograph Series, 20 (Cambridge, 1972).

INDEX OF PASSAGES TO FIRST EDITION

OLD TESTAMENT

APOCRYPHA

INTERTESTAMENTAL WRITINGS

(*Order of books* as in R. H. CHARLES, *The Apocrypha and Pseudepigrapha of the Old Testament*, vol. 2, Oxford, 1963[2])

DEAD SEA SCROLLS

PAGE

Manual of Discipline
col. xi. line 9 37 n. 49
col. xi. line 12 37 n. 49

NEW TESTAMENT (other than Paul)

NEW TESTAMENT (Pauline References)

329

INDEX OF PASSAGES TO SECOND EDITION

OLD TESTAMENT, INTERTESTAMENTAL AND POST RESURRECTION

NEW TESTAMENT (other than Paul)

NEW TESTAMENT (Pauline References)

INDEX OF AUTHORS TO FIRST EDITION

ADDITIONAL INDEX OF AUTHORS

GENERAL INDEX TO FIRST EDITION

(See also Table of Contents, pp. vii–xi)

GENERAL INDEX TO SECOND EDITION